Speech Communication

ANALYSIS AND READINGS

HOWARD H. MARTIN

AND

KENNETH E. ANDERSEN

UNIVERSITY OF MICHIGAN

ALLYN AND BACON, INC.   *BOSTON*

P
91
.M34

Library of Congress Catalog Card No. 68–20533

Speech Communication

ANALYSIS AND READINGS

3.95

Preface

The accumulation of knowledge has become so rapid that it is termed an information explosion. This accumulation threatens to overwhelm individuals, libraries, educational systems, and to destroy conventional boundaries between academic disciplines. Paradoxically, one of the problems of this information explosion is the increasing difficulty of student and teacher in gaining access to relevant material due to information overload.

Growth of interest in communication has similarly been explosive. Information relevant to communication is pouring from such fields as electrical engineering, linguistics, sociology, psychology, and communication sciences as well as more traditional areas concerned with oral and written communication. Although the methodologies, prior orientations, intent, and language often differ, the intensity of interest and the increase in the number of disciplines studying communication have produced a knowledge explosion in this area.

No one book or series of books can compend this vast amount of material. However, it is the goal of this book to provide an exposure to some of the literature, illustrative both of the range and variety of sources and representative of some of the more basic approaches and data relevant to communication, to attempt some synthesis and integration of this material, and to yield some tentative preliminary generalizations of value to the student seeking to understand communication phenomena either as a practitioner or a critic.

The original essays, selected readings (often excerpted and condensed), the predictive generalizations and study questions are constructed in terms of the question: "What factors influence communication effects?" The text treats the nature of the communication process, settings and modalities of communication, strategies in and limitations on communication effects, and methods of evaluating effects. The focus is upon purposive human communication, particularly the oral mode, in which a communicator seeks to obtain a predetermined response from his audience.

We have consciously tried to avoid prescription. The predictive generalizations are offered as organizing principles around which an understanding of the communication process may be developed. Hopefully, a student will develop an awareness of the multiplicity of complex and interacting factors that contribute to communication effects. Audience response to any stimulus is variable, yet patterns and relationships are discernible. Descriptive generalizations about speakers, message elements, and audiences in general, or particular speakers, communication settings, appeals, and audiences can be derived from study of communicative behavior just as they can be derived for other aspects of human behavior. While complex, communication should not be viewed as incomprehensible, without pattern or understandable structure. Nor should application of communication skills be allowed to rest upon a set of prescriptions with the implication of unvarying application.

The genesis of this book was in the need felt by the authors in teaching basic and advanced performance courses in general speech and public address. The texts employed focused upon application of "guide lines" as a basis for student improvement without fully involving the student in an attempt to understand the variables in communication that determine the degree of success or failure. Assigned supplementary readings, while of value, were often too scattered or the readings became unavailable. Further, students needed a framework with which the readings could articulate, thus providing the insight to the student that they yielded to us as instructors.

Further, students entering college today are prepared far beyond the levels of a few years ago. Most students have had some formal training in speech and extensive practical experience. Most seek to continue the development of the skills of communication, but they also seek to expand their insights concerning man and his world. A speech course has much to contribute to the understanding of man and the ways in which man relates to and manipulates his environment, particularly in terms of his interaction with other human beings. A knowledge of the communication process, its potential and its limitations, is central to a liberal arts education.

This book is designed to be a supplement to the textbook typically employed for a basic speech course. It may, of course, be found relevant by many instructors in more advanced or specialized courses. The material is of value to anyone concerned with the nature of communication and the process by which communication effects are achieved. The material is thus relevant to argumentation, persuasion, sales and advertising, some areas of sociology, psychology, and public opinion.

Any textbook must have some degree of flexibility. The various articles reprinted can stand alone and be used or omitted as an instructor desires. Spatial limitations were such that we could not include the number and variety of readings we would wish. Spatial limitations also made it impractical to develop the basis for many of the generalizations offered. Over one hundred bibliographical references could be cited revelant to source credibility alone. However, we have attempted to provide material that represents the state of knowledge of the field and to reflect our judgment of that material as reliably and validly as possible.

The introductory essays found with each section are progressive: they draw upon previous essays and readings as well as seek to integrate and develop the topics of the various readings that follow in a given section. The essays will prove more effective if read in sequence. While flexible and responsive to a variety of uses, the text hopefully achieves coherence and unity in a natural progress of the ideas and concepts developed.

In terms of a given section, some readers may wish to read the material in the order in which it is presented. Some may find it profitable to read the predictive generalizations to provide an overview and hypotheses for testing while reading the material of the section. Still others may find that rereading the introductory essays after the entire section has been read not only provides useful review but also enriches the insights derived from the introductory material.

Ann Arbor, Michigan   HOWARD H. MARTIN
August, 1967   KENNETH E. ANDERSEN

Contents

Speech Communication

ANALYSIS AND READINGS

SECTION I

Views of the dynamics
of communication

VARIANT VIEWS OF THE COMMUNICATIVE ACT

Kenneth E. Andersen

Communication at some level is a process common to all living things. Although not unique to man, the communication process is a particularly key vantage point for the study of *homo sapiens*. While the development of complex communication instrumentalities may not have been a prerequisite to the development of the species, man, it was certainly a necessary concomitant. Further, man's evolution is incomprehensible without awareness of the role of communication in the complex interactions of the family, in the growing complexity and interrelationships of social, economic, and political structures, in improved ability to solve problems, and in the ability to gain understanding of and control over relevant elements of his environment. Communication is the key instrumentality of man.

It is not surprising, then, that among the earliest writings of man, the nature of communication and the problem of enhancing man's effectiveness in achieving his private and social goals should receive significant attention. Rhetoric, defined broadly as the art of persuasion, received attention in the earliest recorded history of man. The writings of Homer bear testimony to the importance of persuasion in propitiating the Gods or changing the behavior of men. The Egyptian manuscript *The Instruction of Ptah-hotep* of about 3550 B.C. stressed the importance of effective communication.[1] Plato, particularly in his dialogues *Gorgias* and the *Phaedrus,* focused upon the methods of communication, the proper role and function of persuasion in human affairs and the proper teacher and teaching of these skills. Aristotle, seminal thinker of many disciplines, provided the first codified, relatively complete theory in his *Rhetoric,* a theory that not only survives as a key historical treatise but also as a surprisingly modern work in many respects.

Despite the long, rich tradition of writing and teaching dealing with the theory and practice of communication, we might almost feel that *communication* is a recent construct of the twentieth century and that attention to and growth of communication theory and knowledge is but a few decades old. The last thirty years have witnessed a tremendous upsurge of interest in communication by scholars in many disciplines. Diligent study of communication theory and effective use of communi-

---

[1] Raymond G. Smith, *Principles of Public Speaking* (New York: Ronald Press Co., 1958), p. 7.

cation skills have been variously urged as the key to world survival, wedded bliss, the understanding of philosophy, the understanding of human behavior, the means to man's reformation, the cure for mental illness and the magic key to wealth, power, and influence.

Communication is legitimately of concern because it is necessary both for the functioning of every individual and of every academic discipline. Since communication is involved in every individual's life, anyone should desire the ability to utilize that process more effectively. Every academic discipline employs the communication process to prepare new scholars, to exchange information, to seek new answers. Just as no one man may properly claim to know all the answers necessary to achieve success in every instance, no one academic discipline can claim hegemony over the formulation of communication theory, the study of the communication process, or the imparting of communication skills.

It is patent that every individual uses communication and that every discipline uses communication; yet some men and some disciplines are more interested in certain aspects of communication than are others. To gain a clearer perspective, we may examine communication in terms of three different but interrelated levels: use, study, and application.

1. *Level of use.* Man normally employs his communication skills automatically and uncritically as if communication were as natural as breathing. "Is it raining?" "Cats and dogs." A moment's thought suggests that the question and answer involve a process that is by no means simple. The process involved reflects not only very complex mental activities but also the accumulated experience of both the questioner and the responder as well as the experience of generations with the English language. Without this backlog of experience, the "simple" question and answer would have no meaning at all. And surely, the precise understanding of the rain conditions that you have differs to some degree from that of others reading about this brief exchange.

The somewhat elusive point which we seek to index by the concept *level of use* is that once the process is mastered to a certain degree, all humans tend to accept communication as the *natural thing,* as if speaking English were more natural than speaking French. We employ communication uncritically, without conscious awareness of the process involved. Only when the differences between meanings held by two individuals become so large that a "breakdown" in communication occurs do we focus upon communication as a factor.

Communication skills and abilities, once acquired, become the means by which we learn most of what we know about our world. They become the means by which we seek to modify our environment in order to meet our needs by obtaining desired responses from others.

The Platonic dialogues stressed the Socratic method. "What do you mean by . . . ?" "What is the essence of . . . ?" On an examination when asked to define *rhetoric* you might write, "Rhetoric is the art and science of the persuasion process." The dialogues and the examination question are concerned with the level of use. They focus, not on the problems of the process of communication, but ask questions about *things*, the *things* presumably symbolized by these words.

Thus, the level of use is concerned with communication as the normal currency of human interaction in which the communication is used to focus upon subjects or topics without significant awareness of the process of communication being involved.

2. *Level of study.* Increasingly, scholars in many disciplines are not simply employing communication as a tool to talk about their subject matter but are seeking to learn about the communication process itself for the contribution such study can make to understanding human behavior, the patterns and structures of social situations, patterns of influence, the impact of the mass media, or other effects associated with communication.

Study of the process of communication is germane to many disciplines. The physicist is concerned with the communication between the thermostat and the furnace that heats a house. The computer programer is concerned with the problem of communicating with the computer. The psychologist is concerned with communication as the central factor in human behavior: How does learning occur as a result of these symbols on this piece of paper? What elements induce or facilitate attitude change? How does a student raised in a conservative environment suddenly become an effective, recognized leader of the campus radicals? The cyberneticist may study the similarities between communication between machines and the thinking process within a man. The linguist may be concerned with studying the various patterns of sounds that make up a language. The linguist or the anthropologist may be concerned about the relationship between certain grammatical patterns and the reasoning forms that characterize a given culture. The social psychologist may ask why one Republican candidate wins the county by a landslide while the other Republican candidate loses by a narrow margin. The political scientist may seek to understand the forces that produced the John F. Kennedy victory. Avis wants to know how to replace Hertz as number one.

Anyone can pose several questions concerning communication that he personally would like to have answered. Some of these may be very general questions, some highly specific; some trivial, some of truly ultimate significance. "What difference does looking or not looking at an audience make? What makes the difference? What patterns of leadership typically result in greater amounts of work being accomplished? Does the Bible speak to today's youth? Can it be made more effective in its communication?"

The basis for the answer to such questions lies within what we term the *level of study*. It is at this level that scholars seek to describe communication behavior and to derive and test theories that may serve to make the communcation process more understandable and more predictable.

3. *Level of application.* In one sense the application level is very similar to the level of use discussed above, for the knowledge gained from the study of communication processes can be put to use to improve everyday conversation and communication. The *level of use* implies that communication is employed habitually, uncritically, without real awareness of the process, but at the *level of application* the body of theory and fact about communication is intentionally utilized to achieve some goal.

Ways in which advances in knowledge about the communication process can be utilized are endless: they may lead to other advances in knowledge or they may have highly practical effects. According to some projections, if Bell Telephone had not found more efficient ways to perform its role, every woman in the United States would now be employed as a telephone operator. (Perhaps employing all the women would reduce the amount of telephone conversations; thus a computer might project an optimum point short of employing all women.)

Knowledge of the communication process has enabled the physicist to develop equipment to handle more messages, more swiftly and more accurately. It has helped in the development of new families of computers. Study of the communication process has led government researchers to new techniques to increase the comprehension of information transmitted from control towers to pilots.

Knowledge of patterns of normal communication is of value to the speech therapist seeking to aid a student in correcting a lisp, of value to the psychiatrist in diagnosing and treating mental illness. Knowledge of the strengths and weaknesses of various patterns of information transmission and decision making may permit a systems analyst to restructure the organizational table of a large corporation with some confidence in the success which may be predicted. Such knowledge may enable an historian to present a more authoritative explanation of Lincoln's effectiveness or permit an anthropologist to offer a new insight concerning a primitive culture.

Knowledge of the communication process provides those who are concerned with developing improved communication skills in their students with the understanding needed to accomplish that task more effectively. The teacher who has some evidence of the relationship between certain classes of stimuli and certain patterns of audience response is capable of providing more insight into potentially effective communication behavior than the teacher forced to rely upon dogmatic presuppositions. And the advice or suggestions offered can be defended on the basis of evidence.

Thus, while communication is a process utilized by all, communication is also a subject of intensive study by people working in many disciplines. The fruits of such study can improve the ability of man to fulfill his goals more efficiently and fully, whether these goals are greater understanding of the past, more rapid growth of knowledge and technology in the present, or greater success in obtaining his goals in the future.

A POINT OF VIEW

This book does not purport to present an encyclopaedic survey of the process of communication as it exists in all living things nor does it summarize the manifold approaches to human communication. The essays and readings supplied, the generalizations attempted, and the questions posed are relevant to many communication forms, but the focus is upon communication as it occurs among humans. Although we recognize the analogies between machine and human communication and between the thought process within an individual and the communication process among individuals, our focus is interpersonal communication.

It is our view that all communication is ultimately persuasive in that it seeks to win a response to the communicator's ideas.[2] A play, a poem, a painting, a piece of music may be persuasive in that each may reinforce or modify someone's perceptions, attitudes or behavior. But our focus' is generally upon more *direct* communication in which the source has some lively sense of his audience and in which, among the persuasive stimuli, *language* plays a significant role. This focus is identified with prose, written or oral, as contrasted to poetry.

As an aid in analysis, various purposes of communication are often identified: to inform, to entertain, to stimulate, to convince, to actuate, with the latter three often subsumed under the term to persuade. Although useful for some purposes, we have avoided discussing communication in terms of these purposes. In everyday communication, it is often difficult to discern meaningful differences in terms of the various purposes: what one speaker, or listener, or critic may view as informative, another may see as persuasive. While a particular speech may stimulate great emotional response from one listener, it may stimulate reflective thinking in another.

Rather, we have focused upon various factors involved in communication with particular emphasis on the processes of attention, perception and comprehension, and acceptance. These processes are basic keys to the success of a communicator in reaching his goal with the receivers. This goal may range from being noticed, being accepted,

---

[2] This point will be clarified by examining the "Sampling of Definitions" which is included at the close of the readings provided with this section. Greater similarities exist between some definitions of *communication* and *persuasion* than among the definitions of *communication*.

sharing a feeling or experience, communicating some element of information, to winning support for a new bond issue, a political candidate, or obtaining a new job. This book seeks to examine the process in which one person seeks to influence one or more other persons in some significant way, i.e. to communicate.

In short, we stress an area often indexed by the term *rhetoric*. As Aristotle employed the term, rhetoric was the search for the available means of persuasion, including all possible sources available to the speaker to "demonstrate" something to the satisfaction of the listener. The essays, readings, generalizations and problems included in this book should contribute to some estimate of what is known about communication as a key form of human interaction.

Although restricting our focus to communication as a mode of human interaction and influence, many alternative emphases are still possible. Analysis could center entirely upon what is said, the message stimuli. Or analysis could center upon the speaker or writer: what he does, how he responds to various external and internal stimuli. Or analysis could center upon the impact of channels or situations: their properties, their restrictions. This book emphasizes the communication effects produced in receivers as the key to analysis of the communication process. This emphasis is often identified as *audience-centered* in that the attempt to understand the process of communication involves isolating the various elements involved and describing the ways in which these interact to produce effects in the audience. The audience is made the key through which elements in the communication can be evaluated as effective or ineffective. The tension a speaker may feel in communicating can be studied in terms of the impact on the speaker himself, but with an audience-centered or effects approach, the ultimate concern is with the effect such tension has upon the receivers.

The remainder of this book is the operationalization of this approach. The concluding section of this essay and the readings which accompany it examine some of the ways in which communication has been approached historically and contemporarily. Later sections discuss the effects of various communication settings; the strategies of manipulating attention, perception and comprehension, and acceptance; the limits imposed upon communication effects; and, finally, some of the varied methods of discovering and/or assessing effects in communication.

MODELS OF THE COMMUNICATION PROCESS

In order to describe and study the communication process, it is useful to isolate the factors involved in communication and attempt to relate them one to the other. Whether done verbally or diagrammatically, this technique provides an opportunity to visualize potential relationships and to pose hypotheses about the process. In the remainder of this essay we will be examining various approaches to communication in terms of the elements seen as involved in the process and the dynamic interaction of those elements in producing communication effects.

The Classical Tradition

As mentioned previously, rhetorical theory was the subject of many early writings. Rhetoric was a more overtly important academic discipline in classical and renaissance education than it is at the present time.

The evolution of the rhetorical tradition can be followed from Ancient Greece through Roman and medieval writers to a resurgence in England during the Renaissance and a second resurgence in the late 1700's and early 1800's. Key English writers of this latter period, Hugh Blair, George Campbell, and Richard Whately, were influential forces in the rhetorical tradition which was transmitted to the United States during this period. Rhetorical theory as applied in oral or written communication has remained an important element in America with some of the most stimulating additions to the tradition being made in the last few decades.

Such a long tradition obviously involves many different contributors and shows the impact of many diverse influences.[3] Some elements have tended to remain central and important over the "long-view," although these elements were at times overshadowed or forgotten and then later rediscovered. In almost every era, however, the writing of Aristotle has remained the central criterion in the rhetorical tradition, a standard against which the theory and practice of other times has been measured.

It is our view that the modern additions to communication theory are in some respects very much in consonance with the essence of the rhetorical tradition. Two brief excerpts included as readings with this section are drawn from that tradition: *The Rhetoric of Aristotle* (translated by Lane Cooper) and *The Philosophy of Rhetoric* by George Campbell. Both are quite contemporary in their emphasis upon speakers framing messages in terms of a psychology of their auditors. While attempting to provide useful generalizations about the nature of man, they remain sensitive to the differences among men in terms of the various forces the respective authors perceive as shaping the responses of the human animal.

Aristotle's rhetoric focussed upon those forms of public communication which were the chief means of achieving social consensus in his

[3] For a condensed but relatively comprehensive summary of the evolution of the classical tradition see Chapters 2, 3 and 4 in Lester Thonssen and A. Craig Baird, *Speech Criticism* (New York: Ronald Press Co., 1948), pp. 27–145.

time: pleading in the courts, deliberation in the legislative setting and celebration of men and events in popular assemblies. Since each of these forms of discourse was persuasive, his definition of rhetoric stressed the means of discovering the available means of persuasion. Aristotle, while concerned with transmitting an understanding of the persuasion process, was essentially concerned with providing prospective speakers with a knowledge of the skills involved in becoming more effective persuaders.

The three key elements in the Aristotelian view of communication seem to be the speaker, the speech, and the listener(s). Further, his treatment places relatively little emphasis upon any interaction between the speaker and his audience in the communication act; rather he treats communication in large part as a one-way affair in which the speaker presents his speech to his listeners. This view is represented graphically in Figure I.

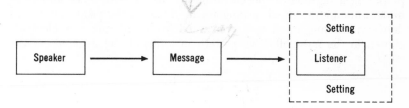

Figure 1. Aristotle's View of the Communication Process.

Presumably, Aristotle saw communication as a dynamic process in which the speaker sought to alter the perceptions, attitudes, and actions of his receivers through the medium of a speech. In providing guidelines and insights concerning the preparation of an effective speech, Aristotle provides the basis for a more elaborated model of the communicative act in the overtly persuasive situation.

Aristotle saw four stages in the preparation and delivery of persuasive speeches: invention, arrangement, style, and delivery. The most important of the stages was that of invention. In the process of invention the speaker sought to find those materials which he could include in his speech which would serve as proofs. Proofs, the reasons why people believe things to be demonstrated, were of three kinds: logical, emotional, or ethical. These proofs were to be supplied by the speaker and were in addition to the facts available on the subject of the speech. Since Aristotle saw persuasion as dealing with matters of probability and doubt rather than matters of pure fact on which certainty was achieved simply as the result of demonstrations, proof became the key to success. The task of the speaker was to select from among the possible proofs those which were most likely to win the belief of the audience he faced.

Although Aristotle wished to underscore the importance of the logical proofs, in an extended treatment of a psychology of man he discussed human emotions and those characteristics of men that presumably determine their response to events: their age, economic and social status, and the goals they seek. He sought to provide generalizations which would help a speaker to understand the various types of listeners or, as his teacher, Plato, had said, to know the soul of man.

Since Aristotle dealt with only three public advocacy settings, there is little basis for conjecture about the role Aristotle attributed to settings for other communication acts. Aristotle did see the setting as meaningful in terms of the topics that might be treated and the nature of the listeners one was likely to have, and he provided advice on the types of proof likely to be maximally effective as a result of these factors.

Although invention was the most significant part of the process of preparing a persuasive speech, three additional steps were important in determining the effect: arrangement, obtaining the proper style, and delivery. Arrangement was concerned with ordering the elements chosen in the most effective pattern in terms of the demands of the

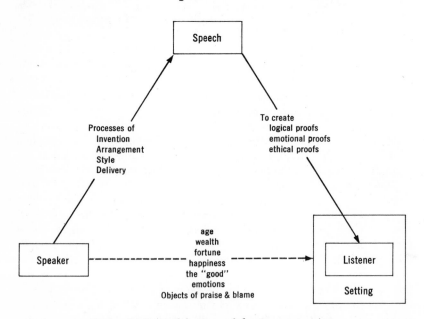

Figure 2. Aristotle's View of the Persuasion Act.

The speaker forms expectations about his audience in terms of the things he knows about audiences in general and this particular audience in this particular setting. He then plans his speech seeking to gain maximum effectiveness by building into the speech material to serve as logical, emotional and ethical proofs to his audience—thus inducing belief.

subject, the audience, and other factors in the setting. The perfecting involved attention to ensuring the maximum clarity and impact of the language employed. Finally, the fourth step was the actual delivery of the speech to the audience.

Figure 2 provides a representation of the more complex set of processes which Aristotle seemed to perceive as operating.

The Aristotelian model, as suggested previously, provided the dominant standard against which the variations of succeeding writers or rhetoric have been measured. Although our summary of the classical tradition tends to stress the importance of content in producing effects, at times the content has been treated as largely irrelevant except as a basis for adornment in fantasy of invention, richness of style, or the showiness of delivery. In part these latter conditions seem to match periods in which the freedom of speech is placed under restrictions or when discourse becomes valued more as a medium of entertainment or verbal play rather than a medium of influence and persuasion.

To attempt generalizations about the contribution of this classical tradition to contemporary theory and research is dangerous. But the influence of the tradition can be seen in speech and English composition textbooks and classroom instruction today.[4] And much of the experimental research as well as evaluations of the effectiveness of communication by those within and without the speech discipline has functioned within a theory of communication akin to that of the classical tradition. Therefore, certain generalizations about the contribution of the classical tradition will be offered although these generalizations should be limited and qualified more carefully than space permits.

1. Mastery of rhetorical theory and its allied skills has generally been thought to be basic to the functioning of society and of utility to all men, but a requirement for an educated man as a means of personal influence.[5]

2. Although given writers have varied emphases, rhetoric has typically been seen as a process involving components of a source, message, and a receiver. For many writers the setting functions as a fixed element to which the speaker adjusted, and not as a variable element influencing the dynamics of opinion change.

3. Rhetoric has tended to focus upon the nature of the listener both generally and particularly. Thus, writings of a period tend to reflect the psychological theories of that period. Rhetorical theorists try to offer useful generalizations about the nature of man and to recog-

---

[4] This development is traced in Karl Wallace, ed., *A History of Speech Education in America* (New York: Appleton-Century-Crofts, Inc., 1954).

[5] Often writers or critics of rhetoric have been concerned with the relationship of rhetoric to the effective propagation of truth, sacred or secular. Most writers have suggested that rhetoric has either an ethical component or concomitant, although most authors refer the reader to other sources or to his own ethics as a basis for this ethical code.

nize the individual differences possible among men due to their education, age, attitudes, and status.

4. Most writers seem aware of the interaction of the elements in the rhetorical situation with the speaker responsible for adjusting to these differences. Thus, a hostile audience demands a different treatment than a friendly audience; a speech on a formal occasion demands a different treatment than informal conversation. This view gives rise to the doctrine of appropriateness, adjusting elements to fit the demands of the situation.

5. Although most writers here seemed to be aware of the importance of adjusting to the particular differences in each communication situation, the generalizations they provided have frequently been treated by later writers as prescriptions. Often what began as an attempt to describe communication culminated in pedantic prescriptions.

6. Although a knowledge of rhetoric as a methodology is important for the successful speaker, he needs a broad education in many fields.

In summary, although the rhetorical tradition has stressed a communication model which seems to overtly involve a speaker, a message, a situation-environment-setting, and a listener, it has tended to focus upon the application of the understanding of communication to the preparation and delivery of an effective speech.

Contemporary Models

As noted previously, the communication process has become a prime target of study and research by scholars in many disciplines during recent decades. Not surprisingly, somewhat different emphases have emerged in the various fields. We shall explore a few models drawn from the fields of psychology, the physical sciences, and public address. These models tend to consider a broader range of communication possibilities than the formal advocacy situation of speaker to audience stressed by the classical tradition.

Psychological Models. Social psychologist Theodore Newcomb approached communication from the standpoint of human interaction. The goal of his model was to focus on "the essential function of enabling two or more individuals to maintain simultaneous orientation toward one another as communicators and toward the objects of communication."[6]

Unlike Aristotle, Newcomb is highly concerned with the two-way interaction potential in the communication situation—the direct relationship existing between a speaker (A) and a listener (B) as well as

[6] Theodore M. Newcomb, "An Approach to the Study of Communicative Acts," *Psychological Review*, LX (1960), 393.

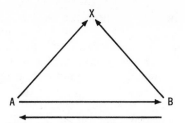

Figure 3. Newcomb's Representation of the Minimal Elements in the Communication Act.*

* Reprinted from Theodore M. Newcomb, "An Approach to the Study of Communicative Acts," *Psychological Review*, LX (1953), 394. By permission of the American Psychological Association, Inc.

their individual perceptions of the matters treated in the communication. This model suggests the potential of frequent alternation of the roles of speaker and listener, an element ignored by Aristotle. The message or the communicative act is not represented as an element in this model, for it is the totality of the relationships pictured in the model that is the communicative act.

The Newcomb model has been elaborated into more complex structures. Of particular interest is the model of Westley and MacLean

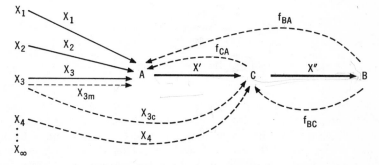

Figure 4. The Westley and MacLean Communication Model.*

The messages C transmits to B (X'') represent his selections from both messages to him from A's (X') and C's selections and abstractions from Xs in his own sensory field (X_{BC}, X_3), which may or may not be Xs in A's field. Feedback not only moves from B to A (f_{BA}) and from B to C (f_{BC}) but also from C to A (f_{CA}). Clearly, in the mass communication situation, a large number of Cs receive from a very large number of As and transmit to a vastly larger number of Bs, who simultaneously receive from other Cs.

* Reprinted from Bruce H. Westley and Malcolm S. MacLean, Jr., "A Conceptual Model for Communications Research," *Journalism Quarterly*, XXXIV (1957), 35.

which represents the role of messages as a part of reality and also which is particularly applicable to mass communication settings.

Most communications are the result of a man's prior stimulation by other messages. The communication which C directs to B may not only incorporate elements of the communication received from A; that communication from A may be the cause of the communication to B.[7] Furthermore, the factors operating upon the various persons in the communication situation are not the same. Different perceptions of reality may exist, different external forces may be acting upon the different people as well as different internal forces.

Information Theory Models. Although a variety of writers have worked with information theory models, the credit for the initial impetus for this model belongs to Claude Shannon and Warren Weaver.[8] Shannon, working in the Bell Telephone Laboratories, was concerned with the problem of message transmission: what happened to the information in a message from the time it was transmitted by a source until it was received at a destination. A somewhat elaborated representation of the model is seen in Figure 5.

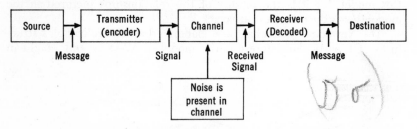

Figure 5. An Information Theory Model.

Although the impact of this model is more fully explained in the article by Broadhurst and Darnell which is reprinted in this section, a brief summary will be helpful. In essence this model describes a process in which a transmitter acts upon information from a source to put it into a channel in the form of a signal. This signal together with additional stimuli (noise) is picked up by the receiver at the destination.

The model drew attention to several factors. Among them:

1. It gave a rather precise meaning to the concept of *information.* Information was defined in terms of the reduction of the degree of uncertainty, randomness, or what Shannon termed entropy. Material

---

[7] This model also serves conveniently as a representation of the "two-step" flow of communication in which a communication to one person is then transmitted to other persons by the initial receiver. Thus the spread of influence goes beyond the audience originally reached by the initial communication.

[8] Claude E. Shannon and Warren Weaver, *The Mathematical Theory of Communication* (Urbana: The University of Illinois Press, 1949).

which provided no reduction in the uncertainty present for the destination contained no information. This approach permitted a mathematical measure of information. It also led to the concept that when the information of source and receiver are equal, communication ceases.

2. Noise, viewed as additional but unwanted stimuli, was indicated as always being present in the channel to be picked up by the receiver along with the desired signal. By analogy, in a crowded room with everyone talking, the stimuli irrelevant to and interfering with desired stimuli, constitute noise. Of course, noise is not a totally negative concept. What is noise at one moment may be key information at another moment. Further, noise has positive values in that it causes people to work to overcome the problem, thus to some extent improving communication potential.

3. The concept of noise led to a focus on problems relative to the ability of a channel to transmit information, adequacy of receivers and transmitters, and other problems relative to improving the adequacy of signal transmission.

Compared to the previous models, the information theory model focused quite specifically upon the problem of accuracy of signal transmission. In discussing Shannon's contribution, Warren Weaver distinguished three levels at which communication problems may be studied. The first level focuses upon the technical question: how accurately can symbols be transmitted? The second level focuses upon a semantic question: how accurately can meaning be communicated? The third and most complex level, which involves both of the previous two levels, focuses upon the strategic question: how can the desired communication effect be achieved?[9]

To a large degree information theorists have concentrated upon questions related to the transmitter, channel, receiver, and noise sources, that is, upon the *technical* problems of communication. The semanticist and the psycholinguist have focused more generally upon the problems related to language and meaning, the *semantic* problems of communication. Finally, psychologists and those concerned with attitude change engendered by communication have stressed the relationship between effects and the manipulation of stimuli by sources, the *strategic* problems of communication. These latter researchers have drawn upon the findings concerning the technical level to some degree and matters relative to the semantic level to a more marked degree in the study of strategic problems of communication.[10]

[9] Warren Weaver, "Recent Contributions to the Mathematical Theory of Communication," in *The Mathematical Theory of Communication* by Claude E. Shannon and Warren Weaver (Urbana: The University of Illinois Press, 1949, 1963), pp. 96–97.

[10] You may find it interesting to compare these models with that of Wendell Johnson in *Your Most Enchanted Listener* (New York: Harper and Brothers, 1956), back leaf.

Communication Effects Models. Many models could be presented which aid in conceptualizing the elements involved in the communication process that contribute to the effects obtained.[11] Our discussion will be limited to three models, each of which provides somewhat different emphases.

The first model (see Figure 6) is an information theory model modified to place more emphasis upon the nature of human communication.

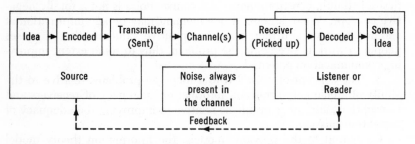

Figure 6. A Modified Information Theory Model.

The *source* is the originator of the message. The source may be a man arguing with a friend on the street, a news commentator or the corporate entity called the *New York Times.*

Presumably, *an idea* exists in the mind of this source. The source may have become conscious of the idea as a result of stimuli wholly within the source or as a response to stimuli largely outside the source. Often the idea is a response to some communication from another.

The idea must be *encoded,* that is, it must be put into some kind of symbol system. Perhaps the idea came to the source in one pattern of symbols but, due to any of a variety of reasons, the source may decide to express the idea differently. He may well weigh two or three alternative patterns for the expression.

The *transmitter* takes the code and puts it into the channel, usually in the process changing the code in some way. The symbols inside one's head are not the same as the physical movements and the sound patterns that are transmitted.

The *channel* is the medium through which the code or signal is sent. It may be air, water, or print on a newspaper page. What is normally called the *message* has physical reality in the channel as distinct from the meanings that the source or the receiver may attach to the stimuli that constitute the message.

[11] F. Craig Johnson and George R. Klare, "General Models of Communication Research: A Survey of the Developments of a Decade," *Journal of Communication,* XI (March, 1961), 13–26.

Noise, defined as distracting stimulation, is present in the channel and picked up by the receiver.

The *receiver* picks up the stimuli in the channel and sends them to the decoder. Often the receiver is *tuned,* whether electronically or as a result of the attention process, selectively to accept or to reject given stimuli.

The *decoder* translates the stimuli picked up by the receiver into some type of "meaning" for the receiver.

Some idea results from the decoding process. This idea goes beyond that provided by the decoding process in that the listener provides added meanings from his store of previous experiences. The idea would be identical to that intended by the source if the communication process were perfect. In the best of situations the ideas of source and listener are relatively comparable. At times the communication process may "break down" so that little or no similarity of ideas is present.

Feedback describes the response which the listener may make to the stimulation which he receives. This response may provide a cue to the success or failure of the communication and provide a basis for correction or modification of future or additional communication.[12] This response may be quite unconscious on the part of the listener or may be conscious. The student falling asleep in the lecture provides feedback for the teacher just as the student who says, "Could you clarify that?" This is not to suggest that feedback is totally determined by the stimuli provided by the source. Feedback results from the complex mental processes that mediate the response which any listener may make. The no-doze pills taken yesterday may be far more the cause of the student's falling asleep than the lecture. Still, the feedback has utility in that it enables the lecturer to modify succeeding communication efforts.

This model is a useful representation of many communication situations. For example, when two people are engaged in conversation, the speaker functions to provide the idea, the encoding, and the transmitting. Each of these stages involves very complex processes, none of which is fully understood. The source may be conscious of limited elements of these processes, but like the proverbial iceberg, far more is hidden and unconscious. Similarly, the auditor functions to provide the receiver which picks up the signal, the decoding, and the derivation of some idea, all of which may be followed by feedback, often by his becoming the communicator. This interrelated set of processes normally occurs without conscious awareness of the processes.

This model can also be generalized to more complex and involved communication situations such as those of the mass media. Section II

[12] Norbert Wiener has been a key figure in the emphasis given to feedback. For example, see Norbert Wiener, *Cybernetics* (New York: John Wiley & Sons, 1948).

of this book devotes extensive space to a discussion of the differences between various communication settings in terms of the relationship of these elements.

Although this model may be employed to represent many communication situations, it gives emphasis to the various elements involved in the technical and semantic areas of communication, and is a useful model to employ in discussing problems associated with the communication of meaning at the various stages of the process as represented by the model.

The model presented in Figure 7 places very limited emphasis upon the technical and semantic aspects of the communication act and stresses the interaction of various complex factors that are involved in the understanding and explanation of communication effects. This model gives particular stress to the interactive possibilities present in the dynamic act we call communication.

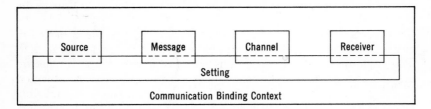

Figure 7. An Elements in Effects Model.

Source Elements
1. Ideas
2. Experiences
3. Attitudes & beliefs
4. Communication abilities
5. Knowledge
6. Interests
7. Group memberships
8. Goals, needs, values

Message Elements
1. Ideas
2. Organization
3. Language
4. Delivery
   a. spoken
   b. written

Channel Elements
1. Face-to-face stimuli
2. Vocal stimuli
3. Visual stimuli
4. Print
5. Mass media—TV, radio, magazines

Receiver Elements
1. Ideas
2. Experiences
3. Attitudes & beliefs
4. Communication abilities
5. Knowledge
6. Interests
7. Group memberships
8. Goals, needs, values

Communication Binding Context
1. Process nature of communication
2. Impact of time
3. Interactive effects of one element upon another
4. Differences in perceptions

Setting
1. State of the world
2. State of the problem
3. Environment
4. Audience size
5. Public or private

The *source* is the presumed originator of the message. This does not suggest, however, that the source is totally free to formulate any message. He must draw upon such ideas and information as he has available to him. He brings a complex of ideas, attitudes, and beliefs that he accepts at some level of certainty and that he acts upon as *truths*. He possesses a vocabulary and a variety of skills in communication. He also brings his needs, his goals, and his aspirations which he seeks to fulfill through the medium of communication. In general, we may hypothesize that a source's communication attempts result from a *need* to communicate. If the effort of communication far exceeds the possible reward, communication will not occur.

Obviously the source makes many conscious decisions. In some instances he may feel that he is weighing every word—painfully tearing them out of his being. But each decision he makes rests upon the limits imposed by his perceptions and his ability to respond appropriately to the many factors involved in the communication. Many of the elements relevant to communication cannot be consciously controlled, and of those that can, only a few can be the object of careful, conscious control at any given time. And the factors that will contribute to the ultimate effect are so varied that the source cannot hope to perceive all of them and if he could, would lack sufficient knowledge to shape all of them to his end.

The *message,* if it is a speech, is a complex of audible and visible stimuli which are originated by the source and which exist in the channel. Whatever the source might have said, intended to say, or thinks he said, the message is what he did say. Although many of the elements in the message were probably consciously included, many others are present without any volitional act by the source. A speaker may not have intended to pronounce the *t* in *often,* he may not have meant to sway back and forth, he may not have realized just how a particular idea was being worded, but these things may be in the message.

For purposes of analysis it is important to separate and distinguish the message from the source. It is hard to think of a smile by a speaker being a part of the message and separate and independent of the source, but such a conception is useful, particularly for purposes of experimental research. Messages can be captured on film, videotape, cinerama or in print and reproduced without variation. No other element in the communication process as suggested by this model can be held so constant and reproduced without change.

It is important to remember that the message itself is simply a complex of stimuli, whether characters on a page or sound waves. Messages *mean* only to people—any meanings this stimuli may have are products of human response. The stimuli in the message may be studied in terms of elements other than meaning, duration, repetition of certain symbols, sentence structure, number of gestures, for example;

but questions of meaning must be discussed in terms of human judgments.

The *channel* has already been discussed. It should be noted that different channels transmit different kinds of stimuli: the face-to-face situation provides some stimuli which a radio broadcast does not. Words on a printed page are not the same stimuli as those words spoken orally. Also, channels may have a direct effect on the results of communication: some people believe what they hear on the news while others trust only the printed word to give the "whole truth."

The *setting* is the context in which a communication takes place; communication does not occur in a vacuum. The setting includes the immediate environment: the temperature of the room, the presence of a large, noisy fan, tea being served at the back of the room, the events which have preceded the communication and provide a psychological setting. The setting also includes a larger context: the state of the world, the status of the item under discussion, the conditions under which the people involved are operating. Section II discusses the impact of settings upon communication.

The *receiver* is the term used in this model to designate the person or persons who hear, read, or otherwise receive the communication. They may be intended recipients or accidental receivers. Each individual receiver gives a *meaning* to the stimuli in the message. Each receiver brings to the communication situation his prior experiences, attitudes, beliefs, needs, group memberships, his vocabulary and skills in communication.

In what we normally term influence situations, the receiver is presumed to be free to respond as he *chooses*. In some situations the receiver is perceived as having no choice, for example, when a gun is held to his head or the life of his child is threatened. But even in normal communication situations, choices are obviously not *free* in the sense that certain results do follow. A student may refuse to report when drafted. He is *free* to do this, but certain things are likely to follow in the wake of this choice. And, within limits, the persuader seeks to manipulate the elements in the communication framework so that the choice is predetermined to the maximum degree possible within the persuader's capabilities.

⌈This book adopts an audience-centered view which means that communication effects are studied in terms of the responses of receivers to communication stimuli.⌋ But humans are both receivers and sources. Often through feedback a receiver provides the means to accomplish his own persuasion if these means are understood and acted upon by the persuader. Further, although every man is different, men do respond in generalized patterns based on such things as general culture, shared experiences and past habits.

The concept of the *communication binding context* is used to stress the complex process that is communication. This process involves not one or two of the five elements discussed above, nor the five acting independently, but all five dynamic elements interacting to produce the communication effect. Like many processes, it is useful for the purpose of analysis to *freeze* the activity and to focus on one stage or one element in the process. However, to stop the action, to examine one element out of context with the others, is to alter the actual process. One of the major problems in studying communication is the need to maintain a *real* communication process while attempting to isolate the effect of one or two elements in the process.

The communication binding context also directs attention to the fact that the perceptions of elements within the communication process may vary greatly. One receiver may see the setting as a time for prayer and thanksgiving. Another receiver may view the setting as an invitation to simply having a good time. But for the source, the setting may suggest the opportunity to celebrate the Fourth of July by announcing his candidacy for reelection and detailing at great length his service to the assembled audience. Each of these perceptions may contribute to the ultimate effects of the communication process.

Starting from this point that perceptions of the various elements in the communication situation may be different in terms of the various participants, the communication binding context may be useful in considering the effects of time in the communication process. What were Aristotle's perceptions of the elements in the communication process as he created the *Rhetoric*? What is your perception as you read it? How and in what sense are the two of you bound together in communication?

Failures in communication often become understandable if an observer studies communication, not from the point of view of the speaker or the listener, but by standing as it were outside the process itself and looking at communication in terms of the communication binding context.

The final model to be presented is provided by Carl Hovland and his associates. As seen in Figure 8 this model stresses the processes that occur within the receiver to mediate between the stimuli impinging upon him during the communication process and his response, if any, to these stimuli. Hovland's model groups those items we have focused upon individually in some of the previous models as elements within what he terms the communication situation. The stimuli arising from these sources are affected by various predispositions or tendencies which the receiver has derived from previous experiences. These predispositions are *givens* which the listener brings to a speech, a reader to a newspaper article. Three internal mediational processes—attention, comprehension, and (possibly) acceptance—operate upon the stimuli as the basis for the response to the communication. Such attention, comprehension and acceptance as may occur are linked to the predispositional factors as well as the communication stimuli. Thus a receiver may be predisposed to give attention to anything relevant to one given issue. Or acceptance may result because of the situation in which many in the audience are being enthusiastically carried along with the speaker and the particular listener is quite suggestible in such situations.

Attention, comprehension and acceptance are interrelated processes: if no attention is given to the stimulus, comprehension and acceptance are unlikely to occur; if comprehension proves too difficult, attention may be withdrawn. Ultimately these processes may result in some form of attitude change which may be manifested in various

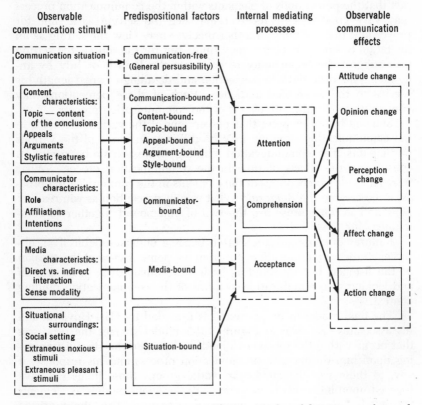

Figure 8. Major Factors in Attitude Change Produced by Means of Social Communication.*

The categories and subcategories are not necessarily exhaustive, but are intended to highlight the main types of stimulus variables that play a role in producing changes in verbalizable attitudes.

* Irving L. Janis and Carl I. Hovland, "An Overview of Persuasibility Research," in *Personality and Persuasibility*, eds. Carl I. Hovland and Irving L. Janis (New Haven: Yale University Press, 1959), p. 4. By permission of Yale University Press.

ways. These mediational processes are normally not thought of as directly observable although indications of these processes or cues to their existence may be present. But an awareness of these processes proves useful in understanding the various stages of response within a reader or a listener who is subjected to communication attempts. Again, it must be remembered that these processes are normally inferred, particularly during the communication process itself, and a speaker attempting to form some estimate of his success in terms of these processes may well be misled by the sources of feedback available.

SUMMARY

The introductory essay has emphasized the process of communication as a rich and complex field of study. The recent emphasis given to this process by many academic disciplines has resulted in a rapid expansion in knowledge about communication.

Communication, as the various models have attempted to show, is a complex, dynamic process in which a variety of elements and processes interact to produce effects. From Aristotle to the present day, communication theorists have stressed the dynamics of the process although contemporary writers are much more aware of the complexity of the interplay of the elements and individuals involved in communication. With an increasing understanding of the nature of man and his psychological processes, new opportunities to examine communication phenomena become available.

Once the majority of writers on communication seemed to emphasize the problems of creating a speech: finding the arguments, arranging them, putting them in suitable language and finding an effective method of delivering the material to the auditors. Now many communication scholars are more interested in the process itself and relatively less concerned with specific applications of their findings. The emphasis is now more often upon the characteristics of listeners and the processes of attention, comprehension and acceptance as these mediational processes interact with communication stimuli to produce communication effects. The latter approach is the one that we wish to emphasize in the pages that follow.

From THE RHETORIC

ARISTOTLE

I.1. [SCOPE AND PURPOSE OF THE ART.] [1] Rhetoric is the counterpart of
Dialectic [that is, the art of public speaking and the art of logical discussion are co-ordinate, but contrasted, processes]; for both have to do
with such things as fall, in a way, within the realm of common knowledge, things that do not belong to any one science. Accordingly, everybody to some extent makes use of both Dialectic and Rhetoric; for all
make some attempt to sift or to support theses, and to defend or attack
persons. Most people do so, of course, either quite at random, or else
merely with a knack acquired from practice. Success in either way
being possible, the random impulse and the acquired facility alike
evince the feasibility of reducing the processes to a method; for when
the practised and the spontaneous speaker gain their end, it is possible
to investigate the cause of their success; and such an inquiry, we shall
all admit, performs the function of an art.

Now hitherto the authors of 'Arts of Speaking' have built up but a
small portion of the art of Rhetoric truly considered; for this art consists of proofs [persuasions] alone—all else is but accessory. Yet these
writers say nothing of enthymemes, the very body and substance of
persuasion, and are concerned in the main with matters external to the
direct issue. Thus the arousing of prejudice, of pity, of anger, and the
like feelings in the soul, does not concern the facts, but has regard to
those who decide. Consequently, if trials were everywhere conducted
as at present they are in some cities—and especially in those that are
best-governed—pleaders who were guided by the handbooks would
have nothing to say; for by common consent the laws should forbid
irrelevant speaking, and some courts, as that of the Areopagus, actually
do forbid it. This certainly is right reason; the man who is to judge
should not have his judgment warped by speakers arousing him to
anger, jealousy, or compassion. One might just as well make a carpenter's rule crooked before using it as a measure. And obviously in a
dispute there is nothing to do beyond showing that the alleged fact does
or does not exist, has or has not occurred. The question whether it is

---

From: *The Rhetoric of Aristotle* (pp. 1–18), translated and edited by Lane
Cooper. Copyright, 1932, 1960 by Lane Cooper. Reprinted by permission
of Appleton-Century-Crofts.

[1] The brackets provide explanatory additions made by Cooper.

24

important or trivial, the question whether there is justice or injustice, so far as the legislator has not defined these points, that is precisely what the judge is there to decide; he is not supposed to learn his lesson from the disputants.

. . . it is clear that our authors of handbooks, in attempting to define the proper content of the Proem, the Narration, and the other divisions of the speech, and the like, are dwelling upon irrelevant matters, for their rules have to do, simply and solely, with the production of a certain mental attitude in the judge. These authors tell us nothing about artistic proofs—nothing, that is, about the way in which one is to become a master of the enthymeme. [By 'artistic' proofs or persuasions we are to understand systematic proofs by 'enthymeme' and 'example,' as opposed to 'non-artistic' proofs such as 'laws, witnesses, compacts (=documents), tortures (=ordeals, inquisitions), and oaths,' as distinct also from the emotional appeals (already noted) to the judges, and as distinct from evidence drawn from character. Aristotle here anticipates his explanation of 'artistic proofs.' By 'artistic' he means *appertaining to the art of Rhetoric proper;* by 'non-artistic,' what is external to the art—adventitious and adjunct means of persuasion that are not involved in the essential issue, which is the subject of the speech. Similarly he anticipates his explanation of 'enthymeme,' the rhetorical syllogism, drawn, not from the principles of the exact sciences, but from propositions, or probabilities, relating to everyday affairs. When he objects so vigorously to existing handbooks for their preoccupation with 'non-artistic proofs,' we are hardly prepared for Aristotle's own attention to them in the present treatise, which probably deals more systematically with the means of arousing emotion in the audience than did any of its predecessors. His extended treatment of the emotions is partly an inevitable concession to practice, for the orator must deal with an audience, and an audience necessarily is emotional; you may work on their emotions in a better way or a worse, but neglect them you cannot. Yet his method is also justified on grounds of perspective since he does subordinate the 'non-artistic' to the 'artistic' proofs, the accessories to the main issue; whereas, he contends, his predecessors wholly neglected what was fundamental. Accordingly, though he owes some actual debt to them, his perspective is good, where theirs doubtless was bad.] . . .

It is clear, then, that the artistic method has to do with proofs [persuasions] in the stricter sense. Now proof [persuasion] is a kind of demonstration; for we entertain the strongest conviction of a thing if we believe that it has been 'demonstrated.' Rhetorical proof, however, [is not scientific demonstration]; it takes the form of an enthymeme, this being, in general, the most effective among the various forms of persuasion. The enthymeme, again, is a kind of syllogism; now every kind of syllogism falls within the province of Dialectic, and must be examined under Dialectic as a whole, or under some branch of it.

Consequently the person with the clearest insight into the nature of syllogisms, who knows from what premises and in what modes they may be constructed, will also be the most expert in regard to enthymemes, once he has mastered their special province [of things contingent and uncertain such as human actions and their consequences], and has learnt the differences between enthymemes and logical syllogisms. [The latter are complete, and yield an absolute demonstration.] Truth and likeness to truth are discerned by one and the same faculty; while human nature, let us add, has aptitude enough for discerning what is true, and men in most cases do arrive at the truth. Consequently one who is skilled in discerning the truth can do well in weighing probabilities [matters of opinion].

It is clear, then, that our handbooks have limited the art to extraneous matters; and it is clear, too, why they have leaned to forensic speaking.

But the art of Rhetoric has its value. It is valuable, first, because truth and justice are by nature more powerful than their opposites; so that, when decisions are not made as they should be, the speakers with the right on their side have only themselves to thank for the outcome. Their neglect of the art needs correction. [A proper knowledge and exercise of Rhetoric would prevent the triumph of fraud and injustice.] Secondly, [Rhetoric is valuable as a means of instruction]. Even if our speaker had the most accurate scientific information, still there are persons whom he could not readily persuade with scientific arguments. True instruction, by the method of logic, is here impossible; the speaker must frame his proofs and arguments with the help of common knowledge and accepted opinions. This method has been noted in the *Topics*, in our remarks on popular discussion. [See Aristotle's *Topica* I. 2.] Thirdly, in Rhetoric, as in Dialectic, we should be able to argue on either side of a question; not with a view to putting both sides into practice—we must not advocate evil—but in order that no aspect of the case may escape us, and that if our opponent makes unfair use of the arguments, we may be able in turn to refute them. In no other art do we draw opposite conclusions; it is characteristic of Rhetoric and Dialectic alone that, abstractly considered, they may indifferently prove opposite statements. Still, their basis, in the facts, is not a matter of indifference, for, speaking broadly, what is true and preferable is by nature always easier to prove, and more convincing. Lastly, if it is a disgrace to a man when he cannot defend himself in a bodily way, it would be odd not to think him disgraced when he cannot defend himself with reason [in a speech]. Reason is more distinctive of man than is bodily effort. If it is urged that an abuse of the rhetorical faculty can work great mischief, the same charge can be brought against all good things (save virtue itself), and especially against the most useful things such as strength, health, wealth, and military skill. Rightly employed, they work the greatest blessings; and wrongly employed, they work the utmost harm.

We have seen that Rhetoric is not confined to any single and definite class of subjects, but in this respect is like Dialectic, and that the art has its uses; and we see that its function is not [absolutely] to persuade, but to discover the available means of persuasion in a given case. [Not outward success, but a correct method, is the criterion of art; the correct method will bring success in proportion. An unwarranted appeal to the emotions might win an undesirable success.] Herein Rhetoric is like all other arts. Thus the aim of medicine is not, strictly speaking, to restore a sick man to perfect health, but to bring him as near to health as the case admits; people who never can be well may yet be properly treated. Further, we see that it is the office of one and the same art to discern the genuine means, and also the spurious means, of persuasion, just as it is the office of Dialectic to discern the truth, and also the sham, syllogism; for sophistical dialectic, or sophistical speaking, is made so, not by the faculty, but by the moral purpose. [The faculty is the same in both arts.] There is this difference, however: we apply the term 'rhetorician' alike to describe a speaker's command of the art and a speaker's moral purpose; whereas, in the field of Dialectic, the term 'sophist' refers to the moral purpose, while 'dialectician' applies to the faculty [the normal function].

[Having thus made clear that Rhetoric is an art, and when rightly practiced an honest and useful art,] we must now proceed to discuss its method—the mode and the means that will enable us to attain to the proper ends. Accordingly, let us start afresh, as it were, first defining, and then going on to the rest.

I.2. [DEFINITION OF RHETORIC, MODES AND MEANS OF PERSUASION.] So let Rhetoric be defined as the faculty [power] of discovering in the particular case what are the available means of persuasion. This is the function of no other art [save Dialectic]. The others are each instructive or persuasive with regard to some special subject-matter. Thus medicine informs us about the conditions of health and disease; geometry about the properties of magnitudes; arithmetic about numbers; and so with the rest of the arts and sciences. But Rhetoric, it would seem, has the function of discovering the means of persuasion for every case, so to speak, that is offered; and hence we say that the art as such has no special application to any distinct class of subjects.

Proofs [persuasions] are of two kinds, artistic and non-artistic. [Or we might call them 'scientific' and 'unscientific.' Aristotle distinguishes means of persuasion that inherently belong in the art, and those that, while associated with it, are really external and adventitious.] By 'non-artistic' proofs are meant all such as are not supplied by our own efforts, but existed beforehand, such as witnesses, admissions under torture, written contracts, and the like. By 'artistic' proofs [means of persuasion] are meant those that may be furnished by the method of Rhetoric through our own efforts. The first sort have only to be used; the second have to be found.

Of the means of persuasion supplied by the speech itself there are three kinds. The first kind reside in the character [*ethos*] of the speaker; the second consist in producing a certain [the right] attitude in the hearer; the third appertain to the argument proper, in so far as it actually or seemingly demonstrates. [Under all three heads, and explicitly under the third, Aristotle makes room, with the scientific branch of Rhetoric, for devices related to those of the sophistical branch. As in the *Poetics*, we see that the artist may use elements that are somewhat external to the art itself, in a more artistic way rather than a less.]

The character [*ethos*] of the speaker is a cause of persuasion when the speech is so uttered as to make him worthy of belief; for as a rule we trust men of probity more, and more quickly, about things in general, while on points outside the realm of exact knowledge, where opinion is divided, we trust them absolutely. This trust, however, should be created by the speech itself, and not left to depend upon an antecedent impression that the speaker is this or that kind of man. It is not true, as some writers on the art maintain, that the probity of the speaker contributes nothing to his persuasiveness; on the contrary, we might almost affirm that his character [*ethos*] is the most potent of all the means to persuasion.

Secondly, persuasion is effected through the audience, when they are brought by the speech into a state of emotion; for we give very different decisions under the sway of pain or joy, and liking or hatred. This, we contend, is the sole aspect of the art with which technical writers of the day have tried to deal. We shall elucidate it in detail when we come to discuss the emotions.

Thirdly, persuasion is effected by the arguments, when we demonstrate the truth, real or apparent, by such means as inhere in particular cases.

Such being the instruments of persuasion, to master all three obviously calls for a man who can reason logically, can analyze the types of human character [*ethe*], along with the virtues, and, thirdly, can analyze the emotions—the nature and quality of each several emotion, with the means by which, and the manner in which, it is excited. Thus it follows that Rhetoric is a kind of offshoot, on the one hand, of Dialectic, and, on the other, of that study of Ethics which may properly be called 'political.' [With Aristotle, Ethics, the science dealing with individual conduct, shades off into Politics (a broader subject), which deals with the conduct and activities of men in groups—of the State.] And hence it is that Rhetoric, and those who profess it, slip into the guise of Politics [and political experts], whether from defects of education, or through quackery [imposture], or from other human failings. As we said at the outset, Rhetoric is a branch of Dialectic, and resembles that. Neither of them is a *science*, with a definite subject-matter; both are *faculties* for providing arguments. On their function, and on their relation to each other, perhaps enough has now been said.

[Let us turn to the instruments of persuasion.] As for real or apparent demonstration, there are in Rhetoric two modes, corresponding to the two modes in Dialectic. As in Dialectic we have, on the one hand, induction, and, on the other, the syllogism and apparent syllogism, so in Rhetoric: the example is a form of induction; while the enthymeme is a syllogism, and the apparent enthymeme an apparent syllogism. 'Enthymeme' is the name I give to a rhetorical syllogism, 'example' to a rhetorical induction. Whenever men in speaking effect persuasion through proofs, they do so either with examples or enthymemes; they use nothing else. Accordingly, since all demonstration (as we have shown in the *Analytics*) is effected either by syllogism [that is, deductively] or by induction, it follows that induction and syllogism [deduction] must be identified respectively with example and enthymeme. [See Aristotle's *Prior Analytics* 2. 23; *Posterior Analytics* I. 1, I. 18, 2. 19.] The difference between example and enthymeme may be inferred from the *Topics* [I. 1, 12]. There, with reference to syllogism [deduction] and induction, it has already been observed that to derive a general law from a number of like instances is in Dialectic induction, in Rhetoric example; whereas to conclude from certain assumptions that something else follows from those assumptions (something distinct from them, yet dependent upon their existing) either universally or as a rule—this in Dialectic is called a syllogism, and in Rhetoric an enthymeme. And of the corresponding two types of oratory it is plain that each has some advantage. What is said of Dialectic in our *Methodology* [a lost work of Aristotle] likewise holds true here; for, of the two kinds of speeches, in one the enthymeme predominates, in the other the example; and similarly some speakers are more given to examples, and others to enthymemes. Arguments through examples are not less persuasive, yet arguments in the form of the enthymeme are more applauded. The reason for this, and the right way of using both enthymemes and examples, will be discussed later. At present let us define the processes themselves more clearly.

'Persuasive' means persuasive to a person. To him, a statement may be persuasive and credible by itself, immediately, or it may become so when it seems to be proved from other statements that he believes. No art, however, has regard to the individual case. Thus medicine does not investigate the question what is a cure for Socrates or for Callias—for the individual as such—but asks what will cure a person or persons of such and such a type; the latter inquiry comes within the province of art, whereas, particulars being infinite, the individual fact cannot be scientifically known. And hence Rhetoric will consider, not what seems probable to the individual—to Socrates or to Hippias—but what seems probable to a given class; the same being true of Dialectic. [Conceivably, both Rhetoric and Dialectic might be used to argue any question or problem, but practically both are restricted.] Dialectic does not form its syllogisms out of any chance notions (such as the notions of crazy people), but takes problems that merit discussion; and similarly Rhetoric is applied to recognized subjects of deliberation. It has to do with things about which we commonly deliberate—things for which we have no special art or science; and with the sort of hearers who cannot grasp many points in a single view, or follow a long chain of reasoning. Now we deliberate about such things as appear to admit of two possibilities. [Is a course expedient or inexpedient, a deed just or unjust, a statement true or false?] On matters which admit of no alternative, which necessarily were, or will be, or are, certainties, no one deliberates, at least not on that supposition—for nothing is to be gained by it.

It is possible to construct syllogisms and draw conclusions in a chain, working successively with the results of those that precede; or you may draw upon propositions that have not been thus proved, yet need proof because they are not commonly accepted. But, necessarily, the first of these processes will be hard to follow because of its length, for we assume the judge [audience] to be of but ordinary intelligence; and the second method will be unconvincing because the conclusions are drawn from premises that are not admitted nor commonly believed.

Accordingly, the enthymeme, and likewise the example, must deal with matters which as a rule are variable (the example corresponding to an induction, and the enthymeme being a syllogism); and the links in the chain must be few—seldom as many as the links in a normal chain of deductions. Thus, if one of the premises is a matter of common knowledge, the speaker need not mention it, since the hearer will himself supply the link. For example, in showing that Dorieus was victor in a contest where the prize is a chaplet, it is enough to say, 'He has won a victory at the Olympic games.' The speaker need not add that the prize there was a chaplet, for everyone knows it.

Let us grant that only a few of the premises of rhetorical deductions are necessarily admitted, and that the majority of cases on which we must decide, and into which we must inquire, may lie this way or that; for men deliberate and raise questions about the things they do, and human actions all belong to this class [of uncertainties or mere probabilities]; no human action, so to speak, is inevitable. And we see that, in Rhetoric, for the most part merely usual and contingent conclusions must be drawn from premises of the same sort; just as, in Logic, necessary conclusions must arise from premises that are determined—a matter that has been settled for us in the *Analytics* [*Prior Analytics* I. 8]. All this being granted, it is clear that the premises from which a speaker derives his enthymemes are sometimes necessarily true, but in the main only generally true. In fact, the materials of enthymemes are (1) probabilities . . . and (2) signs. . . .

1.3. [THE KINDS OF ORATORY.] The kinds of Rhetoric are three in number, corresponding to the three kinds of hearers to which speeches are addressed; for, a speech being the joint result of three things—the speaker, his subjects, and the person addressed—the end or object has reference to this last, namely the hearer; and the hearer must be either (1) a mere observer [critic], or (2 and 3) a judge [decider], and, if the latter, then either (2) a judge of things past or (3) a judge of things to come. One who (3) decides about the future is, for example, an ecclesiast [member of the Assembly]; one who (2) judges about the past is, say, the dicast [juror in a court of law]; while the person who (1) decides about the force and merit of the speech [the 'faculty' or art displayed in it] is the critic [observer, 'theorist']. It follows that there must be three kinds of speeches in Rhetoric, (1) deliberative, (2) forensic, and (3) epideictic. [That is, there are (1) speeches of counsel or advice (deliberation)—as political speeches addressed to an assembly or to the public on questions of State, but also, for example, a speech addressed to an individual (a ruler, or, indeed, any person who is to be advised); (2) judicial speeches, used in prosecution and defence (more generally, in any kind of attack or defence); and (3) panegyrical or declamatory speeches, in the nature of an exhibition or display, eulogies—in general, speeches of praise (or blame).]

(1) The elements of deliberation [counsel] are (a) exhortation [encouragement], (b) dissuasion; for, as advice given in private always has one or the other aspect, so is it with those who discuss matters of State in public—they either exhort or dissuade. (2) The elements of forensic speaking are (a) accusation, (b) defence, since the parties to a legal action will necessarily be engaged in either one or the other. (3) The elements of an epideictic speech are (a) praise and (b) blame. As for the divisions of time which severally belong to these several kinds of speakers, to the deliberative speaker belongs the future, for he gives advice about things to come, exhorting or dissuading; to the judicial pleader belongs the past, for it is always with regard to things already done that the one party accuses and the other defends; and to the epideictic speaker, above all, belongs the present, for every one praises or blames with regard to existing conditions [qualities], though a speaker often adds to his resources with reminiscences from the past and conjectures about the future. [See, for example, the *Funeral Oration* by Pericles in the *History* of Thucydides; and compare Shakespeare's Antony in *Julius Caesar*, 3. 2. 76-7.]

For these three kinds of Rhetoric there are also three several ends. (1) The aim of the deliberative speaker concerns advantage and injury; for the one who exhorts recommends a course of action as better, and the one who dissuades deters us from it as worse; other considerations

—of justice and injustice, of honor and dishonor—he makes subsidiary to this end [of the expedient]. (2) The aim of judicial pleaders concerns justice and injustice, and they in like manner make the other considerations subsidiary to these. (3) The aim of those who praise and blame concerns honor and dishonor, and such speakers likewise subordinate the other considerations to these.

From THE PHILOSOPHY OF RHETORIC

GEORGE CAMPBELL

CHAPTER VII

*Of the Consideration which the Speaker ought to have of the Hearers,
as men in general*

RHETORIC, as was observed already, not only considers the subject,
but also the hearers and the speaker. The hearers must be considered
in a twofold view, as men in general, and as such men in particular.

As men in general, it must be allowed there are certain principles
in our nature, which, when properly addressed and managed, give no
inconsiderable aid to reason in promoting belief. Nor is it just to
conclude from this concession, as some have hastily done, that oratory
may be defined, "The art of deception." The use of such helps will be
found, on a stricter examination, to be in most cases quite legitimate,
and even necessary, if we would give reason herself that influence
which is certainly her due. In order to evince the truth considered by
itself, conclusive arguments alone are requisite; but in order to convince me by these arguments, it is moreover requisite that they be
understood, that they be attended to, that they be remembered by me;
and in order to persuade me by them to any particular action or conduct, it is further requisite, that by interesting me in the subject, they
may, as it were, be felt. It is not therefore the understanding alone
that is here concerned. If the orator would prove successful, it is
necessary that he engage in his service all those different powers of
the mind, the imagination, the memory and the passions. These are
not the supplanters of reason, or even rivals in her sway; they are her
handmaids, by whose ministry she is enabled to usher truth into the
heart, and procure it there a favourable reception. As handmaids they
are liable to be seduced by sophistry in the garb of reason, and sometimes are made ignorantly to lend their aid in the introduction of falsehood. But their service is not on this account to be dispensed with;
there is even a necessity of employing it, founded on our nature. Our
eyes and hands and feet will give us the same assistance in doing mischief as in doing good; but it would not therefore be better for the

George Campbell, *The Philosophy of Rhetoric,* New Edition (London:
William Tegg & Co., 1850), pp. 71–81, 95–96.

world, that all mankind were blind and lame. Arms are not to be laid aside by honest men, because carried by assassins and ruffians; they are to be used the rather for this very reason. Nor are those mental powers, of which eloquence so much avails herself, like the art of war or other human arts, perfectly indifferent to good and evil, and only beneficial as they are rightly employed. On the contrary, they are by nature, as will perhaps appear afterwards, more friendly to truth than to falsehood, and more easily retained in the cause of virtue, than in that of vice.

Section I—Men considered as endowed with Understanding

But to descend to particulars; the first thing to be studied by the speaker is, that his arguments may be understood. If they be unintelligible, the cause must be either in the sense or in the expression. It lies in the sense if the mediums of proof be such as the hearers are unacquainted with; that is, if the ideas introduced be either without the sphere of their knowledge, or too abstract for their apprehension and habits of thinking. It lies in the sense likewise, if the train of reasoning (though no unusual ideas should be introduced) be longer, or more complex, or more intricate, than they are accustomed to. But as the fitness of the arguments, in these respects, depends on the capacity, education, and attainments of the hearers, which in different orders of men are different, this properly belongs to the consideration which the speaker ought to have of his audience, not as men in general, but as men in particular. The obscurity which ariseth from the expression will come in course to be considered in the sequel.

Section II—Men considered as endowed with Imagination

The second thing requisite is that his reasoning be attended to; for this purpose the imagination must be engaged. Attention is prerequisite to every effect of speaking, and without some gratification in hearing, there will be no attention, at least of any continuance. Those qualities in ideas which principally gratify the fancy, are vivacity, beauty, sublimity, novelty. Nothing contributes more to vivacity than striking resemblances in the imagery, which convey, besides, an additional pleasure of their own.

But there is still a further end to be served by pleasing the imagination, than that of awakening and preserving the attention, however important this purpose alone ought to be accounted. . . . Belief commonly enlivens our ideas; and lively ideas have a stronger influence than faint ideas to induce belief. But so far are these two from being coincident, that even this connexion between them, though common, is not necessary. Vivacity of ideas is not always accompanied with faith, nor is faith always able to produce vivacity. The ideas raised in my mind by the Œdipus Tyrannus of Sophocles, or the Lear of Shakespeare, are incomparably more lively than those excited by a cold but faithful historiographer. Yet I may give full credit to the languid narrative of the latter, though I believe not a single sentence in those tragedies. . . .

Section III—Men considered as endowed with Memory

Further, vivid ideas are not only more powerful than languid ideas in commanding and preserving attention, they are not only more efficacious in producing conviction, but they are also more easily retained. Those several powers, understanding, imagination, memory, and passion, are mutually subservient. . . .

Section IV—Men considered as endowed with Passions

To conclude; when persuasion is the end, passion also must be engaged. If it is fancy which bestows brilliancy on our ideas, if it is memory which gives them stability, passion doth more, it animates them. Hence they derive spirit and energy. To say that it is possible to persuade without speaking to the passions, is but at best a kind of specious nonsense. The coolest reasoner always in persuading addresseth himself to the passions some way or other. This he cannot avoid doing, if he speak to the purpose. To make me believe it is enough to show me that things are so; to make me act, it is necessary to show that the action will answer some end. That can never be an end to me which gratifies no passion or affection in my nature. You assure me, "It is for my honour." Now you solicit my pride, without which I had never been able to understand the word. You say, "It is for my interest." Now you bespeak my self-love. "It is for the public good." Now you rouse my patriotism. "It will relieve the miserable." Now you touch my pity. So far therefore it is from being an unfair method of persuasion to move the passions, that there is no persuasion without moving them.

But if so much depend on passion, where is the scope for argument? Before I answer this question, let it be observed that, in order to persuade, there are two things which must be carefully studied by the orator. The first is, to excite some desire or passion in the hearers; the second is to satisfy their judgment that there is a connexion between the action to which he would persuade them, and the gratification of the desire or passion which he excites. This is the analysis of persuasion. The former is effected by communicating lively and glowing ideas of the object; the latter, unless so evident of itself as to supersede the necessity, by presenting the best and most forcible arguments which the nature of the subject admits. In the one lies the pathetic, in the other the argumentative. These incorporated together (as was observed in the first chapter) constitute that vehemence of contention, to which the greatest exploits of eloquence ought doubtless to be ascribed. Here then is the principal scope for argument, but not the only scope, as will appear in the sequel. When the first end alone is attained, the pathetic without the rational, the passions are indeed roused from a disagreeable languor by the help of the imagination, and the mind is thrown into a state which, though accompanied with some painful emotions, rarely fails, upon the whole, to affect it with pleasure. But, if the hearers are judicious, no practical effect is produced. They cannot by such declamation be influenced to a particular action, because not convinced that that action will conduce to the gratifying of the passion raised. Your eloquence hath fired my ambition, and makes me burn with public zeal. The consequence is, there is nothing which at present I would not attempt for the sake of fame, and the interest of my country. You advise me to such a conduct; but you have not shown me how that can contribute to gratify either passion. Satisfy me in this, and I am instantly at your command. Indeed, when the hearers are rude and ignorant, nothing more is necessary in the speaker than to inflame their passions. They will not require that the connexion between the conduct he urges and the end proposed be evinced to them. His word will satisfy. And therefore bold affirmations are made to supply the place of reasons. Hence it is that the rabble are even the prey of quacks and impudent pretenders of every denomination.

On the contrary, when the other end alone is attained, the rational without the pathetic, the speaker is as far from his purpose as before. You have proved, beyond contradiction, that acting thus is the sure way to procure such an object. I perceive that your reasoning is conclusive: but I am not affected by it. Why? I have no passion for the object. I am indifferent whether I procure it or not. You have demonstrated that such a step will mortify my enemy. I believe it; but I have no resentment, and will not trouble myself to give pain to another. Your arguments evince that it would gratify my vanity. But I prefer my ease. Thus passion is the mover to action, reason is the guide. Good is the object of the will, truth is the object of the understanding.[1]

It may be thought that when the motive is the equity, the generosity, or the intrinsic merit of the action recommended, argument may be employed to evince the reasonableness of the end, as well as the fitness of the means. But this way of speaking suits better the popular dialect than the philosophical. The term *reasonableness*, when used in this manner, means nothing but the goodness, the amiableness, or

---

[1] Several causes have contributed to involve this subject in confusion. One is the ambiguity and imperfection of language. Motives are often called arguments, and both motives and arguments are promiscuously styled reasons. Another is, the idle disputes that have arisen among philosophers concerning the nature of good, both physical and moral. . . .

moral excellency. If therefore the hearer hath no love of justice, no benevolence, no regard to right, although he were endowed with the perspicacity of a cherub, your harangue could never have any influence on his mind. The reason is, when you speak of the fitness of the means, you address yourself only to the head; when you speak of the goodness of the end, you address yourself to the heart, of which we supposed him destitute. Are we then to class the virtues among the passions? By no means. But without entering into a discussion of the difference, which would be foreign to our purpose, let it suffice to observe, that they have this in common with passion. They necessarily imply an habitual propensity to a certain species of conduct, an habitual aversion to the contrary: a veneration for such a character, an abhorrence of such another. They are, therefore, though not passions, so closely related to them, that they are properly considered as motives to action, being equally capable of giving an impulse to the will. . . .

Section V—The circumstances that are chiefly instrumental in operating on the Passions

These are perhaps reducible to the seven following, probability, plausibility, importance, proximity of time, connexion of place, relation of the actors or sufferers to the hearers or speaker, interest of the hearers or speaker in the consequences. . . .

CHAPTER VIII

Of the Consideration which the Speaker ought to have of the Hearers, as such men in particular

It was remarked in the beginning of the preceding chapter, that the hearers ought to be considered in a twofold view, as men in general, and as such men in particular. The first consideration I have despatched, I now enter on the second.

When it is affirmed that the hearers are to be considered as such men in particular, no more is meant, than that regard ought to be had by the speaker to the special character of the audience, as composed of such individuals; that he may suit himself to them, both in his style and in his arguments. Now, the difference between one audience and another is very great, not only in intellectual but in moral attainments. That may be clearly intelligible to a House of Commons, which would appear as if spoken in an unknown tongue to a conventicle of enthusiasts. That may kindle fury in the latter, which would create no emotion in the former but laughter and contempt. The most obvious difference that appears in different auditories, results from the different cultivation of the understanding; and the influence which this, and their manner of life, have both upon the imagination and upon the memory.

But even in cases wherein the difference in education and moral culture hath not been considerable, different habits afterwards contracted, and different occupations in life, give different propensities, and make one incline more to one passion, another to another. They consequently afford the intelligent speaker an easier passage to the heart, through the channel of the favourite passion. Thus liberty and independence will ever be prevalent motives with republicans, pomp and splendour with those attached to monarchy. In mercantile states, such as Carthage among the ancients, or Holland among the moderns, interest will always prove the most cogent argument; in states solely or chiefly composed of soldiers, such as Sparta and ancient Rome, no inducement will be found a counterpoise to glory. Similar differences are also to be made in addressing different classes of men. With men of genius the most successful topic will be fame; with men of industry, riches; with men of fortune, pleasure.

But as the characters of audiences may be infinitely diversified, and as the influence they ought to have respectively upon the speaker must be obvious to a person of discernment, it is sufficient here to have observed thus much in general concerning them.

AN INTRODUCTION TO CYBERNETICS AND INFORMATION THEORY

ALLAN R. BROADHURST AND DONALD K. DARNELL

NORBERT WIENER's now-classic work entitled *The Human Use of Human Beings: Cybernetics and Society* reveals the thesis that "society can only be understood through a study of the messages and the communication facilities which belong to it."[1] Communication is assuming not only an important role in our society, but in the society of the world. It is not surprising that the science of communication now includes many diverse fields of interest. In addition to the applied science of rhetoric, we now have the basic science of communication theory. As reported in a recent article by Wayne N. Thompson, entitled "A Conservative View of a Progressive Rhetoric," "Logic, ethics, politics, and philosophy are the antecedents of rhetoric, whereas engineering, electronics, mathematics, biology, sociology, and psychology are among the sources of communication theory."[2] It no longer seems strange for rhetoricians, experimental psychologists, communication theorists, and communication engineers to work side by side on common problems.

One of the principal contributions in the last two decades to the field of communications has been in the area of cybernetics—from which information theory is derived. Cybernetics is a field of study which seems destined more and more to find its way into the periodicals and literature of the speech scholar. . . .

The late Norbert Wiener, professor of mathematics at the Massachusetts Institute of Technology, first coined the term "cybernetics" from the Greek word *kubernetes*, or "steersman," the same Greek root from which we get our word "governor." Though the word was first used publicly by Wiener in 1948, it has now been used retrospectively to cover the whole field of communication and control which originated

---

Allan R. Broadhurst and Donald K. Darnell, "An Introduction to Cybernetics and Information Theory," *Quarterly Journal of Speech*, LI (December, 1965), 442–453. By permission of the Speech Association of America and the authors.

[1] Norbert Wiener, *The Human Use of Human Beings: Cybernetics and Society* (New York, 1954), p. 16.

[2] Wayne N. Thompson, "A Conservative View of a Progressive Rhetoric," *QJS*, XLIX (February 1963), 5.

years before. Cybernetics is a philosophy which insists that, from the point of view of communication, the human organism is not essentially different from a machine. It emphasizes the resemblances between living organisms and man-constructed machinery, and points out that even though the components differ, in theory their operation is essentially the same. In effect, this means that the scientist can treat the human communication process as if it were being conducted by machines, and he is concerned with the building of machines that can "think," "learn," and "communicate."[3] As Norbert Wiener commented, "When I give an order to a machine, the situation is not essentially different from that which arises when I give an order to a person. In other words, as far as my consciousness goes I am aware of the order that has gone out and of the signal of compliance that has come back. To me, personally, the fact that the signal in its intermediate stages has gone through a machine rather than through a person is irrelevant and does not in any case greatly change my relation to the signal."[4] It is not surprising, then, that Mr. Wiener thought of messages between "man and machines," "machines and man," and "machine and machine" as playing an ever-increasing part in our society. . . .

. . . Computers are one of the chief reasons for the cybernetics hypothesis about machinery and organisms. These and similar machines are capable of making deductive inferences, solving mathematical problems, classifying information, and making predictions that are based on inductive reasoning. In effect, they are being taught to "think," "learn," and "communicate."

Thus, one notes that a new theory of information was being developed. The theory was concerned with the problem of defining the quantity of information contained in a message to be transmitted, and how to go about measuring the amount of information communicated by a system of electronic or machine-like signals. Largely through the independent efforts of Norbert Wiener and Claude Shannon, this new theory of information has been applied to a mathematical theory of communication. This mathematical theory of communication refers to every conceivable kind of transmission of information—from the first words of a baby to the complicated theories of an atomic scientist. The units of information are numerous—muscle contractions, sine waves, phonemes, morphemes, syllables, words, phrases, clauses, sentences, paragraphs, letters of the alphabet, numbers, parts of speech, et cetera. The only real restriction is that one must be able to recognize the unit whenever it occurs so it can be mathematically programmed and fed into the machine.[5]

[3] F. H. George, *Automation, Cybernetics, and Society* (New York, 1959), pp. 45–46.

[4] Wiener, p. 17.

[5] George A. Miller, *Language and Communication* (New York, 1951), p. 82.

The work of the information theorist can be likened to that of the mapmaker who presents a traveler with a record of the important towns, highways, and sites of historical interest. But the towns are only dots and the rivers are only lines and all the exciting adventures along the way are missing—the interesting details and beautiful scenery are deliberately omitted. In a similar way information theory does not involve the value-judgments of the human element. The engineer who designs a telephone system does not care whether this link is going to be used for transmission of gossip, for stock exchange quotations, or for diplomatic messages. The technical problem is always the same— to transmit the information accurately and correctly, whatever it may be. At present, then, information theory treats information as a physically measurable quantity, but it cannot distinguish between information of great importance and a piece of news of no great value for the person who receives it.[6]

What then is this "physically measurable quantity," and how is it achieved? It is what is frequently referred to by communication theorists as a "bit" of information and is achieved through the use of a binary coding system. Gustav Herdan states in his book *Type-Token Mathematics* that "our brain and nervous system work in such a way that a nerve cell is either excited or not, which means that it can assume either of two mutually exclusive states, but not both at the same time."[7] In other words, the nerve cell can make a Yes-No decision, All or Nothing decision, or an 0-1 alternative. This is in accordance with the principle known in logic as that of Contradiction, and, "since language is, in the last resort, only the formulation of logical relations in terms of linguistic forms, it seems sensible to conclude that a dual or dyadic symbol system will be appropriate for language."[8]

A coding system with only two symbols falls neatly into this Yes-No principle. An application is the Morse Code of telegraphy with its Dot-Dash symbol system. If for a number system of this kind one chooses 0 and 1 as symbols, one has the so-called Dual, Dyadic or Binary number system in which all numbers are written by means of 0 and 1 only. In contrast to this, one may consider our decimal number system which makes use of ten digits, 0-9 inclusive. The binary system, however, can be used as the basis for all number codes or alphabets. For example, a possible binary system to replace our decimal system could be as follows: [see next page].

Any determined units of information could be signified by such a binary coding system—whether the units be sine waves, phonemes, syllables, paragraphs, or letters of the alphabet. The only real restriction, again, is that the units must be defined in such a way that they can

---

[6] Leon Brillouin, *Science and Information Theory* (New York, 1956), p. xi.

[7] Gustav Herdan, *Type-Token Mathematics, A Textbook of Mathematical Linguistics* (The Hague, Netherlands, 1960), p. 173.

[8] *Ibid.*

Decimal system	Binary system
0	0
1	1
2	10
3	11
4	100
5	101
6	110
7	111
8	1000
9	1001
etc.	etc.

. . . . .

be recognized whenever they occur so they can be mathematically programmed and fed into the machine.

There are also experimental devices which give the possibility of using positive or negative pulses, in addition to no pulse. This is the case for magnetic tape and for systems using positive and negative current. These systems lead to the possibility of a ternary code which is based on —1, 0, +1. One of the three signals (—1, for example) may be used for the letter space, thus leaving the two remaining signals to be used as binary coding for the letters.[9] . . .

Used in the programming of information, mathematics becomes a precise and well-structured language. It is a language which seems to be quite basic to our descriptions of the world. It is a language that picks out the most general structural relations in any situation capable of description. But it can also be an abstract language capable of dealing with structural relations that exist only as we define them— such as morphemes, phonemes, and syllables.

Information theory, therefore, is not concerned with information at all—not in the common meaning of the term "information." Information theory does not deal with meaning, with message content, with knowledge about a subject. Why, then, is information theory so important to communication? It is because the transmission of "information," eliciting meanings in others, requires a code—a set of symbols and a set of rules for combining them—and information theory is concerned with codes and the capacities of channels.

Information is something we need when we face a choice, and the amount of information needed to make a decision depends on the complexity of the choice involved. If we face many different equally likely alternatives—in other words one is just as apt to happen as the other—then we need more information than if we faced a simple choice between just two alternatives, either this or that.

As Claude Shannon uses the term, *information refers to knowledge*

[9] Brillouin, p. 53.

that one does not have about what is coming next in a sequence of symbols. He thus associates information with *entropy*, which is nothing more than randomness, or the lack of predictability. Warren Weaver referred to entropy in the physical sciences as being a measure of the degree of randomness or "shuffled-ness" in a situation.[10] He goes on to point out that there is a tendency for physical systems to become less and less organized, and for entropy to increase it. As Norbert Wiener stated it, "The commands through which we exercise our control over our environment are a kind of information which we impart to it. Like any form of information, these commands are subject to disorganization in transit. They generally come through in less coherent fashion and certainly not more coherently than they were sent. In control and communication we are always fighting nature's tendency to degrade the organized and to destroy the meaningful; the tendency, as Gibbs has shown us, for entropy to increase."[11]

The relationship between the two terms "information" and "entropy" can perhaps be made clear by the following example. Consider a source who is successively selecting discrete symbols from a set of symbols; if those symbols are independent and equally probable, that source has a maximum freedom of choice, the uncertainty about what the next symbol will be is maximum (therefore, there is maximum entropy in the situation) and X bits of information are required to make the next symbol predictable. Once the source has made his choice there is no longer freedom of choice, no uncertainty or randomness (thus, no entropy), and it is a short leap to the assumption that X bits of information have been transmitted (or received). That assumption, however, is the trigger to a painful and frustrating semantic trap. Having made that assumption, one begins to talk (and think) about information transmitted, and slowly, but almost inevitably, he loses the ability to discriminate between information and "information." A useful memory device is to think of the information of Claude Shannon as coming in units referred to as "bits." The word "bit" as in a "bit of information" is not to be confused with the popular use of the term. "Bit" in information theory is a combination of two shortened words, binary digit, and has a precise mathematical value; whereas, ordinary information comes in "pieces" which are vague undefinable chunks.

To demonstrate how important this difference is, one may consider a source who is going to draw a card from a shuffled deck of playing cards. The deck of playing cards represents a set of fifty-two equally probable, discrete symbols. How many *pieces* of "information" would an astute observer obtain by watching the drawing of one card? It might be said that he obtains one piece—the card which was drawn—

[10] Claude E. Shannon and Warren Weaver, *The Mathematical Theory of Communication* (Urbana, Ill., 1949), p. 103.
[11] Wiener, p. 17.

or fifty-two pieces, because he knows not only the one card that was drawn but the fifty-one cards that were not drawn. He might also observe that the card just drawn is a "higher card" than one drawn previously, that our source is the "winner," that $10.00 will now change hands, and so on. For now, the important point is that information theory does not concern itself with this kind of information. It is more concerned with "bits."

Now, how many *bits* of information are there in this situation? A *bit* is defined as that amount of information required to halve the alternatives; i.e., the number of bits of information in a set of equally probable alternatives is equal to the number of times the set must be divided in half to leave only one alternative. If there were two choices the set could be halved once; thus, there would be one bit of information. If there were four choices the set would have to be cut in two twice to reduce the alternatives to one; that is, two bits of information are required if the source has four equally probable choices. In the deck of cards, fifty-two equally probable choices exist, and it becomes difficult to obtain the number of bits by the halving procedure. There is, however, a simplified procedure for obtaining the answer desired. We find that two to the first power is two, and that two squared is four. We know (through our definition above) that a two-choice situation contains one bit of information, and a four-choice situation contains two bits, so we could infer that the power of two required to produce the number of alternatives is the number of bits of information in the system. As it works out, the power function is an inverse logarithmic function. That is, the logarithm to the base two ($\log_2$) of two is one, and $\log_2 4$ is 2. So, we find that for a set of equally probable alternatives the $\log_2$ of the number of alternatives is the number of bits of information required to predict the one that will be chosen. Since tables are available for this logarithm, one can easily find that $\log_2 52$ is 5.70044, and that approximately 5.7 bits of information are required to predict the card that will be drawn from a shuffled deck of playing cards. To put this another way, one would have to ask, on the average, 5.7 questions to be answered "yes" or "no" by some all-knowing power before he could predict with complete certainty the next card to be drawn; and each question asked would be designed to halve the alternatives.

Thus, he might first ask: "Is it red?" The answer will convey to him one bit of information. If the answer is "yes," he obviously knows the card is either a heart or a diamond. If the answer is "no," he knows it is a club or a spade. For purpose of the example, let us suppose that the answer is "yes." He then would ask "Is it a heart?" The reply is "no"; therefore, two bits of information have been conveyed—and he now knows the card is a diamond. He knows there are thirteen diamonds in a deck and now has the task of finding, with as few questions as possible, which diamond it is. The third question would be "Is the card lower in rank than number eight?" The answer is "no" (third bit). He knows the card is between eight and the ace. Again he halves these alternatives by the question "Is it lower in rank than Jack?" The answer "no" provides him with his fourth bit of information. The fifth question would be "Is it lower in rank than King?" and the reply is "yes" (fifth bit). He now knows the card is either the Jack or the Queen of Diamonds. By now asking "Is it the Jack of Diamonds?" he can be certain by the "yes" or "no" reply (sixth bit) what it really is. If the answer is "no," then he knows it is the Queen of Diamonds. If the answer is "yes," then he obviously knows it is the Jack of Diamonds. Thus, six bits of information have carried him to the solution. With favorable answers he can get it in five—which reduces the average to 5.7.

It can be seen, then, that *bits* of information are not the same as *pieces,* and it can be observed that the bit is an arbitrarily defined unit which serves to quantify the uncertainty in predicting, or the information needed to predict, the next symbol to be drawn from a set of symbols.

So far, we have considered only that situation in which the alternatives are equally probable (i.e., the maximum entropy situation). We should emphasize that the 5.7 bits mentioned above in relation to the deck of cards is only accurate if the fifty-two alternatives are equally probable as in a shuffled deck of cards. We have observed that the number of bits of information is reduced as the number of alternatives is reduced (from fifty-two to four to two). Now, let us observe what happens when the probabilities are shifted.

To simplify the computations in the coming discussion, let us assume that we are interested only in the four suits in our deck of cards. That is, we now define our situation as having four alternatives, each with a probability of 13/52 or .25. We could say from the previous discussion that in this situation, with four equally probable choices, two bits of information are required to predict the suit that will be drawn. To simplify further our computations, let us make one other observation. Four (the number of alternatives) times .25 (the probability of each alternative) times the $\log_2$ of .25 equals two. That is, $P1 \log_2 P1$ plus $P2 \log_2 P2$ plus $P3 \log_2 P3$ plus $P4 \log_2 P4$ equals 2, or, to state the general case $\Sigma p_i \log_2 p_i$ equals the number of bits of entropy in a given set of symbols. (Actually, the logarithm of any number less than one is a negative number so we need a minus sign somewhere in our formula to make the result positive.) The formula for information, entropy, uncertainty, can now be stated (letting H stand for information and i for any alternative): $H = -\Sigma p_i \log_2 p_i$. With this formula and a table of values for $-P \log_2 P$ we can now compute the entropy in any set of alternatives with any set of probabilities.[12]

[12] Edwin B. Newman, "Computational Methods Useful in Analyzing a Series of Binary Data," *American Journal of Psychology,* LXIV (April 1951), 252–262.

Suppose we now take our deck of cards and withdraw four spades and two clubs and add six hearts. Again we are concerned with predicting the suit that will be exposed on the next draw. The probability that the next card will be a heart is approximately .37, a diamond .25, a club .21, and a spade, .17. If we insert these values in the formula given above we find:

$$-.37 \ \log_2 \ .37 = .5307$$
$$-.25 \ \log_2 \ .25 = .5000$$
$$-.21 \ \log_2 \ .21 = .4728$$
$$-.17 \ \log_2 \ .17 = .4346$$

$$\text{Total} \quad 1.9381$$

Thus, the four-choice situation with the probabilities .37, .25, .21, and .17 contains approximately 1.94 bits of information, entropy, uncertainty. We could also show by working some more examples that the more disparate the probabilities become the less entropy there is in the system, the less uncertainty there is in predicting the next symbol. If, for example, the probabilities were .75, .10, .08, and .07, only 1.2 bits of information are required to reduce the uncertainty to zero.

The next thing we might want to know is, "How does this *absolute* value—computed for a specific set of alternatives with a specific set of probabilities—compare with the *maximum* value that could obtain if the set of alternatives were equally probable?" We know that the *maximum* value for a four-choice set is 2 bits, and we have just computed an *absolute* value of 1.94 bits. If we divide 1.94 by 2.00 we will obtain .97. This value we call the *relative entropy* or *relative uncertainty*, and we can say that a four-choice situation which yields an absolute uncertainty value of 1.94 bits is .97 (97%) as uncertain as it might be (i.e., as it would be if the alternatives were equally probable).

With the value we have called relative entropy we can compare systems with different numbers of alternatives and with different probabilities, but it should always be kept in mind that the relative entropy of a system of symbols (or the relative uncertainty of a source who is selecting symbols from the set) defines a relationship between the absolute and maximum entropy of a given set. Thus, a set of sixty-four alternatives and a set of eight alternatives could both have a relative entropy of .50, while the absolute entropy of the first set is twice that of the second.

One other concept from information theory can now be meaningfully defined, and that is *relative redundancy. Relative redundancy* is, simply, one (1) minus the relative entropy. Thus, in the example above where the absolute entropy was 1.94 bits, the maximum 2 bits, and the relative entropy .97, the relative redundancy would be .03. The redundancy figure represents *the degree to which the next symbol in a sequence is determined,* or the degree of certainty we might have about what the next card is going to be.

To summarize: given a source who is successively selecting discrete symbols from a set of symbols; if the symbols in the set have equal probabilities of being chosen next that source has maximum uncertainty, or there is maximum entropy in the situation. Maximum entropy is defined for a given set of symbols as the logarithm to the base two of the number of alternatives ($\log_2 n$). If there is some dispersion in the probabilities of the alternatives, the absolute entropy is computed by the formula $-\Sigma p_1 \log_2 p_1$. In the equally probable set both formulas produce the same result. Relative entropy is obtained by dividing the absolute entropy by the maximum entropy and has a value of one (1) when the alternatives are equally probable and a value of zero (0) when any alternative has a value of unity. One minus the relative entropy is the relative redundancy, which is an index of the *predictability* of any given symbol drawn from the set.

When the set of symbols with which one is dealing is the alphabet or vocabulary of a natural language, and the task of the source is the composition of a message in that natural language, it is readily observable that the probabilities of the alternatives fluctuate as the source proceeds with his sequential selection. The fact that choices made in sequence may not be independent requires that for the computation of the uncertainty involved in any particular choice the probabilities of the various alternatives must be determined taking into account all that has gone before. For example, it has been estimated that the average redundancy of English is approximately 50 per cent. However, given the letter "q" the probability of the next letter being "u" is 1.00; therefore, the redundancy of that particular choice is 1.00. This situation, in which the probabilities involved in a given choice are dependent on the previous choices, is called a *Markoff process*. It is a term frequently encountered in the study of information theory.

In addition to the problems associated with the coding of the message, the information theory engineer has the problem of determining the channel capacity. He looks on information theory as a tool for dealing with the efficiency of coding and code transmission.

Let us consider a source capable of transmitting n symbols per second; and let us assume that this source is selecting his symbols from a set of k equally probable symbols. We can characterize this source as having a capacity for handling ($\log_2 k)n$ bits of information per second. We can perhaps simplify the definition somewhat by recognizing the fact that $\log_2 k$ represents the maximum entropy case for a given set of symbols; that is, each symbol in this set represents m bits of uncertainty, and C (the capacity of a channel for handling bits of information) is equal to m times n; ($C = mn$).

Let us now suppose that n is a constant; if the statistical properties of the symbol set are such that the average relative entropy of the set is less than one (1), the peak of operation level of our source in bits per second handled is necessarily less than mn or rmn (where r stands for the average relative entropy of the symbol set). We can say that the maximum rate at which this source, with this symbol set, can handle information is rmn bits per second, and we redefine C as rmn. . . .

Thus, given a source or channel that can handle n symbols per second: if the symbols are equally probable maximum entropy prevails, and the source can handle m bits of information per symbol or mn bits per second. We find, however, that we can remove the assumption of equal probability of symbols by multiplying by the relative entropy (r) of the symbol set and define the capacity, C, for the general case as rmn. C now accounts for the symbol transmission capacity, the size of the symbol set, and considers the distribution of the probabilities of the symbols. The above refers to the formula for the capacity of the source or channel for handling "bits" of information. We have assumed in this example that the symbol transmission rate n is a constant, but there is reason to believe that the capacity C is more stable in human communicators—that n actually decreases as rm increases.

One other concept that should be treated is the concept of *noise*. There is no man-made or natural communication system which does not have in it the potentialities for error. The electronic signal, the written word, or the spoken word all admit the possibility of foreign elements which will get in the way of the intended meaning—a cough, an illegible handwriting, random fluctuations or perturbations in the mechanical signal. These interferences are referred to as "noise." Noise in its simplest form is the addition or omission of a symbol in the communication chain which results in a discrepancy between the message transmitted and the message received (or in more human terms, the message intended and the message perceived). The fact that communication is carried on through channels in which noise is possible makes redundancy useful. In the definition of a channel-capacity redundancy appeared to be of negative value, acting as a limiting factor on the channel efficiency. However, if we consider a source or channel which is subject to error it is quite evident how redundancy can be beneficial. For example, if we have a source that tends to omit every tenth symbol, but has an average relative redundancy equal to or greater than 10 per cent, the receiver can replace the missing symbols with a rather high probability of success. The exact amount of redundancy necessary to fully compensate for a given amount and kind of noise must be determined for each new channel, source, and purpose, but perhaps the general relation which we have suggested is sufficient for this introductory paper.

By way of conclusion, let us at this point review some of the major concepts discussed. . . .

"Cybernetics" as a word can be compared to the term "behaviorism." It is a method of approach rather than a subject matter treated by the method. The method encompasses the fields of language, logic, mathematics, biology, psychology, physiology, anthropology, and sociology. Physiology, psychology, and the biological sciences have taken notice of cybernetics to investigate human behavior and general physiological function from the machine point of view. They have been able to do this because of a new "theory of information" which is based on a precise mathematical concept.

This new theory of information is more concerned with the technical problem of transmitting signals accurately than the semantic problem of the precision with which transmitted signals convey a desired meaning or the effectiveness with which the received meaning affects the conduct of the recipient. Its appeal is due, in part, to the fact that variables can now be quantified which up to this time had defied quantification. Therefore, to some degree it can be stated that a scientific model of communication is replacing "intuitive" or "clinical" models of communication, and predictions of human behavior are being based on "sound thinking" rather than "mere intuition."

The needs and complexities of today's societies emphasize more and more man's dependency on information. "To live effectively," as Norbert Wiener has put it, "is to live with adequate information." Information theory is an attempt to help man understand and provide "adequate information." The theory is so general that it is applicable to any type of communication—whether written letters or words, spoken words, musical notes, symphonic music, pictures, or electrical impulses. It is an imaginative theory that attempts to get at the real inner core of communication problems—"with those basic relationships which hold in general, no matter what special form the actual case may take."[13] It is a theory which bases its design on the statistical character of the source, and its aim is to compromise both rationally and profitably the excessive redundancy or bulk on the one hand and excessive sensitivity to noise on the other. . . .

Can we further generalize with the concepts herein discussed? Let us take an individual who is concerned with predicting an event—any event. Isn't his ability to predict dependent on the number of possible events and his knowledge of their probabilities? And, does it not seem reasonable to say that his uncertainty is greatest when the possible events are equally probable, and least when one event has a probability of one? What about an individual who is forced to make a series of predictions, all of them under maximum uncertainty conditions—would this lead to a state of anxiety or depression? Is there an optimum level of "redundancy" under which an individual or a society functions most efficiently? Can information theory help to explain human behavior?

We think the answer to all of these questions is a qualified "yes." But, the important thing as far as rhetoric or human communication is

13 Shannon and Weaver, pp. 114–115.

concerned is that information theory provides a basis for a comprehensive theory of *organization*. That theory is not yet fully elaborated, but the lines of development seem clear.

Let us assume that the purpose (or function) of the "patterns of organization" consistently recommended by rhetoricians to beginning speakers is to increase the predictability (redundancy) of the message. That is, a "well-organized" message is one that, when transmitted at a normal rate, is redundant enough not to exceed the "channel capacity" of the receiver. In this sense, good spelling or articulation, acceptable grammar, and a "logical order" of ideas are all part of the same system —all indicate compliance on the part of the source with a set of restrictions which are imposed on the source. Thus, any set of restrictions on the source will serve to reduce the "freedom of choice" of the source, but only those restrictions which are familiar or can be explained to the receiver will reduce his "uncertainty." From this it follows that a message that is "organized" for one person may not be "organized" for a second person. There probably are, however, some patterns of restrictions that are more likely to produce organization for whatever audience may receive the message. Following the thread, it seems reasonable to say that titles, introductions, orienting material, subject sentences, as well as patterns of main heads serve both to restrict the production of the source and to make the audience aware of existing restrictions, either of which would tend to increase the ability of the audience to predict what the speaker is going to say next—to reduce the receiver's uncertainty about what to expect.

From this rudimentary extension of information theory it should be clear that the patterns of organization we teach may not work outside the classroom; they may not be necessary "among friends"; and there may be other ways of accomplishing the same ends that we have not considered. . . .

A SAMPLING OF DEFINITIONS

1. "Communication is a term used to refer to any dynamic, information-sharing process."
> Theodore Clevenger, Jr., "What is Communication," Taskgroup Letter No. 2, NSSC Committee on Extant Theory, *Journal of Communication*, 9 (March, 1959), 5.

2. "Communication is the form of interpersonal exchange through which, figuratively speaking, persons can come in contact with each others' minds."
> Theodore M. Newcomb, Ralph H. Turner and Philip E. Converse, *Social Psychology* (New York: Holt, Rinehart and Winston, Inc., 1965), p. 219.

3. ". . . the connecting thread appears to be the idea of something's being transferred from one thing, or person, to another. We use the word

'communication' sometimes to refer to what is so transferred, sometimes to the means by which it is transferred, sometimes to the whole process. In many cases, what is transferred in this way continues to be shared; if I convey information to another person, it does not leave my own possession through coming into his. Accordingly, the word 'communication' acquires also the sense of participation. It is in this sense, for example, that religious worshippers are said to communicate. . . . The type of communication that I particularly wish to discuss is the transference of information, in a very broad sense of the term, which may be taken to include not merely the imparting of news, in a factual sense, but also the expression of feelings, wishes, commands, desires, or whatever it may be. It covers all deliberate uses of language by human beings as well as voluntary or involuntary exclamations, movements, gestures, singing, crying, laughing, dancing, in so far as they are informative."

A. J. Ayer, "What is Communication?" *Studies in Communication* (London: Martin Secker and Warburg, 1955), pp. 12–13.

4. "Communication: The transmission of information, ideas, emotions, skills, etc., by the use of symbols—words, pictures, figures, graphs, etc. It is the *act* or *process* of transmission that is usually called communication."

Bernard Berelson and Gary A. Steiner, *Human Behavior* (New York: Harcourt, Brace and World, Inc., 1964), p. 527.

5. "Communication: A process involving the selection, production, and transmission of signs in such a way as to help a receiver perceive a meaning similar to that in the mind of the communicator."

Wallace C. Fotheringham, *Perspectives on Persuasion* (Boston: Allyn and Bacon, Inc., 1966), p. 254.

6. "Communication consists in the communicator's selecting and arranging symbols that have a certain meaning to him and his audience's sensing those symbols and inferring their intended meaning."

Wayne C. Minnick, *The Art of Persuasion* (Boston: Houghton Mifflin Co., 1957), p. 70.

7. "Communication means that information is passed from one place to another. . . . In most communication systems the source of the information is a human being. From his past experience and present needs and perceptions this source has information to pass on to others. The transmitter discussed . . . is the human speech machinery. This machinery operates upon the information and changes it into a pattern of sound waves that is carried through the air. The channel of principal interest to us will be the air medium that connects the talker's speech machinery with the listener's ears. The ear is a receiver that operates upon the acoustic waves to convert them into nervous activity at their destination, the nervous system of the listener."

George A. Miller, *Language and Communication* (New York: McGraw-Hill Book Co., Inc., 1951), pp. 6–7.

8. "Speech communication is a dynamic process, in which the speaker's encoding, and the listener's decoding of a message is affected by his attitudes, skills, knowledge, and interest. The process requires the use

of a code so that the speaker can represent his thoughts and feelings in words. It takes place within an environment—an immediate environment (occasion) and a broad social context."

> Ronald F. Reid, "The Process of Speech Communication," in *Introduction to the Field of Speech*, Ronald F. Reid, editor (Chicago: Scott, Foresman and Co., 1965), p. 12.

9. ". . . communication is here defined as the process by which people interact for the purpose of interpersonal and intrapersonal integration."

> R. Victor Harnack and Thorrell Fest, *Group Discussion* (New York: Appleton-Century-Crofts, 1964), p. 399.

10. "Communication arises out of the need to reduce uncertainty, to act effectively, to defend or strengthen the ego. On some occasions words are used to ward off anxiety. On other occasions they are means of evolving more deeply satisfying ways of expressing ourselves. The aim of communication is to increase the number and consistency of our meanings within the limits set by patterns of evaluation that have proved successful in the past, our emerging needs and drives, and the demands of the physical and social settings of the moment. Communication ceases when meanings are adequate, it is initiated as soon as new meanings are required."

> Dean C. Barnlund, "Toward a Meaning-Centered Philosophy of Communication," *Journal of Communication*, 12 (December, 1962), 200–201.

11. ". . . Let us define communication as being that process through which individuals observe stimuli and react in varying degree to their perceptions of those stimuli through the drawing of inferences with or without observation. Such a definition would seem to be applicable to communication at the intra-personal, inter-personal, intra-group and inter-group levels."

> James H. Platt, "What Do We Mean—'Communication'?" *Journal of Communication*, 1 (Spring, 1955), 23.

12. "Four generalizations regarding communication situations may now be made. (1) They are situations in which human beings enter into certain strategic relationships with each other or with their environment. (2) They are situations the central characteristic of which is the production and utilization of signs, symbols, and symbolic acts. (3) They are situations which provide a maximal opportunity through the use of signs and symbols for the sharing of experience, achievement of goals, gaining of insight and, in general, mastering one's environment. (4) The sign or symbol material used in these situations is subject to the perceptual processes of the individuals involved."

> Franklin Fearing, "Human Communication," in *People, Society, and Mass Communications*, Lewis A. Dexter and David M. White, editors (Glencoe: The Free Press, 1964), p. 42.

13. "In short, we communicate to influence—to affect with intent."

> David K. Berlo, *The Process of Communication* (New York: Holt, Rinehart and Winston, Inc., 1960), p. 12.

14. "By persuasive speaking, I mean that activity in which speaker and listener are conjoined and in which the speaker consciously attempts to influence the behavior of the listener by transmitting audible and visible symbolic cues."

> Thomas M. Scheidel, *Persuasive Speaking* (Glenview, Illinois: Scott, Foresman and Co., 1967), p. 1.

15. "Persuasion . . . is discourse, written or oral, that is designed to win belief or stimulate action by employing all the factors that determine human behavior."

> Wayne C. Minnick, *The Art of Persuasion* (Boston: Houghton Mifflin Co., 1957), p. 33.

16. "[Persuasion is] the conscious attempt to modify thought and action by manipulating the motives of men toward predetermined ends."

> Winston L. Brembeck and William S. Howell, *Persuasion* (Englewood Cliffs, New Jersey: Prentice-Hall, Inc., 1952), p. 24.

PREDICTIVE GENERALIZATIONS

I-A   Communication cannot be understood except as a dynamic process in which listener and speaker, reader and writer act reciprocally, the speaker acting to provide direct and indirect sensory stimulation of the listener; the listener acting on the stimulation by taking it in, investing it with meaning by calling up images in the mind, testing those images against present information and feelings, and sooner or later acting upon those images.

I-B   Accomplishment of the object of communication—recreation in a listener's mind of the image present in the speaker's mind—depends on the degree to which listener and speaker share the same code. Since the code of extended efforts at communication is language, success depends on listeners and speakers having roughly equivalent sophistication in the use of their common language, especially, equal familiarity with the labels for significant categories of experience.

I-C,   Accomplishment of the object of communication depends also upon the degree to which listener and speaker share other things in common than language, including their experiences, education, perceptiveness, attitudes, beliefs, goals and group memberships.

I-D   Accomplishment of the object of communication depends on the effective transmission of the message signal, which in conversation simply means that the speech was audible, but in more complex transmitting arrangements means that the electronic signal or visual image was of sufficient magnitude and clarity to be received by whatever equipment was available.

I-D-1   Successful transmission presumes that whatever "noise" is present is not great enough either to obscure the signal or divert the receiver's attention from it. If the wind carries the sound away or fog blots out the signalman, if the young lady's hair hanging in her face so annoys the listener that he misses her words, the signal will not be able to overcome the interference of "noise."

I-D-2   Successful transmission, therefore, frequently depends on the setting in which communication occurs and the degree to which elements in that setting either amplify or interfere with the message signal.

I-D-3   Concern about the interference of "noise" in the channel seems to increase as the communicator seeks to reach larger numbers of people simultaneously.

I-E   Accomplishment of the object of communication depends on the degree to which listeners and readers are able or motivated to attend, comprehend or accept information offered by the speaker or writer.

I-F   Accomplishment of the object of communication, therefore, frequently depends on the communicator's ability to discover, by means of "feedback," whether his information is being attended, comprehended or accepted, that is, whether it is being received, accurately decoded or producing the behavior he had intended.

I-G   It will usually be safer to assume that the object of communication has not been completely accomplished than that it has. The nature and complexity of the process forces the conclusion that images evoked in listeners' minds will seldom be more than roughly approximate to the images in the speaker's mind.

DISCUSSION QUESTIONS

1. What proportion of the communication that you engage in daily is actually persuasive in that it seeks to influence the beliefs and/or behavior of your listener or reader?

2. Can the process of intrapersonal communication, thinking, in which you serve as both sender and receiver, be viewed as similar to the interpersonal communication models examined? You may wish to compare the Barker and Wiseman model of intrapersonal communication with some of the other models. What are the similarities? What are the differences?

3. Attempt to devise or revise a communication model which reflects your idea of the major elements involved in communication and the ways in which these elements interact.

4. The late Andrew T. Weaver, University of Wisconsin, often discussed the "happy accident of communication," stressing that we should not be surprised that communication breakdowns occur, but rather we should be surprised that we achieve an adequate level of communication as often as we do. In what sense is communication a "happy accident"? Is a one-to-one correspondence in the meanings held by speaker and listener possible? How important is the attempt at such identity?

5. To what extent do a theory of communication and a theory as to the nature of man correlate? If the theory of the psychology of man changes, must the theory of communication also change?

6. Communication may be defined as an attempt or intent on the part of a sender, as a message existing in a channel, or in terms of the receipt of stimuli by the receiver, or the successful recreation of the intended meaning or the achieving of the desired effect. What are the problems in defining communication in terms of an intent by a sender? In terms of the message existing in the channel? In terms of the response or success of the attempt to win a response from a receiver?

7. What are the problems in interpreting feedback? If you are talking to the class with the instructor nodding his head, some students looking at you, some staring straight ahead, one or two writing and two or three lost in thought, what does this mean to you as feedback? How do you determine who is "getting your message"? How do you employ this feedback to modify your present or future communication behavior?

SECTION II

Settings for communication

COMMUNICATION SETTINGS

HOWARD H. MARTIN

WATCHING A FILM COMEDY at home on the television set is a different experience from watching the same movie in a crowded theatre. Hearing one's favorite candidate in a hall packed with partisans is not the same as watching him in a newsreel clip on television at home with one's family. The identical argument for tax relief offered by a co-worker across the lunch table and by an unidentified editor in the columns of a local newspaper will draw different reactions from the same person. While it may be admitted that communication is affected by the setting in which it occurs, the nature and importance of the differences may not be obvious. In this section, we distinguish four settings for communication in order to discover the relative effectiveness of communication that takes place in each setting.

A *setting* is not the same thing as a *medium* of communication in the sense that Marshall McLuhan and others have used the term *medium*. A medium (those interested in communication technology sometimes use the term *channel*) is the vehicle by means of which ideas are borne to listeners or viewers—a flag or banner, print marks on a page, sketches or photographs, moving pictures on a screen, radio signals in voice or code, billboards, phonograph records or handwritten letters. Advertisers identify as media such vehicles as newspapers, magazines, direct mail solicitations, television, radio, carcards and billboards. A setting, on the other hand, is the environment in which communication takes place—the physical and psychological surroundings of the listener or reader. In general, settings differ in the degree to which they suppress or emphasize parts of the total environment, and by doing so, affect the listener's willingness or ability to pay attention to, to understand and to accept what is said to him.

The four settings we intend to discuss are private face-to-face communication involving two people who usually are friends and whose talk is not chiefly related to some assigned task; small group communication which could occur between two people who have to complete some job together, but which usually takes place in a group of three or four to a dozen people who have some understood common object in meeting together; speaker-audience communication where the audience expects to listen and the speaker expects to monopolize the talk in a face-to-face confrontation; and mass communication which involves an organized effort to reach a great many people with the assistance of some technology—radio, television or print circulation. If we can first identify the important variables in any communication setting, we may then be able to distinguish between these several settings for communication.

An understanding of the differences among these four major settings for communication should permit more effective use by a speaker or writer of the setting in which he proposes to work and may, in fact, allow him to select an appropriate setting in which to promote his intentions. If he is aware of the potential advantages and disadvantages of each setting, he may be better prepared to improve the effectiveness of his communicative efforts. The choice of setting and the exploitation of special advantages of the setting are initial strategic decisions any communicator makes.

VARIABLES IN THE SETTING

1) Opportunities for interaction between speaker and listener

Of all the things that distinguish one setting from another, the chance to interact is probably the most crucial. Without the opportunity to monitor listeners' reactions by word or gesture, a speaker cannot tell whether he has their attention, whether they seem to understand him, or whether they seem inclined to accept his remarks. Advertising copywriters and textbook writers, deprived of that chance, can only guess at what might be done to fix the reader's attention or make an idea clear to him. The speaker before an audience is slightly better off for he receives some clues to listeners' responses, but he is still faced with the problem of interpreting movements and gestures which can never be as unambiguous as the questions or comments listeners may interject in a dinner-table conversation. Private face-to-face communication ideally provides the greatest opportunity for the speaker to discover whether he is being attended and understood because it permits the listener to talk back to the speaker, to question him, and to say what he understands the speaker to have said. Although the chance for an exchange of gestures or grimaces may sometimes be a useful sort of interaction, the opportunity for verbal exchange is the sort of interaction we have chiefly in mind during the rest of this essay.

Interaction is related to a listener's acceptance of the speaker's proposition, not only because it permits the speaker to assess his impact and make adjustments if necessary, but also because it provides for immediate rewards to the listener for accepting influence. If a friend asks us to consider giving a dollar to the Democratic party, we are more likely to do it (supposing we are Democrats) in the expectation of his immediate approval, while the same appeal spoken in a television announcement by Gregory Peck, because there can be no immediate reward, would be less likely to extract the dollar. The social rewards from communicative interaction should not be minimized; most people apparently derive great satisfaction from the pleasant relations with other people that result from talk.[1]

2) Opportunities for the listener or reader to gain information about the speaker

People who are the targets of communications often decide either to ignore or to accept recommendations because they are presented by a spokesman whom they either distrust or respect.[2] That judgment is based on scraps of information that answer such questions as: Who is he? How trustworthy is he? Who are his associates? Does he know what he is talking about? In the face-to-face setting a listener can raise those questions directly and quickly satisfy himself. Can he do as well when the magazine article is unsigned, when the news report bears only the AP identification, or when he tunes in late to a radio or television discussion? Sometimes the listener possesses all the information he needs beforehand. Recognizing the voice as Walter Cronkite's or David Brinkley's may be sufficient to remind us of the training, experience, reliability or special skills of the man. At other times, the listener has to rely on information provided in the immediate setting. Conventions of the setting determine how much information may be offered about the speaker to a businessmen's luncheon. The reader's circumstances—whether he is waiting for the barber or riding on the bus—will determine how much he reads of the biographical note on the author of the article. The chance of asking the contributor in a committee meeting what grounds he has for parading that opinion promises both fuller and more selective information about the speaker.

3) Opportunities for the speaker or writer to gain information about his audience

Students who strongly disagreed with a particular proposition were asked, in several classic experiments, to devise and in some cases deliver arguments in favor of that proposition.[3] Quite a few of the group changed their opinions of the proposition after having written the counterargument. This result was explained by the fact that those who had put themselves on record publicly began to feel the need to adjust their opinions to their public behavior. But, even those who only wrote arguments and did not publicly present them changed their

[1] Theodore M. Newcomb, Ralph H. Turner and Phillip E. Converse, *Social Psychology* (New York: Holt, Rinehart and Winston, Inc., 1965), pp. 282–286.

[2] Research on the influence of prestigious sources is summarized in the report of Andersen and Clevenger included in Section III.

[3] Carl I. Hovland, Irving L. Janis and Harold H. Kelley, *Communication and Persuasion* (New Haven: The Yale University Press, 1953), pp. 233–237.

opinions in the direction of their arguments. Why? Because, it was presumed, their arguments were perfectly tailored to the very objections they would have raised; they knew their "audience" thoroughly, hence they were able to develop an argument that met the needs of that audience—themselves—with a completeness and accuracy impossible for any other persuader. The experiments emphasize the importance of a communicator's knowing his audience if he expects to bring about desired effects.

The settings for communication vary greatly in the possibility of the speaker's knowing his audience with any degree of thoroughness or accuracy. It ought to be easier for a man to frame an argument to influence his wife than to frame one that might persuade his friend, and he ought to be able to develop a more persuasive argument for a shop associate of ten years than for the minister who makes an annual parish call. As the target audience grows in size, the communicator's knowledge about that audience necessarily diminishes in completeness and specificity.

In spite of the decrease in information about his audience available to the man who addresses a large political meeting he may not be without effect. Although he may know a great deal about his single listener, he has only one chance of success; with the larger audience about whom he knows less he has a statistically greater chance of having some influence, since some people will respond as he intends them to respond without respect to his communication or, in fact, to any communication. Still, few communicators would be content with statistically increased chances of success. Instead, they bend every effort to collect the relevant pieces of information about the audience and to adjust their efforts accordingly.

4) Opportunities for the speaker or writer to control the salience of group membership of readers or listeners

Many of us belong to a number of social groups—a church, a professional association, a veteran's group, a social fraternity, a choral society, a civic organization, a political party. To the degree that we value our membership in each of these groups, we will consider the group's expectations of us when faced with the need to stand up and be counted or to act on some matter affecting both ourselves and the group. It has been repeatedly demonstrated that attitudes we share with members of groups which we value highly are very resistant to change.[4] When we are reminded of the importance of membership in a certain group, and that membership becomes *salient* for us in the

---

[4] An illustrative study is that of Harold H. Kelley and Edmund H. Volkart, "The Resistance to Change of Group-Anchored Attitudes," *American Sociological Review,* 17 (August, 1952), 453–465.

sense of being present in the mind, we may be more likely to speak and act in conformity to that group's expectations. When Catholic students were gathered separately from other students to determine "basic assumptions which underlie the opinions of all Catholics," they showed more doctrinal conformity than when they considered the same subject in a group including Protestants and Jews and where no reminders were provided of their group membership.[5]

Because the deliberations of the United Nations General Assembly are open to the inspection of national groups from which members come, speakers cannot afford to ignore their constituents' expectations. The United States representative, much as he might wish to think of himself as an instrument of the largest interests of mankind, knows that Americans watching him expect him to put American interests first. When conflicting constituency interests are equally present, decision and action are difficult. National and state legislatures have sought to overcome the ubiquitous presence of group memberships in the minds of legislators by making some steps in legislative deliberation private. In the executive sessions of congressional committees where minutes are not kept and men's positions are not usually publicized, the pressures of various groups on a man's words and acts can be temporarily reduced. Although labor union lobbyists may be busy in the corridors, and their reactions to a man's words and deeds cannot be ignored completely, even where that reaction is delayed by hours or days, the labor-sympathetic congressman who needs labor support for reelection can still minimize the importance of his union membership in order to allow the larger public interest to dominate his thinking in committee session.

Settings differ in the opportunities they offer a communicator to control the salience of audience group memberships. A candidate for congress who is not a member of my political party can stress in private talk with me that we are professional colleagues who share many views as university faculty members. He can stress that same group membership by arranging to speak to a faculty audience composed of members of both political parties, and by not letting us forget that we share membership in that group with him. The privacy of the first setting is probably effective in suppressing conflicting memberships; the public nature of the second setting which exposes my behavior to the scrutiny of members of my political party may make it more difficult for the speaker to make my academic ties exclusively salient. When a man finds himself in a large audience of strangers, or alone on the train reading a newspaper, the dominance of one or another group member-

[5] W. W. Charters, Jr. and Theodore M. Newcomb, "Some Attitudinal Effects of Experimentally Increased Salience of a Membership Group," in *Readings in Social Psychology*, Eleanor E. Maccoby, Theodore M. Newcomb and Eugene L. Hartley, editors (New York: Holt, Rinehart and Winston, Inc., 1958), pp. 276–281.

ship may sometimes be effectively controlled by reminders from the communicator.

5) *Opportunities for the speaker or writer to control the exposure of listeners and readers to his communications*

While any communicator can turn out hundreds of possibly effective messages,.he cannot guarantee that the listeners he wants to reach will actually pay attention to his messages. Studies of voter behavior have confirmed that, while political information offered by speakers, newspapers, radio and television is open to all people indiscriminately, exposure is selective; Republicans read Republican arguments and Democrats listen to Democratic speakers.[6]

A listener's or reader's opportunities for selective exposure are greatest in the mass communication setting. He can buy any newspaper he wishes, read any magazine, switch off the radio or television as he pleases, read a paragraph of the argument and quit, decide to attend one speaker and ignore two or three others. Few meaningful rewards or punishments can be meted out to him by a newspaper editor or a party campaign director. As a result of this great freedom of selection, so-called educational radio and television programs do not reach the uneducated and messages designed to promote group harmony do not reach the prejudiced people at whom they were directed.

There are ways in which persuaders using mass communication settings may reduce the effects of selective exposure. Since many readers develop habits of reading certain magazines or newspapers, the placement of messages in such places may reach intended listeners or readers. Liberal readers of *The Reporter* magazine did not bargain for the editor's strong support of administration policy in Viet Nam. On the same principle, many potentially unsympathetic readers are no doubt reached by full-page advertisements in the *New York Times* by the Committee of One Million in opposition to admission of The People's Republic of China into the United Nations. Sometimes deceptive headlines or titles may tempt readers or viewers who might not otherwise expose themselves to communications that run counter to their beliefs. A 1967 British film about the affairs of a footloose Lothario named Alfie which turned out to be a sermon against callous self-indulgence no doubt attracted many viewers who expected to have their flippant and irresponsible attitudes toward sex reinforced.

Once he is in the audience of a speaker, the listener's opportunities for selective exposure, while they still exist, are reduced. He can "tune out" the speaker if his ideas become irritating or discomforting—but he may already have heard them by the time he has decided that he does

---

[6] Paul F. Lazarsfeld, Bernard Berelson and Hazel Gaudet, *The People's Choice* (New York: Columbia University Press, 1944), pp. 74–93.

not like them. In a group communication setting—a committee meeting, a staff session, or even a family dinner-table conversation—the chance of running into points of view that run counter to one's own are sharply increased, as are the difficulties of avoiding them in any effective way.

6) Opportunities for the speaker to manipulate the physical environment

We began this discussion by pointing to the difference between viewing a film comedy in a crowded theatre and seeing the same film at home on television. Part of the difference between these two experiences is due to the physical environment. The theatre places you elbow to elbow with hundreds of other people, which has the effect of amplifying your responses to the humor of the film. Your expectations are high; you have dressed up and paid money to see the film. The size of the image and the darkness of the rest of the theatre exclude many potential distractions so that your attention is more sharply focussed than it would be on a television screen. In short, the theatre experience is an altogether different experience, and probably a more important experience to you, than the experience at home in front of the television set. Its importance has been enhanced by the controls the exhibitor enjoys over the physical environment.

Other settings offer similar opportunities for control. The speaker at a political rally surrounds himself with flags, banners, placards, a stageful of celebrities, stirring music and the inevitable excitement created by thousands of people crowded together in a small space. The preacher makes use of the atmosphere and decor of the church to reinforce the impact of his ideas, and if he has no church, arranges the hall with flowers, candles, religious symbols, white-robed choirs and sombre-garbed ushers. The department head who calls a staff meeting just before the lunch hour in a room without chairs may effectively discourage long-winded discussion of the matters placed before the group. When representatives of two contesting groups come together to negotiate, the man who seats himself on the side of the table occupied by the "opposition" may play down rather than emphasize potential antagonism.

7) Presumed purposiveness of the communication

Some of the most effective persuasive communications are those which listeners conclude have not been calculated to influence their opinions—overheard conversations, discussions that come up unpredictably and naturally in personal contacts with friends and acquaintances, and accidentally encountered persuasion that could not have been designed with them in mind. Television commercial advertisers seem increasingly to prefer dramatized conversations between two average-looking housewives about a new cleaner to the use of an announcer who addresses the customer directly with a persuasive message. The viewer is expected to accept these dramatizations as overheard conversations between two people neither of whom is apparently seeking to persuade *him*.

Communication settings differ in the degree to which listeners can identify the persuasive intentions of the speaker. Many mass communication efforts, unless disguised in ways such as that described, are seen as intentionally manipulative. The speaker-audience setting is probably recognized as manipulative where the subject is policy or politics, otherwise listeners do not usually perceive the speaker as seeking to influence them. The remarks of speakers in a small group setting may more often be taken to be off-hand, thereby enhancing their potential effectiveness in altering views of the group members. And, as we have seen, the extemporaneousness of the private face-to-face conversation may mask manipulative intentions.

O course, people do respond to many communications which they recognize as manipulative, because, as David Riesman has observed, we are flattered by the fact that someone has taken the time to try to win our support.[7] But when the persuader is seen as seeking his own ends at our expense, we usually avoid him.

8) Personal characteristics of the listener

Another variable in the communication setting is one or more personal traits of listeners or readers. Studies of voting behavior and of the differential impact of the mass media of communication suggest that certain kinds of people are more often found in some communication settings than in others. For example, the study of the 1940 presidential campaign in Erie County, Ohio, showed that people who exposed themselves to political information in newspapers were more likely to be Republicans than Democrats, and therefore were likely to be of higher socio-economic status, more educated, white collar rather than blue collar workers, and Protestants rather than Catholics. Those who took their political information chiefly from the radio were more likely to be Democrats and therefore of lower socio-economic status, less well educated, blue collar rather than white collar workers, and Catholics rather than Protestants.[8] Apparently women were more likely to rely on their families, especially their fathers or husbands, for political information, hence were more often to be found receiving political information in the small group or private face-to-face setting.

[7] David Riesman, *The Lonely Crowd* (New Haven: Yale University Press, 1950), pp. 22–23.

[8] Lazarsfeld, *People's Choice*, chapter 3.

It was found in the Erie County study and later confirmed and detailed in studies in Decatur, Illinois, that a small but actively interested group of people whom the writers called *opinion leaders* were the largest and most regular users of the mass media of communication —newspapers, radio and television.[9] These opinion leaders picked up information from the mass media and, in personal contacts, passed it on to the majority of citizens who relied on the leaders for information on politics, new products, fashions and movies. Information, then, followed a "two-step flow" process from the mass media to opinion leaders and from them to the majority of citizens. We conclude that the mass communication setting, therefore, is likely to find a concentration of interested and active people in its audiences who in turn mediate between publisher or broadcaster and individual citizen or consumer.

9) *Numbers of people reached by the communication*

For a long time the size of the audience was thought to be the only important difference between one communication setting and another. Gathering a small crowd on a street corner was more efficient than carrying a message door-to-door. Hiring a crew of boys to throw handbills on every porch in town was still more efficient, but could not match the numbers reached by radio broadcasts when that means of distributing information became available. How many people can be reached in one setting as compared with another is still an important consideration but one that cannot be stressed apart from the relative effectiveness of the various settings determined by the other measures already discussed. An advertisement in the *New York Times* may reach several hundred thousand people potentially sympathetic to the cause of Puerto Rican nationalism but may not have anywhere near the drawing power of solicitation letters mailed to a selected list of 10,000 people who previously gave money to an organization promoting independence for Portuguese colonies in Africa. Personally meeting voters at coffee hours in private homes, although it is time-consuming, may be a more efficient means of winning votes than several 15-minute voter interview sessions broadcast over a local television station with a potential listenership of 65,000 people.

The choice of setting may be made on the basis of cost. A candidate with limited financial support may have to schedule more talks to lodge meetings and service clubs, more coffee hours and more shopping-center visits than the well-heeled candidate who can afford to purchase

---

[9] Elihu Katz and Paul Lazarsfeld, *Personal Influence* (Glencoe: The Free Press, 1955).

television time. Merchandisers face similar choices. But it should not be forgotten that the more economical setting may turn out on other grounds to be the more effective. A recent campaign for the senate in Oklahoma was designed on economic grounds to include a personal visit by the candidate to every town marked on the state highway map. The resulting personal contact with a high proportion of the state's voters proved successful at the polls. Unfortunately, not all states have small enough populations to permit a candidate that kind of campaign even if he had unlimited stamina.

Having considered the variables that distinguish one communication setting from another, we are now ready to consider briefly each of those four settings.

DISTINCTIVE SETTINGS

Private face-to-face communication

Communication between two friends over dinner, between a lawyer and his client, or between a psychiatrist and his patient is markedly different in terms of the variables just considered from communication between members of the board of the Community Chest at a scheduled board meeting or between the pastor and elders of his congregation. The first situation we have defined as private face-to-face communication; the second, as small group communication. In the first setting, two people who know and like each other, or who are attracted by mutual interest, talk together in private. *Opportunities for interaction* ought to be at a maximum here, although interaction may be qualified by the personal traits, status, or different roles of speaker and listener. If the two are on equal footing, a listener may easily talk back to the speaker, and the speaker may try to adjust his talk to objections or may express immediate approval or disapproval of the listener's responses. Moreover, the roles of speaker and listener alternate frequently.

When there is much verbal interaction, there are plentiful *opportunities for the listener to gain information about the speaker* and vice versa. Most people who get into such a setting already know and like the other person, or expect that they will like him, and as a result of the interaction, often find that they do. Studies of personal attraction have so regularly demonstrated this fact that Homans has proposed that "If the frequency of interaction between two or more persons increases, the degree of their liking for one another will increase."[10] Newcomb found the same situation when he studied the attraction between roommates in a university residence; even roommates whom

[10] George C. Homans, *The Human Group* (New York: Harcourt, Brace and World, 1950), p. 112.

experimenters predicted would not get along increased liking for each other as a result of frequent communication.[11]

The privacy of the face-to-face setting simplifies the influence of conflicting group memberships. Where members of other groups to which he belongs cannot observe his actions, the listener can allow the group membership he shares with the speaker to dominate. It is this *increased salience of shared group membership* that often increases the effectiveness of communications in the private face-to-face setting. Psychiatrist Jerome Frank argues that shared membership in the middle-class by patient and therapist accounts for the effects of psychiatric treatment. Therapists, he explains, "attribute considerable healing power to self-knowledge and, to this end, require the patient to verbalize his inner feelings and personal problems. This activity may be totally unfamiliar to lower-class persons, and they cannot perceive it as treatment. Nor do they attach any value to increased self-understanding." What therapeutic effect psychotherapy may have, he says, "derives from his [the psychiatrist's] membership in the group to which patients belong or aspire to belong."[12]

We have already said that speakers have very little chance of controlling *exposure to their communications by listeners* since people do not usually come together under these conditions unless they already know and like one another, that is, already know or expect that their views will harmonize. In fact, even when communications may expose differences of opinion, these differences are ignored or minimized by the listener.[13] On the other hand, having begun to talk with a friend about politics or snow tires or movies, one can resist exposure to unwanted ideas on religion or social welfare only by rudely turning away or stopping the speaker—a difficult and unpleasant expedient.

The speaker is often able to control the time and place of face-to-face discussions and in this way to *manipulate the physical environment*. You can button-hole a colleague during business hours or raise the matter over lunch, speak with him in his rooms or yours, meet him in the hall or in the parking lot. Time and place, anthropologist Edward Hall points out, because of our expectations and the meanings we give them, often make a crucial difference in the effectiveness of communication in this setting.[14] Some kinds of communications, proposals of marriage for example, require that we "set the scene." Speakers in the private face-to-face setting have considerable opportunity to do that.

[11] Theodore M. Newcomb, *The Acquaintance Process* (New York: Holt, Rinehart and Winston, Inc., 1961), pp. 210–220.

[12] Jerome D. Frank, *Persuasion and Healing* (New York: Schocken Books, 1963), pp. 117, 119.

[13] Newcomb, *Social Psychology*, p. 174.

[14] Edward T. Hall, *The Silent Language* (Greenwich, Connecticut: Fawcett Publications, Inc., c. 1959), chapters 1, 9 and 10.

An important characteristic of the private face-to-face setting is that *listeners do not see speakers as intending to manipulate* their conduct. Conversations between acquaintances are usually impromptu and natural, not calculated, and the speaker is not seen as having anything exclusive to gain from the listener's adopting his recommendations. A study of the factors influencing doctors' use of new drugs showed that colleagues most often named as friends were those to whom doctors turned for help in drug therapy; questioners, it seemed, did not expect to be "used" but to receive aid. Physicians who had few friends among their colleagues seem to have regarded the pharmaceutical salesman as "a near-professional companion," going to him for advice on drug therapy without perceiving him as a persuader.[15]

Since everyone but a social isolate can be found frequently in such a setting, *personal traits* do not seem as important a variable here as in some other settings. There are, of course, some people who get more of their information from talking with people than from reading, and who are at the same time less well educated and less certain of their capacity to make up their own minds. Women, because of their social role, may be more dependent on personal talk for political information. Studies of *opinion leaders* who are frequently found in private face-to-face settings revealed that marketing leaders were married women with comparatively large families, fashion leaders and movie leaders were young women of high gregariousness, and public affairs leaders were women of high social status.[16] It is difficult to generalize beyond observing that the purpose of the private face-to-face encounter may determine what sorts of people are to be found in it most often.

Communication in the small group.

A major interest of communication specialists, human and industrial relations consultants, sociologists, anthropologists and psychologists for the past three decades has been small group behavior. Information has been sought on the dynamics of group behavior, the effect of personality types on the works of groups, the effect of longstanding groups on the attitudes and opinions of members, the means of increasing the efficiency of problem-solving committees and boards, and a host of other topics. At the moment, we are interested in looking at the small group of three or four to a dozen people, where these people have some understood common object in meeting together, as a setting for communication. The group may be a committee charged with recommending policy, a seminar engaged in exploration of a cluster of ideas, or a group designed to provide for

[15] Herbert Menzel and Elihu Katz, "Social Relations and Innovation in the Medical Profession: the Epidemiology of a New Drug," *Public Opinion Quarterly*, 10 (1955–56), 337–352.

[16] Katz and Lazarsfeld, *Personal Influence*, pp. 331–332.

self-exploration as therapy for personality disorders. In such a group, people meet face-to-face and every person may talk with every other person.[17]

The most important feature of such a setting, as was true of the private face-to-face setting, is the *opportunity for verbal interaction* between speaker and listener. Although opportunities for interaction decrease as groups grow larger, in the size group we are considering, the chance to talk back and forth seems adequate to provide the pleasant experience people derive from interaction and to produce satisfaction with the decisions reached. Of course, interaction can be suppressed by a dominating member, or by collusion among members. For example, when there are people present who hold views very different from what seem to be majority views, the majority members at first direct much of their talk to these "extremists" in efforts to draw them toward the central view; failing in this, the group may reject the extremists and give up talking to them.[18]

The sense of pleasure and satisfaction people draw from interaction in small groups seem to derive from three sources. First, interaction offers opportunity to gain approval and status. Questions, refutations, denials, criticism, praise or approval which threaten punishment or promise reward to a speaker in the private face-to-face setting have a greatly amplified effect in the small group. Criticism is now public and therefore may threaten the social stability of a person unsure of the responses of other members. Approval is also public and therefore may seem to promise the speaker acceptance by this new group and, if he prizes that acceptance, improved status. Either of these probable results might encourage a member to persist in or to adopt certain views presumably approved by respected group members, or to watch his step in publicizing views likely to be attacked.

Second, interaction provides members with a means of finding out the group's standards. A young man elected by his social fraternity to represent that group on the interfraternity council may discover that membership in the IFC becomes important to him because it provides him with improved status and opportunities for larger influence. In order to become a respected member of the new group he needs to discover what it expects of members in order, up to a point, to do what it expects.

Finally, interaction implies a degree of individual responsibility for decisions reached by the group which seems to be an important reason

[17] The effects of other communication networks is outside our discussion here, but see Alex Bavelas, "Communication Patterns in Task-Oriented Groups," *Journal of the Acoustical Society of America*, 22 (November, 1950), 725–730; Harold J. Leavitt, "Some Effects of Certain Communication Patterns on Group Performance," *Journal of Abnormal and Social Psychology*, 46 (1951), 38–50.

[18] Leon Festinger and John Thibault, "Interpersonal Communication in Small Groups," *Journal of Abnormal and Social Psychology*, 46 (1951), 92–99.

why group decisions are better received and more faithfully supported than decisions handed down by administrators. A series of interesting studies demonstrated the superiority of group discussion to individual instruction or lecture in gaining acceptance of recommended behavior. A maternity hospital that gave mothers instruction in child care before they were discharged substituted guided discussion of child care procedures for groups of six women while retaining individual instruction for others. The discussions closed with a show of hands by those willing to try the recommended procedures, and follow-up interviews after two weeks and one month disclosed that women who took part in group discussions adhered more closely to recommended procedures than those who were given individual instruction.[19] Attempts to increase wartime use of unpopular cuts of meat and to increase milk consumption proved that group discussion was more effective in changing behavior than the lecture method.[20] The results of other studies of the differential effects of lecturing and group discussions as teaching techniques, reported by W. J. McKeachie in an accompanying reading, suggest that responsibility for the outcome of the discussion in the small group setting increases its effectiveness in motivating learning and influencing behavior.

Interaction in this setting provides *opportunities for listeners to gain information about speakers* and vice versa, since these roles reverse frequently in small group interaction. Apparently it does not take long for members of a group to gain information sufficient to judge each other's competence. The University of Chicago Law School, studying the operation of the jury system, found that members of mock juries quickly identified the status of other members by the clues of dress, speech and casual references to experiences and, on the basis of that identification, judged a person's competence to perform the jury task.[21] Other studies found that members of groups managed within a short time to fix on leaders by judgments of task competence and likeableness.[22]

The small group as an agency for change offers a communicator some *opportunity to control the salience of group memberships.* Two kinds of membership are involved: membership in the present group and membership in other groups whose aims may be partly at odds

[19] M. Radke and D. Klisurich, "Experiments in Changing Food Habits," *Journal of the American Dietetic Association,* 24 (1947), 403–409.

[20] A. Bavelas, L. Festinger, P. Woodward and A. Zander, "The Relative Effectiveness of a Lecture Method and a Method of Group Discussion for Changing Food Habits," *Bulletin of the Committee on Food Habits* (National Research Council).

[21] Fred L. Strodtbeck, Rita M. James and Charles Hawkins, "Social Status in Jury Deliberations," in *Readings in Social Psychology,* Maccoby, editor, pp. 379–388.

[22] R. Victor Harnack and Thorrell B. Fest, *Group Discussion* (New York: Appleton-Century-Crofts, 1964), pp. 193ff.

with those of the present group. Those interested in increasing the efficiency of problem-solving groups have regularly urged that members should think of their group role and accept responsibility for the satisfactory outcome of the group's deliberations. In the minds of such people, external loyalties—that is, membership in groups outside the present one that retain their importance for the member—are an obstacle to group productivity. No doubt they are; external loyalties may prevent the adoption of the present group's aims, if those are in conflict with aims of an outside group, and if the member prizes his membership in that outside group more than membership in the present group. The Boy Scout Council representative on the Community Chest Board whose chief rewards are in the Boy Scout movement will resist claims of the Community Chest if they undercut scouting interests. Still, as we have argued, because the present group may approve or disapprove, may offer or rescind status, membership in it may be prized and it may therefore require a degree of conformity to its standards.

Controls over the salience of group membership are exerted in various ways. In the effort to increase use of unpopular cuts of meat, to which we referred on page 71, housewives were reminded of their role as patriotic citizens to which role the use of recommended cuts of meat was relevant. The group discussions of child care methods developed recommended methods as a *norm* of the group of new mothers who worked out these methods, under guidance, for themselves. Outside loyalties are sometimes suppressed by preventing a member's actions from being closely observed; two Boy Scout Council representatives on the Community Chest might form an opposition bloc by keeping scouting loyalties always in view for each other; one representative might become a cooperative board member. The privacy of deliberations may also minimize the pressures of outside loyalties.

The listener's *opportunity to expose himself selectively to communications,* which was present to a degree in the private face-to-face setting, is seriously curtailed in the small group setting. There is no way to avoid being thrown in with people whose views one can predict when he accepts nomination to a committee or joins a professional group. The chance of being exposed to views one disapproves is, unfortunately, substantial. Probably this feature of the small group setting recommends it to persuaders interested in converting others to their views. Because listeners in the small group setting cannot exclude disagreeable communications, this setting offers a rare opportunity for possible conversion.

The one who schedules the meetings of a group has the initial *opportunity to manipulate the physical environment* of the small group setting. He may, as the communicator in the private face-to-face setting, choose the time and place. He may try to reinforce a sense of solidarity by arranging the seating of members, although his efforts may be frustrated by other members who have other ideas. Imagine the effect upon deliberations where young members and older members segregate themselves in clumps, or where women members take one side of the table and men the other. A degree of control can be exercised by any member who can gain group support for any physical arrangement of the meeting.

The hospital experiment illustrates another advantage of the small group setting—*listeners do not usually perceive communications in such a setting as purposefully manipulative.* Mothers did not assume that the discussion leader was seeking to alter or reinforce their behavior. Group therapy seems to work for the same reason; patients do not assume that the therapist is trying to get them to do what he has decided is right. Because communication is spontaneous and unprepared, listeners do not see the talk of other members of the group as calculated to influence their opinions or behavior.

Although there does not seem to be a concentration of people having certain *personal traits* in committees or seminars established to accomplish some common objective, some small groups may attract certain types of people. The faculty protest against the Viet Nam war on a midwestern university campus in the spring of 1965 adopted as persuasive tactics public rallies, letters to the press, teach-in seminars, and frequent faculty-student organizational meetings. Some faculty members appeared regularly at the large student rallies to give rousing orations designed to whip up enthusiasm for anti-war activity. Often these men took little part in other phases of the protest; they gave their speeches and went back to their offices. Other men worked long hours in committees and took active parts in seminars for discussion of war issues. One admitted a preference for seminar talk and a distaste for public speech-making. Perhaps the personality differences here rest on the motivation to direct or influence others, need for public approval, or simply recognition of personal skills. I would suspect that many people who operate effectively in the small group setting—and therefore seek it out—are more permissive, more open-minded people who are willing to tolerate diverse opinions; more dogmatic people would be uncomfortable in and frustrated with the small group setting.

The numbers of people reached by communication in a small group setting are not much greater than the private face-to-face setting so there is not often an advantage in efficiency to be gained by seeking to change behavior by this means. In fact, the much greater time consumed by group discussions may make it even less efficient than individual contact. The decision to use this setting will always be made on other grounds than numbers reached.

Speaker-Audience communication

Although more words have been written about the speaker-audience setting for communication—the public speaking situation—than any other of the communication settings, writers have not sought to identify the singular characteristics of this setting. Aristotle distinguished public speech from conversation largely in terms of the subjects appropriate to it. Probably its efficiency as a means of reaching many people at once, in the days before the electronic media, recommended its superiority over conversation, and no other differences seemed crucial. A surprising number of twentieth century critics have concentrated on the differences in language use between the written and spoken styles, although this factor is hardly a dependable means of determining that something was spoken rather than written to be read. One might have supposed that the advent of radio and television would have forced recognition of the differences of setting between a speech delivered in a crowded hall or broadcast to listeners sitting in their living rooms. But very little attention has been given to these differences.

Except in rare instances, the *opportunity for verbal interaction* between audience and speaker is slight. Because it is relatively formal, and listeners accept its formality, the speaker-audience setting encourages listeners to be quiet and listen while the speaker speaks. Neither the lecture nor the sermon, the most common examples of the speaker-audience setting, permits much interaction of any sort between listener and speaker. The lack of opportunity, as McKeachie points out in an accompanying reading, while it may not keep the listener from acquiring information if he is motivated, does present an obstacle to the learning of concepts or the development of problem-solving skills.[23] Most lecture audiences are so sedate that even their amusement is damped. When circumstances produce a more excited audience—a political rally or union strike meeting—listeners may shout approval, applaud wildly, laugh out loud, whistle, boo and hiss, either rewarding a speaker and inciting him to more vigorous verbal attacks on the opposition or, by conveying disapproval, letting him know that he had better adjust his views, keep silent, or get off the podium. Some groups gathered in circumstances where the usual formal conventions for the behavior of audiences do not apply—a protesting band of property owners resisting a highway department crew about to break ground for a new freeway, an incensed assemblage of students objecting to an administration ban on the appearance of a communist speaker—may talk back to the speaker. People may interrupt, shout questions, wisecrack about the speaker to the delight of the crowd, or heckle him in any number of ways. But this sort of interaction occurs in the United States only when the audience is unusually excited, when it feels free of the customary restraints on audiences, or where provision has been made for heckling or custom condones it as in Pershing Square in Los

---

[23] W. J. McKeachie, "Procedures and Techniques of Teaching: A Survey of Experimental Studies," in *The American College*, R. Nevitt Sanford, editor (New York: John Wiley and Sons, 1962), p. 320.

Angeles or "Bug House Square" in Chicago. Most audiences sit tight and listen passively.

A rather special circumstance affects interaction in this setting: the effect on an individual listener of reactions to speaker and setting by all of those other people of whose feelings and behavior he is aware. The simplest illustration of this effect is the one used earlier of watching a comic film alone in the living room via television contrasted with watching the same film in a packed theatre. When others around us laugh, it is easier for us to laugh and laugh out loud. The perceptions we have of the behavior of others work upon us as suggestions to act in a similar way. A half century ago, French sociologist Gustav Le Bon observed, and others since have confirmed his observation, that individuals in large crowds are often more suggestible than when they are alone, more suggestible even than some hypnotized subjects "from the fact that, the suggestion being the same for all the individuals of the crowd, it gains in strength by reciprocity. The individuals in the crowd who might possess a personality strong enough to resist the suggestion are too few in number to struggle against the current."[24] We do not often see audiences carried away by contagious enthusiasm to the sorts of irresponsible acts Le Bon feared and decried, but we all occasionally experience the impact of the suggestion borne upon us by the actions of those around us at a religious meeting, at a party victory rally, at the performance of some celebrated popular singer or musical group, or at an especially large or noisy celebration of the New Year. In such situations as these, the slightest suggestion of the speaker may have remarkable effect on an audience's behavior.

People in audiences feel confident that they can size up a speaker with information they have been given in advance publicity, the re- marks of the chairman who introduces the speaker, and the clues in dress, language, manner and ideas offered by the speaker himself as he talks. Whether this confidence is justified may be argued, but regard- less of the correctness of their judgments, listeners do judge and believe in their judgments. A speaker is forced to reckon with the fact that he will be judged by making appropriate use of *opportunities for listeners to gain information about him.*

Many who join an audience have already gathered enough infor- mation to identify the speaker. Partisans identify their candidates be- fore they go to hear their speeches. The interested or initiated go to a lecture by Barbara Ward or Louis Lomax because they have already identified the speaker and have favorable expectations of him. That this kind of prior identification determines attendance would be con- firmed by any booking agency; the celebrity no matter what his topic outdraws the unidentified speaker with a compelling subject.

A speaker has relatively little control over information an audience

[24] Gustave Le Bon, *The Crowd* (New York: The Viking Press, 1960), p. 32.

receives in advance from his reputation or publicity, but he can provide more information about himself in two ways. The chairman who
introduces him may relate to the audience facts about the speaker's
experience, professional preparation, and the endorsements others have
given him and his ideas—matters the speaker cannot always discuss
without seeming immodest. And, the speaker presents information
about himself in the words he chooses, the ideas he develops, and the
approaches he makes to subjects vital to his audience.[25] Where the information listeners have about him beforehand may be misleading, a
speaker has opportunities to change the impression people have of him.
No doubt Ronald Reagan was glad that thousands who thought of him
as a film celebrity came to hear him campaign for governor of California; once they had come, his job was to provide information about
himself that would allow voters to think of him as a capable public
servant.

The speaker-audience setting, when it is fairly formal and the audience orderly, gives the speaker an advantage communicators in the
small group do not usually enjoy. Because no one talks back, raises
questions or offers conflicting information, the speaker can effectively
control—if he has the skill—the kind of information listeners gain about
him. What is said of him and what he says about himself as well as
the impression he makes by his manner may present a consistent image
of the thoughtful, sympathetic, diligent, well-informed and trustworthy
man; under the fire of hecklers, or measured against the performances
of other advocates in a group, the image may not be so well controlled. While a speaker in this setting may sometimes be able to
present a misleading impression of himself, when listeners are suspicious they will not allow him to protect himself by exploiting the
formality of the setting. Presidential news conferences, the format of
"Meet the Press" and other inquiry shows, and news staff pressures on
all public figures who prefer to utter "statements," threaten the com-
placency of the speaker who seeks to mislead audiences about his
capabilities or motives.

While listeners have adequate opportunities to gain information
about speakers in the setting, *speakers have much less chance of gaining information about their audiences.* Limited interaction prevents
the speaker's receiving much feedback from listeners. But even if
feedback were provided, the heterogeneity of most audiences would
make it difficult for the speaker to decide how to interpret individual
reactions. The few nodding heads may mislead him into thinking that
the audience accepts his views when, in fact, those not reacting out-
wardly are unmoved or alienated. Most of the judgments speakers
make about their audiences are guesses, some good and some faulty,
depending largely, one writer wisely declares, upon the speaker's

[25] Other clues have been discussed relative to the private face-to-face and
small group settings on pages 60 and 71.

COMMUNICATION SETTINGS 77

education and experience in sizing up audiences.[26] Without much time, assistance or organized effort, the speaker can do little more than guess, first, at the kind of things he ought to know about the audience and, second, the interpretations of the information when he has it. Demographic characteristics of an audience—sex, age, occupation, ethnic background, political party preference, socio-economic status, religion and the like—may or may not be useful as a basis for inferences about the audience's disposition toward the speaker's proposition, its level of knowledge, language sophistication and other matters important to the speaker's strategy. Direct collection of relevant information about listeners is not often conveniently undertaken. Often the best guide a speaker can secure is the opinions of two or three people who think they know something about the audience. Without underestimating the importance for a speaker of such impressions, we can appreciate the severe limitations on his ability to know his audience which this setting imposes.

The *salience of certain group memberships* may be established for an audience before the speaker says a word. That all are Republicans may be most important at a partisan rally; that all are indignant citizens resisting encroachments on their rights may be most important to pickets demonstrating. Many audiences possess some sense of group identity at their formation with which the speaker must cope. He may wish to reinforce the saliency of that identity—as keynote speakers seek to do at presidential nominating conventions. Or, he may wish to substitute another group membership as most important in the listeners' minds, as the successful candidate seeks to do in his acceptance speech by reminding those who opposed his nomination that party unity must now supplant former loyalties to other candidates.

The *opportunities of the listener selectively to expose himself* to a speaker's ideas are seriously limited once he has become part of an audience. Whether he listens to the speaker or not is now largely within the skilful speaker's control; he can direct the listener's attention, can in many ways help him to understand what is said, and while he cannot guarantee it, he can facilitate acceptance of his proposition. The only major choice open to the listener is whether or not to join the audience and that choice, as has been said before, is usually made on the expectation that the speaker will or will not say things with which he expects to agree. Norman Thomas no doubt spends most of his time lecturing because in that way he can get a hearing from people unconverted to socialism, while those who might read his books or articles are almost certain to be those already convinced or at least sympathetic with his cause.

A few people will go out of the way to hear speakers with whom they expect to disagree, but either they do so to gather ammunition

[26] Theodore Clevenger, Jr., *Audience Analysis* (Indianapolis: Bobbs-Merrill Co., Inc., 1966), pp. 50–51.

with which to attack the speaker's cause, or they are genuinely in search of information on an unresolved problem and can afford a certain amount of discomfort in order to satisfy their need to know.[27]

Speakers in this setting have considerable *opportunity to manipulate the physical environment.* The decision to have speakers at the end of the Washington civil rights march in August, 1963, address the the crowd from the steps of the Lincoln Memorial represents an effort to reinforce the spirit of the occasion. Soviet political and military leaders who address army units massed in Red Square from the top of Lenin's tomb amid clustered flags, giant portraits of socialist heroes, bands and displays of military hardware give dimension to their words for listeners in Russia and around the world. The frequent opportunity to pick the place, to surround listeners with symbolic reminders of the urgency of the moment or of important group memberships, to arrange listeners for maximum suggestibility, and to reinforce important feelings and beliefs of listeners by means of music and simultaneous performance of symbolic actions may often enhance the effectiveness of communications in this setting.

Although political speeches are usually seen as *purposeful,* most lectures and sermons are not seen by listeners as calculated to influence their opinions. The fact that many lectures are seen as informational or diverting rather than manipulative has caused concern among educators that students will uncritically accept the personal interpretations of events offered by professors. As a result, instructors who are more anxious to develop the independent critical skills of students than to win converts to private causes have tried to alert students to the need to question ideas offered by speakers. Some have argued that because the lecturer enjoys high prestige, listeners may be even more exposed to influence. But it now seems that these fears may be exaggerated; over a period of time, listeners forget the prestigious source of the message and look at the ideas on their own merit.[28] Speakers seeking political office or selling a product are generally recognized as having ulterior motives and therefore required to reassure listeners of their disinterestedness, honesty, and sense of the larger public interest.

The all but universal participation in the speaker-audience setting, at least in this society, forces the conclusion that no distinctive constellation of *personality traits* is likely to be found among listeners in this setting.

An obvious advantage of this setting over the other two we have discussed is the larger *numbers of people reached* by communications. Audiences of several hundred can be accommodated easily in most towns and cities, while indoor political rallies at Madison Square Gar-

[27] Leon Festinger discusses "tolerance for dissonance" in *A Theory of Cognitive Dissonance* (Stanford: Stanford University Press, 1957), pp. 266–271.

[28] Hovland, Janis and Kelley, *Communication and Persuasion,* pp. 254–259.

den seat 20,000 people. Billy Graham has addressed twice that number in many places, and an estimated 200,000 people heard Martin Luther King speak to the marchers on Washington, D.C. in August, 1963.

Mass communication

Studies during the past two decades have changed our image of the mass media from the source of a barrage of communication penetrating and standardizing every phase of our lives to an informational source, one among many, that has far less direct impact on most readers, listeners and viewers than was once feared or hoped. To understand that altered image, we may look at mass communication by means of radio, television and print as a communication setting affected by the familiar variables.

Time and technology prevent much *interaction between speaker and listener, writer and reader.* Only the most strongly motivated people reply, and then the delay in exchanges of letters often renders such reply innocuous. Even if he were anxious to adjust his messages to reacting listeners, the television broadcaster cannot make changes until the 13-week contract runs out, the editor cannot react until the next monthly issue of the magazine. Radio and television *talk shows* have tried to stimulate interaction between broadcaster and listener but often at the most trivial and local level.

One way of initiating feedback is the pre-test of communications by broadcasters and advertisers. Proposed television shows are screened for selected audiences in order to get reactions before contracts are signed. Similar procedures are frequently followed with television commercial messages.[29] What are called *split runs* of print advertisements provide feedback in terms of differential sales. One advertisement is used in a publication in one market area, and another is used in a different area; differences in sales are taken to be an indication of the relative effectiveness of the alternative versions of the ad.

Although listeners may not be able to *gain information about particular writers or speakers,* adequate identification is often made possible by secondary judgment of the medium itself ("Television is more trustworthy than the newspaper in presenting political information, especially information about Democratic party candidates") or of the carrier ("*Time* magazine gives the Republicans more than a fair shake but is often unfair to Democrats"). No doubt identification of this sort precedes exposure; only the most conscientious voter—or unrepentant masochist—would regularly read partisan journals taking positions contrary to his own or listen to many televised speeches of the opposing candidate.

Once a listener has chosen to expose himself to a speaker on tele-

[29] See page 293.

vision, that speaker has roughly the same resources as a man before a
live audience to provide information about himself, and probably a
few additional means provided by the television setting. For example,
in the Kennedy-Nixon debates of 1960, make-up, contrasts between
clothing and scenery, numbers of *reaction shots* broadcast and the
lighting of the candidates seem to have contributed to listener identification of the two men.[30]

However, there are some species of mass communications that prevent readers from getting accurate information about communicators,
for example, a large volume of political campaign literature. Exploiting anonymity or hiding behind a misleading name, purveyors of
scurrilous charges and dishonest claims have operated in many campaigns. A Senate committee investigating campaign tactics in the
1940 presidential election found that one-third of 400 allegedly scurrilous publications were anonymous or insufficiently identified.[31] A particularly serious example was provided by a pamphlet sent from
Atlanta, Georgia in 1956 to 6,000 Negro voters in Detroit by the
"Council of White Citizens of Atlanta" urging them to vote Democratic
"because the Democratic Party keeps the colored in their place." The
pamphlet was actually sent by John R. McAlpine, a Detroit advertising
man working as a volunteer for Michigan Minutemen for Eisenhower.[32]
"Front" organizations produce a large amount of political information
which voters cannot identify clearly as to source. "The Pure Water
Committee," "Citizens for Blake," "Stevenson Democrats for Kennedy"
and other such names are as effective as anonymity in keeping voters
from learning the name or other identification of the actual communicator, his intentions and his record for reliability.

Mass communicators exert more effort than speakers or writers in
any other communication setting to *gain information about their audiences.* Newspapers study their readership by various demographic
traits in order to advise advertisers using their pages. Advertisers
themselves carefully identify their potential audience before they select communication media to carry their messages to consumers. Market surveys help identify not only why buyers buy, but who and where
they are, and how they receive information about products. Television
commercials are sometimes pre-tested in local areas before being aired
nationally in order to verify assumptions about prospective buyers.
Thanks to the Nielsen survey and other television audience measuring
agencies, a great deal of information is available about audiences for
various kinds of program material. But all of this information has only

[30] Herbert A. Selz and Richard D. Yoakum, "Production Diary of the Debates," in *The Great Debates,* Sidney Kraus, editor (Bloomington: Indiana University Press, 1962), pp. 83–95.

[31] Stanley Kelley, Jr., *Political Campaigning, Problems in Creating an Informed
Electorate* (Washington: The Brookings Institution, 1960), p. 129.

[32] *Ibid.,* pp. 129–130.

partial utility to mass communicators until they overcome the major obstacle—the selectivity of media users.

Mass communicators have only modest *opportunities to control the salience of group membership* of listeners. The isolated television viewer or newspaper reader keeps intact the various memberships he regards as important. While the advertiser may remind him of his membership in the working class, the independent thinkers, sportsmen, familymen or some other group, he has no very effective way to insist upon it. Efforts to have housewives identify themselves with characters in commercials are obvious, but their effectiveness undetermined. A more effective way of bringing a single group membership into prominence was group listening encouraged by Father Charles E. Coughlin in his radio campaign during the 1930's for the National Union for Social Justice. Coughlin's followers were urged to gather groups of friends and neighbors in their homes to listen to the priest's radio lectures on economics and politics, in order to enhance the feeling of participation in the Coughlin movement. Few similar efforts have been made by speakers using television.

That factor effectively weakening the impact of mass communications is the almost complete lack of *control by the communicator over the listener's selection of messages.* Selective exposure is the theme of V. O. Key's discussion of "Media: Specter and Reality" included among the readings in this section. Listeners and readers choose to attend mass communications that promise to agree with their partisan political preferences or with other beliefs they hold. Even if they should accidentally encounter ideas that make them uncomfortable, they can turn off the set or put aside the newspaper. Whether or not certain voters make use of newspapers or television for political information seems to depend on their level of education, their level of information on political issues and their level of political participation. Such information as Key reports about listener selectivity led to the understanding that information carried by the mass media does not reach most people directly but is attended by a small minority of *opinion leaders,* active media users, who pass on what they have learned to other people by word of mouth in private face-to-face or small group settings. This two-step flow of information, described by Katz and Lazarsfeld, suggests that people talking to other people still play the most significant role in the dissemination of most public information.[33]

Mass communicators have no significant *control over the physical environment* in which people receive their messages; they can only seek to discover the range of possibilities and accommodate themselves in whatever way they can to those possible environments. The over-use of close-up pictures of speakers and the addition of a written message

[33] Katz and Lazarsfeld, *Personal Influence,* pp. 3–4 and passim.

to the spoken message are two ways in which television broadcasters try to overcome their lack of control over the viewer's environment.

Effectiveness of mass communication is sometimes diminished by the fact that *listeners and viewers regard some communication in this setting as manipulative.* For example, Key reports evidence of public skepticism of newspapers as conveyors of political information. A study of United Auto Workers union members in Detroit in 1952 showed 50 per cent of those asked believed television was the most trustworthy medium while only 23 per cent believed newspapers were most trustworthy. It is not surprising that more Stevenson supporters distrusted the press than did Eisenhower supporters.[34] A more recent estimate of the trustworthiness of several mass media comes from surveys of Elmo Roper and Associates. After the television quiz show scandals in 1959, interviewers asked people, "If you got conflicting or different reports of the same news story from radio, television, the magazines and the newspapers, which of the four versions would you be most inclined to believe?"[35] The results were:

Newspapers	32%
Television	29%
Radio	12%
Magazines	10%
Don't know	17%

A later survey in 1961 showed a shift in trustworthiness to television: 39 per cent would have believed the television report and 24 per cent would have believed the newspaper account. In 1964, 41 per cent said they would have accepted the television account as most believable. One would suspect that, as television broadcasters begin to take editorial positions on less innocuous topics than crime and smut, public suspicion of their manipulative character will grow.

Studies of several indoctrination films shown to U.S. troops during World War II revealed that about one-third of those who saw the films as part of the experimental investigation identified the purpose of the film as manipulation of their attitudes. Apparently, the informational format prevented most servicemen from seeing the films as propaganda or one-sided presentations.[36]

No doubt much advertising in print and broadcast is recognized as

[34] V. O. Key, Jr., *Public Opinion and American Democracy* (New York: Alfred A. Knopf, 1963), pp. 355–356.

[35] Speech by Burns W. Roper, December 7, 1965, at public relations seminar of the American Bankers Association, distributed by Television Information Office, 666 Fifth Ave., New York.

[36] Carl I. Hovland, Arthur A. Lumsdaine and Fred D. Sheffield, *Experiments on Mass Communication* (New York: John Wiley and Sons, Inc., 1965), pp. 87–88.

manipulative by most people, although there are certainly many advertisements that are viewed as informational rather than influential. It is unsafe to generalize about the proportion of mass communications that are recognized as calculated to influence the behavior of listeners or readers.

Key's essay indicates that certain *personal traits* are likely to be found among those who expose themselves to various media. Since these generalizations have been suggested on page 65 we need not repeat them.

The audience of mass media, as is well known, numbers in the millions; it is this *potential for reaching numbers of people* simultaneously that has attracted political campaigners and commercial advertisers. While magazines of opinion have circulations in the hundreds of thousands, news and news picture magazines average more than one million copies each issue, and television has attracted audiences of 70 million or more for major events such as the Kennedy-Nixon debates of 1960.

SUMMARY

As a summary of our observations on the relative effectiveness of communications presented in the four settings we might attempt to picture the score for each setting in a graphic suggestion of its *influence potential* (page 84). No carefully quantified conclusions are implied by this graph, only an indication, sometimes tentative where we have little decisive evidence, of the advantages and disadvantages of each setting in terms of the nine variables we have considered. We have assigned an estimated value of *low, some* or *high* on these factors:

1. Opportunities for interaction
2. Opportunities for listener to gain information about speaker
3. Opportunities for speaker to gain information about listener
4. Opportunities for control of salience of group memberships
5. Opportunities for control of exposure to communications
6. Opportunities for manipulation of physical environment
7. Presumed non-purposiveness of the communication
8. Favorable personal traits of listener
9. Numbers reached by communications

A *high* score on any factor is taken as a measure of potential effectiveness of the communication. The *influence potential* of the setting is indicated by the area to the left of the curve.

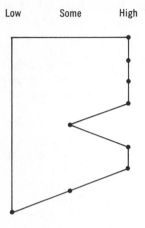

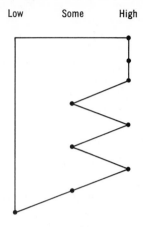

Low   Some   High

Interaction
Know speaker
Know hearers
Group member.
Exposure
Environment
Non-purposive
Favorable traits
Numbers

Private Face-to-Face

Small Group

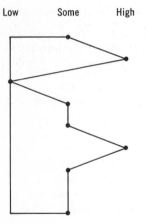

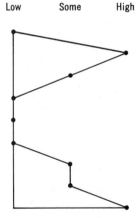

Low   Some   High

Interaction
Know speaker
Know hearers
Group member.
Exposure
Environment
Non-purposive
Favorable traits
Numbers

Speaker-Audience

Mass Communication

THE NATURE OF PERSONAL INFLUENCE

PAUL F. LAZARSFELD, BERNARD BERELSON AND HAZEL GAUDET

THE POLITICAL HOMOGENEITY of social groups is promoted by personal relationships among the same kinds of people. But for a detailed and systematic study of the influence of such relationships—the political role of personal influence—a systematic inventory would be needed of the various personal contacts and political discussions that people had over a sample number of days. . . . Such complete data are not available in the present study,[1] but enough information has been collected to indicate the importance of personal relationships so far as their direct political influence is concerned. . . . The significance of this area of political behavior was highlighted by the study but further investigation is necessary to establish it more firmly.

In comparison with the formal media of communication, personal relationships are potentially more influential for two reasons: their coverage is greater and they have certain psychological advantages over the formal media.

Reprinted with permission of Columbia University Press from Paul F. Lazarsfeld, Bernard Berelson and Hazel Gaudet, *The People's Choice* (New York: Columbia University Press, 1948), chapter 11.

[1] In two respects it is more difficult to get an index of personal exposure as compared with one of radio listening and newspaper reading. One involves a memory factor. Radio speeches are rather distinct events and people are not likely to listen to too many of them. Therefore if they are asked to remember those they have been exposed to, they are bound not to make too many mistakes. With newspapers it is still simpler because we can place the entire paper before them and their recognition is fairly reliable, as we have seen in various studies using this method. But people meet people the whole day long, and it is not nearly so likely that they can remember everything that passed between them in discussion. At least it would first be necessary to do some experimentation with personal contact diaries as suggested in the text.

To this we have to add the element of self-consciousness. If people know that they have to keep a record of what they talked about with other people, they might very well be affected in their selection of topic. Radio diaries have been tested and it seems that keeping such diaries makes people record their radio diet substantially. But this might be due to the fact that radio listening is a much more standardized pursuit; talking with people is much more flexible and might therefore be more affected by a request for systematic recording.

It is hoped that experimentation in this direction will be furthered.

PERSONAL CONTACTS REACH THE UNDECIDED

Whenever the respondents were asked to report on their recent exposure to campaign communications of all kinds, political discussions were mentioned more frequently than exposure to radio or print. On any average day, at least 10% more people participated in discussions about the election—either actively or passively—than listened to a major speech or read about campaign items in a newspaper. And this coverage "bonus" came from just those people who had not yet made a final decision as to how they would vote. Political conversations, then, were more likely to reach those people who were still open to influence.

For example, people who made up their minds later in the campaign were more likely to mention personal influences in explaining how they formed their final vote decision. Similarly, we found that the less interested people relied more on conversations and less on the formal media as sources of information. Three-fourths of the respondents who at one time had not.expected to vote but were then finally "dragged in" mentioned personal influence. After the election, the voters were given a check list of "sources from which they got most of the information or impressions that caused them to form their judgment on how to vote." Those who had made some change during the campaign mentioned friends or members of their family relatively more frequently than did the respondents who kept a constant vote intention all through the campaign.

THE TWO-STEP FLOW OF COMMUNICATIONS

A special role in the network of personal relationships is played by the "opinion leaders." . . . They engaged in political discussion much more than the rest of the respondents. But they reported that the formal media were more effective as sources of influence than personal relationships. This suggests that ideas often flow *from* radio and print *to* the opinion leaders and *from* them to the less active sections of the population.

Occasionally, the more articulate people even pass on an article or point out the importance of a radio speech. Repeatedly, changers referred to reading or listening done under some personal influence. Take the case of a retired school teacher who decided for the Republicans: "The country is ripe for a change . . . Willkie is a religious man. *A friend read and highly recommended* Dr. Poling's article in the October issue of the *Christian Herald* called 'The Religion of Wendell Willkie'."

So much for the "coverage of personal contacts." The person-to-person influence reaches the ones who are more susceptible to change, and serves as a bridge over which formal media of communications extend their influence. But in addition, personal relationships have certain psychological advantages which make them especially effective in the exercise of the "molecular pressures" finally leading to the political homogeneity of social groups. We turn now to a discussion of five such characteristics.

NON-PURPOSIVENESS OF PERSONAL CONTACTS

The weight of personal contacts upon opinion lies, paradoxically, in their greater casualness and non-purposiveness in political matters. If we read or tune in a speech, we usually do so purposefully, and in doing so we have a definite mental set which tinges our receptiveness. Such purposive behavior is part of the broad area of our political experiences, to which we bring our convictions with a desire to test them and strengthen them by what is said. This mental set is armor against influence. The extent to which people, and particularly those with strong partisan views, listen to speakers and read articles with which they agree in advance is evidence on this point.

On the other hand, people we meet for reasons other than political discussion are more likely to catch us unprepared, so to speak, if they make politics the topic. One can avoid newspaper stories and radio speeches simply by making a slight effort, but as the campaign mounts and discussion intensifies, it is hard to avoid some talk of politics. Personal influence is more pervasive and less self-selective than the formal media. In short, politics gets through, especially to the indifferent, much more easily through personal contacts than in any other way, simply because it comes up unexpectedly as a sideline or marginal topic in a casual conversation. For example, there was the restaurant waitress who decided that Willkie would make a poor president after first thinking he would be good. Said she: "I had done a little newspaper reading against Willkie, but the real reason I changed my mind was from *hearsay*. So many people don't like Willkie. Many customers in the restaurant said Willkie would be no good." Notice that she was in a position to overhear bits of conversation that were not intended for her. There are many such instances. Talk that is "forbidden fruit" is particularly effective because one need not be suspicious as to the persuasive intentions of the speakers; as a result one's defenses are down. Furthermore, one may feel that he is getting the viewpoint of "people generally," that he is learning how "different people" think about the election.

Such passive participation in conversation is paralleled in the case of the formal media by accidental exposure, e.g., when a political speech is heard because it follows a favorite program. In both conversation and the formal media, such chance communication is particularly effective. And the testimony to such influence is much more frequent in the case of personal contacts. The respondents mentioned it time and again: "I've heard fellows talk at the plant . . . I hear men talk at the shop . . . My husband heard that talked about at work. . . ."

FLEXIBILITY WHEN COUNTERING RESISTANCE

But suppose we do meet people who want to influence us and suppose they arouse our resistance. Then personal contact still has one great advantage compared with other media: the face-to-face contact can counter and dislodge such resistance, for it is much more flexible. The clever campaign worker, professional or amateur, can make use of a large number of cues to achieve his end. He can choose the occasion at which to speak to the other fellow. He can adapt his story to what he presumes to be the other's interests and his ability to understand. If he notices the other is bored, he can change the subject. If he sees that he has aroused resistance, he can retreat, giving the other the satisfaction of a victory, and come back to his point later. If in the course of the discussion he discovers some pet convictions, he can try to tie up his argument with them. He can spot the moments when the other is yielding, and so time his best punches.

Neither radio nor the printed page can do anything of the kind. They must aim their propaganda shots at the whole target instead of just at the center, which represents any particular individual. In propaganda as much as in other things, one man's meat is another man's poison. This may lead to boomerang effects, when arguments aimed at "average" audiences with "average" reactions fail with Mr. X. The formal media produced several boomerangs upon people who resented what they read or heard and moved in the opposite direction from that intended. But among 58 respondents who mentioned personal contacts as concretely influential, there was only one boomerang. The flexibility of the face-to-face situation undoubtedly accounted for their absence.

REWARDS OF COMPLIANCE

When someone yields to a personal influence in making a vote decision, the reward is immediate and personal. This is not the case in yielding to an argument via print or radio. If a pamphlet argues that voting for the opposite party would be un-American or will jeopardize the future, its warning may sound too remote or improbable. But if a neighbor says the same thing, he can "punish" one immediately for being unimpressed or unyielding: he can look angry or sad, he can leave the room and make his fellow feel isolated. The pamphlet can only intimate or describe future deprivations; the living person can create them at once.

Of course all this makes personal contacts a powerful influence only for people who do not like to be out of line. There are certainly some people who gain pleasure from being non-conformists, but under normal circumstances they are probably very much in the minority. Whenever propaganda by another person is experienced as an expression of the prevailing group tendencies, it has greater chances of being successful than the formal media because of social rewards. For example, here is a woman who was for Roosevelt until the middle of the campaign: "I have always been a Democrat and I think Roosevelt has been all right. But my family are all for Willkie. They think he would make the best president and they have been putting the pressure on me." She finally voted for Willkie. This aspect of personal contacts was especially important for women.

The rewards of compliance to other people are learned in early childhood. The easiest way for most children to avoid discomfort is to do what others tell them to do. Someone who holds no strong opinions on politics and hence makes up his mind late in the campaign may very well be susceptible to personal influences because he has learned as a child to take them as useful guides in unknown territory. The young man who was going to vote for Roosevelt because "my grandfather will skin me if I don't" is a case in point.

TRUST IN AN INTIMATE SOURCE

More people put reliance upon their personal contacts to help them pick out the arguments which are relevant for their own good in political affairs than they do in the more remote and impersonal newspaper and radio. The doubtful voter may feel that the evaluations he reads or hears in a broadcast are plausible, for the expert writer can probably spell out the consequences of voting more clearly than the average citizen. But the voter still wonders whether these are the issues which are really going to affect *his own* future welfare. Perhaps these sources see the problem from a viewpoint entirely different from his own. But he can trust the judgment and evaluation of the respected people among his associates. Most of them are people with the same status and interests as himself. Their attitudes are more relevant for him than the judgments of an unknown editorial writer. In a formal communication the content can be at its best; but in a face-to-face contact the transference is most readily achieved. For example, here is the case of a young laborer who professed little or no interest in the campaign and who did not even expect to vote until late October: "I've been discussing the election with *the fellows at the shop* and I believe I'll vote, but I haven't decided yet who for." His constant exposure to the views of his fellow-workers not only brought him to the ballot booth but also brought out his final Democratic vote in line with his colleagues.

A middle-aged woman who showed great interest in the campaign was undecided until late October and then voted for Willkie: "*I was talking politics just this morning with a friend, a businessman.* He says business will improve if Willkie is elected and that Willkie promises to keep us out of the war. FDR is getting too much power. He shouldn't have a third term." Her friend had apparently run out for her what amounted to a small catalogue of Republican arguments and he was impressive enough to clinch her vote, which had been in the balance throughout the campaign. Her trust in his judgment settled her mind.

Trust in another person's point of view may be due to his prestige as well as to the plausibility of what he has to say or its relevancy to one's interests. It is obvious that in all influences prestige plays a considerable role. The degree of conformity is greater the higher the prestige of the person in our group who seeks to influence us. The plausibility of the consequences he presents will seem greater if he is important. (Of course, the formal media are also important in this respect.) The heightening of trust through the prestige of certain personal contacts was clear in the case of the driver of a bread truck who changed to Willkie because the prominent president of a business firm had done him the honor of persuading him in that direction. Then, too, there is the case of a middle-aged housewife with little education who was for Willkie from May through September, became undecided in October, and finally voted for Roosevelt. She left Willkie because of the statements of people whom she considered authorities: "I talked with *a college student* from Case, in Cleveland, and students are for Roosevelt because he has helped recreation. I talked, too, with a *man from Chicago who is very interested in politics,* and he doesn't seem to think that Willkie is a big enough man to handle international affairs."

PERSUASION WITHOUT CONVICTION

Finally, personal contacts can get a voter to the polls without affecting at all his comprehension of the issues of the election—something the formal media can rarely do. The newspaper or magazine or radio must first be effective in changing attitudes related to the action. There were several clear cases of votes cast not on the issues or even the personalities of the candidates. In fact, they were not really cast for the candidates at all. They were cast, so to speak, for the voters' friends.

"*I was taken to the polls* by a worker who insisted that I go."

"*The lady where I work wanted me to vote.* She took me to the polls and *they all voted Republican so I did too.*"

In short, personal influence, with all its overtones of personal affection and loyalty, can bring to the polls votes that would otherwise not be cast or would be cast for the opposing party just as readily if some other friend had insisted. They differ from the formal media by persuading uninterested people to vote in a certain way without giving them a substantive reason for their vote. Fully 25% of those who mentioned a personal contact in connection with change of mind failed to give a real issue of the campaign as a reason for the change, but only 5% of those who mentioned the formal media omitted such a reason. When personal influence is paramount in this way, the voter is voting mainly for the personal friend, not the candidate.

PRACTICAL IMPLICATIONS

In a way the outcome of the election in Erie County is the best evidence for the success of face-to-face contacts. It so happened that for some time the Republican machine in that area worked much more vigorously than its Democratic opponent. When asked whether they knew people who had good ideas about politics, our respondents mentioned considerably more Republican than Democratic local politicians. A few people who did not expect to vote but finally went to the polls mentioned Republican canvassers as the main influence, but we could not trace a similar success for the Democratic machine.

However, one should not identify the personal contacts discussed in this chapter with the efforts of the *professional* political machines. These personal contacts are what one might call *amateur machines* which spring up during elections—individuals who become quite enthusiastic or special groups that try to activate people within their reach. One might almost say that the most successful form of propaganda—especially last-minute propaganda—is to "surround" the people whose vote decision is still dubious so that the only path left to them is the way to the polling booth. We do not know how the budget of the political parties is distributed among different channels of propaganda but we suspect that the largest part of any propaganda budget is spent on pamphlets, radio time, etc. But our findings suggest the task of finding the best ratio between money spent on formal media and money spent on organizing the face-to-face influences, the local "molecular pressures" which vitalize the formal media by more personal interpretation and the full richness of personal relationships into the promotion of the causes which are decided upon in the course of an election.

In the last analysis, more than anything else people can move other people. From an ethical point of view this is a hopeful aspect in the serious social problem of propaganda. The side which has the more enthusiastic supporters and which can mobilize grass-root support in an expert way has great chances of success.

RESEARCH ON METHODS OF TEACHING

W. J. McKeachie

Lecturing

COLLEGE TEACHING AND LECTURING have been so long associated that when one pictures a college professor in a classroom, he almost inevitably pictures him as lecturing. The popularity of the lecture probably derives from a conception of the instructor's primary goal as transmitting knowledge.

Since lectures typically provide few opportunities for students to respond, there is little opportunity for students to receive feedback except through periodic tests. Delay of feedback may not, however, be a major factor in acquiring knowledge if the learner is motivated and the material is not too difficult. We would, however, expect lack of feedback to be a greater handicap if the lecturer's goal were to develop concepts or to teach problem-solving skills. There is experimental evidence that when these are the goals active participation on the part of the learner is more effective than passive listening or observing. Consequently the passive role of the student in the lecture would be expected to be a handicap in achieving these objectives.

Lecture vs. discussion

The lecture has usually been compared in effectiveness with discussion. Since discussion offers the opportunity for a good deal of student activity and feedback, it could, according to theory, be more effective than lecture in developing concepts and skills in problem solving. Since, however, the rate of transmission of information is slow in discussion classes we would expect lecture classes to be superior in attaining these objectives.

Unfortunately, although there have been many studies of the lecture as compared to the discussion or other methods, few have used independent measures of outcomes in the different cases. The results of the experimentation are generally in line with our hypotheses but are certainly not conclusive. For example, using tests of information, several experimenters have found no significant differences or slight differences

Reprinted with permission from Nevitt Sanford, editor, *The American College* (New York: John Wiley and Sons, Inc., 1962).

in favor of the lecture (Spence, 1928; Remmers, 1933; Husband, 1951; Ruja, 1954; Eglash, 1954). In one of the earliest comparisons of lecture and discussion, however, Bane (1925) found little difference between the methods on measures of immediate recall but a significant superiority for discussion on a measure of delayed recall. In all of these experiments, the information measured by the examination could be obtained from a textbook and in only one was a discussion group smaller than thirty-five students used.

When we turn to measures of more complex outcomes, the results are somewhat different. Hirschman (1952), using a measure of concept learning, compared the effectiveness of presenting material by dictation with that of presenting written materials followed by discussion and rereading. The reading-discussion method resulted in superior ability to identify examples of the concepts presented. Barnard (1942) compared the effectiveness of a lecture-demonstration teaching method with that of a problem-solving developmental discussion in a college science course. In this experiment the lecture-demonstration method proved superior on a test of specific information but the discussion method proved to be superior on measures of problem solving and scientific attitude. Other evidence favoring discussion was the experiment of Elliott (Beardslee, Birney, and McKeachie, 1952) who found that students in his discussion groups in elementary psychology became interested in electing more additional courses in psychology than did students in a large lecture course. Similarly, Casey and Weaver (1956) found no differences in knowledge of content but superiority in attitudes (as measured by the Minnesota Teacher Attitude Inventory) for small group discussions as compared to lectures. Thus the results point to the superiority of lectures for information learning and of discussion for achieving higher level objectives.

Many universities and large colleges use a method of distributing class meetings between lectures and discussions. Other studies, by Warren (1954), Becker et al. (1958), and Klapper (1958), indicate that in courses in which the instructors must not only give information but also develop concepts, the use of both lectures and discussions would seem to be a logical and popular choice.

The chief competitor of the lecturer is not the teaching machine, television, or film, but rather a much older invention—writing. If rate of transmission of knowledge is important, a good book is hard to beat. Not only can the reader control his own rate, but the motivated, skilled reader can traverse the printed page much more rapidly than even the fastest lecturer can deliver the material. Over a generation ago Greene (1928) conducted an experiment demonstrating that college students learned as much from reading a passage as from hearing the same material in a lecture.

Although printed materials have been almost as popular as television for a much longer time, lectures have survived. Even the advent of picture-book textbooks did not dislodge the lecturer. If we had stopped to think about this, we probably would not have been surprised that dozens of researches have not had much impact upon lecturers' attitudes toward television.

Perhaps the lecturer's arguments are rationalizations, for there is little research to support them. Nevertheless psychologists may have underestimated important factors in our usual analyses of the learning situation. Because we wish to maintain good experimental controls, rate and sequence of presentation are carefully controlled in most of our experiments. The materials used are meaningless to the learner. The results lead us to stress the importance of feedback to the learner. Lecturing, however, is largely devoted to communicating meaningful materials to somewhat motivated learners. Apparently such learning can take place with relatively infrequent checks on the progress of the learner. In fact, he can to some extent obtain feedback by himself. By our experimental controls we miss the important fact that when knowledge is presented by a teacher he is able to respond to feedback from the learners. This may be an important asset of the instructor. Although films and television present material at a relatively fixed rate, an instructor can go faster or slower when he gets cues of inattention, glares, or blank confusion from his class.

The reader too can pace himself, but the inexperienced student may not be able to separate the meat of a book from the fat. Even though lecturers are slower than books, a good lecturer may be able to give his students all they need from a book in much less time than it would take them to read it.

Textbooks, films, and teaching machines must be organized to fit average students if they are to be economically feasible. The lecturer can not only plan his lecture for his own class but he can also respond to feedback from his class as he delivers it. This responsiveness to cues from the class is probably the reason that material can be covered less rapidly in "live" classes than in television classes. Because the instructor responds to feedback, his presentation may appear to be unorganized. Yet one might hypothesize that this very responsiveness may make for greater effectiveness than that of a carefully organized, inflexible presentation.

Although there is little relevant evidence from research, we would thus expect live lecturing to be most effective in situations where there is considerable variation among groups in ability, relevant background, or motivation and where flexible adjustment to the group is thus important.

Most lecturers avow aims beyond transmission of information. College instructors often say that they provide the integration lacking in the text. Again one would expect that other means of communication could also provide integration. Probably what the instructor really does is to provide his own system of integration. Whether or not this is preferable to integration provided by textbooks, acceptance of the frame of reference of the instructor does at least make a difference in the grade received by the student. Runkel (1956) measured the structure of instructors' and students' attitudes in beginning college courses in psychology and zoology. He found that *agreement* with the instructor's position *did not* predict students' grades, but students whose attitudes were *colinear* with the instructor *did* earn higher grades. What we do not yet know is whether or not the instructor can communicate his structure to students who do not already have it.

Probably the most careful attempts to measure attitudinal and motivational outcomes have been those comparing live instruction with television instruction in the research programs at Penn State and Miami. In neither case does the live instructor seem to be very superior. Still if the students' tendency to identify with the instructor has anything to do with personal interaction with the instructor, it may be an ominous finding that students do not seek personal conferences with television instructors as much as with "live" instructors. . . .

Size of lecture classes

The monumental studies of class size conducted at Minnesota in the 1920s indicated that large classes are actually superior to small classes. Fifty-nine well-controlled experiments were reported by Hudelson (1928). The experiments involved such widely varying subject matter as psychology, physics, accounting, and law. In forty-six of the experiments results favored the large classes. Although many of the differences were not statistically significant, the majority of significant differences favored large classes. In these experiments small classes tended to be 25 to 30 students, but they ranged from 12–60 in size while large classes ranged in size from 35–150. Extreme differences in size were no more favorable to small groups than were small differences. Although most of the criterion measures were tests of knowledge, some experiments also attempted to measure higher level intellectual changes with similar results.

More recent experiments are less favorable to large classes. Rohrer (1957) found no significant differences. In experiments by Macomber and Siegel (1957, 1960), the only statistically significant differences favored the smaller classes (particularly for high ability students) on achievement tests and on measures of change in misconceptions in psychology, on a case test of problem solving in a course in marketing, and on the measures of student attitudes toward all the courses. When retention of knowledge was measured one to two years after completion of the courses, large classes did not prove to be significantly inferior to small classes in any one course. In eight of the nine courses compared, however, differences favored the small classes (Siegel, Adams, and Macomber, 1960).

At Grinnell students give instructors higher ratings in smaller classes (Lovell and Hainer, 1955); at Brooklyn (Riley, 1950) and Purdue (Remmers, 1927), there is no significant difference in ratings of small and large classes generally, although Remmers reports in a controlled experiment at Purdue (1933) that the students involved preferred a small recitation to a large lecture. The weight of the evidence seems to be toward small classes if one uses student or faculty satisfaction as criterion.

We have stressed the role of the lecturer as a communicator of information. Insofar as information is a one-way process, size of group should be limited only by the audibility of the lecturer's voice. In fact, as Hudelson suggests, a large class may have sufficient motivational value for an instructor to cause him to spend more time in preparation of his lectures resulting, we would hope, in better teaching and in greater student achievement. But if the effective lecture involves some interaction between instructor and students, the large class may be inferior even for lectures, for most lecturers report that fewer students raise questions or interpose comments in large classes than in small.

If there is less participation in large classes, some of the results of the Minnesota research may suggest that we hark back to the criterion problem mentioned earlier. Let us examine the evidence more closely. Were the achievement tests used biased against teaching that introduced varying points of view? If our tests place a premium upon exact recall of the materials presented by the teacher or textbook, the student who hears other points of view may be at a disadvantage.

To sum up, lectures of large size are not generally inferior to smaller lecture classes if one uses traditional achievement tests as a criterion. When other objectives are measured, large lectures are on somewhat shakier ground but are not consistently inferior. However both students and faculty members feel that teaching is more effective in small classes. Probably of more significance than class size per se is its relation to the teaching method used. For example, one would expect class size to be of minimal relevance in television teaching, of slight importance in lecturing, but of considerable significance in discussion teaching.

Discussion methods

We have anticipated our discussion of discussion methods in the previous review of research comparing the effectiveness of lecture and discussion. We implied there that discussion may be ill-adapted for communicating information because the rate of communication from instructor to student is slow. This implication, however, should hastily be countered by pointing out that not all information must come from the instructor and, in addition, not all information is eagerly received. When information encounters intellectual or emotional resistance, discussion methods may be necessary in order to bring the source of resistance to light so that it may be treated.

Moreover, if we are trying to achieve application, critical thinking, or some of the higher level cognitive outcomes, it seems reasonable to assume that students should have an opportunity to practice application and critical thinking and to receive feedback on the results. Group discussion provides an opportunity to do this. Although teaching machines may also be programmed to provide prompt feedback, a group discussion permits presentation of a variety of problems enabling a number of people to gain experience in integrating facts, formulating hypotheses, amassing relevant evidence, and evaluating conclusions. In fact the prompt feedback provided by the teaching machine may actually be less effective than a method in which students are encouraged to discover solutions for themselves with less step-by-step guidance (Della-Piana, 1956). Since problem solving ordinarily requires information, we might expect discussion to be more effective for groups with more information than for those lacking in background. Some remote support for this hypothesis is provided by a study of the learning of children in visiting a museum. Melton, Feldman, and Mason (1936) found that lectures were more effective than discussions for children in grades 5, 6, and 7, but discussions were more effective for eighth graders.

In discussing the liabilities of lecturing, I mentioned that lectures usually place the learner in a passive role and that passive learning is less efficient than active. We would expect discussions to promote more active learning, and we have some relevant evidence. Bloom and his colleagues at Chicago used recordings of classes to stimulate students to recall their thoughts during class (1953). As predicted, it was found that discussion did stimulate more active thinking than did lecture classes. Unfortunately, no one has followed this up to see in what way active thinking relates to gains in knowledge or cognitive skills.

The idea that discussion methods should help overcome resistance to learning is difficult to verify. Essentially the argument is that some desired learning encounters emotional barriers that prevent it from affecting behavior. For example, a psychology student may learn that distributed practice is effective, but not change his study methods because his anxiety about grades is so great that he does not dare try anything different. In such circumstances experiments on attitude change suggest that the instructor must either bring about changes in underlying attitude and motivation or must change the individual's perception of the instrumental relationship between his belief and his motives. Psychotherapists believe that expressing one's attitude in a nonthreatening situation is one of the steps in the process of change. A group discussion may provide such opportunities for expression as well as give opportunities for other group members to point out other instrumental relationships. Also the presence of a group is a real advantage in bringing about changes in motivation and attitudes, as Lewin showed (1952).

Student-centered vs. instructor-centered teaching

The theories of client-centered counseling and of Lewinian group dynamics have led to an increased interest in discussion techniques. A wide variety of teaching methods are described by the labels "student-centered," "nondirective," "group-centered," or "democratic," discussion. They have in common the desire to break away from the traditional instructor-dominated classroom and to encourage greater student participation and responsibility. In Table 1, I have attempted to list some of the ways in which the student-centered method has been supposed to differ from the traditional "instructor-centered" class.

TABLE 1   DIMENSIONS UPON WHICH STUDENT-CENTERED AND
INSTRUCTOR-CENTERED METHODS MAY DIFFER

Student-Centered	Instructor-Centered
Goals	
Determined by group (Faw, 1949)	Determined by instructor
Emphasis upon affective and attitudinal changes (Faw, 1949)	Emphasis upon intellectual changes
Attempts to develop group cohesiveness (Bovard, 1951)	No attempt to develop group cohesiveness
Classroom Activities	
Much student participation (Faw, 1949)	Much instructor participation
Student-student interaction (McKeachie, 1951)	Instructor-student interaction
Instructor accepts erroneous or irrelevant student contributions (Faw, 1949)	Instructor corrects, criticizes, or rejects erroneous or irrelevant student contributions (Faw, 1949)
Group decides upon own activities (McKeachie, 1951)	Instructor determines activities
Discussion of students' personal experiences encouraged (Faw, 1949)	Discussion kept on course materials
De-emphasis of test and grades (Asch, 1951)	Traditional use of tests and grades
Instructor interprets feelings and ideas of class member when it is necessary for class progress (Axelrod, 1955)	Instructor avoids interpretation of feelings
Reaction reports (Asch, 1951)	No reaction reports

From the standpoint of theory, student-centered teaching in its more extreme forms might be expected to have some serious weaknesses, at least in achieving lower-level cognitive goals. With the instructor's role as information giver reduced, his role as source of feedback virtually eliminated, his opportunity to provide organization and structure curtailed, it is apparent that a heavy burden falls upon the group member to carry out any of these functions that are necessary. We would expect that these functions could best be assumed by groups that not only have some background experience in the academic discipline involved but also have had experience in carrying out these functions in "democratic" groups.

Since student-centered teaching attempts to reduce dependence upon the instructor, it would be expected to diminish his influence as a prestige figure, and consequently the instructor's power to bring about attitudinal changes might be reduced. However, in terms of our earlier discussion this may be more than compensated for by increased freedom of expression and increased potency of group norms as sources of influence. Participation in discussion gives students an opportunity to gain recognition and praise which should, according to learning theory, strengthen motivation. Some support for this comes from Thistlethwaite's (1960) finding that National Merit Scholars check as one of the outstanding characteristics of the teachers who contributed most to their desire to learn, "allowing time for classroom discussion." Other characteristics mentioned included "modifying course content to meet students' needs and interests," "treating students as colleagues," and "taking a personal interest in students." In line with our earlier discussion of feedback, another trait mentioned was "providing evaluations reassuring the student of his creative or productive potentialities."

The advocates of student-centered or group-centered teaching also introduce another category of objectives, not usually considered in traditional classes. This is the goal of developing skills in group membership and leadership.

Since student-centered teachers often stress group cohesiveness, a possible explanation for the contradictory results in the experiments to follow may be found in the studies of group cohesiveness and productivity in industry (e.g., Seashore, 1954). These studies indicate that it is not safe to assume that a cohesive group will be a productive one. Cohesive groups are effective in maintaining group standards, but may set either high or low standards of productivity. Since cohesive groups feel less threatened by management than less cohesive groups, it may be difficult to change their standards. With this as an introduction let us review the experimental attempts to demonstrate the effectiveness of student-centered teaching.[1]

[1] Much of the following material on student-centered discussion is based on Birney and McKeachie (1955) and is used with the permission of the American Psychological Association.

Faw (1949) studied a class of 102 students which met two hours a week to listen to lectures and two hours a week in discussion groups of 34. One of the discussion groups was taught by a student-centered method, one by an instructor-centered method, and one group alternated between the two methods. Scores on the objective course examination based on the textbook showed small but significant differences favoring the student-centered method.

In a very similar experiment Asch (1951), like Faw, taught all the groups involved in his experiment. Three sections of about 30 to 35 students were taught by an instructor-centered method, half lecture —half discussion. One section of 23 students was taught by a nondirective method, quite similar to that of Faw. There were, however, certain differences between Faw's and Asch's experiments. In Faw's experiment both student-centered and instructor-centered classes also spent two hours a week listening to lectures. Although Faw does not mention grading, one assumes that grades were determined by the instructor on the basis of the coursewide examination. In Asch's experiment, students in the student-centered class were allowed to determine their own grades.

Asch's results do not completely agree with Faw's. On the final examination in the course, students in the instructor-centered class scored significantly higher than members of the student-centered class, not only on the objective portion of the test, but also on an essay portion. Note, however, that the student-centered class was specifically told that this examination would in no way affect their grades in the course, and the two groups were thus probably not equivalent in motivation. As measured by the Bogardus Social Distance scale, attitude change in the two sections was not significantly different. As compared with the instructor-centered class, a greater percentage of members of the student-centered class improved in adjustment as measured by the Minnesota Multi-Phasic Inventory.

Following the model of Lewin, Lippitt, and White's (1939) study of authoritarian, democratic, and laissez faire group climates, the staff of the University of Michigan's general psychology course set up an experiment using three styles of teaching: recitation, discussion, and group tutorial (Guetzkow, Kelly, and McKeachie, 1954). As compared to discussion and tutorial methods, the more autocratic recitation method not only produced superior performance on the final examination, but also produced greater interest in psychology, as measured by the election of advanced courses in psychology. Furthermore, students liked the recitation method better than the other methods. The greater gains in knowledge produced by the recitation method fits in with the general principle that feedback aids learning, for students in the recitation sections had weekly or semiweekly quizzes. McKeachie (1951) suggests that the popularity of this method is related to student anxiety about grades, which is most easily handled when students are in familiar, highly structured situations. Another factor in these results may be the inexperience of the instructors involved, most of whom had had less than a year of previous teaching experience. . . .

Student-centered teaching: conclusions

The results of the research on student-centered teaching methods are not impressive, but tend to support the theory with which our discussion began. We had suggested that student-centered methods might be ineffective in achieving lower-order cognitive objectives. There seem to be few instances of such a loss. Students apparently can get information from textbooks as well as from the instructor. The possible advantages of student-centered instruction in achieving the goal of application of concepts is supported by the experiments of Bovard, McKeachie, Patton, Carpenter, and Davage. The theory that student-centered teaching is effective in producing noncognitive changes is supported by the experiments of Popham and Moore, Raw, Asch, and Gibb and Gibb. Finally, the only experiment in which group membership skills were measured (Gibb and Gibb) did find the group-centered students to be superior. . . .

Automated techniques

The impending shortage of college teachers has sparked several hotly contested skirmishes about the virtues or vices of various techniques of teaching with devices substituting for a portion of the usual face-to-face interaction between instructors and students. Since some college faculty members are anxious about technological unemployment and resist innovations, research has often been used as a technique of infiltration rather than as a method of developing and testing educational theory.

TELEVISION.[2] The most glamourous of the newer technological aids to education is television. Before reviewing the research on teaching by television, let us consider two hypotheses that may help in analyzing the research results.

Television is not a method of instruction in the sense that discussion and lecture are methods of instruction. Rather it is a means of giving the student a clear view of the instructional situation. Therefore we would expect that (1) the relative effectiveness of teaching via television will vary depending upon the importance of being able to see

[2] Some of this section was previously published in McKeachie, W. J., TV for college instruction. *Improving college and university teaching,* 1958, 84–89, used by permission of the publisher, Graduate School of Oregon State University, Corvallis, Oregon.

clearly. For example, we would expect television to be effective when it is important for students to see demonstrations, visiting lecturers, or films, but to have little advantage when the communication is primarily verbal.

Television reduces the opportunity for students to communicate with teachers and for teachers to interact with students. We would thus expect that (2) the effectiveness of television will vary inversely with the importance of two-way communication not only for feedback to the student but also particularly for feedback to the teacher. . . .

Uses of Television. From our hypothesis that television would be of most value in courses depending upon visual presentation of information we might expect it to be more effective in science and engineering courses than in social sciences and humanities courses. From our hypothesis that television would be of less value in classes where interaction between students and instructor is important, we might expect it to be relatively less effective in psychology, speech, and languages than in courses usually taught by lecture. Such comparisons are difficult to make, however. As we have seen, students learned as much by television as in conventional classes in chemistry at Penn State and this was also true at Purdue (Seibert and Honig, 1959), but in general psychology the television students both at Purdue and Penn State did more poorly than students in conventional classes. This evidence is in line with our assumption. Similarly, if we simply look at the direction of the differences about half the experiments in science classes favor television and half favor conventional instruction. In nonscience courses well over two-thirds of the differences favor conventional teaching.[3]

Insofar as student-instructor interaction is important for teaching a course, television would appear to be of little help. Television does not permit more students to talk, even with two-way audio connections. It is apparent that the student's opportunity to participate is an inverse function of the number of students in the class. If actual participation is important, larger classes should be less effective whether they are taught in one classroom or by television. . . .

It seems safe to conclude that television instruction is inferior to classroom lectures in communicating information, developing critical thinking, changing attitudes, and arousing interest in a subject but that this inferiority is probably not great. Although differences favoring conventional teaching appeared in about two-thirds of the studies

[3] The preceding comments have been primarily concerned with closed-circuit television instruction on campus. Although it is difficult to do adequately controlled studies of the educational effectiveness of broadcast television, it seems quite clear that students motivated enough to take a television course for credit at home learn well and have favorable attitudes toward television (LePore and Wilson, 1958; Dreher and Beatty, 1958; Evans, Roney, and McAdams, 1954).

reviewed, only a fifth of the differences were statistically significant. One's view of these results depends a good deal upon one's bias toward or against television. When compared with research comparing other instructional methods, the consistency of results favoring conventional instruction over television is unusual. However, when one weighs heavily the necessity for accommodation of higher education to large numbers of students, the differences between television and conventional instruction seem small.

FILMS. The great mass of research on instructional films is relevant to our topic, even though most of it has not been concerned with college teaching. Although it would be impossible for us to summarize all of the relevant studies, certain principles have emerged. (For a more complete analysis, see Miller, 1957.)

1. Students can learn from films, and usually do learn at least as much as from a poor teacher (VanderMeer, 1950).

2. Such learning is not confined to details, but may include concepts and attitudes (Kishler, 1950; Mertens, 1951; Hoban and Van Ormer, 1950).

3. Repeating the film increases learning (McTavish, 1949).

4. Students learn how to learn from films; i.e., students with previous experience in learning from films learn more than those with no previous experience with instructional films (VanderMeer, 1951).

5. Presenting pictures is more effective than presenting words as stimuli in rote association tasks such as learning a foreign language (May and Lumsdaine, 1958; Kopstein and Roshal, 1954).

6. Participation increases learning (Hovland, Lumsdaine, and Sheffield, 1949).

Much of the preceding discussion of instructional television is also relevant to teaching by films. The chief differences seem to be in the greater mobility of movie cameras than of television cameras, the greater expense of producing a film than a television lesson (assuming that the television equipment is already available), and the presumed greater immediacy of "live" television. Unfortunately, we have very little evidence on the educational importance of immediacy. Intuitively it would seem that students would feel more involvement in watching a television professor on their own college's staff knowing that they are seeing him at the actual moment of performance than they would feel in watching a film made at some earlier time. Whether or not such differences in involvement do occur (and if they occur whether it makes any difference educationally) is still unknown.

REFERENCES

ASCH, M. J. Nondirective teaching in psychology. *Psychol. Monogr.*, 1951, *65*, No. 4 (Whole No. 321).

AXELROD, J. Group dynamics, nondirective therapy, and college teaching. *J. higher Educ.*, 1955, *26*, 200–207.

BANE, C. L. The lecture vs. the class-discussion method of college teaching. *Sch. and Soc.*, 1925, *21*, 300–302.

BARNARD, J. D. The lecture-demonstration versus the problem-solving method of teaching a college science course. *Science Educ.*, 1942, *26*, 121–132.

BEARDSLEE, D., BIRNEY, R., AND McKEACHIE, W. Summary of conference on research in classroom processes. (Mimeo.) Unpublished manuscript, Department of Psychology, University of Michigan, 1952.

BECKER, S. L., MURRAY, J. N., AND BECHTOLDT, H. P. *Teaching by the discussion method.* Iowa City: State University of Iowa, 1958.

BLOOM, B. S. Thought processes in lectures and discussions. *J. gen. Educ.*, 1953, *7*, 160–169.

BOVARD, E. W., JR. Group structure and perception. *J. abnorm. soc. Psychol.*, 1951a, *46*, 398–405.

BOVARD, E. W., JR. The experimental production of interpersonal affect. *J. abnorm. soc. Psychol.*, 1951b, *46*, 521–528.

CASEY, J. E., AND WEAVER, B. E. An evaluation of lecture method and small group method of teaching in terms of knowledge of content, teacher attitude, and social status. *J. Colo.-Wyo. Acad. Sci.*, 1956, 4(7), 54.

DELLA-PIANA, G. M. Two experimental feedback procedures: a comparison of their effects on the learning of concepts. Unpublished doctoral dissertation, University of Illinois, 1956. (*Diss. Abstr.*, 1956, *16*, 910–911.)

EGLASH, A. A group discussion method of teaching psychology. *J. educ. Psychol.*, 1954, *45*, 257–267.

FAW, V. A. A psychotherapeutic method of teaching psychology. *Amer. Psychologist*, 1949, *4*, 104–109.

GIBB, LORRAINE M., AND GIBB, J. R. The effects of the use of "participative action" groups in a course in general psychology. (Abstract) *Amer. Psychologist*, 1952, *7*, 247.

GREENE, E. B. Relative effectiveness of lecture and individual reading as methods of college teaching. *Genet. Psychol. Monogr.*, 1928, *4*, 457–563.

GUETZKOW, H., KELLY, E. L., AND McKEACHIE, W. J. An experimental comparison of recitation, discussion, and tutorial methods in college teaching. *J. educ. Psychol.*, 1954, *45*, 193–209.

HIRSCHMAN, C. S. An investigation of the small groups discussion classroom method on criteria of understanding, pleasantness, and self-confidence induced. Unpublished master's thesis, University of Pittsburgh, 1952.

HOBAN, C. F., AND VAN ORMER, E. B. *Instructional Film Research*, 1918–1950. Tech. Rep. No. SDC 269-7-19. Special Devices Center, Dec. 1950.

Hovland, C. I., Lumsdaine, A. A., and Sheffield, F. D. *Experiments in mass communication*. Princeton: Princeton University Press, 1949.

Hudelson, E. *Class size at the college level*. Minneapolis: University of Minnesota Press, 1928.

Husband, R. W. A statistical comparison efficacy of large lecture vs. smaller recitation sections upon achievement in general psychology. *J. Psychol.*, 1951, *31*, 297–300.

Kishler, J. P. The effects of prestige and identification factors on attitude restructuring and learning from sound films. Instructional Film Res. Rep. SDC 269-7-10. Spec. Devices Center, Office of Naval Res., March, 1950.

Klapper, Hope L. Closed circuit television as a medium of instruction at New York University. New York: New York University, 1958.

Kopstein, F. F., and Roshal, S. M. Learning foreign vocabulary from pictures vs. words. *Amer. Psychologist*, 1954, *9*, 407–408.

Lewin, K. Group decision and social change. In G. E. Swanson, T. M. Newcomb, and E. L. Hartley (Eds.) *Readings in social psychology*. (2nd ed.) New York: Holt, 1952, pp. 330–344.

Lovell, G. D., and Haner, C. F. Forced choice applied to college faculty ratings. *Educ. psychol. Meas.*, 1955, *15*, 291–304.

McKeachie, W. J. Anxiety in the college classroom. *J. educ. Res.*, 1951, *45*, 153–160.

McTavish, C. L. Effect of repetitive film showings on learning. Instructional Film Research Report, SDC 269-7-12, Special Devices Center Office of Naval Research. Nov., 1949.

Macomber, F. G., and Siegel, L. Experimental study in instructional procedures. Progress Report No. 2. Oxford, Ohio: Miami University, 1957b.

Macomber, F. G., and Siegel, L. Final report of the experimental study in instructional procedures. Oxford, Ohio: Miami University, 1960.

May, M. A., and Lumsdaine, A. *Learning from films*. New Haven: Yale University Press, 1958.

Melton, A. W., Feldman, N. G., and Mason, C. N. *Experimental studies of the education of children in a museum school*. Washington: Publ. Amer. Assoc. Museums. No. 15, 1936, pp. 1–106.

Mertens, Marjorie S. The effects of mental hygiene films on self regarding attitudes. Instructional Film Res. Rep., SDC 269-7-22, Special Devices Center Office of Naval Res., July, 1951.

Miller, N. M. Scientific principles for maximum learning from motion pictures. *Audio-Visual Comm. Rev., Graphic Comm.*, 1957, *5*, 61–113.

Remmers, H. H. Learning, effort, and attitudes as affected by three methods of instruction in elementary psychology. *Purdue University Studies in Higher Educ.*, 1933, *21*.

Remmers, H. H., and Bradenburg, H. C. Experimental data on the Purdue rating scale for instructors. *Educ. Adm. Sup.*, 1927, *13*, 519–527.

Riley, J. W., Ryan, B. F., and Lifshitz, Marcia. *The student looks at his teacher*. New Brunswick: Rutgers University Press, 1950.

Rohrer, J. H. Large and small sections in college classes. *J. higher Educ.*, 1957, *28*, 275–279.

RUJA, H. Outcomes of lecture and discussion procedures in three college courses. *J. exp. Educ.*, 1954, *22*, 385–394.

RUNKEL, P. Cognitive similarity in facilitating communication. *Sociometry*, 1956, *19*, 178–191.

SEASHORE, S. E. Group cohesiveness in the industrial group. University of Mich. Survey Res. Center, Pub. No. 14, 1954.

SEIBERT, E. F., AND HONIG, J. M. A brief study of televised laboratory instruction. Purdue University: TVPR Report No. 8, 1959.

SIEGEL, L., ADAMS, J. F., AND MACOMBER, F. G. Retention of subject matter as a function of large group instructional procedures. *J. educ. Psychol.*, 1960, *51*, 9–13.

SPENCE, R. B. Lecture and class discussion in teaching educational psychology. *J. educ. Psychol.*, 1928, *19*, 454–462.

THISTLETHWAITE, D. L. College press and changes in study plans of talented students. Evanston, Ill.: Natl. Merit Scholarship Corp., 1960.

VANDERMEER, A. W. Relative effectiveness of instruction by films exclusively, films plus study guides, and standard lecture methods. Instructional Film Res. Rep. SDC 269-7-13. Special Services Center Office of Naval Res., July, 1950.

VANDERMEER, A. W. Effect of film-viewing practice on learning from instructional films. Instructional Film Res. Rep. SDC 269-7-20. Special Devices Center Office of Naval Res., Nov., 1951.

WARREN, R. A comparison of two plans of study in engineering physics. Unpublished doctoral dissertation. Purdue University, 1954. (*Diss. Abstr.*, 1954, *14*, 1648–1649.)

WHITE, J. R. A comparison of the group-laboratory and the lecture-demonstration methods in engineering instruction. *J. Eng. Educ.*, 1945, *36*, 50–54.

MEDIA: SPECTER AND REALITY

V. O. KEY, JR.

THOSE WEARY with the modern world seem especially disposed to attribute an overwhelming influence over public opinion to the media of mass communication: television, radio, newspapers, magazines, and movies. Their indictment runs to the effect that modern politics— through the interdependence of all parts of the world and through the transfer of decision from local to national authorities—becomes remote from the average man. His information about events and personalities must be acquired through the media, with no possibility of independent check against his own observation or experience. This dependence, the argument goes, makes the public a plastic to be molded by the masters of the media into almost any form they desire. The free and independent citizen beloved of democratic theorists becomes an automaton actuated by impulses transmitted by anonymous rulers through the system of communication. While the capacity of the media collectively to affect public attitudes and behavior cannot be doubted, the luxuriant verbiage on the subject contains a generous component of buncombe. The problem is to separate the fairly well-established propositions from the buncombe.

The fairly well-established propositions, it should be emphasized at the outset, are few. There are especially few on the topics of concern in this discussion. We should like to be able to sum up in some comprehensible way what the media do to make people what they are politically. What are the effects of the media on the policy outlooks, preferences, and expectations of the citizenry as a whole? Even with a plenitude of research resources, such questions would present almost insurmountable problems of observation and analysis. Given the limits of knowledge of the political role and effects of mass communications, about all that can be done is to make educated guesses around the edges of the problem. Those guesses, though, should enable us to define some of the boundaries of the role of mass communications as molders of opinion.

AUDIENCES AND THE OBJECTS
OF THEIR ATTENTION

The literary model of the world of modern mass communications is one in which the messages of the media fall upon the just and the unjust alike, as does the rain; from the relentless clamor of the media modern man has no escape. Moreover, that model in its political versions assumes that the flow of communications includes a large component of political content. In the appraisal of the place of mass media in the political order, a first step is to deflate these assumptions. Modern man fortunately retains a degree of freedom of choice. He may or may not, as he wishes, attend to the mass media. If he listens to the radio or watches television, he may, within the limits of what is available, be selective in his attention. To some extent, each medium of communication has its characteristic audience, and within those audiences the extent of attention to differing types of messages varies enormously.

Choices Among Media. Perhaps the principal incontestable moral of the data about politics and mass communications is that many of the political messages carried by the communications network do not reach many people. The limits of the audience fix the area of direct influence of the mass media; a message unheard is a message unheeded. The audience for mass communications defines itself as people choose that to which they will attend. Some people have a wider range of choice than others, but all people have some control over their intake from the mass media. A major factor in the determination of the information to which one will expose himself is the choice among media, for the range and even the kind of political content differs among the media.

Media audiences are not, of course, sharply divided; they overlap. Some clues to the nature of that overlap and to the relative sizes of the audiences come from studies of campaigns. At such times the level of political attention is doubtless much higher than between campaigns, but the relative importance of media as continuing sources of general political information may resemble that which prevails during campaigns. A rough notion of the relative magnitude of the audiences for the principal media comes from the responses of samples interviewed after the 1952 and 1956 presidential campaigns. Of the total sample:[1]

	1952	1956
Read about the campaign in newspapers	79%	69%
Listened to radio speeches or discussions	69	45
Watched campaign programs on television	49	74
Read about the campaign in magazines	40	31

[1] Data source: Survey Research Center, University of Michigan, 1952 and 1956.

The contrasts between the two years reflect principally the extension of television facilities and the growth of the TV audience at the expense of other media.

Even minimal exposure placed a person in these grossly defined media audiences. A "Yes" reply to the question: "Did you read about the campaign in any newspapers?" qualified a person for inclusion in the 69 per cent of the sample in the 1956 newspaper audience. More of a differentiation of the media audiences came from responses to the question: "Of all these ways of following the campaign which one would you say you got the most information from—newspapers, radio, television, or magazines?" The distributions on this question perhaps define better the relative importance of sources of information. The percentages who said that they "got the most information" from the various media were:

	1952	1956
Newspapers	22%	24%
Radio	28	10
Television	31	49
Magazines	5	5
Combinations of media	5	3
Didn't follow campaign	6	8
Don't Know and No Answer	3	1

Thus, in 1956 by far the largest bloc of people rated television as their most important source of campaign information.[2] About half as many gave that rating to the newspapers; radio fell far behind. Magazines were ranked as the most important source by 5 per cent, and, as we shall see, this audience has special characteristics.

Striking contrasts in political attitude and behavior exist among those chiefly dependent on each of the media. The small group that relies mainly on magazines ranks markedly higher than other media audiences in willingness to express opinions on issues and in disposition to appraise governmental performance on the issues. Twice as high a proportion of this group as of radio listeners—54 per cent against 24 per cent—placed high on a scale of issue familiarity in 1956. Magazine readers, though, are persons who tend also to follow campaigns through several media. Newspaper readers also ranked on the average

[2] The import of television for voting behavior remains to be established. One 1952 analysis based on studies of areas with and without television, failed to isolate any special effect of television.—Herbert A. Simon and Frederick Stern: "The Effect of Television upon Voting Behavior in Iowa in the 1952 Presidential Election," *American Political Science Review*, XLIX (1955), 470–477. One study offers the subversive suggestion that it is what a campaigner says, not the medium of transmission that determines whether people remember the message.—Charles E. Swanson, James Jenkins, and Robert L. Jones: "President Truman Speaks: A Study of Ideas vs. Media," *Journalism Quarterly*, XXVII (1950), 251–262.

considerably higher than radio listeners. Those who reported that they followed the campaign not at all were least informed; yet they included, relatively, almost half as many persons high in issue familiarity as did the radio-listening group. The data appear in Table 14.1.[3]

TABLE 14.1.   MOST IMPORTANT SOURCE OF CAMPAIGN INFORMATION IN
RELATION TO ISSUE FAMILIARITY[a]

ISSUE FAMILIARITY	MOST IMPORTANT SOURCE					
	Magazines	Combinations of media	Newspapers	TV	Radio	Didn't follow campaign
High 4	54%	42%	35%	32%	24%	11%
3	25	32	28	25	23	12
2	14	11	21	20	15	14
Low 1	7	15	16	23	38	64
	100%	100%	100%	100%	100%	100%
N	80	47	423	862	185	147

[a] The question was: "Of all these ways of following the campaign, which one would you say you got the most information from—newspapers, radio, television or magazines?"

DATA SOURCE: *Survey Research Center, University of Michigan, 1956.*

Media audiences also vary in political participation. The magazine audience includes a large proportion of high participators—that is, persons who both vote and participate in some other way, such as by contributing money or talking up their candidate—while those who rely chiefly on radio include relatively only one fourth as many high participators. As might be expected, those who do not follow political campaigns through any of the media are in high proportion nonvoters. In 1956 61 per cent of this group failed to vote. In appraising these differences in proportions of high participators one must, of course, remember that the television audience accounts for a far larger part of the electorate than does the magazine audience. The magazine audience includes only a high concentration of activists. High participators among the magazine readers are far outnumbered by comparable persons in the television audience. Participation figures for the several media audiences are shown in Table 14.2.

An important difference in media audiences is education. The better-educated rely in far higher degree on printed sources for their campaign information than do those with the least formal education;

[3] Many studies establish the high information level of the magazine audience. On a test of familiarity with names in the news, 82 per cent of readers of three or more magazines in Minnesota villages ranked high, but only 39 per cent of those who read no magazines.—R. O. Nafziger *et al.:* "The Mass Media and an Informed Public," *Public Opinion Quarterly,* XV (1951), 105–114.

TABLE 14.2. RELATION OF MOST IMPORTANT SOURCE OF CAMPAIGN
INFORMATION TO LEVEL OF POLITICAL PARTICIPATION

PARTICIPATION LEVEL	MOST IMPORTANT SOURCE					
	Magazines	Combinations of media	Newspapers	TV	Radio	Didn't follow
High 4	56%	56%	34%	32%	13%	5%
3	34	36	46	44	44	34
2	4	4	5	5	5	5
Low 1	6	4	15	19	38	56
	100%	100%	100%	100%	100%	100%
N	80	47	423	862	185	147

DATA SOURCE: *Survey Research Center, University of Michigan, 1956.*

the latter depend more upon radio and television.[4] Formal education
does not drive persons away from the radio and TV but leads them, or
at least many of them, to be attentive to several media. An index of
media exposure during the 1956 campaign provides data on the point.
Those who had paid attention to the campaign through all the media
were ranked high in media exposure; those who had followed the campaign through none of the media earned a low ranking in media exposure; others placed at intermediate points depending upon the
number of media to which they had exposed themselves. As may be
seen from Table 14.3, 40 per cent of those who reported exposure to
all the principal media had at least some college education. Only 3
per cent of the low-exposure group were college persons. Grammar-
schoolers made up almost 60 per cent of the low-exposure category.[5]

The choice among media is also probably related to the degree and
kind of interest in political matters. Persons who seek information
about their political interests soon reach a ceiling on the possibilities if
they rely chiefly on radio. Thus, persons with more than a superficial
interest in international affairs find radio and television singularly un-
satisfying as the sole source of their information. Consider the data of
Table 14.4, which relates the principal source of campaign information

[4] Angus Campbell, Gerald Gurin, and Warren E. Miller, "Television and the
Election," *Scientific American*, CLXXXVIII, 5 (1953), 46–48.
[5] Geographical contrasts also prevail among media audiences, according to a
Minnesota study of five media: newspapers, magazines, books, movies, radio. "The
proportion of people attending all five media decreased consistently from metrop-
olis through small city and village to the farms."—Malcolm S. MacLean, Jr.; "Mass
Media Audiences: City, Small City, Village and Farm," *Journalism Quarterly*,
XXIX (1952), 271–282.

TABLE 14.3.   MEDIA EXPOSURE IN RELATION TO LEVEL OF EDUCATION

EDUCATION	MEDIA EXPOSURE[a]				
	Low				High
	0	1	2	3	4
College	3%	4%	15%	28%	40%
High school	39	48	57	48	51
Grade school	58	48	28	24	9
	100%	100%	100%	100%	100%
N	147	355	559	494	228

[a] Ranks are fixed by the number of media the respondent reported exposure to during the campaign. Thus, those in the high category had read about the campaign in newspapers, listened to radio speeches or discussions, watched political programs on television, and read about the campaign in magazines. The low category consists of those who followed the campaign in none of these ways.

DATA SOURCE: *Survey Research Center, University of Michigan, 1956.*

TABLE 14.4.   RELATION OF MOST IMPORTANT SOURCE OF CAMPAIGN INFORMATION TO POSITION ON FOREIGN ISSUE SCALE

INTERNATIONALISM	MOST IMPORTANT SOURCE					
	Magazines	Combinations of media	Newspapers	TV	Radio	Didn't follow
High	68%	57%	50%	45%	35%	29%
Medium	15	17	25	22	17	10
Low	10	15	12	15	20	12
Not scaled[a]	7	11	13	18	28	49
	100%	100%	100%	100%	100%	100%
N	80	47	423	861	185	147

[a] Respondents with too few opinions to permit placement on scale.

DATA SOURCE: *Survey Research Center, University of Michigan, 1956.*

to position on a scale of favorableness toward involvement in international affairs. Of those persons who rely on radio, over one fourth had so few opinions on the issues constituting the scale that they could not be ranked on it. On the other hand, 68 per cent of the magazine readers placed at the top of the scale of internationalism. It is not to be supposed that such persons have these opinions solely because they read magazines; the odds are that they read magazines in part because they have these opinions.[6]

[6] On the domestic-issue scale a large proportion of the radio listeners, 42 per

All these data on audiences of the media at times of campaigns do not provide any solid information on who relies on what media for their day-to-day political intelligence during the intervals between elections. Yet those who rely principally on radio and television for their campaign information probably are not voracious readers during the periods between elections. If half or more of the population depends heavily on radio and television for its regular supply of political information, a substantial sector of the citizenry places a limit on its own political enlightenment. The technical characteristics of these media, as well as the economic conditions of their operation, affect the kinds and quantities of information they can convey. Despite an occasional production of extraordinary power, television must limit itself to the tidbits of the events of the day. Radio and television can convey a tone toward political events and an impression of the personalities and the human interest, but ordinarily they can carry little analysis in depth. Moreover, the message of the electronic media is as evanescent as the trill of the songbird. Newspaper and magazine readers, or at least the readers of some newspapers and some magazines, have the opportunity to pursue their interests at length and in some depth, an option not open to those who restrict themselves to television and radio.

Selectivity in Attention. A person may, through choice or by force of circumstance, rely principally on one or another of the great mass media for his political information. Other types of self-selection also contribute to the definition of the audience of the media. A person may be a newspaper reader, but he may choose to read one paper rather than another. If he relies on magazines, he may read one, another, or several.[7] If he is a radio listener, commonly he may choose among stations. If he is a TV watcher, he is likely to have his favorite channel. Still further choices fix the boundaries of the media audiences. The newspaper reader may only skim the headlines, or he may peruse the cerebrations of the editors and of Mr. Walter Lippmann with a grim determination. Some radio listeners hang onto the loaded phrases of Mr. Fulton Lewis, Jr. while others hear only scattered sentences from the newscasts interspersed between the rock 'n' roll. The magazine reader may subject himself to the indignant editorials of the *Saturday Evening Post,* he may reflectively linger over its political articles, or he may read only the fiction. Perhaps he reads the lugubrious political

cent, ranked high in "liberalism" or favorableness toward governmental intervention. Only 28 per cent of the magazine readers occupied that position. The moral may be that a sector of the population with most liberal leanings has least facilities for learning what the score is politically. For an instructive analysis of the mass media and the audience for discussion of world affairs, see Alfred O. Hero: *Mass Media and World Affairs* (Boston: World Peace Foundation; 1959).

[7] For an analysis of the types of audiences of a series of magazines, see Paul F. Lazarsfeld and Rowena Wyant: "Magazines in 90 Cities—Who Reads What?" *Public Opinion Quarterly,* October, 1937, 29–41.

analyses with their strange middle-class Hearstian tinge in the *Reader's Digest* or perhaps he concentrates on its joke sections.

When the opportunity exists for readers to choose, newspapers attract somewhat differentiated audiences. A New Yorker, for example, can read the *Daily News* or the *Times* and, on the whole, different interests actuate the readers of such distinctive journals. Newspaper audiences tend to be differentiated by education, by economic status, and probably also by degree and kind of political interests. A clue to the difference comes from an analysis of the reading habits of women in New York in the early 1940's. Of those women who spent on the average $30 or more for a dress, 42.5 per cent read the *Times* and 7.2 per cent, the *Daily News*. Of those women who in those days spent less than $5 on the average for a dress, 8.6 per cent read the *Times* and 46 per cent, the *Daily News*.[8] Thus, in multipaper towns individual newspapers tend to develop their characteristic audiences. The Hearst press has a special attraction for those of lower education and low political interest. In Detroit, for example, Kornhauser found that one half of the nonvoters among UAW members who read any paper read the Hearst *Times*. This paper was read to a much greater extent by nonvoters than either of the other two papers.[9]

TABLE 14.5. "WOULD YOU SAY YOU READ NATIONAL AND INTERNATIONAL NEWS RATHER CAREFULLY OR DO YOU USUALLY READ JUST THE HEADLINES?": METROPOLITAN ALBANY, 1949

CARE IN READING NEWS	ALL ALBANY ADULTS
Do not read news	4%
Just headlines, skim	47
More than headlines, not much	4
Sometimes carefully, sometimes not	14
Carefully, skip some things	19
Very carefully	6
National carefully, international not	3
International carefully, national not	1
Not ascertained	2
	100%

SOURCE: *Survey Research Center*, Interest, Information, and Attitudes in the Field of World Affairs (*November, 1949*), *being a report of a sample survey in metropolitan Albany in April, 1949.*

Readers of newspapers are highly selective in what they pay heed to in the varied fare laid before them. The vagaries of its readers clip

[8] Paul F. Lazarsfeld: "The Daily Newspaper and Its Competitors," *Annals of the American Academy of Political and Social Science*, CCXIX (1942), 32–43.

[9] Kornhauser *et al.*: *When Labor Votes*, 82–83.

the power of the press.[10] Even when editors bring out their boldest display type, faithful readers may not intercept the message. In the summer of 1940 the Cleveland *Plain Dealer*, the paper with the largest circulation in Erie County, Ohio, splashed on the front page an announcement in support of Willkie; it followed up during the campaign with daily front-page editorials. In September, 59 per cent of a sample of Erie County did not know which candidate the *Plain Dealer* was supporting. Only about one in seven of those persons with a Democratic predisposition—those who would have to be converted if the paper was to have influence—knew of the paper's editorial position.[11]

Although the evidence is scant, it suggests that an extremely small proportion of the population follows political news in the press with care. Doubtless attention to this type of news increases during the excitement of a presidential campaign. Day in and day out the odds are that less than 10 per cent of the adult population could be regarded as careful readers of the political news. Some evidence on this point appears in Table 14.5, which shows responses to a survey inquiry in the Albany metropolitan area in April, 1949: 47 per cent of the sample said they read "just the headlines" of the national and international news,[12] while only 6 per cent claimed to read both types of news "very carefully." While Albany is not the United States, similar inquiries of a national sample probably would not turn up larger proportions of persons closely attentive to the political news in the press.[13]

While radio once was and television now is the medium that attracts an audience most dispersed through all social and economic levels, sharp differences apparently exist in the audiences for programs with various types of content. Major speeches by the candidates in presidential campaigns may be heard and watched by an audience spread across the socio-economic spectrum, but serious programs in the lulls between campaigns attract relatively far more persons in the upper socio-economic reaches. In 1937, for example, a controversy developed over the appointment of Senator Hugo Black to the Supreme Court. He was traveling in Europe when it was revealed that in his

[10] Of this fact publishers are well aware. They attempt on occasion to offset the obscurity of the editorial page by transferring their political message to the comics. Consider, for example, the political morals of the adventures of "Little Orphan Annie."

[11] Elmo C. Wilson: "The Press and Public Opinion in Erie County, Ohio," *Journalism Quarterly*, XVIII (1941), 14–17.

[12] The headlines of a paper are an important means for affecting the outlook of readers. For experimental evidence, see Percy H. Tannenbaum, "The Effect of Headlines on the Interpretation of News Stories," *Journalism Quarterly*, XXX (1953), 189–197. A laboratory experiment demonstrated differences in impressions among readers of the same story captioned with different heads. The headline effect was especially marked among scanners.

[13] The comics seem to command wider attention than any other category of newspaper content. See Charles E. Swanson: "What They Read in 130 Daily Newspapers," *Journalism Quarterly*, XXXII (1955), 411–421.

earlier years he had been a member of the Ku Klux Klan and, so the reports went, the country awaited breathlessly the explanatory radio speech to be delivered on his return. The surveys showed that the proportions of various socio-economic classes listening to his speech were:[14]

Socio-economic Class	Listening	N
High	62%	366
Upper-middle	49	934
Lower-middle	42	427
Low	35	452

Similar evidence comes from a survey to identify the listeners to two speeches in the same year by President Roosevelt on his proposal to reform the Supreme Court. These are the proportions of urban listeners to these speeches within socio-economic classes:[15]

Socio-economic Class	Listening	N
High	43%	187
Upper-middle	38	433
Lower-middle	35	210
Low	28	255

In short, when learned (or even exciting) political discourses begin to move over the electronic waves, a great many listeners and viewers turn off the power or tune in another station.[16]

Still another process in individual selection of items in the mass media for attention may be of the greatest significance for the political role of the mass media. People seem to pay attention to those items with which they agree, not those that seek to convert them.[17] Insofar as campaign propaganda is concerned, it has repeatedly been found that people tend to pay heed to those communications supportive of their own predispositions.[18] A good Republican tends to listen to sound

[14] Paul F. Lazarsfeld: *Radio and the Printed Page* (New York: Duell, Sloan, and Pearce; 1940), p. 26.

[15] *Ibid.*, pp. 27–28.

[16] In 1956 the average audience for nighttime political programs on CBS was about 60 per cent below the usual audience for entertainment programs. The size of the audience for individual political broadcasts varied with the size of the audiences for the entertainment regularly scheduled for the time period.—Richard S. Salant: "Political Campaigns and the Broadcaster," *Public Policy*, VIII (1958), 336–367.

[17] Katz and Lazarsfeld put the matter wryly: "Perhaps the most important generalization in this area—at least as far as an understanding of the process of effective persuasion is concerned—is that those groups which are most hopefully regarded as the target of a communication are often least likely to be in the audience."—*Personal Influence* (Glencoe: Free Press; 1955), pp. 21–22.

[18] Paul Lazarsfeld, Bernard Berelson, and Hazel Gaudet: *The People's Choice* (New York: Duell, Sloan and Pearce; 1944), 129–133; and Wilbur Schramm and R. F. Carter: "Effectiveness of a Political Telethon," *Public Opinion Quarterly*, XXIII (1959), 121–127.

Republican oratory; Democrats listen to their own brand of propaganda. Campaigns are not, of course, entirely a matter of Republicans talking to Republicans and Democrats talking to Democrats. The tidings of the day manage to seep across party lines and to make some converts. The information on whether this same selective process operates as people winnow the day-to-day flow of political communications in non-campaign periods is limited. It is perhaps not practicable for even the most alert and agile person to avoid communications content divergent from his own notions; yet the best guess is that the audiences of the mass media tend toward a selectivity that supports rather than weakens their pre-existing outlooks. A bit of evidence comes from a study of an intensive campaign of education in Cincinnati about the United Nations. Those most exposed to the campaign turned out, regrettably, to be those already most favorably disposed toward the United Nations. The same study found that interest in international affairs tended to be a function of a sense of personal concern. Of those, for example, who felt that "they would be better off personally" if foreign trade increased, 57 per cent had an interest in international affairs. Of those who did not see this personal advantage, only 37 per cent had an interest in international affairs by the tests used in this study.[19] From what is known of the generally low levels of interest in political matters, we should expect that factor to be of continuing influence on the nature and extent of popular attention to the flow of political communications.

Even though a person pays attention to a medium of communication, he may regard it with a defensive skepticism. In many localities it has long been a maxim of practical politics that press opposition is a positive asset. Perhaps among some people, who may at times be numerous, newspaper communications have an inverted effect: such people either do not believe what they read in the papers, or they believe that the opposite is true. The extent of this mistrust in the national population is not known,[20] but small-scale inquiries throw some light on the matter. In his study of a random sample of United Auto Workers in Detroit, Kornhauser found that 50 per cent ranked television as the most-trusted source of political information; only 23 per cent placed newspapers in the first rank. When asked which source they trusted least, 42 per cent ranked newspapers first. Distrust of the

[19] S. A. Starr and H. M. Hughes: "Report on an Educational Campaign: The Cincinnati Plan for the United Nations," *American Journal of Sociology*, LV (1949–50), 389–400. For a thoughtful discussion of individual selection of communications for attention, see W. Phillips Davidson: "On the Effects of Communication," *Public Opinion Quarterly*, XXIII (1959), 343–360.

[20] Quite apart from the defense of conscious skepticism, some people under some circumstances unconsciously misinterpret propaganda messages and thereby sidetrack them. For experimental evidence, see Eunice Cooper and Marie Jahoda: "The Evasion of Propaganda: How Prejudiced People Respond to Anti-Prejudice Propaganda," *Journal of Psychology*, XXIII (1947), 12–25.

press was especially high among Stevenson voters in 1952; Eisenhower voters among UAW members on the average regarded newspapers more favorably. While these levels of trust and distrust of the media reflect the peculiarities of the sample and of the Detroit press, they suggest that many people build for themselves a defensive shell against the mass media, especially the press.[21]

The sources of information to which an individual attends fix the range of content to which he may choose to subject himself. An extremely small proportion of the flow through the channels of mass communication has an overtly political content. To expose himself extensively to political content, a person must search for it and, having found it, exert himself at least to the extent of reading beyond the newspaper headlines or the captions of magazine articles. Even the passive radio listener or televiewer with political concerns has to go to the trouble of remembering to tune in at the right time if he wishes to sift political items out of the flow of information. In the heyday of radio, in 1946, only 13 per cent of the total air time of a sample of members of the National Association of Broadcasters was dedicated to news and comment; another 3 per cent went for "talks."[22] Although newspapers give political news prominent position, it constitutes only a small proportion of the items in the paper; other kinds of items compete for space (more successfully in some papers than others) and for the attention of the reader. Sports contribute the largest proportion of newspaper items, 11.6 per cent in a sample of 130 daily newspapers. Items about national government accounted for 2.8 per cent of the items; politics, 2.5 per cent; social and economic international relations, 1.2 per cent; and political international relations, 1.9 per cent.[23] In many communities the political content of the local daily is so thin that the most persevering quest for political information of any depth is certain to be futile.

Stratification of the Audience of the Mass Media. Though these data on who attends to what in the mass media are sketchy, they suffice to support some observations about the politically significant characteristics of the media audience. They modify the conception of mass man as one upon whom the impulses of the media strike without pity

[21] Kornhauser: *When Labor Votes*, pp. 89–90. These findings suggest also that the mass of people have yet to learn that television reports of events can be doctored. The public-relations men have developed the practice of generously providing TV stations with films on newsworthy events, including political events; such films rarely show the clients to disadvantage. See Maurice Schonfeld: "Seeing Is Not Believing," *The Reporter*, June 25, 1959.

[22] Kenneth Baker: "An Analysis of Radio's Programming," in Paul Lazarsfeld and Frank Stanton: *Communications Research 1948–1949* (New York: Harper; 1949).

[23] Swanson; *op. cit.*

and without defense. The flow of the messages of the mass media is rather like dropping a handful of confetti from the rim of the Grand Canyon with the object of striking a man astride a burro on the canyon floor. In some measure chance determines which messages reach what targets.

Although information is scant on who pays how much attention regularly to what political content of the media, a fruitful way to visualize the audience for political communications is to regard it as stratified. It is stratified according to interest and involvement in politics. The greater the sense of political involvement, the greater the exposure to political communications tends to be. Strata also differ in the types of communications to which they attend. The highly and continuously attentive stratum includes relatively large numbers of magazine readers, book readers, and readers of the quality newspapers. The same group listens in higher proportion to radio and TV programs with a high assay of political content than do other strata. This upper stratum doubtless includes most of the political activists, probably no more than 10 per cent of the population at the most.

At the opposite extreme of the communications audience are those who pay little or no attention to the political content of the flow of communications. The size of this group depends on where one locates the cutting point as he defines the bottom stratum. Almost 10 per cent of a national sample confessed that it had followed the 1956 campaign in none of the major media. For at least a quarter of the population the day-to-day attention to politics must be slight indeed. To the extent that this group is attentive at all, it includes large proportions of persons who rely in high degree upon the radio or the tabloid and tabloid-like press for their information. It includes many persons whose interest in politics is insufficient to bring them to the polls. Their average level of education is low. Obviously the kinds of political communications, as well as the quantities, to which these people expose themselves also differ from those to which the upper 10 per cent devote their attention.

Between these two strata are intermediate strata whose characteristics cannot well be defined for lack of data. They certainly include large proportions of persons who rely on the newspapers as their principal source of political information. They are made up of persons more likely to vote than are those of the bottom stratum and less likely to be active in other ways politically than are members of the top stratum. All of these observations find some support in the relationship between media exposure and political involvement. Those who are highly exposed to the media tend to rank high on the scale of political involvement that has been used at several preceding points; those who rank low in exposure also have on the average a low level of political involvement. Doubtless the relationship works in both ways. Exposure

may produce involvement and, in turn, highly involved persons may expose themselves more to the media. (See Table 14.6.)

Doubtless the audience for political communications also varies in
size through time. The great regular pulsation in size occurs with the
quadrennial presidential campaigns. Other events and episodes may
bring huge but temporary enlargements of the political audience; the
telecasts of the Kefauver crime investigations and of the Army-
McCarthy hearings held the attention of large audiences. The marginal

TABLE 14.6.   EXPOSURE TO MEDIA IN RELATION TO LEVELS OF POLITICAL
INVOLVEMENT

LEVEL OF POLITICAL INVOLVEMENT	MEDIA EXPOSURE				
	Low				High
	0	1	2	3	4
High 4	5%	10%	23%	41%	46%
3	13	24	32	30	31
2	33	35	27	21	17
Low 1	49	31	18	8	6
	100%	100%	100%	100%	100%
N	147	335	559	494	228

DATA SOURCE: *Survey Research Center, University of Michigan, 1956.*

or in-and-out audience probably makes up a larger proportion of each
subsequent lower stratum of the audience for political communications.
Probably the upper 5 or 10 per cent, the most politically attentive, are
also the most nearly continuously attentive. Those least intimately connected with the communication system tend to be intermittent in their
attention.

PREDICTIVE GENERALIZATIONS

II-A   The settings in which it takes place affect the impact of a communication by contributing to or detracting from the attention listeners give
to it, their comprehension of it, and their acceptance of recommendations contained in it.

II-B   Opportunities for verbal interaction between speaker and listener
tend to increase the satisfactions both draw from the experience of
communicating and potentially increase the effectiveness of communications by permitting immediate adaptation by speaker to listener
in order to improve attention, comprehension and acceptance.

II-C   Opportunities for listeners to gain information about speakers are important to the effectiveness of communication since the words of

respected speakers will often be given more serious attention than those of unknown or unrespected speakers.

II-D   Opportunities for speakers to gain information about listeners may be important to the effectiveness of a communication since listeners' experiences, social roles, beliefs and attitudes determine whether they will attend, comprehend or accept a communication.

II-E   Because a listener's or reader's group membership, if important to him, may prevent his believing or acting inconsistently with the expectations of the group, the speaker's opportunities for emphasizing or suppressing the importance of certain group memberships may determine the effectiveness of a communication.

II-F   Listeners or readers who ignore communications render them ineffective. The degree to which a speaker can control a listener's exposure to his messages, therefore, will help to determine their effectiveness.

II-G   Since certain features of time and place may enhance the effectiveness of a communication, a speaker's opportunity to control these aspects of the physical environment will be important to the success of the communication.

II-H   Often listeners or readers who perceive a speaker's efforts as calculated to influence them will avoid such communications or respond less often to them than to those of speakers whom they believe have no ulterior motives.

II-I   A listener's personal traits may, in some cases, determine what communication settings he may frequent for certain purposes.

II-J   Although communication settings certainly differ in the numbers of people that can be reached by a communication, effectiveness will not necessarily be affected by the size of audience provided by the setting.

II-K   Because it provides for unlimited interaction between listener and speaker and consequent opportunities for each to gain information about the other, because the speaker can in some degree control the salience of group membership, manipulate time and place and a listener's exposure to his communications, the private face-to-face setting may increase the effectiveness of communications.

II-L   Because it often provides a high degree of interaction among members and consequent opportunities for exchange of information about each other, because membership in the present group can be stressed while conflicting group memberships are suppressed, and because members may be exposed to divergent views, the small group setting may often be an effective tool for changing opinions and behavior.

II-M   The effectiveness of the speaker-audience setting, which has generally been considered to rest on the speaker's ability to reach fairly large numbers of people simultaneously, probably is related more often to the speaker's control over time and place, his indirect control over the salience of group membership, his ability to get listeners to expose themselves to dissonant ideas, and the fact that listeners frequently accept his objectives as the provision of information or diversion rather than persuasion.

II-N   Although mass communication settings may often be deprived of direct effect by limited opportunities for interaction between speaker and listener and the resultant difficulty listeners may sometimes have in gaining information about the speaker, because of the tendency of listeners to regard certain mass communications as manipulative and the absence of much control by the communicator over listeners' exposure to his efforts, the large numbers of people reached may improve the statistical probability of success, and the fact that certain active opinion leaders relay mass communicators' messages to other people by word of mouth may ultimately give these messages a greatly enhanced effect.

DISCUSSION QUESTIONS

1. What would be a layman's explanation of the reasons why communication between psychiatrist and patient serves as a "cure" for emotional ills? Would the explanation illuminate the nature of other private face-to-face communication situations?

2. Suppose that a friend of yours accepted the job of contacting people in your building for the blood bank appeal. Would you advise him to make a short presentation to the residents at dinner, to send out a printed sheet describing the program and offering to answer questions, to speak to everyone in the building personally, or to talk to groups gathered in rooms during evening hours? What factors would determine your recommendations concerning various settings?

3. How stable would you estimate the role of *opinion leader* to be? On the basis of your experience in choosing people to consult and having others consult you, can you say whether the relationship is stable or unstable? Why?

4. The writers who originally discovered the *two-step flow* of information distribution have subsequently wondered whether there may not be, in many instances, a three-, four-, or more step flow. Do you see any evidence for such an idea?

5. Many teachers who say they recognize the advantages of small group discussion explain their reliance on lectures as an efficiency measure ("I have too many students to permit discussion"). Are there any ways of gaining some advantages of the small group setting while retaining the efficiency of the lecture?

6. It is argued that students prefer lectures because they know how to deal with them, and would rather avoid the frustration of having to work out an understanding of the material for themselves. On the other hand, we have seen evidence that people gain satisfaction from small group interaction and seek the sense of responsibility for group decisions which is a feature of that communication setting. Is the contradiction genuine? If so, how can it be reconciled?

7. Consider the appropriateness of the small group setting for such projects as these:

    a. winning support for a tax millage increase for public school teachers' salaries

    b. harmonizing the working relations between three or four people whose jobs are interdependent and who have not been getting along

    c. presenting a candidate for the state legislature to the voters

8. V. O. Key declares that "technical characteristics of these media, as well as the economic conditions of their operation, affect the kinds and qualities of information they can convey." Does such a view seem a realistic appraisal of radio and television as news sources or does it reflect resignation or despair that is not justified by experience?

9. Can Key's observations on the flow of political information in the mass communication setting be generalized to other kinds of information? If so, why? If not, why not? How would one prove one's answer?

10. Considering the potential advantages of one setting over another in accomplishing particular communication objectives, how would you judge recent political campaigns that have spent more money for 30-second and 15-second spot radio and television announcements and less for televised speeches of a half-hour or more? How would you regard the emphasis on more money for mass communication efforts and less grass roots doorbell pushing or neighborhood coffee hours to introduce the candidate?

11. Can you categorize the frequency with which you receive or offer information on certain subjects in certain communication settings? For example, do you rely on magazines for information on movies, certain acquaintances for political information, television for information on products you use, etc.? Could your experience be generalized to other people? Why or why not? Is there any suggestion here that certain settings are more effective for certain kinds of influence?

SECTION III

*Strategies of
communication*

COMMUNICATION STRATEGIES

Howard H. Martin and Kenneth E. Andersen

Everyone who talks or writes wants something; he would not go to the trouble of communicating if he did not. We do not mean to deny that some behavior is *expressive* as well as *instrumental,* that we sometimes simply gesture or vocalize, juggle colors or words, for our own satisfaction rather than for any effect they may have on others. But almost all of the talking or gesturing we do in the presence of other people, all of the writing we willfully expose to others' view, is directed toward the accomplishment of some goal, in short, is motivated. Therefore, "communication" and "persuasion" are nearly synonymous terms. Since the communicator is most interested in gaining his object by means of communication, presumably he wants to know what means are most likely to secure that object for him. Having implied in the last section that the choice of setting may be an initial decision, we can now turn to a consideration of those *strategies* available to the speaker or writer by means of which he may facilitate the listener's or reader's attention, comprehension and acceptance of his communication.[1]

MANAGEMENT OF ATTENTION AND PERCEPTION

All communicators are painfully aware that unless listeners and readers give their close attention to messages, those messages are useless. Unless the communication, for however short an instant, occupies a listener's mind at the expense of other stimulation, it will not be perceived (that is, detected or recognized), and if not perceived, will not be understood, and if not understood, can have no effect upon attitudes or behavior. Therefore, much effort is expended to seize and hold listeners' or readers' attention, effort that is likely to be successful only if the communicator has managed to accommodate two characteristics of attention, the *fluctuation* of attention, and the *selectivity* of attention. M. D. Vernon, in an essay included in this section, discusses these matters in some detail.

[1] A word about *strategy* as the term for the means of producing desired effects with communications. Strategy, in the original military sense of the word, meant a grand design framed to accomplish stated objectives by means of intelligent deployment of a host of resources. Strategic decisions involved knowledge of available alternatives and the judgment and "art" to bring all of one's available resources to bear in the most advantageous and economic way. This seems exactly the task of the persuasive speaker or writer.

126

The fluctuation of attention was of interest to students of attention at the beginning of the century, several of whom found that the length of time one could attend to a simple stimulus before his attention wandered to something else was a matter of a few seconds.[2] If no more than such elementary stimulation were involved in communication, problems of sustaining attention would be overwhelming. Of course, communication often provides complex stimulation which, as we shall see in a moment, is one of the ways in which the fluctuation of attention can be accommodated.

Attention does not shift indiscriminately from one object to another but is directed by the individual to those features of the environment that become important for him. For convenience we might say that attention is directed either *involuntarily* by mechanisms probably defensive in character to aspects of the environment that pose a potential threat to the individual, or *voluntarily* by the individual's interests as he sees them in terms of more complicated goals than mere survival. Things to which attention is directed involuntarily include bright lights, loud noises, sudden movements and other *novel events* occurring in the environment which people automatically attend until removed or recognized as harmless. (See page 156.) We pay only momentary attention to such stimulation; as soon as the source of the light is identified and we adjust to it, we can afford to ignore it. Things to which attention is directed voluntarily are always connected with some *interest* we can see in them. Because they promise to reward us by supplying directly or indirectly the means of accomplishing some personal goal, we attend them. In other words, attention is a form of motivated behavior in that it is directed toward the achievement of goals. An object of *interest* should be taken to mean anything in which we have a personal investment, share, or commitment, either because of some past experience of the matter (some investment of time in it), or because we see it as relevant to the achievement of goals we are now pursuing. It is safe to say that, unless an object is perceived as interesting in that sense, it will not be attended for more than the moment it takes to discover that it is not harmful.

Strategies exist for the accommodation of these two features of attention. "No one can possibly attend continuously to an object that does not change," William James declared.[3] M. D. Vernon goes even further than James in declaring that "normal consciousness, perception, and thought, can be maintained only in a constantly changing environment."[4] The strategy, therefore, must be to provide, in delivery, the

[2] William James, *Talks to Teachers on Psychology* (New York: W. W. Norton and Co., Inc., 1958), p. 78.

[3] William James, "Attention," in *Attention*, Paul Bakan, ed. (Princeton: D. Van Nostrand Co., Inc., 1966), p. 13.

[4] M. D. Vernon, *The Psychology of Perception* (Baltimore: Penguin Books, 1962), p. 183.

stimulation of a changing milieu and, in selection and arrangement of ideas, to present the subject in an ever-novel view.

(1) *Strategies for managing attention: delivery*

The extravagant vocal inflections of the children's story-teller are only slightly less necessary to maintain the attention of an adult audience. Whatever other virtues it may possess, movement or gesture, by introducing novelty and variety into the visual part of communication, may serve at least to *seize* attention for the speaker if not to *hold* attention on the substance of his message. Probably communicators using print materials make more use of the visual elements of novelty and variety than do speakers. Advertisements that picture the product in the corner of a large white page expect that attention will be seized by the novel visual effect in a magazine otherwise having little white space. Colors, startling images, unusual or unexpected perspectives serve to arrest the wandering attention momentarily perhaps because of some generalized response to the strange or novel in our environment, although no "danger" is obviously posed by white space in an advertisement. But even those communicators who use print cannot depend on novelty to sustain attention; the listener's or reader's mind must be engaged by the substance of the essay or publication.

(2) *Strategies for managing attention: invention*

Engaging the minds of listeners or readers means touching their vital interests by associating, as James has explained, the speaker's ideas with ideas already present and important in the listener's mind.[5] The examples and illustrations chosen by the speaker to illuminate his topic are not only vital to comprehension, as we shall see in a moment, but are the chief means of sustaining attention. Thoreau's *Walden* is currently a piece of underground literature carried about and thumbed by high school boys whose natural rebelliousness provoked by the argument over the legitimacy of American involvement in Viet Nam has made compelling Thoreau's celebration of self-sufficiency and his rationalization for disobedience to bad laws. The examples of contemporary social rebellion, in other words, have established the relevance of *Walden*; attention is paid because the reader's personal interests in it are apparent. A knowledge of the interests of listeners will direct the choice of examples and illustrations by this maxim: what touches the listener's or reader's experiences and interests most directly will gain and hold his attention.

(3) *Strategies for managing attention: arrangement*

The strategy of accommodating listeners' or readers' interests has another aspect. Where listeners are potentially uninterested in the

[5] James, *Talks to Teachers*, chapter 9.

topic of the speaker's communication, he may be able to adjust to their tendency to ignore his efforts by arranging his materials in anti-climactic order.[6] The most interesting details or strongest arguments will be presented first in order to engage attention. Where lively interest in the topic already exists, speakers may be advised to place details in climactic order as a means of sustaining the attention willingly granted at the start. Where listeners are in disagreement with the speaker's proposition, in order to prevent them from avoiding his communications, the speaker may be advised to present agreeable ideas first, and follow them with elements of his communication that he expects will arouse the most antagonism.[7] Attention will be secured by those ideas promising to satisfy a reader's interests and will tend to encourage attention to other ideas offered later on by the speaker.

Attention is a prerequisite to perception. Vernon has declared that "an observer's perception of the field, or of any particular aspect of it, may be made more rapid and accurate in so far as his attention is directed towards it. The more narrowly and specifically attention is directed, the greater the improvement."[8] However, attention is not the only factor affecting accurate perception; a number of personal characteristics will determine whether a listener or reader will perceive the communicator's message. Although it is difficult at some points to distinguish between perception and comprehension of the message, we consider perception to be the process of detecting or recognizing the message or, in terms of the information-theory model of section I, the process of receiving the signal, and comprehension the process of making sense out of the message, that is, of decoding it.

What are some of the personal characteristics that affect a reader's or listener's perception of the message? One is his disposition toward new information. People have been classified as open-minded or closed-minded by their disposition to regard new information as either potentially useful or as potentially threatening. Those who look upon new information as dangerous may take steps to protect themselves from it either by avoiding it or, if they cannot avoid it, by distorting it.[9] One's interests, while they may focus attention on a communication, may also cause him to distort that communication in order to render it more agreeable. This is especially true of political partisans who understand the statements of their favorites to agree more with their own views than is actually the case and the statements of oppo-

[6] Carl I. Hovland, Irving L. Janis and Harold H. Kelley, *Communication and Persuasion* (New Haven: Yale University Press, 1953), p. 115; Carl I. Hovland, et. al., *The Order of Presentation in Persuasion* (New Haven: Yale University Press, 1957), p. 136; Arthur R. Cohen, *Attitude Change and Social Influence* (New York: Basic Books, Inc., 1964), chapter 1.

[7] Hovland, Janis and Kelley, *Communication and Persuasion*, p. 129.

[8] Vernon, *Psychology of Perception*, p. 165.

[9] Milton Rokeach, *The Open and Closed Mind* (New York: Basic Books, Inc., 1960), pp. 67–68, 400–401.

nents to disagree more sharply with their own views than they really do.[10] A number of other studies have suggested that our personal values affect what we perceive. The study by Postman, Bruner and McGinnies described on page 233 found that people more quickly perceived words related to personal values than words unrelated to such values. And, an interesting account of reactions of Dartmouth and Princeton students to films of a particularly "rough and dirty" football game between their two schools showed that Dartmouth students saw fewer of their team's infractions of the rules than did Princeton students, and more of Princeton's infractions than did Princeton students.[11]

Some experiments have suggested that our membership in groups will affect our ability to perceive objects accurately; if we are aware of the group's consensus on an object, we will tend to see it the same way.[12] Also, the perceptive capabilities of many people are affected by their aroused emotional state. Painful experiences or the emotional conflict produced by asking subjects to identify a series of sexual words flashed on a screen seem to impair accurate perception. The latter conflict induced researchers to identify a phenomenon they called "perceptual defense," the tendency of some people to resist perceiving objects unpleasant to them.[13] Finally, we perceive details more accurately when we expect to see them, have been alerted to them, have been "set" to perceive them. The navy plane-spotter in World War II saw the planes and was able to identify them as friend or enemy because he had been alerted to observe them. When "set" to observe one kind of detail, however, we tend to ignore others; the driver of the car notices the traffic signal but misses part of the conversation.

The strategies for accommodating personal characteristics that affect perception lie in language choice and the use of redundancy.

(1) Strategies for managing perception: language choice

Some interpreters of the results of those studies mentioned earlier of the effects of values on perception have argued that the familiarity of the words rather than motivational factors speeded perception. Such a view suggests strategy for producing accurate perception: familiar vocabulary may make perception more rapid and accurate. If he knows

[10] Robert E. Lane and David O. Sears, *Public Opinion* (Englewood Cliffs: Prentice-Hall Inc., 1964), pp. 50–51.

[11] Albert H. Hastorf and Hadley Cantril, "They Saw a Game," *Journal of Abnormal and Social Psychology,* 49 (January, 1954), 130–132.

[12] S. E. Asch, "Effects of Group Pressure upon the Modification and Distortion of Judgments," in *Group Dynamics,* Dorwin Cartwright and Alvin Zander, eds. (Evanston: Row, Peterson, 1953), pp. 151–162.

[13] A summary of these experiments can be found in William N. Dember, *The Psychology of Perception* (Holt, Rinehart and Winston, 1960), pp. 314–317.

the general linguistic sophistication of his audience, the speaker or writer will be able to adjust his language to insure that it is familiar to them.[14] The tendency of partisans to distort political information suggests another strategy: neutral language will be less likely to provoke distortion than emotionally loaded language. John Kennedy adressing the Protestant Greater Houston Ministerial Association on the subject of his Catholicism avoided loaded labels for the anti-Catholic literature that had been circulating in the South, referring to it as "these pamphlets and publications we have all seen" rather than as "irresponsible, defamatory or lying hate literature."[15]

(2) Strategies for managing perception: invention and delivery

Perhaps the best insurance against distortion, as well as the best means of accommodating the variety in perceptual abilities represented in any audience, is the introduction of redundancy. The English language is, of course, already redundant in the sense that more information is presented in the usual sentence than is necessary to meaning. But even that level of redundancy may be insufficient; the speaker or writer may need to restate ideas in a variety of ways in order to insure that his ideas will be accurately perceived by most of his hearers or readers. The use of gesture, vocal inflections and supplementary materials—charts, photographs, films, graphs, tables, drawings, objects, demonstrations—are frequently means by which the speaker or writer introduces redundancy in order to insure that his message will be accurately perceived.[16]

MANAGING COMPREHENSION

It is easier to say what comprehension is than to describe how it comes about. We all know the moment when we can declare with elation, "Yes, I see what you're getting at!" But what brings us to that moment is not completely understood. Basically, the ability to make sense out of a communication seems to rest on two things: our knowledge of the words or other symbols being used, and our ability to associate, in some useful way, unfamiliar ideas with familiar ideas.

[14] Vernon, *Psychology of Perception*, pp. 199, 218.

[15] A transcript of Kennedy's statement may conveniently be found in the appendix of Theodore H. White, *The Making of the President 1960* (New York: Atheneum Press, 1961).

[16] Incidentally, the conventional wisdom that "a picture is worth a thousand words" has not been confirmed by experimentation. School children who saw instructional films were often confused by them; students who looked at charts and graphs often could not make head or tail of them without accompanying verbal explanations. Such methods may, however, be useful means of introducing redundancy. See Vernon, *Psychology of Perception*, pp. 104–105, for a summary of the research.

Both of these skills are related, in turn, to what Jerome Bruner and his associates have called *concept formation* and *concept attainment*.[17]

The language we use reflects the categories into which we have divided the world. The process of establishing these categories is the process of *concept formation*. For example, having received a number of reports of strange aircraft moving at great speeds and giving off a brilliant glow, some air force officer established the category of "unidentified flying objects" and put all such subsequent reports into the same folder. UFO is now a legitimate part of the language and appears in recent dictionaries. Most people could describe that category as containing fast flying objects, often saucer-shaped, illuminated, appearing usually at night, which cannot be identified as commercial or military aircraft or as any other known vehicle. Now that we have such a category, we can deal more efficiently with each subsequent observation by relating it to a collection of known phenomena. All nouns are names for such categories formed by grouping individually different objects together in classes on the basis of certain similarities. In other words, language provides us with a collection of concepts or, to put it another way, language is an end-product of concept formation.

The other half of the process is performed when we encounter a new instance, examine its characteristics, and assign it to one of the existing categories; this is *concept attainment*. When he discovers an unfamiliar plant, the biologist examines it closely until he is able to assign it to one of the existing species and varieties of live-oak. In order to do that, of course, he has to be thoroughly familiar with the available categories and know which of the plant's characteristics to emphasize in deciding to which group it belongs. Making that identification associates the new plant in useful ways with familiar ideas.

Consider the problem of explaining the system of musical notation to someone who does not already understand it. In order to make clear the relationship between the notational system and the musical notes produced, for example, by the pianist, we would have to explain the results of concept formation—"the note on the middle line of the staff represents the musical note, B; the note in the space above, C," and so forth. After all the relevant categories had been identified, we might then provide some exercise in concept attainment—"play the note I point to." In the course of the explanation we would have to indicate also the notations for time-value categories of notes, loudness and softness of phrases, methods of attack by the pianist, etc. But the two processes for producing comprehension are the same as in the first example: we set forth the categories—report the results of concept formation, and provide practice in fitting instances into those categories

[17] We are indebted in this discussion to Chapters 2 and 3 of Jerome S. Bruner, Jacqueline J. Goodnow and George A. Austin, *A Study of Thinking* (New York: Science Editions, 1962).

—practice in concept attainment. Again, familiarity with the language of the teacher is important; the Italian phrases describing expressive qualities of the music will have to be translated into familiar vocabulary before the student comprehends.

This example raises another problem: does it make any difference in what order various aspects of the notational system (frequency-, time-, style-notations) are discussed? There does not seem to be any basis for choosing one order rather than another. Although it seems more logical to consider which notes to play before considering how to play them, the reverse order might not affect a student's ability to comprehend the notational system after it had been explained completely.[18] One kind of order that could be predicted to be ineffective would be the consideration of the meaning of each successive notational mark on a sheet of music—"The 2/4 means it's a march, this means the first beat is a rest, the first note is E-flat played as a staccato note," etc. While either of the first two orders keeps the discussion of separate categories distinct, the last order mixes categories and moves on to a new category without having indicated the characteristics of the first. Similar confusion would result from trying to follow a pint of gasoline through an operating eight cylinder automobile engine in the hope that students would then understand the operation of the internal combustion engine.

Educators assume that "structure," understood as an organized pattern, even an orderly pattern, is an important component in educational curricula. And there may be some subject-matters that are best learned in some progressive way—mathematics is everyone's prize example. But the "new math" has pretty thoroughly upset what we used to think was the order in which mathematics ought to be learned, so that even that prize example may be difficult to press. Those who declare that "structure" is a prerequisite to comprehension mean by "structure" the opportunity for students to relate new information to familiar informaion in useful ways, which is less a function of "order" than of "discreetness" of categories. Jerome Bruner seems to have had that idea in mind when he said, "Grasping the structure of a subject is understanding it in a way that permits many other things to be related to it meaningfully. To learn structure, in short, is to learn how things are related."[19] If one new category is taken up at a time, the characteristics of its members explained in terms of those in similar familiar categories, and practice provided in fitting unidentified instances into

[18] See K. C. Beighley, "An Experimental Study of the Effect of Four Speech Variables on Listener Comprehension," *Speech Monographs*, 19 (November, 1952), 249–258.

[19] Jerome S. Bruner, *The Process of Education* (New York: Vintage Books, c. 1960), p. 7. A discussion of the values of structure beyond its contribution to comprehension may be found on pp. 23–26.

the new category, students may be able to comprehend material presented in communications.[20]

From this consideration of the nature of comprehension we can identify several strategies speakers or writers may adopt for improving the comprehension of their messages by listeners or readers.

(1) Strategies for managing comprehension: language choice

First, language must be familiar to the audience. Irving Lee speaks of this crucial matter in an essay in this section. It is easy for a speaker to assume that the meanings he attaches to words are the same as his listener's, but he may easily be mistaken unless he knows his man. The speaker who makes use of feedback from his audience may not have to proceed in the dark; he can discover that his language is not understood and try again.

(2) Strategies for managing comprehension: invention

Like perception, comprehension depends on the listener's ability and motivation to understand. His ability is usually related to his breadth of experience and his verbal sophistication. Efforts of a speaker to adjust vocabulary to a listener's language level will often improve the listener's ability to comprehend. But comprehension is also a product of the listener's interest in the subject of the communication. The strategy of sustaining motivation is selecting examples and illustrations that tie the present subject to listeners' or readers' personal interests; the motivation to attend will also provide motivation to comprehend.

Since structure of discourse aids comprehension by keeping categories distinct, speakers who want to be clear will see to it that aspects of a subject are dealt with separately. A discussion of the causes for the rise of the novel in England would be more comprehensible if such contributing factors as the increasing leisure of middle-class women, the rising literacy of the merchant class, the increase in newspaper reading, and the growing interest in serious realistic portrayal of life were treated one at a time rather than muddled together. But this is such an elementary truth of rhetoric that we need not labor it.

Perhaps the most important strategy for inducing comprehension is providing useful associations between the new ideas and familiar ideas. This is done chiefly by means of examples and illustrations designed to relate the new concept to familiar concepts or the new instance to

[20] Of the central importance of concept formation and concept attainment, Bruner, Goodnow and Austin declare that "the task of isolating and using a concept is deeply imbedded in the fabric of cognitive life; that indeed it represents one of the most basic forms of inferential activity in all cognitive life," *A Study of Thinking*, p. 79.

other familiar instances already categorized. Consider the following two explanations:

1. What is a euphemism? It's a name given to something in order to make it seem less offensive or unpleasant. To say that a woman is "in that delicate condition" instead of "pregnant," to use "expectorate" rather than "spit," "inebriated" rather than "drunk," or "pass away" for "die" is to employ euphemisms. Undertakers are called "morticians," life insurance salesmen are called "underwriters," what used to be referred to as "relief" or "the dole" is called "social security." H. L. Mencken was asked by Georgia Southern, a strip tease dancer, to find a better name for her professional activities. After discarding "moltician" because of its similarity to "mortician," he hit upon a euphemistic term having biological roots—"ecdysiast"—which referred to the practice of molting one's outer coverings. The magazine, *Nation's Business,* reported that "ten times more women buy a shade of hosiery when it is called *Gala* than when it is offered as plain beige. A diplomatic hosiery company calls its short-legged lengths *Brev,* long-legged ones *Duchess,* while the stoutish lady unembarrassedly asks for *Classical* and feels understood." Although some of these efforts at re-naming objects or programs in order to arouse more favorable attitudes toward them may seem silly, many of us do indeed feel better with a euphemism that softens an unpleasant reality.

2. Under what conditions will the price of durable goods rise? By durable goods we mean cars and large appliances such as refrigerators, stoves and dishwashers. When the cost of labor goes up, the prices of the finished goods have to go up. After the last round of steel wage increases, the price per ton of steel went up $6.00. If the cost of materials goes up, so do prices. Automakers who had to pay $6.00 more per ton of steel passed their cost on to the consumer by hiking passenger car prices by $50.00 to $200.00. Or, if the demand for the product is much larger than the supply, prices will soar, as was the case after the Second World War when everyone wanted a car but the automakers had not converted to civilian production; new cars were sold off the showroom floor at great profit to "used" car dealers who turned around and charged exorbitant prices of people unwilling to wait months for a factory order. Or, where the seller has a monopoly of production or sales, prices will rise. Imagine what would happen if only one company made clothes dryers; it could charge whatever the traffic would bear. There have been few such monopolies in the area of durable goods, but we have seen them in the drug market. A new drug like penicillin was very expensive when first introduced and sold only by one company. Competition slimmed down the price. Is there going to be a hike in prices of durable goods? We need only look at the increasing costs of labor—the UAW will win wage boosts and we will feel it in car prices. Steel will cost more, and so will glass and tires. But, except in boats and camping equipment, demand is not out of line with supply.

Notice that in the first explanation, the new concept, "euphemism," is said to be a category which contains things possessing certain subjective qualities. Those distinctive qualities are presented: "seem less offensive or unpleasant," "unembarrassing," "arouse more favorable attitudes," "feel better," "softens an unpleasant reality." In other words, the writer reports the results of concept formation. He also provides some exercise in concept attainment by fitting several instances into the category. Whether he has done enough to insure comprehension can be judged only by each reader.

The second explanation employs the same two strategies. The concept category is presented: "periods in which durable goods prices rise." Since the category is probably not unfamiliar to the audience, and the main difficulty will be concept attainment, that is, discovery of whether the time referred to is one of those periods, the writer spends his effort in relating each of the characteristics of that category to the interests of his audience by means of examples—the last round of steel wage increases which boosted steel prices, the hike in steel prices that affected auto prices, the situation after the war when demand outstripped supply, the hypothetical example of a seller's monopoly. Finally, he tries to fit the unidentified instance—the time referred to—into the concept category. The reader may now comprehend why the writer places that period in the concept category of "periods in which durable goods prices will rise"; whether he *accepts* that proposition will depend on factors we have yet to discuss.

A second strategy for inducing comprehension in invention is *explicitness*. Studies of the relative effectiveness of stating one's conclusion vs. allowing the reader or listener to draw the conclusion himself have shown that, insofar as comprehension is concerned, it is invariably better to state the conclusion explicitly. Especially when listeners are less intelligent and where the issue is complex, unless the communicator states his propositions explicitly they will be missed.[21] Consider what readers might have concluded about the nature of "euphemisms" if the writer in our earlier example had only presented a list of terms he had classed as euphemistic. On the other hand, the writer in the example about consumer prices does not state his conclusion explicitly; is there some reason why he can get away with that? Or, does he? The example mentioned earlier in a footnote to page 131 of the ambiguity of instructional films also confirms the wisdom of stating one's propositions explicitly where comprehension is the objective.

MANAGEMENT OF ACCEPTANCE

Securing attention and comprehension are only means to the objective all communicators seek—*acceptance*. The speaker wants his audience to do something about his proposition, either now or later—recognize that it meshes with other beliefs they hold, know more completely why they believe it, begin to act in harmony with it, discard

[21] Hovland, Janis and Kelley, *Communication and Persuasion*, pp. 103–104.

a notion that contradicts it, turn it over in their minds, talk about it with other people, seek more information about it, join a group that seeks to advance it, give time or money to promoting it. *Acceptance* in most experimental studies of communication effects has been taken to mean the *expression of favorable attitudes* toward the speaker's or writer's proposition on the assumption that a favorable state of mind or feeling toward a proposition must precede action consistent with it. On the other hand, agreement with a proposition does not guarantee action on it. We will discuss more fully the implications of attitude change as a measure of acceptance in Section V (see page 288); here it is necessary only to keep in mind that communication research has, in many instances, given us data on the way communications may affect the acceptance of new or strengthened attitudes but has not yet described the predictable relationship between attitudes and actions.

A great deal of interest has been shown by journalists, broadcasters, students of speech, political scientists, social psychologists, psychotherapists and anthropologists in the question: what aspects of the communication situation that are under some control by the communicator cause listeners or readers to accept his propositions? As a result, our growing understanding of these causal relationships suggest a number of strategies by means of which a communicator may induce acceptance—acceptance understood either as the strengthening of a belief or pattern of behavior already held (reinforcement), or altering a belief or pattern of behavior by substituting a new one (conversion). Because of the phenomenon of selective exposure, most communications reinforce already held beliefs rather than change them.

Why does one accept the recommendations of a speaker or writer? He does it for three main reasons:

1. because he respects the person making the recommendation,
2. because information provided him demonstrates that those recommendations are consistent with other things he believes or does, and
3. because acceptance promises to lead to the achievement of one or more of his personal goals.[22]

In a sense, the first two reasons are included in the third, but it is convenient to talk about them separately.

(1) Strategies for managing acceptance: ethos of speaker or writer

In an early experiment, Franklyn Haiman discovered that it made quite a difference in listeners' willingness to change their opinions on public health insurance whether the speech they heard was attributed to

---

[22] For a related explanation see Herbert C. Kelman, "Processes of Opinion Change," *Public Opinion Quarterly,* 25 (Spring, 1961), 57–78.

Eugene Dennis, Secretary of the Communist Party in the United States, to Thomas G. Parran, Surgeon-General of the United States, or to a college sophomore.[23] Subsequently, considerable attention has been given to investigations of the effect of *prestige, credibility* or *ethos* of the source, the results of which Andersen and Clevenger report in an accompanying reading.[24] Investigators trained in rhetoric have frequently used the Aristotelian term, *ethos,* to designate the speaker's character or trustworthiness, his intelligence or competence, and his goodwill or consideration for his hearers. Psychologists and political scientists have used the terms *credibility* and *prestige* to denote audience perceptions of the communicator's knowledge, intelligence and sincerity or, in other language, *technical trust* and *ethical trust.* The phenomena investigated are identical.

These studies have led to several conclusions. First, identical arguments have greater effect in inducing acceptance when attributed to a speaker or writer of high prestige rather than one of low prestige. Second, listeners' judgments of the *ethos* or credibility of the speaker are affected by indications in his speech of his apparent social status; by clues in his voice to "sincerity" or "moderation"; by clues provided by his appearance and dress to his competence and likeableness. And, third, that although a communication may be immediately accepted or rejected because it was presented by a person of either high or low prestige, after a period of time, the effect of the prestigious source wears off, unless reinstated, and as a result the opinion change originally produced by the communication declines.

These findings suggest several available strategies. Since the speaker's reputation affects the acceptance of his communications, he has been advised that "A good name is rather to be chosen than great riches, and loving favor rather than silver and gold.[25] But, assuming that he already possesses that strategic advantage, there still remain a few things to be done. Listeners must understand that he does possess the competence he claims. Where relevant information about his competence cannot be presented by someone else in a biographical note or a few introductory remarks, he will have to see that listeners have it from him. Since it is easy to appear immodest, tact will be required in the indirect revelation of his competence by what he says of his past work and interests, of the attention others have given it, and of the respect in which he is held for it by people whom listeners know and respect. Beyond what he says explicitly about his competence, the speaker should be aware that his dress and speech, his manner and physical appearance, provide clues by means of which audiences judge

[23] Franklin S. Haiman, "An Experimental Study of the Effects of Ethos in Public Speaking," *Speech Monographs,* 16 (September, 1949), 190–202.

[24] Cohen, *Attitude Change and Social Influence,* pp. 23–36 also summarizes studies of credibility.

[25] *Proverbs* 22:1.

his competence and trustworthiness. He cannot afford to have listeners
see him as a person of inferior status or a member of an unliked or
unrespected group. We have shown before (see page 71) that one's
speech is an index to social status, and that judgments of social status
are directly related to judgments of competence. Uneducated speech,
colloquial speech, regional speech may cause listeners to judge one
man to be less competent than another. We all have several levels of
language use which we adjust somewhat to those we are with at the
moment; this almost unwitting strategy stresses our membership in the
present group and encourages members to look upon us with greater
respect which increases chances that our communications will be accepted. Argument laced with coarse language may be one way of
seeming to be "one of the boys" in the fraternity thereby enhancing
one's prestige; a rather more formal and less colloquial style would
probably improve judgments of competence by one's professor.

There is not much one can do about physical appearance but one
can, of course, do something about dress and manner. Haiman tried
delivering the same speech to different audiences, at one time clean-
shaven and neatly dressed, at another, unshaven and unkempt. That
his neat appearance led to greater acceptance than his unkempt appearance probably means that college students in 1949 were more
likely to be offended by sloppy appearance than might be the case
today.[26] The implicit strategy is that of identifying oneself with the
group he is addressing, not in a phony way—as some presidential candidates have done by wearing their American Legion caps when addressing that group's convention—but by revealing that he actually is
a member of the audience by virtue of sharing in its values and respect-
ing its standards.

Having done what he can to establish his prestige, the speaker or
writer may consider strategy for gaining maximum effect from listeners'
or readers' inclination to accept his communications. People remember
arguments they have heard whether or not they came from a highly
respected source; after a while, however, they do forget which arguments came from the prestigious source and which came from the
little-respected source.[27] For the speaker's prestige to affect acceptance
of his proposition, listeners must be clearly aware which arguments
were his. Therefore, he would be advised to secure some kind of
commitment from his audience immediately after they have heard and

[26] Haiman, *Speech Monographs* 16:190–202.

[27] This phenomenon, called a "sleeper effect," was noticed by Herbert C.
Kelman and Carl I. Hovland in their report, " 'Reinstatement' of the Communicator
in Delayed Measurement of Opinion Change," *Journal of Abnormal and Social
Psychology*, 48 (1953), 327–335; a study of the effects of the Kennedy-Nixon television debates of 1960 revealed that viewers were as able to recall arguments of
the opposing candidate as of their own man. See Richard F. Carter, "Some Effects
of the Debates," in Sidney Kraus, ed., *The Great Debates* (Bloomington: Indiana
University Press, 1962).

accepted his communication, or he must, at the moment the audience does act, remind them that the arguments they recall came from a person whom they highly respect.

When most people accept the recommendations of a speaker or writer because of their respect for him, they reinforce existing beliefs and actions, attitudes and behavior. The chief reason for this result is selective exposure. However, it is also a likely result because a person given the option of changing his opinion of the speaker's proposition or changing his evaluation of the speaker's competence will frequently find it easier to discredit the speaker than alter his own opinion, particularly if that opinion is firmly imbedded in his belief system. That this choice is before the listener is the assumption of the various forms of balance theory which we will have occasion to mention again. Briefly, the theory is this: when he encounters a bit of information that contradicts one he already holds, an individual will try to regain a state of *cognitive balance*. For respected persons to make statements we agree with is an expected situation; the two cognitions are in balance. For unrespected persons to make statements we disagree with is also expected and no imbalance results. When a respected person, however, says things we disagree with, the imbalance created causes pressures to reduce or remove it. Between these two options—changing one's opinion to agree with that of the respected source or discrediting the source—especially if one's opinion is important, it will be easier to change one's evaluation of the source. That most people take that option explains why prestige effects are not often involved in producing conversion. It has, in fact, been asserted that the less high one's prestige, the less change one can safely recommend to an audience that already has strong opinions on the matter. If the audience has weak opinions and the speaker, high prestige, however, the greater the change recommended the greater the change produced.[28]

(2) Strategies for managing acceptance: evidence

A second reason one accepts the recommendations of a speaker or writer is that the information provided demonstrates that those recommendations are consistent with other things one believes or does. Such information may either serve to *reinforce* or support the things he already believes or does, or to provide the grounds for *conversion* to some new belief.

Robert Lane and David Sears in a brief essay in this section stress the fact that people frequently form opinions without having much information. Surveys relating the possession of political information and the possession of political opinions have shown that many people

[28] Lane and Sears, *Public Opinion*, p. 49.

hold opinions on foreign and domestic policy issues without knowing what the government is doing about the issue. An example is provided by Table 1.[29]

After a single humiliating experience with, say, a plumber we may find ourselves collecting all the information we can to provide a rational

TABLE 1. OPINIONS AND INFORMATION, 1956

ISSUE	% No Opin- ion	Hold Opinion but Do Not Know What Gov't Is Doing	Hold Opinion and Know What Gov't Is Doing	% Total
Foreign Policy				
Give aid to neutral countries	28	19	53	100
Send soldiers abroad	20	13	67	100
Economic aid to foreign countries	17	16	67	100
Act tough toward Russia, China	20	11	69	100
Avoid foreign involvement	14	15	71	100
Friendliness toward other nations	12	10	78	100
Domestic policy				
Firing of suspected communists	16	39	45	100
Leave electricity, housing to private industry	30	19	51	100
Segregation of schools	12	34	54	100
Influence of big business in government	28	18	54	100
Influence of unions in government	25	20	55	100
Insure medical care	12	29	59	100
Cutting taxes	19	18	63	100
Government guarantee of jobs	10	23	67	100
Racial equality in jobs and housing	14	19	67	100
Government aid to education	10	23	67	100

[29] Table reprinted with the permission of John Wiley and Sons from Angus Campbell, Philip E. Converse, Warren E. Miller and Donald E. Stokes, *The American Voter, an Abridgment* (New York: John Wiley and Sons, 1964), p. 101.

foundation for our dislike and mistrust of plumbers. Something like this process may be illustrated in the formation and rationalization of prejudices against national, religious or racial groups.[30] But many other beliefs provide incentives for us to seek supporting information; the often-mentioned phenomenon of selective exposure reflects the directed character of information-seeking activities. Information gathered in this way supplies rationalizations for beliefs and opinions we already hold, helps us to fit the opinion into a harmonious relationship with our other beliefs, helps us to satisfy ourselves that we have arrived at the position by logical means, and places all of our cognitions on this subject in balance.

When beliefs or opinions grow intense and momentarily salient they can produce consistent action. To encourage such consistent action is usually the object of speakers to friendly audiences, that is, audiences that already agree tacitly with the speaker's proposition. Certain kinds of information seem to bring the belief into focus and intensify it, especially information that reminds a listener or reader of the emotional experiences that underpin his belief—his first shocking visit to an under-staffed mental institution, the barbaric conditions he saw as a child in migrant labor camps, or the original trauma he felt at learning of a friend's death in an auto accident. Such information brought back into the mind may make the belief salient and encourage action.

When new ideas are proposed, information has a slightly different use. As Gerald Miller points out in an accompanying essay on "Evidence and Argument," testimony is intended "to induce a sense of belief in the proposition" where there was previously no belief. The function of such information for the reader or listener is to exhibit the consistent relationships between the new proposition and other things he believes and does. In a section of Miller's essay not included here, he discusses two forms of testimony, *testimony composed of statistical data* and *testimony composed of authority-based assertion*. Statistical data, while it indicates the extent to which a proposition is true, seems to induce belief by demonstrating *that* the proposition is true because the tools of "science," in which we already believe, have shown it to be true. In other words, testimony composed of statistical data exhibits consistency between the new belief and our established belief in particular *ways of knowing*. We would prefer, we twentieth century Americans, to accept propositions for which the methods of science provide some confirmation.

Testimony composed of authority-based assertion draws its initial impact, as we have already seen, from the respect we bear for the person testifying. In the case of a respected source's uttering senti-

[30] Gordon W. Allport, *The Nature of Prejudice* (Garden City: Doubleday and Company, Inc., 1954), pp. 22–26, 161–172.

ments we share, the information reinforces our conviction because it is seen immediately to be consistent with previously held views of the source. In the present case, where a respected speaker provides information that at first seems contradictory to our opinions, he will have to provide more information in order to demonstrate the consistency between the new proposition and other things we believe and do. If he has enough prestige to induce us to hear his ideas, the information we receive may finally disclose the harmony between new and old beliefs. And, if several people whom we respect advocate the same proposition, we may be compelled to admit it.

What we have said about the relation of information to opinions and beliefs suggests several strategies. First, when the speaker or writer addresses a friendly audience intending to reinforce a belief already held tacitly, he would be advised to provide information to shore up that belief. This, of course, is what keynote speakers do at national presidential nominating conventions. By reciting the shortcomings of the opposition party and illustrating their own party's achievements, they expect to supply listeners with ammunition for defending party policies and attacking opposition proposals. Well-chosen examples, illustrations, statistical data and authority-based assertions are all employed to provide rational bulwarks for the listeners' beliefs.

Second, where the speaker's aim is to make the belief salient in order that action may result, he may be required to remind listeners or readers of those emotional experiences which prompted the belief. Information in the form of examples or illustrations that stir the imagination to experience again the fear or pity, the anger or indignation associated with the belief may remind the listener of the importance of the belief for him and may motivate him to do something about it.

Finally, where the speaker or writer seeks to win assent from those who are not already convinced of his proposition, he may need to present information demonstrating that acceptance of the proposition is consistent with accepted ways of knowing, or is consistent with their other beliefs and actions. Evidence both in informal argument and in law courts has these functions for listeners, readers or jurymen. Consider, for example, the kinds of evidence offered for the "conspiracy" version of the assassination of President Kennedy. Initially, the writers of several "revisionist" accounts of the assassination encouraged doubt by reciting a number of allegedly unexplained facts—a bullet hole in a traffic sign that was later removed, testimony that people and smoke bursts were seen ahead and to the right of the President's vehicle, and an alleged acquaintance between Lee Oswald and Jack Ruby. Then, they offered statistical data about the poor performance of National Rifle Association "experts" who tried to duplicate Oswald's feat of striking a moving target with two bullets within the space of a few seconds. And, they offered testimony composed of authority-based assertions—the Marine Corps reports showing Oswald's performance as a marksman, the reports of the National Rifle Association on the possibility of accomplishing what the assassin accomplished, testimony of ballistics specialists who have declared that the bullet found could not have done the damage it did and remained undeformed. By means of such evidence, the advocates performed two functions: first, they sought to destroy the reader's sense of the consistency of information already accepted from the report of the Warren Commission; second, they sought to establish a new consistent picture of the assassination that included all of the "new" and all of the "old" information. By relying on accepted ways of knowing, and by exhibiting the consistency of new propositions with already held beliefs, the advocates hoped to induce belief in their proposition.

(3) Strategies for managing acceptance: motivation

A final reason for accepting the recommendations of a speaker or writer is that acceptance promises to lead to the achievement of one or more personal goals. Like attention, perception and comprehension, acceptance is a form of motivated behavior. What can confidently be said about the nature of motivated behavior as it may be influenced by communications? In the first place, it is clear that people generally expect that their beliefs or actions will lead to the attainment of goals. One may go to a film in order to reach a goal as modest as an hour and a half's entertainment, or spend four or more years in a university to reach a goal as complex as "a better life." How people develop these tendencies to act is not wholly understood, but it is supposed that certain *primary drives,* such as hunger, thirst and sexual desire, provide the bases for a number of *acquired drives* that direct behavior toward the attainment of goals such as mastery over some problem, the favorable opinion of other people, or the possession of a lot of money. Human motivation is understood chiefly in terms of these acquired drives, large numbers of which have been identified for the would-be persuader.[31] One attempt at the categorization of human motives that is more than a list and which has useful implications for those seeking to understand the relation of communications to the induction of acceptance is Abraham Maslow's proposal that human needs constitute a hierarchy.[32]

At the base of the ladder are those *physiological needs* (hunger, thirst, sex, etc.) which, if none of the individual's needs were satisfied,

[31] See, for example, Wayne C. Minnick, *The Art of Persuasion* (Boston: Houghton Mifflin Co., 1957), p. 206; Winston L. Brembeck and William S. Howell, *Persuasion* (New York: Prentice-Hall, Inc., 1952), pp. 83–91; Robert T. Oliver, *The Psychology of Persuasive Speech* (New York: Longmans, Green and Co., 1957), pp. 254–255.

[32] A. H. Maslow, *Motivation and Personality* (New York: Harper and Brothers, 1954), pp. 80–103.

would dominate his behavior. But since most physiological needs are satisfied in a well-ordered society, Maslow argues, the next higher group of needs becomes dominant, the *safety needs* (desire to escape from illness or injury, need for a stable world free of dangers from war, catastrophe, crime waves, and general social disorder). Again, when safety needs are somewhat satisfied, those of the next rank, the *belongingness and love needs* (need to give and receive affection, need to hold a place in the group), may direct behavior. Next in the hierarchy are *esteem needs* (desire for a sense of personal worth, achievement, mastery, desire for prestige or status). And, when all these four levels of needs have been somewhat satisfied, a final group of needs may dominate behavior, the *self-actualization needs* (to fulfill one's capacities, to do with one's life all that one is able physically and intellectually to do).

Maslow makes two points that are especially relevant to communicators. The first is his observation that those needs highest in the hierarchy are least satisfied in the lives of most people. While perhaps 85% of physiological needs are satisfied and 70% of safety needs, except in emergency situations, only 50% of belongingness needs, 40% of esteem needs and 10% of self-actualization needs are satisfied. In short, since behavior is dominated by unsatisfied needs, communications related to the achievement of the higher goals may strike at more potent motives. Second, behavior is determined not by a single motive but by efforts to reach a number of goals simultaneously by means of a single course of action. For example, one may go to a musical concert to please a friend, to think well of one's self, as well as to live up to one's capabilities. Communications which relate to the achievement of a variety of goals, therefore, may seem more useful to listeners or readers than those relating to the attainment of a single goal.

Much of the laboratory experimentation on the motivating effects of communications has dealt with fear-arousing appeals, on which C. William Colburn reports in one of the essays in this section. In terms of Maslow's hierarchy, the effects of messages promising to lead to the achievement of safety needs have been more thoroughly investigated than those of messages promising attainment of esteem needs, respect and affection needs or self-actualization needs. There may be some theoretical justification for this concentration of attention on the motivational effects of fear; one writer observed that "fear might be the underlying mechanism in a number of instances" of acquired drives, but explained that ignorance of other sources of motivation may have tempted investigators "to place such a heavy theoretical burden on fear."[33] In fear-arousing communications, the goal is defined as the absence of unpleasant stimulation (the specter of disease or injury) rather than the presence of pleasant stimulation (a knotty problem to

---

[33] Neal Miller, "Comments on Selected Controversial Issues," in *Theories of Motivation in Learning*, Richard C. Teevan and Robert C. Birney, editors (Princeton: D. Van Nostrand Co., Inc., 1964), pp. 198–199.

be solved, the affectionate or deferential responses of other people).
Apparently, we could view the possibility of frustration of *any goal*
as productive of "fear" in a rather general sense of that term, this
seems to be the rationale behind many of the studies of fear-arousing
communications.

A final observation about the nature of motivated behavior is that
as long as the means of achieving a goal are *rewarding* in that they do
achieve the goal, those means will be chosen. For example, if by voting
Republican one were to continue to enjoy low taxes, or if by using a
cosmetic one increased one's social invitations, both of these choices of
means would continue to be made.

To this point, we have said regarding the nature of motivated behavior (1) that people generally believe or act in the expectation that
action will lead to the attainment of a goal, (2) that human behavior
is understood in terms of a number of acquired drives, based upon
primary drives, which direct behavior toward learned goals, (3) that
these goals may be defined either as the absence of unpleasant stimulation (fear) or the presence of pleasant stimulation (affectionate responses of others), and (4) that as long as a means does attain a goal,
it will continue to be chosen. We may now ask: how may a communication induce motivations to accept a speaker's recommendations?
Usually, this happens in two ways. First, a speaker or writer either
reminds his listeners or readers of goals they seek (to be tolerant, adapt-
able, socially useful), or, he creates a situation in which a goal becomes
salient (arouses fear that a goal may be frustrated). Second, the
speaker promises that acceptance of his proposition will lead, sooner
or later, to the attainment of one or more goals sought by listeners.
In short, the speaker either offers a *reward* in goal-attainment or a
punishment in the frustration of goal-attainment. The television commercial picturing a young man pampered by two young ladies because
he used "a little dab" of hair cream, the magazine advertisement illustrating the luxury in which one will live if one drives a certain automobile, the political candidate's speech evoking an image of "the great
society" are attempting to make salient certain goals presumably held
by their readers or listeners. Each of these communications is designed
to make the goal as attractive as possible so that its achievement will
become urgent. Each, also, tries to show that acceptance of recommendations will bring about achievement of the goal—using the hair
cream will bring female attention, driving the car will bring social
status, a vote will lead to social rebirth. Examples of communications
that offer punishment for failure to accept recommendations are the
commercial picturing the girl left on the dock because her breath is
bad while the gang goes boating, the advertisement showing the
stunned family huddled on the roadside after an accident without insurance against injury or disablement, and the candidate's calling up
the specter of social disorder if the opposition party's man is elected.
Obviously, many such efforts fail to motivate acceptance either because

the goal proposed was not as important as the speaker imagined, or listeners refused to believe that it could be accomplished by accepting the speaker's recommendations. All successful strategies depend on thorough understanding of the audience, and sound judgment born of experience. The first is not always possible, and the second is never in great supply.

Several possible strategies are suggested for motivating the acceptance of communicators' recommendations. Since it will first be necessary for listeners or readers to appreciate the worth of the goal to be attained by accepting communicators' recommendations, speakers and writers must first picture the satisfactions of the achievement of the goal or the miseries of failing to attain it. Many of the same means—examples, illustrations and authority-based assertions—appropriate as strategies for reinforcing beliefs may be relevant here, since making a belief salient is precisely what one wishes to do in picturing the worth of a goal in which the listener presumably believes. Having first presented information to arouse awareness of needs, the communicator is able to offer information demonstrating that adoption of his proposal will satisfy those aroused needs. Studies of various orders of presentation have shown that acceptance is enhanced by the need arousal-need satisfaction order.[34] Finally, when fear is aroused in listeners or readers that failure to adopt the speaker's recommendations will frustrate the attainment of a goal, it is well to remember that very frightening communications may produce defensive avoidance by listeners or aggressive feelings toward a communicator that result in his devaluation rather than any change in opinion of the proposition. Therefore, as Colburn's study confirms, the strength of fear-arousing appeals will induce acceptance only when proportionate to the importance of the topic in listeners' minds.

SUMMARY

Most current research on communication has sought, in one way or another, to identify those strategies in discourse that affect certain kinds of listeners and readers in predictable ways. We have not been able here to do more than suggest the major strategies and to indicate illustrative experimental research or summaries of research. Our plan has been to identify those strategies relating to speakers' or writers' three goals, (1) to fix and sustain listeners' attention so that they may be more apt to perceive the message swiftly and accurately, (2) to facilitate listeners' comprehension of the message, and (3) to facilitate listeners' acceptance of the proposition where acceptance implies either reinforcement or conversion. The readings that follow should give the reader a more detailed understanding of the strategies of managing attention and perception, managing comprehension, and managing acceptance.

[34] Cohen, *Attitude Change and Social Influence*, pp. 11–12.

ATTENTION AND PERCEPTION

M. D. Vernon

1. CONCENTRATION OF ATTENTION

WE HAVE NOTED from time to time that what people perceive in any given situation may vary according to their previous experience, especially in so far as this affects what they expect to see. A very important instance of this variation arises in cases in which their attention varies. Attention is difficult to define; but we are all perfectly aware that when we wish to perceive something clearly and correctly, we concentrate our attention upon it. On the other hand, if we are idly contemplating the scene of view, with no great desire to perceive anything in particular, we may notice very little and overlook many things around us because, as we say, we are not attending.

In point of fact, the degree of attention may vary greatly from time to time, and with it the amount we perceive. We may concentrate upon a narrowly restricted view, as, for instance, in looking through a microscope, and perceive clearly and accurately almost everything within that field. If the field of view is wider, we may direct our attention upon one particular part of it, and in that case we are unlikely to notice much in the surrounding parts. Or we may look to and fro, deliberately picking out first one thing and then another. Or we may not be attending at all, but thinking of something other than the field of view. Then we perceive very little unless an event occurs which attracts our attention and forces itself upon our consciousness. We then concentrate on this event and endeavour to perceive it clearly. In all these cases, the total number of objects and events perceived varies, and the manner with which we perceive them.

Sometimes a pattern in the field of view may actually appear different when we attend to it "figurally" and when we perceive it merely as the background of another figure. The *Gestalt* psychologists presented patterns made up of dots arranged in vertical columns and horizontal rows, and found that there was a tendency to notice either the rows or the columns according as to whether the dots were nearer together horizontally or vertically; that is to say, those in closer proximity to one another were grouped together. But it was necessary to

---

Reprinted with permission of the author from M. D. Vernon, *The Psychology of Perception* (Baltimore: Penguin Books, 1963).

make a considerable difference between the vertical and the horizontal separation of the dots before observers perceived the column or row structure. However, this structure was more readily perceived (with a smaller difference in separation) when the observers looked attentively at the dot pattern than when they perceived it merely as the background of another figure, superimposed upon it. This indicates that perceptual "organization" of the field of view takes place more easily when it is attended to focally.

If the field of view is relatively unchanging, and we have plenty of time at our disposal, we may be able by glancing to and fro to perceive a great deal of it, though it is unlikely that we shall observe everything there. We tend to overlook anything relatively uninteresting and unimportant, unless it moves or changes in some way. But, as we saw, a sudden movement is likely to attract attention and stimulate us to try to perceive as clearly as possible what moved and how it moved. There are other events which produce a similar effect—bright lights or loud noises, for instance. As we shall see, these effects appear in part to result from certain concomitant physiological changes. Furthermore, they may be signals of something potentially dangerous to us. Therefore we are throughout life set, as it were, to become rapidly aware of such events, in order that we may respond to them and avoid them as quickly and effectively as possible.

There are other situations in which the time available to us for perceiving is extremely limited. If we know beforehand that this will be so, then we are able to concentrate our attention and make ourselves ready to perceive as quickly and accurately as possible. Obviously if we also know beforehand where to look, we shall perceive more than if we are obliged to waste time searching the field of view for the significant event. Moreover, the smaller the area which we are attempting to perceive, the greater the accuracy with which we shall perceive it. In experiments on tachistoscopic perception, . . . the observer is directed to concentrate his attention upon what will appear within a limited area for a short interval of time. Thus he knows both where and when to look, and his perceptions within that area are maximally clear and accurate. But not unnaturally if attention is concentrated upon a particular point in the field of view, the perception of other parts of the field will be correspondingly less clear. Thus if letters or digits are presented in various positions in the field of view, and the observer instructed to direct his attention to one particular point in the field, what appears at that point will be perceived accurately; but letters appearing at other points are likely to be overlooked or reported inaccurately.[1] Thus a rough generalization may be made that the total amount which can be attended to at any one moment is constant. If

[1] Meisenheimer, J., "Experimente im Peripheren Sehen von Gestalten," *Arch. f. d. ges. Psychol.*, 1929, 67, 1.

attention is concentrated on a small part of the field, little will be perceived in other parts; if attention is diffused over a larger area, no one part will be very clearly and accurately perceived.[2]

So also if a complex field is viewed, to one aspect of which the observer's attention is directed by particular instructions, so that he has some idea or some expectation of what will be shown him, he will perceive it more quickly and accurately than if he has no such expectation. For instance, differently arranged groups of letters were presented, and different observers were instructed to report either the number of letters, or the positions of the letters, or what the letters were.[3] Each of these characteristics was reported most accurately by the observers who had been given the corresponding instructions. But in such circumstances the other characteristics tended to be disregarded. Again, sets of four nonsense syllables were shown printed in different colours and differently arranged in different sets.[4] The observers were given one of four tasks: to report the number of syllables, or their colours, or their arrangement, or the letters composing them. Afterwards they were asked to report all these characteristics; and it was found that those not mentioned in the task which had been set were overlooked or forgotten. In general, it appeared that the amount of information which could be obtained and reported from a given field of view was approximately constant; but it was differently distributed according to the instructions. Thus the greater the number of features an observer is required to perceive and remember, and the greater the complexity of these, the less his accuracy in doing so. The following results were obtained from the tachistoscopic perception of coloured shapes or letters: when only the number of shapes or letters were required, about eight were reported correctly; when numbers and names of letters were required, six to eight; with numbers and shapes of forms, four; with numbers, colours, and shapes of forms, three.[5]

However, there is some evidence to show that the limitation on perception of many features in a complex field is imposed less by the original intake of information than by the necessity of storing it in memory for more than a very short period of time. Thus when observers were shown various numbers of different shapes in various colours, and given instructions to attend primarily to number, or shape, or colour, it was found that the observers could report some information about the features to which they had not been directed to attend (or even told specifically not to attend), provided that this was done

[2] Grindley, G. C., "Psychological Factors in Peripheral Vision," *Medical Res. Counc. Spec. Rep. Series*, 1931, No. 163.

[3] Chapman, D. W., "Relative Effects of Determinate and Indeterminate *Aufgaben*," *Amer. J. Psychol.*, 1932, 44, 163.

[4] Külpe, O., "Versuche über Abstraktion," *Ber. I Kongress exp. Psychol.*, Giessen, 1904.

[5] Dallenbach, K. M., "The 'Range of Attention'," *Psychol. Bull.*, 1928, 25, 152.

quickly.[6] But this information could not be retained in memory over more than a very brief period of time.

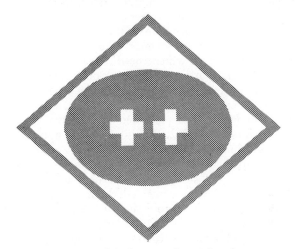

Figure 1. Classification of complex shapes

Again, in perceiving certain parts of a complex field and making judgments about the figures shown, the observer will be considerably affected if he does not know beforehand just which parts of the field will be relevant to his judgments. Observers had to classify a series of complex shapes primarily in accordance with the shape and size of the central figure (the ellipse in Fig. 1); but in certain cases they had also to take into account the inner figures (the crosses) and the outside border (the diamond).[7] When they were instructed beforehand which of these features were relevant and which irrelevant, they were quicker in making their judgments than when they were uncertain which features were or were not relevant. The time taken increased with the amount of irrelevant information presented. But it decreased with practice, which presumably enabled the observers to discard irrelevant information more rapidly and concentrate their attention upon the important aspects of the task.

In a situation in which it is difficult to perceive what is being shown, irrelevant and distracting information may be produced by the incorrect guesses of the observer. Thus a series of pictures was presented;

[6] Lawrence, D. H. and Laberge, D. L., "Relationship Between Recognition Accuracy and Order of Reporting Stimulus Dimensions," *J. Exper. Psychol.*, 1956, 51, 12.

[7] Henneman, R. H., "The Effect of Irrelevant Information upon Complex Visual Discrimination," in *Form Discrimination as Related to Military Problems*, edited by Wulfeck, J. W. and Taylor, J. H. (National Academy of Science, Washington, D. C., 1957).

the first of these were extremely blurred, but they became clearer as the series progressed.[8] Observers were liable to make incorrect guesses as to what the pictures represented and to stick to these as the series progressed. Thus they took longer to identify the clearer pictures than did other observers who had begun in the middle of the series, with less blurred pictures, and had not made the earlier incorrect guesses.

There are other cases in which the direction of attention towards the perception of some particular shape or object causes an observer to perceive what he expected to see rather than what is actually presented. Such a direction may be given by special instructions; or by what the observer has been accustomed to perceive in such circumstances and therefore he thinks will most probably appear in the present case. An experiment demonstrating the effect of instructions was one in which groups of letters were presented tachistoscopically, such as "sael" and "wharl."[9] Observers who had been told that they would see words related to "boats" perceived these as "sail" and "wharf"; while observers who had been told they would see words related to "animals" perceived them as "seal" and "whale." Such an effect may occur without any deliberate instructions being given and without any intention on the part of the observer. Thus in one experiment, observers were given to read a story of a feud between two families; a reconciliation effected by the betrothal of the son of one family to the daughter of the other; and the wedding feast which marked the uneasy truce.[10] Three days later the observers were shown some pictures including a reproduction of *The Village Wedding* by Pieter Breughel. They were asked to pick out from these the picture which depicted an incident described in the story; and they all selected *The Village Wedding*. On a subsequent occasion when they were asked to recall the picture, they stressed in their recalls the features most closely related to the story, and they sometimes introduced items which were in the story but not in the picture. In particular, they attributed to the picture the atmosphere of uneasiness which had occurred in the story. But another group of observers who had seen the picture but not read the story saw it simply as a scene of merriment and gaiety. Now it is true that this effect was in part a function of the remembering and recall of the picture; but it also seems probable that even in the first case the observers who had read the story must have perceived the picture in a somewhat different manner from those who had not.

More frequent are the cases in which an observer's general familiarity with a situation causes him to perceive what he expected would

[8] Wyatt, D. F. and Campbell, D. T., "On the Liability of Stereotype or Hypothesis," *J. Abn. Soc. Psychol.*, 1951, 46, 496.

[9] Siipola, E., "A Group Study of some Effects of Preparatory Sets," *Psychol. Monogs.*, 1935, 46, No. 210.

[10] Davis, D. R. and Sinha, D., "The Influence of an Interpolated Experience upon Recognition," *Quart. J. Exper. Psychol.*, 1950, 2, 132.

appear. Instances of this have already been given in Ames's two demonstrations of the distorted room which was seen as a normal rectilinear room . . .; and the rotating trapezoidal window which appeared as an oscillating rectangular window. . . . Another example is afforded by the experiment . . . in which observers were shown playing cards with the colours of the suits reversed. Here their perceptions of the cards shown them were frequently falsified by their expectations based upon the familiar colours of playing cards. In everyday life an instance of this tendency appears in the so-called "proof-reader's illusion," in which misprints in a text are completely overlooked, even when the reader is looking out for them, because he is so habituated to perceiving normally printed words.

However, in this and other cases observers may be trained, or given special practice, to acquire the ability to perceive something unlike that which they had previously perceived. Thus the professional proof-reader learns to perceive misprints, in part by ignoring to a considerable extent the meaning of what he is reading. So also by practice observers can learn to perceive the distortion in the Ames distorted room. We noted that one way of doing this was for the observer to touch the walls of the room with a stick, or to bounce a ball against them.[11] In this case, sensory data other than those of vision are used by the observer to modify his perceptions. A slower way of achieving the same result is to observe carefully the movements of an object of familiar size across the back wall of the room.[12] A cigarette packet, for instance, will at first appear to change its size as it moves. But after a time the observer perceives the size as remaining constant; and then he can see that the back wall slopes obliquely backwards. Again, in the experiments on the effects of wearing inverting or reversing spectacles, over long periods of time . . ., it was found that in time the observers saw the field of vision in its normal orientation; and that this occurred most quickly when they made voluntary movements. Thus again additional non-visual information was utilized in learning a new way of perceiving.

Many examples occur in ordinary everyday life of people learning to perceive particular aspects of the visual scene which they had hitherto overlooked. Thus botanists, zoologists, and geologists learn to notice flowers, animals, and geological formations which persons uneducated in these sciences do not perceive at all, and which in some cases they may be unable to perceive even when their attention is drawn to them. We noted instances of this in the perception of pictures and diagrams, and of X-ray photographs. An experiment which demonstrates this phenomenon was one in which students were shown pictures of medie-

[11] Kilpatrick, F. P., "Two Processes in Perceptual Learning," *J. Exper. Psychol.*, 1954, 47, 362.
[12] Weiner, M., "Perceptual Development in a Distorted Room," *Psychol. Monogs.*, 1958, 70, No. 16.

val armour, and required to describe the armour afterwards.[13] Students who were instructed beforehand about how the armour was constructed were able to perform this task much better than the others, provided they had thoroughly understood and assimilated what they were told. But if they had not done so, they were merely confused.

In all these cases, it seems that an observer's perception of the field, or of any particular aspect of it, may be made more rapid and accurate insofar as his attention is directed towards it. The more narrowly and specifically attention is directed, the greater the improvement. Thus the greater the amount of training and experience, and the clearer and more defined it has been, the greater the effect is likely to be. It is also true, however, that in some cases the emphasis seems to lie more upon practice and training in a particular form of attending, rather than upon attending to a particular aspect of the field. In some cases, this may be the narrowly concentrated type of attention which is needed in tachistoscopic perception. . . .

It is sometimes supposed that highly gifted individuals can attend to more than one activity at once; for instance, they can perceive simultaneously two or more different series of events. There do appear to be cases in which two series of events can be combined in some way which enables the observer to perceive both of them, though this happens more commonly in auditory than in visual perception. Thus a listener can sometimes hear two different messages conveyed to him simultaneously provided that they are differentiated in some way—for instance, they are spoken by different voices.[14] But since the eyes are more narrowly directed in space than are the ears, simultaneous perception of different visual stimuli is harder to carry out. Thus what usually happens is that the observer's attention alternates rapidly between the two series of events. Indeed, it has been shown that absolutely simultaneous perception of a visual and an auditory message was impossible.[15] An observer was required to locate places on a map in accordance with information about their positions, part of which was presented visually, four words at a time; and part of which was spoken. The places could be located accurately only if both these sets of instructions were received. It was clear that when the words of the spoken message coincided exactly with the visual presentation, one of the messages was always overlooked. Some observers received the visual messages correctly, others the auditory messages; on the whole, the visual messages were perceived better than the auditory ones. Now it is true that this experiment did not make use of simple percepts but of the perceiving and understanding of quite complex information.

[13] Fox, C., "A Study in Preperception," *Brit. J. Psychol.*, 1924, 15, 1.

[14] Broadbent, D. E., *Perception and Communication*, chap. 2 (Pergamon Press, London, 1958).

[15] Mowbray, G. H., "The Perception of Short Phrases Presented Simultaneously for Visual and Auditory Reception," *Quart. J. Exper. Psychol.*, 1954, 6, 86.

Also, the information was presented through two different sensory modalities, vision and hearing. There is some evidence that two series of visual events may be combined to some extent; for instance, an observer may be able to count the number of lines in two series presented simultaneously.[16] But it is not clear whether in this case the observer may not be alternating his attention rapidly between the two series. . . .

In general, then, these experiments indicate that it is not possible to perceive and attend to two events separately and independently if these coincide too nearly in time or space. Either one will cancel out the other, or they will be combined in some way if this is at all possible. It appears that a time interval of the order of one-fifth of a second is necessary to transfer the direction of attention from one event to another, in the sense of perceiving them as different.[17] This time appears to be about the same whether attention is being transferred from one part of the visual field to another, or from a visual to an auditory stimulus. So also it has been shown that if an individual thinks he may have to modify his reaction to a given stimulus in the light of information given him by another stimulus, he can react correctly when the latter appears at an interval of one-fifth to two-fifths of a second before the former; that is to say, he can perceive both stimuli correctly when they are separated by this interval of time.[18] However, the time is lengthened if the observer is uncertain whether or not the second stimulus will appear.

2. FLUCTUATION OF ATTENTION

Up to the present we have been considering in the main how observers perceive events upon which their attention is focused. However, we noted that although such events were perceived more clearly than any others, yet things to which attention was not principally directed were perceived, and remembered, for at least a short period of time afterwards. Now it is clear from everyday experience that we do in fact perceive many things and many aspects of the visual field without directing attention upon them. In fact, the theory has been put forward that there is a large number of "levels of attention," varying from the highest, at which attention is focused and narrowly concentrated upon a particular part of the field, to the lowest, a bare consciousness of the marginal parts of the field. It would perhaps be preferable to say that our awareness of our surroundings varies continually, from place to place and from time time, from a maximal to a minimal amount. We have seen that much is known as to the con-

[16] Hylan, J. P., "The Distribution of Attention," *Psychol. Rev.*, 1903, 10, 373.

[17] Mager, A., "Neue Versuche zur Messung der Geschwindigkeit der Aufmerksamkeitswanderung," *Arch. f. d. ges. Psychol.*, 1925, 53, 391.

[18] Poulton, E. C., "Perceptual Anticipation and Reaction Time," *Quart. J. Exper. Psychol.*, 1950, 2, 99.

ditions of maximal awareness. Far less is known with regard to lower degrees of awareness.

In discussing the effects of the background upon perception, for instance of size, shape, colour, etc., it was noted that our perceptions of this background did in fact affect considerably the manner in which objects attended to were perceived. In these cases, the background in itself might not be perceived at all; it merely formed a setting or framework for the objects. But it also seems that parts of the background may be perceived as such, without attention being directed upon them, at least at that moment; though it may pass to them subsequently.

It is clear that events sometimes occur in the first place outside the central focus of attention, and then rapidly become focal. It was noted that we may be scarcely conscious of a familiar scene in which little or no movement or change is occurring. But if some aspect of this scene or some object in it is altered, and particularly if the change is sudden and involves movement, we immediately become aware of it, and *then* direct our attention upon it, investigating it and responding to it as rapidly as possible. Such events are said to force themselves upon our consciousness.

So also when we are endeavouring to direct awareness, with the maximum degree of concentration, upon a task on which we are engaged, irrelevant events may intrude into consciousness which we call distractions. Whether or not this happens depends in part upon the nature of these events. Sudden loud noises or sudden blows are almost invariably distracting. Bright lights and moving objects are also distracting if they happen to "catch the eye." But we are better able to preserve the direction of attention in visual than in auditory or tactile perception because of our capacity voluntarily to control the sense organs themselves. However, we know that it is impossible to maintain the direction of attention, even in visual perception, for an indefinite period of time upon a single aspect of the visual scene. After a period, a shorter or longer time, the direction alters and attention "wanders" spontaneously to something else. In an intermediate period, events become distracting which at an earlier period would have been ignored. But all these fluctuations of attention depend to a greater or less extent upon conditions within the individual himself—his general health, his state of fatigue, his interest in his task, and the strength of his motivation for maintaining attention.

Let us consider first some cases in which attention seems to fluctuate very readily. When a stimulus, a light or a sound, of very low constant intensity is exposed for some length of time, and the observer is required to say whether or not he perceives it, he may report that it appears at one moment and disappears the next. In other words, the perception of stimuli at threshold intensity fluctuates.[19] If two stimuli

[19] Guilford, J. P., "'Fluctuations of Attention' with Weak Visual Stimuli," *Amer. J. Psychol.*, 1927, 38, 534.

are presented, one very slightly more intense than the other, and the observer is asked to adjust their intensity so that one is perceptible and the other is not, it is found that his adjustments vary regularly over a certain range of intensity.[20] No amount of effort of attention on the part of the observer can prevent the stimulus at threshold intensity from disappearing from time to time. This phenomenon probably depends on certain physiological processes which we shall discuss below.

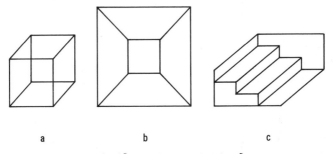

a   b   c

Figure 2. Alternating perspective figures

Other instances of fluctation are given by the phenomena of the alternating "figure" and "ground," alternating perspective and retinal rivalry. . . .

The same type of effect occurs in alternating perspective figures, some of which are shown in Fig. 2. In these, one part of the figure appears to stand out in front of the rest of the figure; but there is alternation, first one part standing out and then the remainder. Thus Fig. 2a may be seen with the cube alternately facing to the left and to the right. Fig. 2b can be seen as a receding hollow or a protruding boss; and Fig. 2c as a staircase or an overhanging cornice. Again, voluntary direction of attention to one aspect may make it predominate in awareness, but cannot altogether suppress the other aspect. Introducing complicating details, such as windows, a door, and other objects, in Fig. 2b, tends to make it look like a receding passage and increase the dominance of that aspect, but this seldom altogether suppresses the other aspect.

These effects have been attributed by some psychologists to an effect called "satiation." This is little more than a name for this effect, in which an observer seems unable to attend to one aspect for more than a limited period of time. However, as we shall see, there is some possibility that events in the central nervous system may be responsible for the effect. It cannot be due to any form of retinal fatigue. Nor can binocular retinal rivalry be attributed to retinal factors, in spite of its

[20] Dixon, N. F., "Apparatus for Continuous Recording of the Visual Threshold by the Method of 'Closed Loop Control'," *Quart. J. Exper. Psychol.*, 1958, 10, 62.

name. In this phenomenon, different fields of view are presented simultaneously to the two eyes, for instance, two differently coloured fields. If these are fairly similar in brightness and wave length (i.e. they are neighbouring colours in the spectrum), the two fields may fuse and a mixture of the colours be perceived.[21] But if their unlikeness is increased, they will tend to alternate with each other; though sometimes a black and a white field will produce a shimmering or lustrous effect. If one field is figured and the other plain, the former will dominate and the latter may be altogether suppressed.[22] The same things occur if one field is more structured or brighter than the other, or if one is more "meaningful." Thus it was found that if the photograph of a face was presented to one eye, and the same photograph upside down to the other eye, the upright photograph tended to dominate and the inverted photograph was sometimes completely suppressed.[23] Again, pairs of photographs were presented stereoscopically, a Mexican scene to one eye and an American one to the other, to Mexican and American observers.[24] The Mexican scenes tended to dominate for the Mexican observers, the American ones for the Americans. The more nearly equal the degree of figuration of the two fields, the greater the tendency to alternation between them. Voluntary direction of attention towards one field may increase its dominance, but seldom produces complete suppression of the other field. However, the rate of alternation can be increased by voluntary effort.

Somewhat similar effects have been demonstrated recently in the "stabilized image" phenomenon. . . .[25] When shapes of different kinds were projected continuously onto the central area of the retina, the speed and amount of fading and regeneration varied according to the nature of the figure. In the first place, meaningful figures faded less. With a line and a profile face side by side, the latter faded more slowly and remained for a larger proportion of the time than did the former. A letter with an irregular line across it remained when the line disappeared. Specific attention to any part of a figure would restore it to awareness. Again, different parts of meaningless figures faded in different ways; but curved figures remained as a whole to a greater extent than did straight line figures. With a square, certain lines might disappear while others remained; in particular, parallel lines tended to

[21] Pickford, R. W., "Binocular Colour Combinations," *Nature*, 1947, 159, 268.
[22] Gellhorn, E., "Über den Wettstreit im Nachbild," *Arch. f. d. ges. Physiol.*, 1928, 218, 54.
[23] Engel, E., "The Role of Content in Binocular Resolution," *Amer. J. Psychol.*, 1956, 69, 87.
[24] Bagby, J. W., "A Cross-Cultural Study of Perceptual Predominance in Binocular Rivalry," *J. Abn. Soc. Psychol.*, 1957, 54, 331.
[25] Pritchard, R. M., Heron, W., and Hebb, D. O., "Visual Perception Approached by the Method of Stabilized Images," *Canad. J. Psychol.*, 1960, 14, 67.

ATTENTION AND PERCEPTION 159

fade and regenerate together. These observations are interesting as showing that the fading tendency is affected firstly by attention and interest; and secondly by some of the *Gestalt* factors of "goodness" of form. . . . But the "wholes" into which parts of a complex shape were organized appeared to be somewhat different from those postulated by the *Gestalt* psychologists.

These effects may at first sight seem to have little relevance to everyday experience. Nevertheless they all appear to be related to fluctuations in attention. What does occur frequently in everyday life is that, if the field of view contains a number of objects all of which are interesting and attractive to the observer, his attention is likely to alternate between them. He will automatically glance to and fro, looking first at one and then at another. In such a situation also he may find it difficult to concentrate and maintain his gaze on one object or part of the field, although voluntary effort may assist him up to a point.

In all these cases, interest in and attractiveness of objects play an important part in the direction of attention. Experiments have shown that variation, surprise, and incongruity are also liable to attract attention.[26] Observers were shown sets of pictures containing one or two items which were quite incongruous with the others, and told that they could prolong the exposure of any of the items as long as they were interested in looking at it. They spent more time in looking at the incongruous items than at the others; and also in looking at irregular figures among a series of regular ones. Other figures were presented in pairs, one a regular and the other an irregular figure; or one a picture of a normal animal and the other an animal with incongruous parts. Again, the irregular and incongruous figures were studied for a longer time than were the regular and familiar ones. Presumably longer time was required to perceive the exact nature of the unusual and irregular items than of the normal ones.

It is true also that lack of interest makes attending more difficult and distraction easier. An important instance of this appears in the kind of boredom which results from lack of change or variety in the environment, and especially from the monotonous repetition of an event at intervals over a considerable period of time. If a stimulus pattern is repeated sufficiently often and unchangingly, at length the observer may cease to be able to attend to it; or if he has to respond in exactly the same way, he may be unable to continue doing so. It seems, however, as if it is the perceptual activity which breaks down, before the response. A test called the "clock test" was designed by Mackworth to

[26] Berlyne, D. E., "Conflict and Information-Theory Variables as Determinants of Human Perceptual Curiosity," *J. Exper. Psychol.*, 1957, 53, 399; "The Influence of Complexity and Novelty in Visual Figures on Orienting Responses," *J. Exper. Psychol.*, 1958, 55, 289.

find how long observers could go on perceiving a repeated event.[27] A pointer rotated round a dial like that of a clock, in successive small jumps, one every second; and at irregular and comparatively infrequent intervals it made a double jump. The observer had to notice and signal each of these double jumps. After only about half an hour observers began to miss these; and the number of omissions increased steadily throughout a two-hour period. In another experiment, observers had to signal the occurrence at intervals of an "echo" on a mock-up radar screen.[28] There was a marked increase in omissions when the echo was dim and difficult to see, but relatively little when it was bright and clear. Thus attraction of attention by the more striking perceptual event was effective in preventing wandering of attention from the task. So also was lengthening of the time over which the signals were visible, in another similar task. Keeping the observer continuously active in the clock test, by requiring him to press a key at every one of the smaller jumps (as well as another key at the larger jumps) did not keep up his efficiency. And if a continuous loud sound was maintained throughout the period of testing, this enhanced the decline. Thus clearly there are certain conditions of perceptual stimulation which make it particularly difficult for the observer to maintain attention, of which the most important are low intensity, short duration, and repetition.

These effects may however be counteracted in various ways by making the situation more interesting and more generally stimulating. Having another observer in the same room, or alternating one observer with another, prevented increase of failures to respond. So also did signaling to the observer whenever a double jump occurred, whether he responded to it or not. But also an increase in the rate and regularity at which signals appeared sometimes seemed effective, by increasing the probability of their appearance and hence the observer's expectancy. Clearly, however, the factors involved in the maintenance of attention to tasks of this kind are complex.

It is of course well known that a state of fatigue is liable to make it harder for an observer to maintain his attention on any task, even a complex and variable one. Indeed, performance of such tasks may itself engender states of fatigue which make it more and more difficult for the performer to keep up his efficiency. This was strikingly demonstrated by experiments carried out during the war on aircraft pilots in an experimental cockpit.[29] The pilots had to make coordinated movements of the hand and feet, as in flying an aircraft, in response to the

[27] Mackworth, N. H., "Researches on the Measurement of Human Performance," *Medical Res. Counc. Spec. Rep. Series*, 1950, No. 268.
[28] A fuller discussion of these and the following experimental findings is given in Broadbent, D. E., *Perception and Communication*, chap. 6, see note 14.
[29] Bartlett, F. C., "Fatigue Following Highly Skilled Work," *Proc. Roy. Soc. B*, 1943, 131, 247.

readings on a series of dials similar to those on the instrument panel of an aircraft cockpit. In addition, distracting lights were introduced at intervals. Towards the end of a two-hour period, certain characteristic changes appeared in the mode of responding: (a) the pilots became relatively indifferent to small changes in dial readings, attended to them sporadically and unsystematically, and sometimes not until they had passed a "danger" reading; (b) the pilots tended when they did respond to make correct responses but in the wrong order; (c) there was a funnelling of attention towards those dials to which response was most frequent, with a consequent failure to notice other dials less frequently used, for instance, the petrol gauge; (d) the distracting stimuli, which in earlier stages could be ignored, or allowed for, became increasingly obtrusive and annoying. In general the fatigued individuals were seldom aware of the deterioration in their performance, but thought that they were attending and responding quite adequately. If because of the deterioration in efficiency, something went wrong, they tended to attribute this to faults in the machinery and not to their own actions.

It is clear therefore that there are several situations in which the power to attend is only partially under voluntary control, and in which the observer cannot deliberately maintain his attention for an indefinite period. It appears to become temporarily inhibited, and his strongest efforts cannot preclude this happening. Some strong interest or other motive may prevent it for a time, but not indefinitely. The principal condition in which this failure of attention occurs is that of lack of change or variation in the perceptual situation; the more pronounced the invariability, the greater the deterioration. We shall now consider some particularly striking instances of this.

Under the direction of Hebb, at the University of MacGill, experiments were carried out to investigate the effects of keeping people for periods up to five days in a completely homogeneous and unvarying environment.[30] In a small room they lay on a bed; they heard nothing but the monotonous buzz of machinery; they had translucent goggles over their eyes so that they could see only a blur of light; and they wore long cuffs which came down over their hands and prevented them from touching anything. Some observers were able to stay in these surroundings continuously for five days; others could not endure them for more than two days, in spite of the very high rate at which they were being paid for performing the experiment. Although at first they slept a great deal, after about a day they were unable to sleep except in snatches. They became bored and restless, and could not think in any

[30] Bexton, W. H., Heron, W., and Scott, T. H., "Effects of Decreased Variation in the Sensory Environment," *Canad. J. Psychol.*, 1954, 8, 70; Heron, W., Doane, B. K., and Scott, T. H., "Visual Disturbances After Prolonged Perceptual Isolation," *Canad. J. Psychol.*, 1956, 10, 13.

concentrated fashion about anything. In fact, when their intelligence was tested, it was found to have deteriorated. They frequently suffered from visual and auditory hallucinations. When they emerged from their incarceration, their perceptions of their surroundings were impaired. Objects appeared blurred and unstable; straight edges, such as those of walls and floors, looked curved; distances were not clear; and sometimes the surroundings moved and swirled round them, causing dizziness.

In another rather similar experiment, the observers were kept in a completely silent room.[31] Here few hallucinatory phenomena were experienced. But after a period of sleepiness, there was again an increasing disturbance of thought, beginning with loss of power of concentration, and progressing in some cases to complete disorganization. Thoughts became incoherent, and the observers developed erroneous ideas about their own bodies including feelings of unreality and depersonalization. These were accompanied by growing anxiety leading to states of panic such that they were compelled to give up the experiment. But no after effects were noticed.

Somewhat similar phenomena were experienced by observers who placed themselves in the tank type of respirator used for poliomyelitis patients.[32] In these, they were kept motionless, and could perceive little of their surroundings. They experienced hallucinations and loss of concentration, accompanied sometimes by acute anxiety such that many of them could not endure the experience for more than thirty-six hours. Similar hallucinatory phenomena have been experienced by poliomyelitis patients themselves, and also by patients immobilized for fractures and cardiac disorders, when their environment was restricted and monotonous. . . .

Recent studies have indicated that the behaviour of infants may be affected if they are kept for a period of time in surroundings which lack variation.[33] The infants were under seven months of age, and were in hospital for periods of one to two weeks. On removal from hospital, they appeared to be almost unaware of objects and people, even their mothers, and spent their time continually gazing around them with blank and bewildered expressions on their faces. This behaviour might continue for a few hours, or as much as two days. It did not appear while they were in hospital unless they were moved from one ward to another. The behaviour seems to have been caused by their prolonged exposure to monotonous and unchanging surroundings in the hospital, where they could see little, and were seldom lifted up and played with.

[31] Smith, S. and Lewty, W. "Perceptual Isolation Using a Silent Room," *Lancet,* 1959, ii, 342.

[32] Leiderman, H., et al., "Sensory Deprivation," *A.M.A. Arch. Internal Medicine,* 1958, 101, 389.

[33] Schaffer, H. R., "Objective Observations of Personality Development in Early Infancy," *Brit. J. Med. Psychol.,* 1958, 31, 174.

Thus apparently they became as it were rigidified and set in the unchanging perceptual environment. When they were moved, this rigid environment was disrupted; and they had difficulty in adapting to the change and becoming orientated to the more normal type of varying surroundings. Hence their prolonged inspection of these. Moreover, the resulting stress often produced disorders of eating and sleeping.

Thus we must conclude that normal consciousness, perception, and thought, can be maintained only in a constantly changing environment. When there is no change, a state of "sensory deprivation" occurs; the capacity of adults to concentrate deteriorates, attention fluctuates and lapses, and normal perception fades. In infants who have not developed a full understanding of their environment, the whole personality may be affected, and readjustment to a normal environment may be difficult.

THEY TALK PAST EACH OTHER

Irving J. Lee

"It takes," says Thoreau, in the noblest and most useful passage I remember to have read in any modern author, "two to speak truth—one to speak and another to hear."—Robert Louis Stevenson, "Truth of Intercourse," *Virginibus Puerisque,* J. M. Dent & Sons, 1925, p. 32.

HOW MISUNDERSTANDING HAPPENS

THE ONE THING people tend to take for granted when talking to others is that they understand each other. It is rare, indeed, in a meeting to have someone hold up his own argument long enough to say, "I think you said . . . Did you?" or "Was I right in thinking you meant . . .?" We found people ever so eager to parry what a man says without ever wondering whether *that* is what the man said.

In the give-and-take of talk things go fast, and one is so busy organizing his reply that he doesn't take the time to make sure he knows what he is replying to. This is unfortunate because it often means that, instead of talking with others, people talk past or by-pass each other.

Note some by-passings.

1. The British Staff prepared a paper which they wished to raise as a matter of urgency, and informed their American colleagues that they wished to "table it." To the American staff "tabling" a paper meant putting it away in a drawer and forgetting it. A long and even acrimonious argument ensued before both parties realised that they were agreed on the merits and wanted the same thing.[1]

2. I remember a worrisome young man who, one day, came back from the X-ray room wringing his hands and trembling with fear. "It is all up with me," he said. "The X-ray man said I have a hopeless cancer of the stomach." Knowing that the roentgenologist would never have said such a thing, I asked, "Just what did he say?" and the answer was on dismissing him, the roentgenologist said to an assistant, "N. P." In Mayo clinic cipher this meant "no plates," and indicated that the X-ray man was so satisfied

Reprinted from Irving J. Lee, *How to Talk with People* (New York: Harper & Row, Copyright 1952), pp. 11–26. By permission of Harper & Row, Publishers, Inc.

[1] Winston Churchill, "The Second World War," Vol. III, Book II, *The New York Times,* February 28, 1950, p. 31.

with the normal appearance of the stomach on the X-ray screen that he did not see any use in making films. But to the patient, watching in an agony of fear for some portent of disaster, it meant "nothing possible:" in other words that the situation was hopeless![2]

3. A foreman told a machine operator he was passing: "Better clean up around here." It was ten minutes later when the foreman's assistant phoned: "Say, boss, isn't that bearing Sipert is working on due up in engineering pronto?"

"You bet your sweet life it is. Why?"

"He says you told him to drop it and sweep the place up. I thought I'd better make sure."

"Listen," the foreman flared into the phone, "get him right back on that job. It's got to be ready in twenty minutes."

. . . What [the foreman] had in mind was for Sipert to gather up the oily waste, which was a fire and accident hazard. This would not have taken more than a couple of minutes, and there would have been plenty of time to finish the bearing. Sipert, of course, should have been able to figure this out for himself—except that something in the foreman's tone of voice, or in his own mental state at the time, made him misunderstand the foreman's intent. He wasn't geared to what the foreman had said.[3]

4. Lady recently ordered some writing paper at a department store and asked to have her initials engraved thereon. The salesgirl suggested placing them in the upper right-hand corner or the upper left-hand corner, but the customer said no, put them in the center. Well, the stationery has arrived, every sheet marked with her initials equidistant from right and left and from top and bottom.[4]

5. In a private conversation with Mr. Molotov, it became apparent that another difficult misunderstanding in language had arisen between ourselves and the Russians. At the San Francisco Conference when the question of establishing a trusteeship system within the United Nations was being considered, the Soviet delegation had asked Mr. Stettinius what the American attitude would be toward the assumption by the Soviet Union of a trusteeship. Mr. Stettinius replied in general terms, expressing the opinion that the Soviet Union was "eligible" to receive a territory for administration under trusteeship. Mr. Molotov took this to mean we would support a Soviet request for a trusteeship.[5]

In each case a word or phrase or sentence was used one way by the speaker and interpreted in another way by the listener. This is possible because words are versatile. Except for those intended for highly specialized purposes (like tetrasporangium, icosahedron, bisulfite), it is not unusual to find most words put to rather varied uses. A seventh-

[2] Walter C. Alvarez, *Nervousness, Indigestion and Pain,* Paul B. Hoeber, Inc., 1943, p. 74.

[3] *The Foreman's Letter,* National Foreman's Institute, Inc., February 8, 1950, p. 3.

[4] "The Talk of the Town," *The New Yorker,* January 28, 1950, p. 21. Reprinted by permission. Copyright, 1950, The New Yorker Magazine, Inc.

[5] James F. Byrnes, *Speaking Frankly,* Harper & Brothers, 1947, p. 96.

grade class in English was able to make up thirty sentences in which the word "set" was used differently each time. Even "word" is listed in sixteen different ways in *The American College Dictionary*.

The naïve speaker of a language usually has the feeling that, in general, words have a meaning, and he is seldom conscious of the great "area" of meaning for all except highly technical words. It is in this respect that the student's observation first needs widening and sharpening. . . . He must be made aware, for example, that the statement "The children did not *count*" can mean that they did not *utter the words* for the numbers in a series, or that the children *were not considered*. Ordinarily we just don't believe without considerable careful examination that for the five hundred most used words in English (according to the Thorndike *Word Book*) the Oxford Dictionary records and illustrates from our literature 14,070 separate meanings.[6]

At different times the same words may be used differently.

When Francis Bacon referred to various people in the course of his *Essays* as *indifferent, obnoxious*, and *officious*, he was describing them as "impartial," "submissive," and "ready to serve." When King James II observed that the new St. Paul's Cathedral was *amusing, awful*, and *artificial*, he implied that Sir Christopher Wren's recent creation was "pleasing, awe-inspiring, and skilfully achieved." When Dr. Johnson averred that Milton's *Lycidas* was "*easy, vulgar*, and therefore *disgusting*," he intended to say that it was "effortless, popular, and therefore not in good taste."[7]

The role of experience also affects the varieties of usage. Brander Matthews provided an example from a dinner-party conversation:

The second topic . . . was a definition of the image called up in our several minds by the word *forest*. Until that evening I had never thought of forest as clothing itself in different colors and taking on different forms in the eyes of different men; but I then discovered that even the most innocent word may don strange disguises. To Hardy forest suggested the sturdy oaks to be assaulted by the woodlanders of Wessex; and to Du Maurier it evoked the trim and tidy avenues of the national domain of France. To Black the word naturally brought to mind the low scrub of the so-called deer forests of Scotland; and to Gosse it summoned up a view of the green-clad mountains that towered up from the Scandinavian fiords. To Howells it recalled the thick woods that in his youth fringed the rivers of Ohio; and to me there came back swiftly the memory of the wild growths bristling up unrestrained by man, in the Chippewa Reservation which I had crossed fourteen years before in my canoe trip from Lake Superior to the Mississippi.

[6] Charles C. Fries, "Using the Dictionary," *Inside the ACD*, October, 1948, p. 1.
[7] Simeon Potter, *Our Language*, Pelican Books, 1950, p. 116.

Simple as the word seemed, it was interpreted by each of us in accord with his previous personal experience.[8]

This conclusion about the range and possible uses of a word is easily verified. When it is forgotten, a listener just as easily comes to believe that (1) there is but one way to use a word—his—and (2) the speaker is doing with his words what the listener would were the listener doing the talking.

Can you see these beliefs at work in the examples given above?

In short, what *you* understand by any word or statement may not be what someone else intends to say. In a way, this is so obvious that most of us feel no obligation to think more about it. However, when one is aware of the fact it does not necessarily follow that he will act in terms of it. And there is some evidence that, unless people can be made sensitive to the possibility of by-passing, they make only meager efforts to stop it.

IT TAKES TWO TO MAKE COMMUNICATION

I have no wish here to give comfort to the bore who gets so much pleasure squelching discussions with his defiant "Define your terms." His maneuver results in shifting the burden in communication to the other fellow. Both must be brought into the act. We would have the listener work just a bit, too. So we urge him to state his notion of what was being said. Incidentally, that bore may sometimes be routed with this: "What definition of my words have you in mind? Perhaps we are thinking together after all." . . .

It is helpful to think of the radio in this. The performer in the studio can talk his heart out, but if the man in the easy chair is tuned in elsewhere it really makes no difference what is being said. Unless the receiver is on same wave length, the character of what is sent out hardly governs the communication process.[9]

This is not to imply that a speaker cannot help by putting what he has to say in clear, listenable language. Anything he does to define, simplify, amplify, illustrate, is all to the good. But it is only part of the process. The listener has a job to do, too. He must make the effort to come to terms with the speaker to keep from assuming that he in-

[8] Brander Matthews, *These Many Years: Recollections of a New Yorker*, Charles Scribner's Sons, 1917, pp. 287–288. Quoted from the essay by Allen Walker Read, "Linguistic Revision as a Requisite for the Increasing of Rigor in Scientific Method," read at the Third Congress on General Semantics, July 22, 1949.

[9] This image is well developed in the article by Charles T. Estes, "Speech and Human Relations in Industry," *The Quarterly Journal of Speech*, April, 1946, pp. 160–169.

evitably knows what the speaker has in mind. At the very least he might temper his arrogance with a question now and then just to make sure.

It takes two to make communication.

ARE YOU ON HIS COMMUNICATION LINE?

The preceding pages of this chapter were mimeographed and given to three groups, one meeting for study of the Bible, one considering matters of policy in a business corporation, and one working on problems in the administration of a college fraternity. Every member of each group read a portion out loud. We then talked about the main point—it takes two to make communication. We agreed that this was rather simple stuff and that we would try to talk with the possibility of by-passing in mind. We agreed, further, that no one of us would be insulted if asked to clarify or "talk some more" on any doubtful point. Nor would anyone feel hesitant about trying to get on the same wave length with anyone else. We gave each a small card with the inscription, "Are you on *his* communication line?"

What happened?

In each case the business of the meeting was slowed down. Only half as many items on the agenda could be covered. There was a certain amount of unfruitful wrangling about small points. Some members became tongue-tied in the face of so much freedom. Others became impatient with what seemed a waste of time, this trying to get to the speaker. The first sessions were always the worst. Most members felt comfortable only after the second or third.

And then we came upon something interesting. A man was being listened to. He found that others were actually waiting until he finished. He felt flattered in turn by the fact that another was trying to reach him rather than argue at him. He found himself trying to make his points so that his hearers would have less trouble with them. They were trying harder to read the cards he was putting on the table. The ornery member, normally so quick to doubt, stayed to question. The timid member found that the social pressure about the participation was all on his side.

We are inclined to think that the long-run results were worth the time and trouble.

THE PURIST'S DOGMA

In a number of experimental discussion groups generous enough to submit to such instruction there was a curious resistance to this seemingly obvious doctrine. I would be asked questions like these: Do you mean to say that a word doesn't have some definite, accurate meaning of its own regardless of the person who uses it? Isn't there a right or correct use for each word? If somebody fails to use a word exactly isn't he violating some rule in rhetoric or grammar? . . .

Regardless of the source, they used this dogma as the basis for a theory of their own about the cause of misunderstanding. If a speaker didn't use a word correctly it was only natural if a listener who did know the exact meaning was misled. Just get people to use words in their right meaning and then everyone will understand everyone else.

Indeed, this might be a way—but how can we do it? Who has the authority to declare *the* correct use and who has the time to learn it? There are more than 600,000 words in the Merriam-Webster una-bridged dictionary and perhaps half as many more in the technical vocabularies of medicine, engineering, law, etc. And when the diction-ary gives several meanings, which is *the* one? . . .

And what is more crucial, why do we look at words alone? Are words not most often used with other words in phrases, clauses, sen-tences? May not the setting affect the word?

We tried to get around this ill-advised zeal for exactness by sug-gesting that a word might be compared with a tool which can be used in a variety of ways. Thus, a screwdriver might be designed to drive screws, but once available it can be used to stir paint, jimmy a tight window, or, lacking any other weapon, to defend oneself with. You might, if you wish, insist that the screw function is the "right" or "cor-rect" one and that a pistol is a much more effective weapon. But your insistence will hardly stop me from using the screwdriver in these other ways if I find it convenient or necessary to do so. . . .

Within limits, especially in technical disciplines, it is possible to standardize word usage. One is usually safe in assuming that the workers in specialized areas will conform to some established, stipu-lated word usages. In the military establishment and in legal affairs, for example, it is often possible as well as necessary to insist that par-ticular words be used in particular ways.

Once outside the range of the specialist's interests, however, we are wise if we expect words to be used variously. A speaker's concern at any moment is not to use a word but to make a statement. In his eagerness to speak his piece he is more concerned with his continuous expression than with his total effect. If he happens to range outside his listeners' conventional usage, they will get nowhere lamenting his lexi-cographical heresy. And if they do not get to his usage they are likely to assume that he said what he never intended to.

We have come to see wisdom in this advice: Never mind what words mean. What did *he* mean?

It may take time to find out what a man means. It may demand a patient listening and questioning. It may be an unexciting effort. But it should help to bring people into an area of awareness which they are too often on the outside of. Mr. Justice Jackson's experience in a situation more momentous than anything we were exposed to adds to our confidence in the advice:

It was my experience with the Soviet lawyers at Nurnberg that the most important factor in collaboration with the Soviet was patiently and persistently to make sure, when a proposition is first advanced, that it is thoroughly understood and that both sides are using their words to express the same sense. When this was done, the Soviet lawyers kept their agreements with us quite as scrupulously as American lawyers would. They may or may not regard that as a compliment, but my intentions are good. But it was my experience that it took infinite patience with them, as they thought it took infinite patience with us, to get to a point where there was a real meeting of minds as distinguished from some textual abstract formula which both could accept only because concretely it meant nothing or meant different things to each. And I have sometimes wondered how much misunderstanding could have been avoided if arrangements between the two countries had not often been concluded so hurriedly, in the stress of events, that this time-consuming and dreary process of reducing generalities to concrete agreements was omitted.[10]

[10] Excerpt from address by Mr. Justice Robert H. Jackson at the Bar Dinner of the New York County Lawyers' Association, December 8, 1949.

THE RELATIONSHIP OF OPINIONS AND INFORMATION

ROBERT E. LANE AND DAVID O. SEARS

THE SAME "BIT" OF INFORMATION is highly useful in some minds—useless in others. The difference, of course, lies in how it is connected to other information, opinions, values. The connecting process is nothing other than *thinking*, something we must touch on briefly here.

One of the things that will make a bit of information useful is *familiarity with an appropriate concept* or category to put it in; without that it may not be noticed, for it may not have much meaning. A man sees in the papers that a local utility has raised its prices and the significance is limited to his regret over his larger outlay. If he is aware of the concept "monopoly" (and 64 per cent of the public has a rough understanding of the meaning of this term—AIPO 6/10/50)[1] there is the possibility of an enlarged understanding. Another man sees the federal government undertake a new service for dependent mothers. If he is among the 36 per cent of the public that can define the term "welfare state," he can more easily put this new bit of information into a framework with broader meaning, and generalize its significance. Thus, the understanding of a wide variety of concepts is, perhaps, the first step in putting information to use.

The comprehension of such concepts, of course, is a product of education and interest. On this latter score, the focus of interest of the public is reflected by the fact that in a 1950 test the three best understood concepts and the three least understood concepts, with the percentages of the public able to define them, were as follows:

Flying saucers	94%
Universal military training	75
Bookie	68
Reciprocal trade agreements	29
Bipartisan foreign policy	26
Point Four	5
(AIPO 6/10/50)	

Reprinted from Robert E. Lane and David O. Sears, "Opinion Without Information," Chapter VI in *Public Opinion* (Englewood Cliffs: Prentice-Hall, Inc., 1964), pp. 66–71. By permission of Prentice-Hall, Inc.

[1] AIPO is the American Institute of Public Opinion.

But conceptual clarity implies more than familiarity with a term, or approximating a dictionary definition; it may also imply *concept formation*. What shall we do, for example with the concept "good citizen," mixing, as it does, an evaluative component with an understanding of a social role? Lane asked his sample of working-class men to say what they thought the term meant. Everybody "knew," but everybody had a different definition, some seeing it as meaning a good, honest, sincere man, others as a friendly person who helped in common neighborhood tasks, others as a good family man, others as a person who fulfilled his political duties faithfully, and still others as a person who did not criticize society. These men were faced with two problems, each illustrating an aspect of conceptualization in political discourse. First, they were confronted with the fact that there is no consensus on the citizen's role in Eastport, where they lived, just as there may be no consensus on the meaning of, say, "imperialism" in international society. It is not necessarily the case that for every word there is an agreed upon referent, something "out there" for which the word is an appropriate symbol. Under these circumstances, everyone creates his own and a babble of voices may result. Political argument and thought as often founder on this obstacle as on the obstacle created by poverty of information.

And second, even if everyone knew exactly what "citizen" meant, there were differences in evaluation, due to the different values each brought to the problem. Value clarity is as important as empirical clarity (defining real world phenomena) in political thinking. It is just as important to ask "What do you mean by 'good'?" as it is to ask "What do you mean by 'citizen'?" Concept formation and concept clarity have at least these two aspects, the empirical and the evaluational.

Third, there is the problem of *concept attainment*, that is, assigning instances to a category or concept.[2] Is Thomas Jefferson a good citizen? Is Aaron Burr? Is John Doe? Are you? A good definition makes it easier, but it often is very difficult, particularly when an object can "earn" concept attainment in several alternative (disjunctive) ways. One strategy is to take the several criteria of the definition and demand evidence enough on each of them to allow some assignment. But what is enough evidence? How much evidence on a person's loyalty is needed to assign him as a "good citizen" to a sensitive job in the Department of Defense? Another way is to look for patterns or consistencies in the various criteria. For example, a person is likely to be a regular voter if he volunteers to canvass in an election, because voting almost always goes along with canvassing (but not vice versa). A third test, not a very good one but often all there is, is the test by con-

---

[2] The following discussion relies upon some of the formulations in Jerome S. Bruner, Jacqueline J. Goodnow, and George A. Austin, *A Study of Thinking* (New York: Wiley, 1956), particularly pp. 17–22.

sensus. "Such categories as 'good citizens' or 'decent fellow' are often in effect consensually validated."[3] And finally, particularly in such emotional areas as patriotism and citizenship, there is a purely subjective test, an inner feeling of certainty. Such "tests" are incapable of disproof, of course, and are expressive in their nature. The degree to which any given public relies upon this fourth kind of test is a measure of its unreadiness for the burden of effective citizenship.

If a person has some information and some more or less clear concepts into which it fits, he is ready to do a little political thinking. His success along these lines depends a good deal on his ideas of causation, especially social causation. Answers to the question "Why?" are causal answers. Policies are advocated because people think certain laws or governmental acts will cause or bring about preferred events — say, prosperity. In this connection, perhaps the most important differences are to be found among those who rely upon (1) fate or chance, or (2) personal agents, "good" or "bad" leaders, or (3) impersonal circumstances or social forces. In asking his sample of working-class men, "what causes war" and "what causes poverty" and "what causes delinquency?" Lane found that relatively few Americans shrug their shoulders and blame "fate" or refer to "Divine providence"; that is the way of the traditional societies of the less developed areas and these societies' passive subjects. On the other hand, many tended to explain everything in terms of the personal qualities of political leaders, their greed, or their stupidity, or their sincerity. Such men also tended to blame poverty upon the poor. Personalized explanations of this kind were not too helpful, for they led up blind alleys when it came to discussions of reform and, moreover, opened up the possibility that change could only be achieved through some "Great Leader." On the other hand, those who saw wars as the products of, say, population pressures, or believed poverty to be caused by the working of an uncontrolled business cycle, opened up avenues of reform through the usual processes of a representative government adjusting a delicate economic mechanism or offering medical assistance to those in need. Those relying on these impersonal concepts of cause were not only the more intelligent, but also had a better command over their own impulses.[4]

Finally, if a man has a piece of information, some useful concepts and a grasp on the nature of social causation, there is still the context into which his information is placed. He may employ some well-formulated belief system to give the information "meaning"; that is, to draw inferences about what is going on and what should be done. Every-

[3] *Ibid.*, p. 19.
[4] Robert E. Lane, *Political Ideology: Why the American Common Man Believes What He Does* (New York: The Free Press of Glencoe, 1962), pp. 308–309.

one has some belief system references of this kind (democratic, socialist, isolationist, etc.). The big difference comes, as we have mentioned before, between those who use all information selectively to bolster a rigid belief system (dogmatists) and those more open to information which challenges their belief system.[5] A more open belief system, such as Lane found his respondents had, gave less help in interpreting events, but also it served less to block new information.

The value of information is often cumulative; within a given field of knowledge, each new "bit" gives added value to related "bits." Knowing the name of a candidate for President may be useless unless one also knows his party, because, for many people, the party label is a cue which tells them who is "for" him. Beyond that, a knowledge of what the candidate stands for may give his name and party additional meaning. In Elmira in 1948 a study found, however, that "only about one third of the voters are highly accurate in their perception of where the candidates stand on the issues," and that others misjudge at least one of four important issues on which the candidates could be assigned positions.[6] Thus they could not link issue and name. But the point can be made with "larger" decisions. Lane asked his sample of working-class men about their opinions on American policy toward the Soviet Union. The wiser respondents did three things. (1) They anticipated Russian responses to American policy, that is, they had an idea of "feedback"; (2) they placed the American policy in a historical framework, that is, they could embrace a longer time period and hence anticipate delayed reactions, and (3) they compared American policy with the policies of other nations; they used a comparative approach, finding, in this search process, alternatives to be weighed and considered.[7] As students of public opinion, therefore, we need to know not merely the extent of the public's information, but the structure of this information, the interrelationships among the informational "bits" which create a pattern of meaning and interpretation.

We have found the informational level of the American public to be rather low; somewhat less adequate to its tasks than has sometimes been imagined. But, as we have tried to show, the level of information possessed by a public achieves its significance in the uses to which it is put. Here lies the major problem of education for democracy, or, as it is now called, the socialization process. Pouring "civics" into the electorate won't help much (it won't be remembered long, either); teaching men how to use knowledge, how to conceptualize, appraise evidence, infer causality — there lies a task worthy of a great teacher.

[5] See Milton Rokeach, *The Open and Closed Mind* (New York: Basic Books, 1960).

[6] Bernard Berelson, Paul F. Lazarsfeld, and William N. McPhee, *Voting* (Chicago: University of Chicago Press, 1954), p. 233.

[7] Lane, *Political Ideology*, pp. 350–356.

OPINIONS OFTEN COME BEFORE INFORMATION
AND REASONS

There is something about this whole process of knowing and thinking about politics which has been treated indirectly on many occasions but now must be faced directly. Do people first decide who or what they are for, and then seek information and arguments to support that position? Or do they acquire information and after thinking about its implications, then decide who or what they are for? It is an interactive process, of course, going back and forth between preference and reason and, perhaps, changed preference, but the importance of inherited political party identification, the use of reference groups in framing an opinion, and the importance of special intra-psychic gratifications derived from certain opinions suggest that a very frequent order is: opinions first, information and reasons later. Now we have strong experimental evidence to support this.

Rosenberg has described two studies in which he implanted, by hypnotic induction, a reversal of the emotional feelings attached to a public issue. For example, one of his subjects had been against Negroes living in white neighborhoods. In the hypnotic induction, the subject was told, "When you awake, you will be very much in favor of Negroes moving into white neighborhoods. The mere idea of Negroes moving into white neighborhoods will give you a happy, exhilarated feeling."[8]

Rosenberg presents ample evidence to show that the hypnotic inductions were effective in reversing the directions of opinions on the issue. For example, this subject then genuinely favored Negroes living in white neighborhoods. More than that, Rosenberg showed that this change was a product of two separate changes in the subjects' thinking. First, they changed their *values* to correspond with their changed attitudes toward Negroes and whites living in the same neighborhood. Second, they changed their ideas of how these values could best be *implemented,* that is, put into practice. As a result, the organization of their thoughts and attitudes was changed by the hypnotic suggestion and a new system of ideas was created to support their changed outlook. In doing this they "discovered" many new arguments for integration which they had not thought about before.

Rosenberg's implantation of radical affective changes toward particular attitude objects was stronger and more rapid than is customary in political life. However, it has very clear implications for those cases in which people learn strong "feelings" (of favor or disfavor) about

[8] Milton J. Rosenberg, "An Analysis of Affective-Cognitive Consistency," in Carl I. Hovland and M. J. Rosenberg (eds.), *Attitude Organization and Change* (New Haven: Yale University Press, 1960).

some attitude object without knowing much about it, or without having much in the way of supporting knowledge. From Rosenberg's research, we can expect that such people will, over time, collect and develop cognitions which will bolster their preferences and will be consistent with them. In a sense, they will "rationalize" the unfavorable or favorable feeling they have by adducing reasons why it is a desirable position.

For example, many Southern white children grow up thinking that Negroes are morally and intellectually inferior, as a race, to Caucasians. These opinions have their origins, of course, both in parental opinions and in the dominant beliefs of the childhood social environment. They are reasonably strongly developed before the child reaches high school; i.e., before he is in an intellectual position to evaluate the matter on a scientific basis. As the child grows up, many challenges to this belief, and to the social system it creates, are issued, many, in particular, by the federal government or by the federal judiciary. The cognitive elaboration of these simple affective tendencies has, however, produced in the subsequent years a comprehensive political ideology concerning the constitutional basis of state vs. federal powers, and so forth. In time, therefore, the individual may well come to think that his position on segregation is based upon a rational consideration of the "constitutional questions." In fact, however, it is more likely to be based on the early learning of an intense affective opinion, and bolstered by the subsequent cognitive elaboration.

On face value, then, much public opinion would seem to be basically "irrational" in nature.

A SUMMARY OF EXPERIMENTAL RESEARCH IN ETHOS

KENNETH E. ANDERSEN AND THEODORE CLEVENGER, JR.

ALTHOUGH the number of quantitative studies employing the term *ethos* in their titles is small, related rubrics such as *credibility* and *prestige* encompass such a quantity and variety of research clearly related to this classical concept that a summary should be valuable to those undertaking further studies. The primary purpose of this paper is to provide such a summary. In this study *ethos* is defined as the image held of a communicator at a given time by a receiver—either one person or a group. The use of the words *communicator* and *receiver* is deliberate, for the writers have chosen to include studies of written and nonverbal communication as well as those involving a speaker-auditor relationship.

The major sections of this paper are summaries of experimental findings pertaining to (1) the influence of ethos upon the effect of the communication, (2) techniques for generating or changing ethos, and (3) measurements of one or more aspects of ethos and attempts to assess the relative levels of ethos of individuals or groups.

INFLUENCE OF ETHOS UPON THE INTENDED EFFECT OF THE COMMUNICATION

Experiments concerning ethos have dealt with many and varied topics: with the effects of differences in prestige, credibility, likeableness, and other variables upon attitudes toward political-social issues, upon evaluations of art and literature, and upon learning; with the relative effectiveness of majority and expert opinion and the relative susceptibility of the sexes, different age groups, and persons of various educational levels to *prestige* suggestion; and with the temporal effects and the permanency of the attitude change and the learning induced by different levels of ethos.

It is important to remember that these studies, which arise from such fields as psychology, speech, sociology, and education, are quite diverse in origin, that many of the experimenters did not use rhetorical

Reprinted with slight revisions from Kenneth E. Andersen and Theodore Clevenger, Jr., "A Summary of Experimental Research in Ethos," *Speech Monographs*, XXX (June, 1963), 59-78. By permission of the Speech Association of America.

terminology, and that many of them also did not perceive a relationship between their studies and ethos. Studies are included, however, if the independent variable is a difference in treatment which is basically related to ethos and if the dependent variable is some measurement which is basically a communication effect index.

Theoretical and Methodological Differences

Studies differ so much in the definition of ethos and in certain other theoretical and methodological features that an analysis of these distinctions is a necessary preliminary to reporting the experiments.

1. Fixed ethos vs. congruity hypothesis

In most studies the ethical element is treated as relatively fixed in value during the communication act, and persuasion is construed as the linking of a proposition with an *approved* source for a positive effect or a *disapproved* source for a negative one.[1] However, in some recent studies, especially those using semantic differential measurement, ethos is regarded as flexible, because during the act of communication alterations in the image of the speaker may be caused either by the sender's propositions or by other situational factors.[2]

2. Ethos assumed vs. ethos measured

Early studies of ethical effects commonly followed the pattern of employing two sources (such as Franklin Roosevelt and Herbert Hoover) assumed to differ greatly in credibility, prestige, or some other ethical component and then comparing the attitude change for Group I, which received the message credited to the first source, with that for Group II, which received the same message except that it was ascribed to the second source.[3] This method assumes that for the group of subjects in question, the experimenter can determine intuitively the relative levels of ethos of the given sources. Recent studies, in contrast, have tended to measure ethos. Experimenters have either selected their sources on the basis of pretests of credibility or chosen them arbitrarily and then checked for credibility differences by direct measurement after

---

[1] Such as John Highlander, "Audience Analyzer Measurements and Informational Effects of Speaker Variables in Radio Talks," unpubl. diss. (Wisconsin, 1953); Franklyn Haiman, "An Experimental Study of the Effects of Ethos in Public Speaking," unpubl. diss. (Northwestern, 1948); *SM*, XVI (Sept., 1949), 190–202.

[2] Such as Charles Osgood, George Suci and Percy Tannenbaum, *The Measurement of Meaning* (Urbana: University of Illinois Press, 1957); Erwin Bettinghaus, "The Operation of Congruity in an Oral Communication Situation," unpubl. diss. (Illinois, 1959).

[3] Such as Helen Lewis, "Studies in the Principles of Judgments and Attitudes: IV. The Operation of 'Prestige Suggestion,'" *Journal of Social Psychology*, XIV (1941), 229–256.

the completion of the experiment.[4] The last of these techniques, of course, is valid only if one is willing to espouse the fixed ethos model; for if the image of the speaker may change during the speech, a measurement rendered after the address may be quite deceptive concerning ethos at the outset.

3. Topic-oriented vs. topic irrelevant ethos

The assumption for the majority of the studies apparently is that the prestige, the credibility, or some other ethical characteristic of the speaker varies from one topic to another. Thus, in most of the studies of *expert* opinion the authorities were selected because they were reputed to be well informed on the topic of the experimental message.[5] Some studies, on the other hand, seem to be based on a concept of generalized credibility and to discount or ignore the possibility that the prestige varies from topic to topic.[6]

4. Average vs. individual measure

Although the assumption in most studies is that the experimental group as an entity places the communicator at a certain level of prestige,[7] in some studies ethos is regarded as differing from one subgroup to another, and data are treated separately for such variables as sex, occupation, educational status, and political affiliation.[8] A few studies even consider the prestige of the source in respect to each individual auditor.[9] Whereas in the first two types of experiment the usual statistical test is for the significance of difference between means, in studies of the individual auditor the common method is correlation.

[4] Such as Muzafer Sherif, "An Experimental Study of Stereotypes," *Journal of Abnormal and Social Psychology*, XXIX (1935), 371–375; Herbert Kelman and Carl Hovland, " 'Reinstatement' of the Communicator in Delayed Measurement of Opinion Change," *Journal of Abnormal and Social Psychology*, XLVIII (1953), 327–335.

[5] Such as Malcolm Moos and Bertram Koslin, "Prestige Suggestion and Political Leadership," *Public Opinion Quarterly*, XVI (1952), 77–93; Irving Lorge with Carl Curtis, "Prestige, Suggestion and Attitudes," *Journal of Social Psychology*, VII (1936), 386–402.

[6] Such as Clare Marple, "The Comparative Susceptibility of Three Age Levels to the Suggestion of Group Versus Expert Opinion," *Journal of Social Psychology*, IV (1933), 176–186.

[7] Such as Raymond Bernberg, "Prestige Suggestion in Art as Communication," *Journal of Social Psychology*, XXXVIII (1953), 23–30; William Michael, Bernard Rosenthal, and Michael DeCamp, "An Experimental Investigation of Prestige-Suggestion for Two Types of Literary Material," *Journal of Psychology*, XXVIII (1949), 303–323.

[8] Such as Helen Lewis, *loc. cit.*

[9] Such as Herbert Birch, "The Effect of Socially Disapproved Labeling upon a Well-Structured Attitude," *Journal of Abnormal and Social Psychology*, XL (1945), 301–310; David Cole, " 'Rational Argument' and 'Prestige-Suggestion' as Factors Influencing Judgment," *Sociometry*, XVII (1954), 350–354.

5. *Extent of audience analysis*

Finally, the studies differ in that some examine audience characteristics, whereas others do not. Both approaches have interpretative hazards as well as distinctive advantages. In studies which assess the effect upon attitude change of such audience properties as sex, age, and educational level it is also possible (although infrequently done) to investigate the interaction of ethos with each of the audience variables. Thus, a study in which two levels of prestige are employed with an audience of men and women can include data on the effect of prestige level upon attitude change (ignoring sex), the difference in the persuasibility of the sexes (ignoring prestige), and differences in the relative susceptibility of the two sexes to prestige and nonprestige communication (the interactions). Careful interpretation, however, is necessary: First, the experimenter must distinguish over-all persuasibility differences between the sexes (main effect of sex) from prestige-suggestibility (the interaction). Second, where prestige is taken with reference to the entire sample of subjects, he must note the possibility of confounding prestige level with sex—that is, a source may not have the same prestige for the two sexes, and this difference may result in a spurious sex-by-prestige level interaction if prestige level is measured as a group average. Thus, some of the results seeming to show greater prestige-persuasibility for women than for men may have been products of concealed differences in the prestige level of the source for the two sexes.

Within the limits of the five methodological distinctions described above, the studies of the effects of ethos present a reasonably harmonious body of findings. In the following pages those studies employing the conception of a fixed ethos model will be presented first, and the limited number employing the congruity model will follow.

Studies Assuming That Ethos Is Fixed

A number of studies which employ the relatively common fixed ethos model indicate that certain ethical factors can produce changes in attitude toward political and social issues. Arnett, Davidson, and Lewis found that a group of graduate students shifted significantly toward agreement with graduate educators on Harper's test of liberalism.[10] The study was conducted without a control group, however, and during the lapse of four weeks between the two administrations of the test, factors other than prestige may have operated to produce the observed shifts.

Birch studied the effect of political labels of *Fascist* or *Communist* and *Reactionary* or *Liberal* on college students' judgments of two state-

[10] Claude Arnett, Helen Davidson, and Hallett Lewis, "Prestige as a Factor in Attitude Changes," *Sociology and Social Research*, XVI (1931), 49–55.

ments. No significant differences in preference for the two statements were observed, but this conclusion may be misleading. The fact that ninety-nine per cent of all subjects favored one statement over the other may have masked any possible prestige effect.

While the preceding studies were concerned with the effect of referential group or class prestige upon attitude change, a number of studies have been directed toward an investigation of the prestige of individuals. Saadi and Farnsworth found greater acceptance for dogmatic statements which were attributed to well-liked persons than to the same assertions when attributed to disliked individuals.[11] Lorge and Curtis found a significant tendency for subjects to shift opinion toward the supposed position of a prestige source, but they found no significant negative shift when the proposition was linked with a disapproved source.

In apparent conflict with these findings are the results obtained by Lewis. She reported that college students remained relatively unchanged in the evaluation of statements and that they tried to explain away the "prestige source" through rationalization. Unhappily, the conclusions to the study show the bias of an author who quite evidently hoped to support an hypothesis: for example, she describes rank-order correlations of a magnitude of .50 as "high." This bias renders suspect the assertion that informal interviews with the subjects and free responses revealed that suggestion, when effective, usually redefined an ambiguous situation.

A more satisfactory design for testing a similar hypothesis was that employed by Moos and Koslin, who discovered that vague quotations were those which were the most likely to be influenced by attribution to differing sources.

Hastorf and Piper, using a variety of problems, studied the effects of supposed ratings of businessmen and educators on the attitudes of subjects. They found that all groups, including one which was instructed to duplicate its pretest responses and ignore the supposed ratings, shifted significantly.[12]

Smith found that printed propaganda statements when labeled as fact produced greater belief than when labeled as rumor. The success of the "fact" label, however, clearly varied with the prior attitude of the subject and with the relation of the alleged "fact" to truth.[13]

The objective of all of the above studies was to assess the effects of

[11] Mitchell Saadi and Paul Farnsworth, "The Degrees of Acceptance of Dogmatic Statements and Preferences for Their Supposed Makers," *Journal of Abnormal and Social Psychology,* XXIX (1934), 143–150.

[12] A. H. Hastorf and G. W. Piper, "A Note on the Effect of Explicit Instructions on Prestige Suggestion," *Journal of Social Psychology,* XXXIII (1951), 289–293.

[13] George Smith, "Belief in Statements Labeled Fact and Rumor," *Journal of Abnormal and Social Psychology,* XLII (1947), 80–90.

prestige upon judgment of political and social issues, and the method in all instances was to link a source with a proposition but to provide no message by which the source supported the proposition. A question of more immediate interest to students of speech is whether differences in the speaker's prestige significantly influence the persuasive outcome of a speech.

Haiman presented to three groups a tape recorded speech variously attributed to Thomas Parran, Surgeon General of the United States; to Eugene Dennis, Secretary of the Communist Party in America; and to a "Northwestern University Sophomore." Not only was Parran rated significantly more competent than the other two, but also, as measured by the Woodward Shift-of-Opinion Ballot, his speech was significantly more effective in changing attitude than was either of the other two. The "Dennis" and the "Sophomore" speeches did not differ significantly.

Employing essentially the same techniques—a tape-recorded speech, differing introductions, and the Woodward ballot—Strother and Paulson in separate studies obtained results similar to Haiman's. Not only did Strother find significant differences in the persuasiveness of the "Parran" and the "Dennis" speeches, but also he noted that only those who thought they had been listening to Dennis wrote unfavorable comments concerning the speech techniques employed.[14] Paulson attributed a taped speech to a political science professor and to a student. For female auditors there was no significant difference in the effects of the "two" speeches, but among the male auditors the proportion of those shifting opinion was greater for the group which thought it had been addressed by the professor.[15]

The supposed differences in prestige level in the experiments cited above were assumed to be quite large, and the methods of establishing the prestige levels were straightforward and obvious. On the other hand, Hovland and Mandell, in an effort to assess subtler sources of the speaker's image, manipulated credibility through the *suggestion* of differing degrees of selfish interest and self-motivation. The nonsignificant difference in attitude change which the speakers produced was very small, but the audiences, apparently reacting to their presumed prejudices, rated the "unbiased source" as the significantly fairer and more honest of the two.[16] Since these evaluations were rendered after

---

[14] Edward Strother, "An Experimental Study of Ethos as Related to the Introduction in the Persuasive Speaking Situation," unpubl. diss. (Northwestern, 1951).

[15] Stanley Paulson, "Experimental Study of Spoken Communications; The Effects of Prestige of the Speaker and Acknowledgement of Opposing Arguments on Audience Retention and Shift of Opinion," unpub. diss. (Minnesota, 1952); SM, XXI (1954), 267–271.

[16] Carl Hovland and Wallace Mandell, "An Experimental Comparison of Conclusion Drawing by the Communicator and the Audience," *Journal of Abnormal and Social Psychology*, XLVII (1952), 581–588.

the speech, the initial ethos of the two sources, the point at which the "biases" of one began to emerge, or the ways in which the images of the two speakers changed during the speech are unknown.

A study by Kraus likewise suggests the possibility of evaluating indirect, implicative sources of ethos. Using pairs which were racially homogeneous and others which were racially heterogeneous, he compared whites with Negroes in respect to their persuasiveness in filmed discussions of segregation issues. The results indicated that arguments favorable to integration were more persuasive when advanced by the heterogeneous pairs, and Kraus explained the results in terms of differing levels of credibility.[17]

All the studies mentioned thus far have dealt with ethos as determined by the position or reputation of the source. Messages, if used, have been standardized so that the only variable was the introduction given the speaker.

Other studies, in contrast, have been designed so that some internal message elements have been varied systematically. Gilkinson, Paulson, and Sikkink, who incorporated or excluded authority quotations in two versions of the same speech, found that both versions engendered a significant shift in attitude with only a trend to favor the inclusion of authorities.[18] In another study Sikkink similarly employed quotations, but neither attitude shift nor ratings of convincingness showed significant differences.[19] While the use of authorities certainly has persuasive implications beyond the ethical dimension (and indeed the authors of these experiments apparently did not consider ethos the critical variable), the fact that the speaker was not evaluated as significantly more convincing when he used authorities suggests that citing reputable sources does not necessarily enhance ethos—as some theorists have suggested.

The two studies above are included within the fixed ethos model because the prestige of the authorities seemingly served directly as the basis for the shift in opinion, if any. Other experimenters varied the procedure by apparently employing authorities for the purpose of altering the image of the speaker; this altered image, in turn, was to serve as the warrant for the persuasive effect. (Possibly both effects could occur.) Studies of attitude changes dependent upon such attempts at artistic ethos are reported in a subsequent section of this paper.

[17] Sidney Kraus, "An Experimental Study of the Relative Effectiveness of Negroes and Whites in Achieving Racial Attitude Change Via Kinescope Recordings," unpubl. diss. (Iowa, 1959); *SM*, XXVII (1960), 87–88.

[18] Howard Gilkinson, Stanley Paulson, and Donald Sikkink, "Effects of Order and Authority in an Argumentative Speech," *QJS*, XL (1954), 183–192.

[19] Donald Sikkink, "An Experimental Study of the Effects on the Listener of Anticlimax Order and Authority in an Argumentative Speech," *Southern Speech Journal*, XXII (1956), 73–78.

Historically parallel to the study of the effects of ethos upon political and social attitudes has been the study of its effect upon judgments of literature, art, and matters of personal taste. In three experiments in Turkey and at Harvard Sherif found correlations of .45 to .53 between rankings of authors and subsequent rankings of passages to which authors' names were randomly attached. Sherif asserts that the name of the author exerts an influence upon ratings of passages.

Michael, Rosenthal, and DeCamp matched authors with prose and poetry passages and found little evidence of the effect noted by Sherif. Although they claimed methodological improvements over the Sherif study, their rank-of-summed-ranks technique actually produced a measure of dubious statistical reliability.[20] . . . The interpretation of their inconclusive results as evidence contrary to the Sherif hypothesis seems unjustified.

More recently, in India, Das, Rath, and Das studied the effect of author prestige upon evaluations of poetry. Working with quite small groups and crude statistical measures, they concluded that prestige influenced judgment greatly but that this effect was weakened when the factors of understanding and merit were stressed.[21]

Judgments of art seem to be similar. Data obtained by Farnsworth and Misumi displayed a trend indicating that recognition of the artist's name had some favorable effect on the evaluations of pictures.[22] In another experiment Bernberg found that positive and negative evaluations of alleged art critics significantly affected the judgments by artistically naive students with regard to seven of ten paintings.

Cole presented abstract finger paintings for discussion in small groups. In situations in which the art teacher presented judgments in opposition to those of the group, significant shifts occurred only when the teacher was present. A peer leader, to cite a second finding, secured significant shifts only when he also presented pseudo-rational arguments.

Again, similar effects have been found in the area of personal taste and perceptions. Duncker presented a story to nursery school children in which a fictional hero endorses a food actually less desirable than an alternative selection. The after-effect was decidedly positive—a large percentage of the children selected the endorsed food when given a choice. Over a period of twelve days, however, the selection of the less satisfying food declined to the level of a control group. Some of

---

[20] The problems in the use of a rank-of-summed-ranks technique are discussed by Roger Nebergall, "Some Applications of Measurement Theory to the Judgment of Speech Contests," unpublished paper read at the Central States Speech Association Conference, April 8, 1960.

[21] J. P. Das, R. Rath, and Rhea Das, "Understanding Versus Suggestion in the Judgment of Literary Passages," *Journal of Abnormal and Social Psychology*, LI (1955), 624–628.

[22] Paul Farnsworth and Issei Misumi, "Further Data on Suggestion in Pictures," *American Journal of Psychology*, XLIII (1931), 632.

the initial preference for the less desirable food was reinstated by recalling the story, but this effect degenerated very quickly.[23]

Donceel, Alimena, and Birch presented adults and high school and college students with personality descriptions of themselves. These supposedly came from tests and expert evaluations, but actually were determined by chance. Under mild suggestion a significant number of students accepted these statements as valid, and under strong suggestion all subjects yielded. They accepted as true the false descriptions of their personalities and reversed previous answers to questions in a personality test.[24]

Aveling and Hargreaves found *personal suggestion* capable of affecting performance in a variety of perceptual and psychomotor tasks, but they also secured evidence of strong negative suggestibility among some of their subjects.[25]

Although there is little reason to suppose that those elements of ethos which are designed to obtain attitude change are also capable of producing differences in learning, a small number of studies pertain to this possibility. Weiss taught responses to groups of students, one of which was told that the answers were untrue. No differences in learning occurred, but what was learned correlated with the attitude change which took place during the experiment.[26] Paulson found no significant differences in retention between high and low ethos sources, although certain audience variables did appear to be related to learning. Sikkink's results were substantially the same.

An experiment by Harms shows that cloze test scores are somewhat higher when the speakers are high in status than when they are low. The inferred reason for this result is that high-status speakers are more "comprehensible." A further result, secured through a differential analysis of listener groups, is that listeners respond with greater comprehension to those from their own class than to speakers from either a higher or a lower class.[27]

The above studies were concerned with the effects of the ethos of individual communicators. A smaller number of investigations have attempted to compare the effects of expert opinions with those produced by majority opinion.

[23] Karl Duncker, "Experimental Modification of Children's Food Preferences Through Social Suggestion," *Journal of Abnormal and Social Psychology,* XXXIII (1938), 489–507.

[24] Joseph Donceel, Benjamin Alimena, and Catherine Birch, "Influence of Prestige Suggestion on the Answers of a Personality Inventory," *Journal of Applied Psychology,* XXXIII (1949), 352–355.

[25] F. Aveling and H. L. Hargreaves, "Suggestibility With and Without Prestige in Children," *British Journal of Psychology,* XII (1921–1922), 53–75.

[26] Walter Weiss, "A 'Sleeper' Effect in Opinion Change," *Journal of Abnormal and Social Psychology,* XLVIII (1953), 173–180.

[27] Leroy Stanley Harms, "Social Judgments of Status Cues in Language," unpubl. diss. (Ohio State, 1959); *SM,* XXVII (1960), 87.

Using as a criterion the frequency with which the subjects reversed their preferences so as to conform to the prestige group, Moore measured the relative influence of majority and expert opinions upon judgments of grammar, ethics, and music. The two sources were about equally effective except with respect to grammar, where the majority opinion prevailed by a ratio of 10 to 7.[28] The primitive design of this experiment may have concealed other differences.

An experiment by Marple, who found that both the group and experts influenced opinions about solutions to seventy-five assorted problems, reinforced Moore's results. Majority opinion was roughly one-third more effective than expert opinion with students and roughly one-fifth more effective with adults.

With respect to religious beliefs, Burtt and Falkenburg discovered that opinions of both the majority and experts influenced judgments significantly, that expert (clerical) opinions tended to have greater influence than majority views in some matters of religious belief, and that a contrary tendency existed in other areas.[29]

Incidental findings of a number of studies bear upon the question of the relative susceptibility of various audience types to prestige as a means of suggestion. Within the narrow range which an undergraduate psychology class affords, Hovland and Mandell found that personality and intelligence were not related to prestige-suggestibility. Kersten reports a similar finding for intelligence,[30] but Wegrocki reports a tendency for intelligence to the negatively associated with prestige-suggestibility.[31] Strother discovered no shifts in opinion which correlated with either sex or the urban-versus-rural dimension, but he did find that members of the audience with initially neutral views on the speech topic were significantly more responsive to variations of ethos than were either the pro or the con groups. Studies by Kersten, by Paulson, and by Pross[32] obtained results confirming those of Strother.

Sikkink found that women rated the persuasiveness of all speeches significantly higher than did men, but that women were neither easier nor harder to influence than men. Cathcart also concluded that sex was not significantly related to persuasibility.[33] Pross reported some

[28] Henry Moore, "The Comparative Influence of Majority and Expert Opinion," *American Journal of Psychology*, XXXII (1921), 16–20.

[29] Harold Burtt and Don Falkenberg, Jr., "The Influence of Majority and Expert Opinion on Religious Attitudes," *Journal of Social Psychology*, XIV (1941), 269-278.

[30] Barbara Kersten, "An Experimental Study to Determine the Effect of a Speech of Introduction upon the Persuasive Speech that Followed," unpubl. thesis (South Dakota State College, 1958).

[31] Henry Wegrocki, "The Effect of Prestige Suggestibility on Emotional Attitudes," *Journal of Social Psychology*, V (1934), 384–394.

[32] Edward Pross, "A Critical Analysis of Certain Aspects of Ethical Proof," unpubl. diss. (Iowa, 1942).

[33] Robert Cathcart, "An Experimental Study of the Relative Effectiveness of Four Methods of Presenting Evidence," *SM*, XXII (1955), 227–233.

indication that women were the more suggestible, and Wegrocki also concluded that girls, as compared with boys, tended to be more suggestible and to react more strongly to sympathetic propaganda. Paulson found that women reacted more but retained less information. Freshmen, also according to Paulson, tended to shift less in response to the high ethos source than did upperclassmen, but there was no guarantee that the freshmen and the upperclassmen perceived the high ethos source in the same light. Cathcart found that education, speech training, and subject matter competence had no effect on persuasibility. The discovery of Aveling and Hargreaves of great differences in suggestibility on a number of perceptual and psychomotor tasks leads to speculation that two sharply divided groups, the suggestible and the contrasuggestible, may exist. They found no tendency, however, for suggestibility to correlate with any of a number of psychometric variables.

Marple found that high school and college students shift more than do adults.

A single study has illustrated the possibility of investigating the effects of audience size upon the relationship between ethos and attitude change. Knower compared the effect of delivering a speech in an audience situation with giving the speech to one auditor at a time. The speech in the individual situation was somewhat more effective, women were more influenced than men, and women speakers obtained greater attitude shifts than did men. In the audience situation, however, male speakers obtained greater shifts than did women.[34]

Most of the studies described above deal primarily with the immediate effects of prestige, credibility, and other ethical elements. Hovland and his associates, however, have investigated the temporal effects of the source upon persuasion. In one of these experiments Hovland and Weiss held all of the message elements constant except for factors which produced an impression of high credibility for one source and low credibility for another. The subjects exposed to the former stimulus shifted in significantly greater numbers on immediate posttests of attitude than did those receiving the message with low credibility. Over a period of one month the favorable effect, however, decreased, and the subjects exposed to the "inferior" source moved toward agreement with the attitudes expressed in it. Hovland postulated a "sleeper effect"—than in the absence of further stimuli agreement with high credibility sources decays while agreement with low credibility sources grows. The possible explanation is that the subject forgets the source but retains the information and the essential arguments.[35] In a specific test of the sleeper hypothesis, Kelman and

[34] Franklin Knower, "Experimental Studies of Changes in Attitudes: I. A Study of the Effect of Oral Argument on Changes in Attitude," *Journal of Social Psychology*, VI (1935), 315–347.

[35] Carl Hovland and Walter Weiss, "The Influence of Source Credibility on Communication Effectiveness," *Public Opinion Quarterly*, XVI (1961), 635–650.

Hovland found that a high ethos source, who was rated significantly fairer, better qualified to speak, and of sounder judgment than a supposedly low ethos source, produced significantly greater attitude shifts. Over a three-week period, however, the extent to which subjects agreed with the positive source decreased significantly, and the extent to which they agreed with the negative source increased nonsignificantly. Reinforcing the recall of the sources by playing back the introductions of the tape-recorded messages produced greater agreement with the high prestige speaker and less agreement with the one of low ethos in an experimental group than occurred in a control group which received no repetition of the stimuli.

In a variation of the above approach Weiss determined that a group exposed to a low credibility source showed less regression toward its original attitude than did a group exposed to a high credibility source.

Also supporting the sleeper effect is the finding that over a period of time those who originally disliked a communicator became slightly more positive toward him while those who had originally liked him became slightly less favorable (nonsignificant).[36] The results of Duncker's study of the effect of prestige suggestion upon children's food preferences also confirm the Hovland sleeper effect findings in respect to both the decline of the effect over time and the renewal of strength following reinstatement.

Studies Assuming That Ethos Is Variable

Diverse as the studies discussed above appear to be, they share a common model of ethos—that is, they are all based on the assumption that the speaker's image is relatively fixed throughout the period of communication. In sharp contrast with this view is the ethical model based on a congruity principle enunciated by Osgood.[37] Intended to explain many psychological functions, the congruity principle holds that an image (or meaning) depends upon the other concepts with which it is associated and thus is subject to perpetual change. Among the factors causing these variations are the successive parts of the message.

Drawing upon this generalized congruity hypothesis, Tannenbaum formulated predictions of attitude change toward communication sources and then compared these estimates with the results obtained when college students were exposed to written messages. Since the cor-

---

[36] Arthur Cohen, "Need for Cognition and Order of Communication as Determinants of Opinion Change" in *Order of Presentation*, eds. Carl I. Hovland et al. (New Haven: Yale University Press, 1957), pp. 79–97.

[37] Osgood, Suci, and Tannenbaum, *loc. cit.*; Charles Osgood and Percy Tannenbaum, "The Principle of Congruity in the Prediction of Attitude Change," *Psychological Review*, LXII (1955), 42–55.

relation was .91, the conclusion is that attitude changes of the college students in this experiment conformed to the congruity hypothesis.[38]

A study of the same hypothesis applied to public speakers showed that the congruity model predicted changes in attitude somewhat better than chance alone.[39] This study, however, failed to produce the goodness of fit observed in the Tannenbaum experiment.[40]

Bettinghaus hypothesized that the difference between these results was caused by the presence of a greater number of elements in the cognitive structure for oral than for written messages. Extending the congruity model to four elements—speaker, central proposition, speech composition, and delivery—he obtained results which fit his extended model significantly better than they do the two-element model (speaker and central proposition) employed in the earlier experiments.

GENERATING OR CHANGING ETHOS

Unlike the studies discussed in the preceding section, which typically attempted to assess the utility of a presumed or measured ethos, the experiments discussed below are concerned with the means of generating or altering a receiver's image of a communicator. These efforts, in general, fall into two categories: those which tried to establish extrinsic ethos by techniques employed before the message itself began, and those which attempted to create intrinsic ethos by techniques employed by the speaker during the presentation.[41]

Extrinsic Ethos

The following experiments deal with the generation or the modification of a communicator's image by stimuli which are not part of the actual presentation.

Since the ethos of the individual depends in part upon the reputation of the group to which he belongs, experiments concerning the alteration of group images are relevant to the concept of ethos. One such experiment showed that very short speeches produced immediate

[38] Percy Tannenbaum, "Initial Attitude Toward Source and Concept as Factors in Attitude Change Through Communication," *Public Opinion Quarterly*, XX (1956), 413–425.

[39] David Berlo and Halbert Gulley, "Some Determinants of the Effect of Oral Communication in Producing Attitude Change and Learning," *SM*, XXIV (1957), 10–20.

[40] Compare the results of Berlo and Gulley with those of Osgood, Suci, and Tannenbaum, p. 212.

[41] Extrinsic ethos is the image of the speaker as it exists prior to a given speech. Intrinsic ethos, comparable to Aristotle's artistic ethos, is the image derived from elements during the presentation of the speech, consciously or unconsciously provided by the speaker. In real life speech situations, the final ethos is a product of the interaction of extrinsic and intrinsic ethos.

attitude changes in favor of either China or Japan but that over a five-month period significant regression occurred toward the original attitudes.[42] Wegrocki found Roman Catholic school children were . . . quite persuasible to some but not all items in propaganda covering a wide range of topics. Other conclusions were that attitudes toward well-known individuals seemed about as subject to change as other attitudes and that reactions toward groups outside the students' immediate experience seemed especially subject to the influence of propaganda.

Closely related to the question of changing attitudes toward individuals is that of building an image. Annis and Meier set out to create an image of an unknown source through planted editorials which linked the source with certain opinions and actions. : . . As few as seven planted editorials generated the desired image, and most of the effects persisted over a period of four months.[43]

Berlo and Kumata studied the effect of a dramatic allegory. "The Investigator," in modifying images. Attitudes toward Joseph McCarthy, the subject of the satire, tended to become more favorable, while attitudes toward the source (the Canadian Broadcasting Company) and toward Congressional committees became significantly less favorable. The experimenters felt that the extreme one-sidedness of the presentation may have caused these "boomerang" effects."[44]

Using a single tape-recorded speech, Kersten compared two introductions, one of which employed techniques estimated by experts to focus attention on the speaker and his subject and to build the speaker's prestige and the other of which did not. The persons hearing the speech with the favorable introduction changed opinion significantly more than did those who heard no introduction or the poor one. The confounding involved in the simultaneous manipulation of prestige and attention-focussing elements makes it impossible to conclude that the enhanced prestige of the speaker was the source of the observed difference. Indeed, Pross found that an introduction stressing the character, the reputation, and the intelligence of the speaker added little to the persuasiveness of either "ethical" or "nonethical" forms of speech.

Neither Kersten nor Pross actually measured differences in ethos; they assumed that different introductions would affect the variable. The same is true of Highlander's experiment, which seems to show

[42] William Chen, "The Influence of Oral Propaganda Material upon Students' Attitudes," *Archives of Psychology*, XXIII (1933); "Retention of the Effect of Oral Propaganda," *Journal of Social Psychology*, VII (1936), 479–483.

[43] Albert Annis and Norman Meier, "The Induction of Opinion Through Suggestion by Means of 'Planted Content,'" *Journal of Social Psychology*, V (1934), 65–81.

[44] David Berlo and Hideya Kumata, "The Investigator: The Impact of a Satirical Radio Drama," *Journalism Quarterly*, XXXIII (1956), 287–298.

that variable levels of authoritativeness of the speakers do not affect either the likeableness of radio programs or the amount of information gained from them. In all such studies it is possible that the experimental treatments failed to take effect in the supposed manner.

Andersen constructed three introductions designed to establish varying levels of prestige and authoritativeness for speakers dealing with the farm problem. His conclusions were these: (1) Students perceived significant differences between a college student and a Professor of Agriculture or a Farm Extension Agent on two scales: (a) the evaluative and the dynamism dimensions of a semantic differential designed to measure ethos; (b) authoritativeness as estimated by a Likert-type scale. (2) The expected differences between the professor and the extension agent did not result except on the authoritativeness scale. (3) The more rhetorically sophisticated students seemed to perceive differences in ethos that the rhetorically naive students did not. (4) There was no proof that the variations in ethos and authoritativeness affected persuasiveness.[45]

A speech of introduction, one should note, creates special theoretical problems; for if the audience image of the introducer is low, this attitude through transfer may affect the ethos of the speaker. For instance, at the time of this writing, a laudatory introduction of a political candidate in the United States performed by James Hoffa or Fidel Castro might prove a serious detriment to persuasiveness. Since less obvious factors may also affect the experimental situation, it is conceivable that ethos may be more sensitive to such unforeseen and uncontrolled variables than it is to the verbal content of the introductions.

Intrinsic Ethos[46]

That changes in ethos result from hearing speeches seems clear from a study of the effect of a campaign speech by Thomas E. Dewey. Comparing ratings obtained before a speech with those recorded immediately afterwards, Thompson found that students raised their estimation of Dewey as a public speaker but did not change their opinions significantly concerning the soundness of his ideas and his acceptability as a candidate.[47]

Studies which have altered the presentational elements may be divided into those which have manipulated characteristics of the

[45] Kenneth E. Andersen, "An Experimental Study of the Interaction of Artistic and Nonartistic Ethos in Persuasion," unpubl. diss. (Wisconsin, 1961).

[46] *Intrinsic ethos* is defined in this study as the image of the speaker which is generated during the presentation of the message.

[47] Wayne Thompson, "A Study of the Attitude of College Students Toward Thomas E. Dewey Before and After Hearing Him Speak," *SM*, XVI (1949), 125–134.

manuscript and those which have altered such nonmanuscript stimuli as the speaker's appearance or his style of delivery.

A common type of study is the comparison of the effect of presenting both sides with the effect of giving but one—a distinction which seems to the writers to be ethically significant.[48] In one such investigation Hovland, Lumsdaine, and Sheffield found (1) that the "both sides" presentation was significantly more effective for subjects with a high school education when the weight of evidence clearly supported one side; and (2) that a one-sided presentation was more effective with subjects initially favoring the advocated view and with subjects who had not completed high school.[49]

Similarly, Paulson's experiment involved two speeches, one of which omitted opposing arguments and the other of which made the barest mention of them. Opinion changes did not differ significantly, but the "both sides" speech was significantly superior in respect to the amount of information which was obtained. Shanck and Goodman also tested reactions to propaganda which presented equal amounts of argument on both sides or one-sided pro or con arguments. That no significant difference was observed,[50] might be explained by the extreme subtlety of the propaganda.

Another rhetorical element which is sometimes held to carry ethical implications is the use of authority and citations of source. Three studies described earlier in this paper reported that the inclusion of authority did not increase persuasiveness.[51] Cathcart presented four versions of a speech with variations from form to form in respect to the amount of specific evidence and documentation. He found that the forms which supported but did not document contentions and which supported, documented, and specified that the sources cited were experts produced significantly greater shifts at the five per cent level than did the form which merely supplied generalizations. A fourth form which supported the assertions and documented fully but did not say that the cited sources were experts was not significantly more effective than the one which merely supplied generalizations. That such differences as were observed were attributable to nonethical considerations is suggested by the finding that none of the speeches

---

[48] The presentation of both sides of an issue is often treated as one aspect of ethical proof. The practice also has logical connotations. It is possible to consider the impact of the treatment of both sides on the image of the speaker and the impact of this image on persuasiveness as distinct from the logical value of the treatment and the resultant persuasiveness.

[49] Carl Hovland, Arthur Lumsdaine, and Fred Sheffield, *Experiments on Mass Communication:* Vol. III of *Studies in Social Psychology in World War II* (Princeton: Princeton University Press, 1949).

[50] R. C. Shanck and Charles Goodman, "Reactions to Propaganda on Both Sides of a Controversial Issue," *Public Opinion Quarterly*, III (1939), 107–112.

[51] See the studies previously cited by Sikkink, by Cole, and by Gilkinson, Paulson, and Sikkink.

differed in terms of the audience's evaluations of the speaker's competence, enthusiasm, or clarity of ideas.[52]

Ludlum constructed a speech in which he incorporated several elements designed to increase the credibility of the source. His techniques include the acknowledgment of opposing arguments, "leading thoughts rather than forcing," showing alleged facts to be consistent with known facts, showing material to be recent, and manifesting a "high degree of credibility" by means of self-praising statements. Comparing the persuasiveness of this speech with that of a "straight argumentative" address, he found the latter to be more effective.[53] Since he did not measure received ethos, the effect of the variables in the nonargumentative speech is unknown. Moreover, since all of the variables were incorporated in a single speech, it is impossible to isolate the effect of any one of them. If some of the techniques produced positive effects and others acted negatively, the effects may have counterbalanced one another. Thirdly, some of the self-praising statements in the nonargumentative speech may have had an effect quite different from that intended. Finally, argumentative technique may have an ethical dimension for college students, such as those whom Ludlum employed, with the result that the argumentative talk may well have produced a more favorable speaker image than did the speech employing an assortment of "conciliatory" techniques.

The experiment by Ludlum points up the importance of specifying carefully any differences in content between speeches intended to produce high credibility and those against which their effects are to be compared. This same consideration applies to an early experiment by Pross, who constructed four forms of a speech on a single topic. Two of these employed techniques of "ethical appeal" (as judged by speech experts) and the other two did not. Length was kept constant. The interpretation of Pross' nonsignificant findings is difficult, for matching the lengths necessitated the removal of material in order to make room for the ethical elements. As a consequence the two ethical speeches had almost no logical structure.

This investigation and other studies indicate a confusion in the use of the terms *ethos* and *ethical*. On the one hand, these terms are used to refer to the audience's image of the speaker, as when it is said that Parran is more credible or higher in ethos than is Dennis; on the other hand, certain types of speech content are labeled *ethical appeals*. For example, a speech which employs many self-references and conciliatory elements is described as higher in ethos content than an address which follows a straightforward proposition-and-proof format.

[52] The problem of separating the logical and the ethical effects of the same complex stimulus is again at issue. The writers believe that a complex stimulus may affect both logical and ethical proof and perhaps pathetic proof as well.

[53] Thomas Ludlum, "A Study of Techniques for Influencing the Credibility of a Communication," unpub. diss. (Ohio State, 1956).

Usually, when rhetoricians classify a speech content element as "ethical," they seem to mean that the elements *seem to the classifier* to be calculated to gain the good will of the audience or to enhance the speaker's ethos. In our present state of knowledge concerning audience response, such a judgment is at best only an educated guess. Therefore, when the results of the Pross and the Ludlum studies are cited in support of the proposition that ethical speeches are no more effective in inducing attitude change than are logical speeches, it should be specified very carefully that the results are based upon analysis of speech content and not upon the image of the speaker which the audience holds. The present writers as rhetorical critics believe that some of the Pross and Ludlum "ethical" speech techniques probably had decidedly negative effects on the ethos of the speaker. The basis of this judgment, of course, is intuitive, not empirical.

The message which an audience receives during a speech obviously involves more than verbal (manuscript) stimuli. Several studies indicate that nonverbal factors produce audience judgments concerning the speaker. Haiman found (1) that an audience rated a graduate male speaker higher in competence than it did an undergraduate male and two females; (2) that with content held constant, graduate speakers obtained higher rates of fairmindedness, sincerity, and likeableness than did undergraduates; (3) that in two experiments shifts of opinion within the audience were correlated positively with the speakers' competence ratings and with nothing else; and (4) that although variations in ratings of likeableness and physical attractiveness could be produced through changes in appearance and demeanor, significant changes in attitude did not result.

Many of the variables in the Haiman study are those associated with differences in social status. Harms has shown that, regardless of their own position, listeners in general assign high credibility to speakers of high social status and low credibility to those of low status. Such judgments occur even though the stimulus is nothing more than a short tape-recorded sample of speech. The Harms study further shows that listeners can discriminate class differences with rough accuracy and that they identify the low status speakers somewhat more readily than they do those of superior background.

Consistent with these results is the experimental finding that audiences may construct relatively complete assessments of a speaker's personality and physical characteristics on the basis of his voice. Other conclusions to this study were that personality, physical characteristics and occupation were likely to be perceived correctly, that consistency of response (right or wrong!) was a stronger tendency than accuracy of judgment, and that gross psychological characteristics were judged more accurately than physical features.[54]

[54] Gordon Allport and Hadley Cantril, "Judging Personality from Voice," *Journal of Social Psychology*, V (1934), 37–55; also in Hadley Cantril and Gordon Allport, *The Psychology of Radio* (New York: Harper and Row, 1935).

These findings suggest the plausibility of the "truth-will-out" theory regarding the action of subliminal, nonverbal stimuli upon the ethos of the speaker. As the theory goes, an insincere speaker's sophistry will betray itself through unconscious behaviors which act subliminally upon the auditors. An experiment by Hildreth, however, offers no confirmation for this hypothesis. Defining sincerity in terms of the speaker's expressed preference for one side of a controversial issue and using a large number of speakers who filmed speeches on both their preferred and their non-preferred sides, he discovered that audiences were unable to distinguish the sincere from the insincere speeches and that the ratings of the two types of speeches did not differ significantly in effectiveness. Rather, ratings of effectiveness and of *estimated* sincerity were positively correlated.[55] Unfortunately, methodological considerations render the results of the experiment inconclusive. Since the "sincere" speech was composed, practiced, and delivered first in all instances, the time allowed for composition was very brief, and the making of a film was presumably unfamiliar to a majority of the speakers, a number of factors were operating to enhance performance in the "insincere" presentation as contrasted with the "sincere" one.

Indeed, the role which subliminal perception may play in the establishment of ethos has been little clarified by experiments. Drawing upon the "hidden persuader" approach, Steiner found that placing visually superimposed words on a screen at subliminal intensity levels did not alter either the effectiveness of a filmed speech or the judgment of the sincerity of the speaker.[56]

Combining prior and intrinsic elements, Strother attempted to study a combination of factors. The addition of ethical techniques either singly or in combination did not significantly increase the persuasiveness of a low ethos source. However, as measured by a hostility scale, the combination of elements apparently surpassed a control speech in allaying hostility toward the low ethos source. . . .

In another investigation of combinations of variables Andersen used two tape-recorded speeches, both of which were attributed to three sources described in tape-recorded introductions. The principal results were these: (1) Despite great manuscript variations which speech experts predicted would produce different levels of ethos, the only significant differences between the two speeches were those measured on a dynamism scale. (2) The elements of artistic and inartistic ethos did interact significantly in producing the final image of the speaker. (3) The variations in ethos did not cause a significant difference in persuasiveness.

[55] Richard Hildreth, "An Experimental Study of Audiences' Ability to Distinguish Between Sincere and Insincere Speakers," unpubl. diss. (Southern California, 1953).

[56] George Steiner, "An Experimental Study of the Influence of Subliminal Cue Words on an Audience's Perception of a Filmed Speaker's Sincerity, Effectiveness, and Subject Matter," unpubl. diss. (Southern California, 1959); SM, XXVII (1960), 93–94.

MEASUREMENTS OF ETHOS AND ATTEMPTS TO
ASSESS THE RELATIVE DEGREES OF ETHOS

In a few instances the development of a measure of ethos has been the main goal of a research project, but more often the measurement of prestige, credibility, or some other ethical component has been ancillary to the study of such presumed results of ethos as preferences, attitude change, and information gain. The methods of measurement in both types of investigation are the same: (1) rankings, (2) sociograms, (3) "prestige indexes" obtained from attitude change data, (4) linear rating scales, (5) Thurstone-type attitude scales, and (6) devices similar to Likert scaling techniques, including the semantic differential.

Perhaps the most elementary method of determining differences among sources in respect to prestige, credibility, likeableness, etc., is to require subjects to arrange the sources in rank order. Sherif, for example, presented a list of sixteen authors to a group of undergraduates and asked them to rank the authors according to personal preferences for their writings. A month later the subjects were told to rank sixteen passages in respect to literary merit. Since all of the passages had been written by a single author not included in the list and since literary experts had judged all of them to be of equal merit, the only variable was the false attachment of a different author's name to each excerpt. Correlations between the two sets of ranks were held to represent the effects of "prestige." The replication of the study with similar results in three instances indicates the usefulness of the rank-order technique for simple experiments of this type. The method was to determine the rank order for individuals, to compute rank correlations for individuals, and to draw conclusions from the average correlations. While this technique seems justified, the rank-order method employed by Michael, Rosenthal, and DeCamp was not. In an effort to discredit the "constant stimulus" theory of prestige, these authors worked with mean and median ranks—statistics which are generally meaningless.

Cole demonstrated the possibility of using sociometric data for the determination of certain characteristics of ethos. Using a particular personal characteristic (judgment, personal appeal, etc.) as the basis for sociometric choices, he selected one or more members of a group as "stars" and then assumed that they were more highly regarded than their colleagues. Under some conditions, these preferred members were as persuasive as authorities from outside the group.

Kulp apparently made the first attempt to develop an index of prestige based upon attitude change. In a classic design which was to be repeated with variations many times during the ensuing years, he first administered Harper's test of liberalism to more than three hundred graduate students at Columbia. Later, various subgroups were told that the responses supplied them had been written by social scientists, educators, and other learned persons. The relative amounts of attitude shift toward each of these sources was used as the basis for computing a prestige index for each of the several professional groups.[57] Bowen, Caldwell, and West replicated the essential features of Kulp's study in an experiment using junior high, high school, and college students as subjects and employing a variety of different prestige levels. Sample findings with respect to the economic problems considered were these: "Prestige of the educators seems to increase as progress is made up the educational ladder" and "Ministers received the lowest rank in every case."[58]

Underlying these measuring techniques is the assumption that the prestige of a source is directly proportional to the ability to produce attitude shift. In 1938 Lurie formalized this point of view when he defined prestige as "The change in scale value of certain items brought about by attaching the name of the symbol to these items." He obtained scale values for prestige by administering a test of attitude without attaching prestige labels to the items, by administering the same test two weeks later with prestige labels attached, and by then subtracting the scores on the first test from those on the second. The remainder was the index of prestige.[59]

Naturally, prestige measures obtained in this manner are not pure or independent measures of the variable. Moreover, to use any of these measures to test the hypothesis that prestige induces attitude change is impossible, for the measure of prestige *is* attitude change. In an effort to develop an independent index suitable for testing this hypothesis, Saadi and Farnsworth combined gross ratings of "like," "indifferent," and "dislike" by the formula $100 \left[(L + \frac{1}{2}I) (L + I + D) \right]$ to obtain a score for likeableness based on group data.

The multiple-choice aspect of the Saadi-Farnsworth measure was an early precursor of an obvious means of measuring various aspects of ethos—the rating scale. An early experimenter with this type of measurement was Lorge, whose subjects rated seventy sources on a five-interval scale ranging from "those individuals whose opinions you respect most" to "those individuals for whose opinions you have least respect." More recently, Hovland and Weiss employed a five-point linear scale of "trustworthiness" to evaluate the credibility of two sources.

The well-known study by Haiman used a variety of scales. In one phase of his experiment two nationally prominent public figures were evaluated on nine-point scales of reputation and competence. In other

[57] Daniel Kulp, II, "Prestige, as Measured by Single-Experience Changes and Their Permanency," *Journal of Educational Research*, XXVII (1934), 663–672.

[58] A. O. Bowden, Floyd Caldwell, and Guy West, "A Study in Prestige," *American Journal of Sociology*, XL (1934), 193–203.

[59] Walter Lurie, "The Measurement of Prestige and Prestige-Suggestibility," *Journal of Social Psychology*, IX (1938), 219–225.

parts of the investigation student speakers were rated on similar scales for the qualities of sincerity, fairmindedness, physical appearance, conceit, competence, and likeableness.

In addition to being one of the first experimental research workers to recognize explicitly the multidimensionality of ethos, Walter made the earliest effort to apply recognized test construction methods to the problem of creating a measuring device. His specific project was the development of an instrument to measure a single factor, the evaluation of character. Beginning with nearly 400 character-describing statements and employing both the Thurstone sorting techniques and the Seashore rating methods, he developed two tests of twenty-two items each. When applied to such individuals as Franklin Roosevelt and "The person with the best character I have known," the two forms of the test were normally distributed, distinguished among intuitively perceived gross character levels, and correlated well (.86) with each other. . . .[60]

The Osgood and Stagner use of bipolar nouns in a set of scales to rate occupations and occupational groups was a forerunner of the semantic differential technique. They found that the prestige of jobs and workers could be determined through the use of their scales.[61]

Although Walter asserted the multi-dimensionality of ethos and although Haiman's technique actually employed a polydimensional approach, until recently no practical way of employing multivariate measures of ethos in research seemed to exist. Now the semantic differential technique makes such research possible. Berlo and Gulley, Berlo and Kumata, and Bettinghaus used the differential to measure attitude toward the communicator, but in each instance they reported only one dimension of the semantic space, the evaluative aspect of the image. "Although it does not tap much of the *content* of an attitude in a denotative sense . . . it does seem to provide an index to the location of the attitude object along a general evaluative continuum."[62] Employed in this manner, the semantic differential is similar in many ways to a traditional Likert scale in which a number of judgments concerning the concept are rendered on a linear scale and the sum of the scale values recorded by the subjects is used as a more-or-less unidimensional measure of the single property with which the scale is concerned.

Andersen developed a semantic differential which was specifically designed to measure ethos. Employing terms garnered from theoretical and experimental literature and securing responses to famous living people from freshmen engineering and physical education students, he

[60] Otis Walter, Jr., "The Measurement of Ethos," unpubl. diss. (Northwestern, 1948).

[61] Charles Osgood and Ross Stagner, "Analysis of a Prestige Frame of Reference by a Gradient Technique," *Journal of Applied Psychology*, XXV (1941), 275–290.

[62] Osgood, Suci, and Tannenbaum, p. 195.

obtained two major dimensions (evaluative and dynamism) in the images. Berlo carried out a similar study, but he used a greater number of concepts and more students than did Andersen. Berlo also employed an oblique solution, whereas Andersen's method was the orthogonal factor solution.[63] Inspection suggests that the two structures were not essentially dissimilar if allowance is made for the difference in the factor rotation methods.

SUMMARY

Despite the great number of experimental studies relevant to ethos, the scope of this concept is such that the findings are not yet sufficiently numerous and sophisticated to permit definitive conclusions about the operation of ethical proof.

The finding is almost universal that the ethos of the source is related in some way to the impact of the message. This generalization applies not only to political, social, religious, and economic issues but also to matters of aesthetic judgment and personal taste. Some evidence even shows that "prestige-suggestion" can affect the appetite for certain foods and can influence performances of perceptual and psychomotor tasks. On the other hand, there is not enough evidence to suggest that the amount of information gained from exposure to a message is related to the ethos of the source—at least this lack of relationship seems to be true of college populations. The effect of ethos, again according to many studies, has a temporal dimension. In other words, when the stimulus is not renewed, material presented by a high ethos source loses in persuasiveness and that given by a poor source gains. Recall of the source reestablishes some of the initial effect, but the improvement which renewal produces decays more rapidly than does the original increment.

Some auditors appear to be more susceptible to ethical appeal than others; some may be contrasuggestible. However, there is no evidence to show that suggestibility to prestige correlates well with intelligence, education, speech training, subject-matter competence, age, or sex. The only variable which seems clearly related to differences in suggestibility to prestige is the initial attitude toward the topic or the purpose: consistently, those who are neutral initially shift more often than do those who are at one extreme or the other.

Research shows that expert opinion may be about as influential as majority opinion in inducing attitude change.

While most experimentation has been conducted in a fixed ethos model, recent research shows that a congruity model can be used to predict attitude change toward both a communicator and his topic. Incorporating elements concerning speech composition and delivery increased the usefulness of the model.

[63] David Berlo, "An Empirical Test of a General Construct of Credibility," unpubl. paper presented at the SAA convention, New York City, December 29, 1961.

Printed and oral propaganda can succeed in creating and altering images of groups or of individuals, but attempts to produce unfavorable reactions to individuals may backfire. When this response occurs, the prestige of the criticized person may increase and that of the attacker may decline.

Speeches of introduction probably influence the image of a speaker, but most of the evidence on this point is indirect.

Certain characteristics of a speech affect the ethos of the speaker. No evidence, however, supports the common beliefs (1) that giving "both sides" is a superior way to present controversial material, (2) that citing the sources of evidence increases persuasiveness, and (3) that including conciliatory remarks, statements of self-praise, and other conscious, obvious attempts at ethical appeal enhances the speaker's status.

Such noncontent stimuli as dress, voice, and manner apparently affect the attitude of the audience toward the speaker, but these factors may not be related to persuasiveness on a given occasion. There is no evidence that the audience can perceive lack of sincerity; rather, audiences appear to react to their evaluations of the competence of the speaker.

Many techniques of measurement have been applied to ethos: among these are ranking, sociograms, prestige indexes, linear rating scales, Thurstone scales, and the semantic differential. Each of these has proved useful in assessing one or more of the aspects of ethos.

This preceding body of findings suggests certain possibilities for future research:

1. The dimensions of ethos should be explored through multivariate analysis in terms of different auditors, different speakers, and different speech situations. New measurement techniques, and especially the semantic differential, make this type of research possible.

2. Ethos or ethical proof should be measured in experiments designed so that this variable is not confounded with persuasiveness.

3. The effect upon ethos of the interaction of prior reputation and the artistic elements in the message should be studied. Findings in this area would be of great importance to rhetorical theory.

4. Some research suggests that differences in ethos are not established as easily with some audiences as previous experimenters often assumed. More research dealing with the methods of establishing and modifying ethos is needed.

5. The effect of variations in auditors, situations, and topics upon the function of ethical proof in persuasion should receive renewed attention. The utilization of improved designs and measuring devices can create experimental conditions that may lead to more meaningful results than those obtained in the past.

EVIDENCE AND ARGUMENT

GERALD R. MILLER

THIS CHAPTER deals with the role of evidence in argument. Although the term *evidence* smacks of the courtroom, it should be obvious that its scope is much wider; in fact, we usually demand that most statements or propositions be supported by some form of evidence. You may, for example, assert to a friend (let us call this friend "Skeptic") that you expect to receive an A in argumentation class. Skeptic, being a questioning soul, inquires about the reasons for this claim, whereupon you enumerate the facts that you have received A's on all the speeches you have presented, that you received an A on the midterm examination, that you have participated freely in classroom discussion, and that you have missed no classes or assignments. In enumerating these facts to Skeptic, you are presenting evidence for your claim that you will receive a grade of A in the course. Or, on another occasion, you may remark to Skeptic that college professors are rather peculiar people. When Skeptic asks you the basis for such a statement, you are likely to respond somewhat as follows: "I know Professor X, and he is peculiar; I know Professor Y, and he is peculiar; and I know Professor Z, and he is peculiar; therefore, I have concluded that college professors are rather peculiar people." Your mention of particular professors to Skeptic is an attempt to provide evidence for the generalization that college professors are rather peculiar people.

In the above examples, what is it that you are attempting to accomplish by your enumeration of particulars? I would hold that you are establishing your reasons for believing the assertions that you have made, and even more important, you are attempting to induce in Skeptic a sense of belief in these same assertions. Insofar as Skeptic responds favorably to your evidence, you will be successful in convincing him; insofar as Skeptic, for any number of reasons, views your evidence with distrust, you will be unsuccessful.

If I am correct in my assumption that your primary objective was the development in Skeptic of a sense of belief, and if this assumption holds for most of the communication that occurs among the "Skeptics"

Reprinted from Gerald R. Miller, "Evidence and Argument," Chapter II in *Perspectives on Argumentation*, eds. Gerald R. Miller and Thomas R. Nilsen (Chicago: Scott, Foresman and Co., 1966), pp. 24–37. Reprinted by permission of Scott, Foresman and Co.

of the world, the following may be offered as a useful, tentative definition for the term *evidence: Evidence consists of those data that are intended to induce a sense of belief in the proposition which the data purportedly support.* Thus, the term *evidence* embraces a large body of diverse and varied materials; the common defining characteristic of these materials is to be found in the function they perform.

Several implications of this definition should be explored more fully. First, this definition implies that questions regarding the nature and uses of evidence are essentially psychological and involve considerations of the bases for people's beliefs and of the kinds of materials most likely to induce in a particular person or persons a sense of belief. This approach to the study of evidence is somewhat different from the one most commonly encountered in books on debate and argumentation. Generally, these works have dealt with criteria for evaluating sources of evidence and rules for valid inductive inferences.[1] Although these matters will be considered in this chapter, I believe that such a viewpoint embraces only a part of the general problem of evidence. Specifically, this approach emphasizes the ways in which evidence *ought* to affect people and the ways in which evidence *ought* to be used; to a large extent, it ignores the ways in which evidence often *does* affect people and the ways in which evidence often *is* used. In other words, it minimizes *description* to concentrate on *prescription,* an approach that no doubt stems from a view of argumentation as rational, reasoned discourse, rather than a view which emphasizes the behavioral effects of argumentative discourse on audiences. In treating evidence, I shall try to combine the salient elements of both approaches.

The decision to divide discussion between the psychological and logical aspects of evidence stems from the assumption, considered earlier and explicit in the definition of evidence adopted here, that one's primary purpose in employing evidence is to induce a sense of belief. To illustrate, let us return to the example in which you are detailing to Skeptic your evidence for the assertion that college professors are rather peculiar people. The evidence consists of examples of particular professors of your acquaintance who also qualify for the label "rather peculiar people." In using such evidence—often referred to as *examples* or *specific instances*—you may ask yourself several questions: Have I mentioned a sufficient number of professors who fit the appellation "rather peculiar people"? Are these professors typical? Have I been accurate and truthful in my enumeration of examples? Such questions deal with the logical characteristics of the evidence employed; spe-

---

[1] See, for example, A. Craig Baird, *Argumentation, Discussion, and Debate* (New York: McGraw-Hill Book Company, Inc., 1950), pp. 90–115. A recent work by Douglas Ehninger and Wayne Brockriede, *Decision by Debate* (New York: Dodd, Mead & Company, 1963), pp. 110–125, places some emphasis on the psychological nature of evidence; even so, the primary focus still appears to be on the value aspects of its use.

cifically, they involve considerations of whether one is justified in performing the inductive leap. Probably, however, the paramount question you will consider can be phrased in the following manner: Will the examples I have employed produce in Skeptic a sense of belief in my assertion that college professors are rather peculiar people? This crucial question deals with the psychological characteristics of the evidence employed.

Many times, of course, attention to logical characteristics of the evidence serves to enhance its psychological impact. If Skeptic is a trained logician or a professor of argumentation, he is likely to be quite sensitive to violation of the rules of evidence and inference. Even so, logical factors provide only a means to the psychological end. If both you and Skeptic are acquainted with a single professor of marked idiosyncratic tendencies, you may find it more advantageous, in terms of inducing belief, to allude to this single example and to ignore all others, even though such a decision violates the accepted standards of inductive inference.

A second implication of the above stipulated definition of evidence, and one that is closely related to the preceding point, has to do with the use of the term *belief* in the definition. After Bertrand Russell, I will define a belief as "a certain kind of state of body or mind or both."[2] This definition emphasizes that the term *belief* refers to a psychological condition of the individual. On the other hand, I will use terms such as *fact* and *truth* to refer to empirically ascertainable phenomena that exist as part of the physical world. Thus, to say that one holds a particular belief is or is not a true statement of fact; but the psychological state of the belief and the factual assertion of the belief's existence are not identical, or even roughly synonymous.

Perhaps an example will best serve to illustrate this point. Our friend Skeptic asserts, "I believe in the existence of Centaurs." Being sophisticated and intelligent individuals, we know that the statement, "There exist on this earth creatures known as Centaurs," is a false statement of fact. Consequently, we attempt to induce in Skeptic a new belief, specifically, a belief in the assertion, "Centaurs do not exist." In order to support this latter assertion, we cite evidence, consisting of copious testimony by noted scientists, which asserts the impossibility of the existence of Centaurs. Skeptic responds to our efforts by asserting, "I believe in the existence of Centaurs." We have failed to change Skeptic's belief, even though both our evidence and the proposition it supports are factually true.

The point to be emphasized is that the function of evidence in argument is to induce belief, not necessarily to aid in communicating truth or establishing fact. Granted, fact and truth may sometimes be

2 Bertrand Russell, *Human Knowledge: Its Scope and Limits* (New York: Simon and Schuster, Inc., 1962), p. 145.

consistent with the belief that an arguer hopes to induce; many times, however, this is simply not the case. Almost all of the evidence utilized by the Nazi Party to induce a sense of belief in certain propositions dealing with the superiority of the German people was factually false; even so, the evidence was effective in its function of inducing such a sense of belief. While we can, and should, condemn attempts to induce belief in such ethically repugnant propositions, we should remain aware that our objection involves values; that is, it concerns the way evidence *ought* to be used, not the way that evidence frequently *is* used.

Still another implication of the definition of evidence given above concerns the phrase, "that the data *purportedly* support." What conclusions may be validly drawn from certain items of evidence is a question associated with the logical rules of inference and with the empirical status of certain related propositions. In some cases, this question may be of crucial significance in inducing a sense of belief in the proposition; in other cases, it may be of little import. To illustrate, we will return to Skeptic and his Centaurs and ask how he has come to hold the strange belief that Centaurs exist. Let us assume that Skeptic gained his belief in Centaurs in the following manner: A friend, given to levity, once remarked, "Skeptic, Writer A has written about Centaurs; Writer B has written about Centaurs; and Writer C has written about Centaurs; therefore, I conclude that there exist on this earth creatures known as Centaurs." Henceforth, Skeptic's belief in the existence of Centaurs has been unshakeable.

What may we conclude concerning the role played by evidence in this whimsical example? The data utilized consist of statements of particular writers who have mentioned creatures known as Centaurs; these data are then used to support the proposition that Centaur-objects exist. You and I are aware that no such statement is logically or empirically warranted by this evidence. We know that authors have also mentioned Unicorns, Slithy Toves, Three-Winged Jabberwockies, and a host of other strange creatures, but we also know that inventing a name and stipulating a verbal definition for an animal do not constitute proof of the creature's physical existence. As a result, we would hold that the evidence more logically supports statements such as "Many authors have written about imaginary creatures known as Centaurs" or "The Centaur is a popular figure in mythological literature."

But our rationality may have little effect on Skeptic's belief. If his own psychological posture is such that he is willing to accept these instances as proof for the existence of Centaur-objects, then the evidence has been effective only in inducing belief in the existence of Centaurs. Although the example we have used may seem far-fetched, it is obvious that considerations dealing with the question of what sorts of statements may be inferred from certain data are often significant. We can, for example, collect mountains of evidence demonstrating that a large number of individuals withdrew great amounts of money from the banks during the depression days of the 1930's. Does this evidence support the proposition that our economy was suffering from dire problems, or does it support the proposition that if enough people *believe* the economy is suffering from dire problems, they will, by their behavior, create such problems, i.e., they will engage in behavior calculated to result in what Robert Merton has labeled the "self-fulfilling prophecy"?[3] In other words, were the instances of withdrawal of money a *symptom* of a problem that already existed or a *cause* that contributed to the development of a problem? Among economists, each interpretation has its defenders; the significant point here is that the same evidence may be used to induce belief in two or more greatly disparate propositions.

The above discussion has focused on some of the implications of the definition of evidence offered in this chapter. True, matters have been somewhat exaggerated; after all, how many noninstitutionalized people entertain a serious belief in the existence of Centaur-objects? It may have occurred to you that if Skeptic were a sensible man, he would have sought further evidence to support his belief in Centaurs, once he had been exposed to the negative testimony of eminent and respected scientists. The present discussion, however, has been an attempt to emphasize the psychological complexities associated with any consideration of evidence and its role in argument. Men often do operate from extra-rational considerations, and evidence is frequently employed in a post hoc manner to buttress beliefs that have been derived entirely apart from some ideal, rational model of man. After all, Freud might suggest that Skeptic's belief in Centaurs resulted from a traumatic childhood experience, not from testimony gleaned from any reliable authority nor from instances in literature in which authors referred to Centaur-objects.

Fortunately, however, there is also evidence to indicate that man frequently seeks rationality and that a sense of belief may be induced by employing evidence that appeals to his rational side.[4] We may say,

[3] Robert K. Merton, *Social Theory and Social Structure*, rev. ed. (New York: Free Press of Glencoe, Inc., 1957), pp. 421–439. It should be added that if the evidence more logically supports the latter proposition, it again emphasizes the distinction between *fact* and *belief* outlined above, since the beliefs of these depositors are contrary to the factual state of the economy.

[4] Recently, one of the more interesting areas dealing with man's desire for rationality and order has been that of balance theory in psychology. Basically, theorists of this school argue that man cannot tolerate two inconsistent cognitions and that he must strive to regain balance by eliminating inconsistency. Although such behavior seems reasoned and rational, these same theorists also recognize that the *means* an individual adopts to achieve the *end* of cognitive consistency may be quite irrational in nature. For a discussion of the problem see Leon Festinger, *A Theory of Cognitive Dissonance* (Stanford: Stanford University Press, 1962), and Milton J. Rosenberg and others, *Attitude Organization and Change: An Analysis of Consistency Among Attitude Components* (New Haven: Yale University Press, 1960).

then, that some concern for the logical aspects of evidence may, on numerous occasions, lead the arguer to choose data that are maximally suited to the function of inducing belief. Thus, the logical and the psychological aspects of evidence cannot be separated into discrete categories. . . .

One other preliminary remark is in order. Some may feel that the preceding discussion has strayed from matters involving evidence and has dealt with questions more traditionally covered in discussions of logic and inference. Let me clarify my position by stating that I recognize two modes of inference, deduction and induction. Problems regarding particular *genres* of these two general species are, to me, problems that deal primarily with evidence, not with inference. Thus, the rules of inference for the two inductive forms commonly labeled *argument from authority* and *argument from example* are the same; differences in the analysis of the two forms result from the sorts of evidence employed, not from variations in the inferential format. Although some may disagree with this position, it is a distinction that I shall maintain throughout the entire chapter; consequently, the reader will be aided if he keeps it in mind.

PROPOSITIONS AND EVIDENCE

Having examined some of the implications of the definition of evidence stipulated in the preceding section, let us examine various types of propositions in which men commonly profess belief and discuss the kinds of evidential data that have led to these beliefs. An analysis of some sample propositions should aid in accomplishing this objective.

"The sun rises in the east" and "Columbus discovered America in 1492" are two propositions that all of us believe. You may justifiably say that you no longer demand evidence to sustain your belief in the truth of these assertions; however, as we analyze the statements more fully, it will become apparent that you were led to your belief in these propositions by evidence to which you were exposed, and that for at least one of the propositions you are constantly encountering further evidence which buttresses your belief in its truth.

As a beginning step in our analysis, let us attach the label *statement of fact* to these two propositions and to others like them. After Gustav Bergmann, we may definite a statement of fact as one that "says something about the object or objects it mentions; and depending only on the properties of these objects, . . . is either true or false."[5] Thus, the first proposition above says something about the sun, i.e., that it consistently rises at a point in space designated as *east*, while the second proposition says something about Columbus, i.e., that he was the man who discovered the geographical area designated as *America*.

[5] Gustav Bergmann, "Ideology," *Ethics*, LXI (1951), 206.

Bergmann's definition emphasizes that a statement of fact may be either true or false. Thus, if the first proposition above read, "The sun rises in the west," we would regard the assertion as a false statement of fact, since the sun does not have a property of rising in the west. Consistent with the distinction drawn earlier between *fact* or *truth* as opposed to *belief*, it should be apparent that one can be induced to believe a false statement of fact. Before Columbus discovered America, many people believed the false statement of fact, "The earth is flat." Each time a religious sect predicts the world will end on a certain date, only to have the prediction disconfirmed, we witness another instance of a group of individuals who have professed belief in what has proven to be a false statement of fact.[6]

Before examining the kinds of evidential data that have engendered our belief in the sample propositions given above, it would be well to make one further point about statements of fact. You may be thinking that propositions such as "Columbus discovered America in 1492" are not the stuff of which argument is made. If so, you are unquestionably correct; we usually spend little time disputing such assertions. There are, however, a host of statements of fact that are not amenable to immediate verification; i.e., they cannot be labeled as *true* or *false* at the time they are uttered. Statements such as "The United States is leading the Soviet Union in the missile race," "Cigarette smoking causes lung cancer," and "We can change an individual's intelligence quotient by changing his environment" are examples of statements of fact that have been hotly disputed. We shall discuss such propositions in some detail in the third section of this chapter.

For now, however, we can return to the propositions "The sun rises in the east" and "Columbus discovered America in 1492." We know that we have labeled these propositions *statements of fact,* and we know that we believe they are true. But why do we believe in the truth of these assertions? What kinds of evidential data have induced this sense of belief? Is our basis of belief the same for both propositions? It is to these questions that we will now turn.

Suppose your imaginary friend Skeptic remarks, "The sun rises in the east," and you respond with the question, "How do you know?" The intent of this question may be more fully stated as follows: "What evidence has led you to profess belief in the proposition, 'The sun rises in the east'?"

Let us ignore the problems of induction associated with the statement, "The sun rises in the east," and focus on Skeptic's probable response to your query. Although he may conceivably answer that he read this statement in a science or logic text, his most probable response will be of the order, "Why, I saw it rise in the east this morning," or,

[6] The effects of such a disconfirmation on the attitudes and beliefs of group members have been studied, and the findings make for interesting and informative reading. See Leon Festinger, Henry W. Riecken, Jr., and Stanley Schachter, *When Prophecy Fails* (Minneapolis: University of Minnesota Press, 1956).

"Haven't you ever seen the sunrise?" By means of such statements, Skeptic is asserting that his belief in the proposition, "The sun rises in the east," has been induced by a number of observations of the occurrence of this event; i.e., that he believes the statement because he has directly experienced the physical event labeled "sun rising in the east."

As was implied earlier, there was a time in Skeptic's life when this proposition would have induced no sense of belief. Only after a number of occurrences of the evidential datum, "experiencing the physical event labeled, 'sun rising in the east,'" does Skeptic profess belief in the proposition. Furthermore, each additional instance of experiencing this event provides further assurance that his belief is well founded. In fact, it is interesting, albeit somewhat frightening, to speculate about the way Skeptic would react should he ever experience an instance of a physical event labeled, "sun rising in the west."[7]

Thus, we see that one sort of evidential datum which may induce belief in propositions involving statements of fact is the direct experiencing of the event or events mentioned in the proposition. This is the type of datum employed in science. When scientists wish to test the truth or falsity of a proposition, they establish a set of conditions for observing the event mentioned in the proposition. The results of their observations serve as evidence to induce a sense of belief in the proposition, or to induce a sense of belief in some alternative statement of fact, e.g., the statement, "Our proposition is false."

Sometimes, however, the observations necessary to determine the truth or falsity of a factual proposition are more complex and involved than is the case in the sunrise example discussed above. This occurs when the event or situation mentioned in the proposition is complex and its truth or falsity is dependent upon a number of related observations. What observations must be made to verify the factual proposition, "The United States is leading the Soviet Union in the missile race"? It is possible to conceive of a horrible experiment in which we place a group of observers in space and then have the United States and the Soviet Union fire all of their missiles at each other. Assuming that we could arrive at an objective measure of destruction, our observers could then determine its extent in each nation; and, on the basis of their findings, we could label the original proposition as either true or false. All of us fervently hope, however, that no such experiment will ever take place. In its absence, the missile race proposition

---

[7] The problem of induction mentioned above has to do with the impossibility of observing all of the possible instances of the physical event labeled "sun rising in the east." Thus, though one may have psychological certainty that the sun has risen, and will continue to rise, in the east, he can never have logical certainty that such will be the case. Obviously, this unverifiable assumption of continuity in the physical world underlies all scientific enterprise and should be called to the attention of those individuals who assert naïvely that science is completely objective in nature.

will continue to be an argumentative one, and it will be possible to utilize various kinds of evidential data in attempting to induce belief in its truth or falsity.

We are now ready to examine our second sample proposition of fact, "Columbus discovered America in 1492." Suppose Skeptic has expressed a belief in this statement, and you have again inquired as to his reasons for believing it. Will he respond differently than in the case of the proposition, "The sun rises in the east"?

Obviously, the answer to this question is affirmative. It is difficult to conceive of Skeptic replying, "Why, I saw Columbus discover America," or, "Didn't you see Columbus discover America?" Rather, he is likely to respond, "I learned that from my first-grade teacher," or, "I read about Columbus' discovery in the encyclopedia." In other words, Skeptic will never have directly experienced the physical event labeled "Columbus discovering America"; rather, his belief in the truth of the proposition that asserts the occurrence of this event is occasioned by evidential data consisting of testimony.

It is obvious that using testimonial data to induce Skeptic to believe in the truth of a proposition involves something more than when the data consist of Skeptic's direct experiences. When the evidence consists of testimony, Skeptic must first believe, or be induced to believe, the statement, "X testifies truthfully"; from this will stem his belief in the particular proposition that X has uttered. We might, in fact, suggest that Skeptic's psychological state as expressed in the assertion, "I believe that Columbus discovered America," might be more accurately portrayed by the statement, "I believe that X (and Y, and Z, etc.) consistently utter true propositions."[8]

You may say that, as evidential data, direct experience and testimony differ only in degree, not in kind, and that implicit in the acceptance of evidence based on direct experience is the belief that our senses do not lie.[9] To this I can only reply that the difference, whether of degree or kind, is sufficiently great to be of practical significance. While I seldom have occasion to consciously question the reliability of my senses—unless in the presence of a magician or a

[8] This consideration provides one good reason for the claim that primary source material (i.e., materal taken from the source himself) is superior to secondary source material (i.e., material in which a second party relates what the original source had stated). In the case of the former, one has only to induce the belief, "X testifies truthfully about the event in question," while with the latter, one must induce the twin beliefs that, "(1) Y testifies truthfully about what X has stated, and (2) X testifies truthfully about the event in question." Thus, when secondary source material is utilized the problem of inducing belief becomes psychologically more complex and difficult.

[9] Here, we have touched upon a number of complex philosophical problems having to do with the relative merits of realism and idealism as theories of knowledge. For a discussion of these problems see, for example, A. J. Ayer, *The Problem of Knowledge* (Baltimore: Penguin Books, Inc., 1962).

perceptual illusion—I frequently have reason to entertain consciously the belief, "X does not testify truthfully." Thus, I would hold that for the purpose of analyzing their effects and functions in argumentation, direct experience and testimony differ as evidential data.

We can see, therefore, that for the purpose of inducing belief in propositions involving statements of fact, there are two broad categories of evidential data, direct experience and testimony. It should be obvious, however, that in most instances to which we assign the label *argumentation,* the evidential data consist of some form of testimony. Although it may, on occasion, be possible to arrange an actual demonstration of the physical event, the vast majority of cases require that the disputant rely on testimony about the event as a means of inducing belief.

There is, however, a second kind of proposition in which men often profess belief. Let us take as samples of this type of proposition the statements "Capital punishment is morally reprehensible" and "Communism is the worst form of government." Even before we discuss these propositions, you are intuitively aware that they differ from such statements as "The sun rises in the east" or "The United States is leading the Soviet Union in the missile race." Why is this the case?

Let us attach the label *value judgment* to the first two propositions above, and to others like them. Turning again to Bergmann, we find the following definition for a value judgment:

A value judgment is misunderstood if it is taken to ascribe a property to the object, act, or situation it mentions in the same sense in which a statement of fact is such an ascription; it is, therefore, *literally neither true nor false.* [italics mine] What it involves and misleadingly states as the property of an object, act, or situation alone is the fact that this object, act, or situation causes in the one who makes the judgment a certain state of mind, say, for instance, of positive aesthetic appreciation or of moral approval.[10]

The above definition sets forth the common sense core of ethical relativism, a position to which I shall subscribe in the following discussion. Succinctly put, this position holds that the statement, "The United States is leading the Soviet Union in missile development," differs from the proposition, "Capital punishment is morally reprehensible," primarily because the former says something about the properties of the act mentioned (missile race), while the latter says nothing about the properties of the act (capital punishment); rather, it provides information only about the state of mind of the individual making the assertion.

An example will best serve to illustrate this point. Both you and Skeptic have accepted jobs as newspaper reporters, and you have both been assigned to cover the execution of a convicted murderer. As the

[10] Bergmann, 206.

switch is thrown, Skeptic turns to you and remarks, "Justice has been served." You respond, "Society is once again guilty of a heinous crime."

Have Skeptic and you literally experienced a different event? Common sense suggests that you have not. Each of you has witnessed the execution of the same murderer, in the same electric chair, by the same executioner. Could the two of you, as a result of evidential data resulting from direct experience, agree on your belief in the truth or falsity of such factual assertions as, "The convicted murderer was pronounced dead at approximately 12:05 A.M.," "The convicted murderer was wearing a blue suit," or, "The warden had brown hair"? Undoubtedly you could. Why, then, do you find it impossible to agree on your beliefs regarding the goodness or badness of the act itself?

The reason is not to be found in any objective properties of the act, but rather in the different predispositions and attitudes that you and Skeptic hold regarding the act. Whereas the locus of disagreement concerning propositions of fact lies "out there" in the objects, acts, and situations themselves, the locus of disagreement concerning value judgments lies in the minds of the disputants, i.e., in the different attitudes that they bring to the dispute. Given this distinction, it becomes readily apparent that value judgments are literally *neither* true nor false, in the sense that statements of fact are *either* true or false.[11]

Several implications of the nature of value judgments should be considered. First, it is apparent that almost any value judgment can provide a basis for argument. Suppose, for example, that Skeptic and you attend a movie at the Campus Theater entitled, *Long Is the Night.* Is it likely that the two of you will argue about the title of the movie or about the name of the theater that you attended? Such factual quibbles exemplify the ultimate in triviality. On the other hand, if Skeptic states that *Long Is the Night* is the finest movie he has ever seen and you respond that it was a deplorable picture, a lively and interesting argument is likely to ensue. This is because—contrary to what is implied in the language Skeptic and you have used in making your assertions— you are not arguing about any properties of the film itself, but rather about the esthetic contents of your minds, i.e., your beliefs and attitudes about what constitutes a pleasing movie.

The use of the term *beliefs* in the preceding sentence calls to mind once again our earlier distinction between *truth* or *fact* as opposed to *belief.* The position outlined above denies the possibility of ascertaining the truth or falsity of a value judgment; certainly, however, it does not deny that people can be induced to profess strong beliefs in value propositions. Skeptic is quite confident of his beliefs in the moral desirability of capital punishment and the esthetic perfection of *Long Is*

[11] I am grateful to the editor of *Southern Speech Journal* for permission to quote parts of the above from an article appearing in that journal. See Gerald R. Miller, "Questions of Fact and Value: Another Look," *Southern Speech Journal,* XXVIII (1962), 116–123.

the Night, even though you may be able to demonstrate cogently to him that he can never verify the truth or falsity of such moral and esthetic assertions. In fact, the history of mankind is replete with instances of violent argument about value propositions.

At this point, let us turn to a consideration of the kinds of evidential data that can be used to induce belief in value propositions. Once again, our two broad categories of direct experience and testimony may seem appropriate. Concerning the former category, however, some qualifications and reservations are in order.

While most of us have directly experienced the event designated in the proposition, "The sun rises in the east," I would hold that no one has directly experienced an event corresponding to what is contained in the proposition, "Communism is the worst form of government." In the latter case, what one has experienced is a series of related events (imprisonment for six months, deprivation of property, assertions by one's father that the communists are tyrants, etc.) that have led to a belief in the value implied by the proposition, "Communism is the worst form of government." A second individual, however, may experience a series of related events (twenty years of education, appointment to a prosperous governmental position, high office in the party, etc.) that have led him to a belief in the value implied in the proposition, "Communism is the best form of government." While we would be willing to grant the rationality of both of these individuals (after all, few of us would question that Brezhnev's belief in the latter proposition is rational), we would, on the other hand, have serious doubts about an individual who asserted that his experiences had led him to doubt the truth of the factual proposition, "The sun rises in the east." Thus, while direct experiences may serve as evidential data calculated to induce belief in both factual and value propositions, the nature of these experiences and, even more important, what the experiences themselves imply will differ for factual and value propositions.

Although we could examine the preceding point at greater length, I will dispense with further discussion, since most instances of argumentation concerning value judgments involve evidential data of the kind we have labeled *testimony.* Think, for example, of most of the values you now hold. Are your religious values, for example, a function of direct experiences you have had with the major religions of the world, or are they largely a result of testimony by X, Y, and Z which has induced you to believe the value proposition, "This religion is the best"? For most of you, I am certain that the latter case prevails. The same could probably be said for most of the political and social values you hold and, though perhaps to a lesser extent, for your current tastes in the arts.

It should be apparent that the mechanism for inducing belief by means of testimony is similar for both factual and value propositions; i.e., an individual must first believe the proposition, "X testifies truthfully," after which he is more likely to be induced to believe in the proposition about which X is testifying. Given the fact that testimony embraces similar psychological processes for both factual and value propositions and granted the assumption that most instances of argumentation involve testimony as the sole evidential datum, you may feel that I have been unnecessarily laborious in distinguishing between factual and value propositions. Actually, however, the distinction is a crucial one, since the category *testimony* is a broad one that embraces a number of different kinds of materials. In the next section of this chapter, I hope to show that all kinds of testimonial data are not equally effective for both factual and value propositions; rather, it should become apparent that some kinds of testimonial data are more suited to factual than to value propositions, while for others the converse is true. For this reason, the distinction between the two types of propositions is important.

One final remark is in order. I have made no mention of the type of proposition commonly labeled *policy*, a type frequently discussed in texts on argumentation and debate. This is because I hold that a policy proposition has no distinguishing characteristics which set it apart from fact and value propositions; that is, I believe that if any meaningful argument is to occur, a policy proposition must be disputed as either a proposition of fact or a proposition of value. The key to the choice of a factual or value orientation lies in the definition of the term *should*—a term which occurs in most policy propositions. If *should* is defined in terms of means-ends interests (we would increase our gross national product, we would win the war, etc.), then the issue becomes one of fact, revolving around considerations of whether or not the stipulated ends would occur. If *should* is defined in terms of intrinsic ethical considerations (it would be morally good to do this, men of good will ought to behave this way, etc.), then the issue becomes one of value, revolving around the goodness or badness of these moral precepts. Although the two may overlap, it should be apparent that all parties to the dispute must first agree on where the emphasis should be placed; otherwise, the argument will proceed from different premises, and no clash of ideas can occur. Also, the choice of a factual or value orientation will determine which kinds of evidential data will be maximally effective in inducing a sense of belief on the part of the particular audience involved.

FEAR-AROUSING APPEALS

C. WILLIAM COLBURN

THE PRINCIPAL GOAL of a communicator is to gain auditor acceptance of the recommendations which he advocates. To achieve this goal a speaker must motivate his listeners to understand his proposition and then act upon that proposition in the prescribed manner. While the prerequisites of achieving this goal may be expressed in relatively simple and straightforward terms, those experienced in the practice and study of communication realize the complexity of the process which is involved. Understanding and developing strategies which aid in the successful manipulation of the communication process is a study of considerable substance. It is, in fact, the study of human motivation and behavior. It shall be the purpose of this article to examine one aspect of motivation as it relates to the communication process, and then, to evaluate the use of fear-arousing appeals designed to motivate a listener toward accepting the recommendations advocated within a particular communication.

When we analyze the actions of an individual or a group of individuals who have listened to a communication we are often confronted with the apparently simple question, "Why?" Why did the majority of the listeners pledge a campaign contribution? Why were so many people willing to sign a petition calling for a particular referendum? Why were the students so easily swayed by the leaders of the demonstration? In other words, we are faced with making judgments concerning the *direction of action* chosen by those individuals who were asked to respond to a specific recommendation. Resolving this question, however, produces only a partial picture of the behavior of an individual. If provided information concerning the direction of action that an individual or individuals take over a number of independent instances, we next ask: "Why does the individual *persist* in selecting a particular course of action?" Why is it that a person will continue his support of the local conservative party election after election? Why is it that some people listen to one news analyst over another day after day? Why is it that so many people ignore communications forecasting the dangers of overpopulation, water shortage, nuclear war, cigarette smoking, etc., year

Prepared especially for this volume, based in part upon C. William Colburn, "An Experimental Study of the Relationship Between Fear Appeal and Topic Importance in Persuasion" (Ph.D. dissertation, Indiana University, 1967).

after year? It is this analysis, the combined observation of direction and persistence of action, which constitutes the basis of the study of motivation. In light of this view, we may define motivation as an internal factor which arouses, directs, and integrates a person's behavior.[1]

While it is true that there is general acceptance of a definition of motivation it is equally true that there is widespread disagreement as to the theoretical conception of this factor of human behavior. A brief review of several of the available hypotheses confirms this idea. One view about the motives of man is that he is essentially a rational being. In very simple terms this cognitive theory supports the position that a person has the ability to think of what he wants and a capacity to figure out means of getting it. A second explanation for man's direction and persistence of action is the hedonistic or hedonic theory of motivation. Basically, this philosophy states that man's action can be accounted for by the fact that he seeks pleasure and avoids pain. That which is pleasurable is sought and that which is painful is avoided. The drive theory of motivation is still a third explanation for man's behavior. According to this concept, a state of disequilibrium (homeostatic imbalance) is created whenever the internal conditions of the body deviate from a normal state. This idea is most readily demonstrated by examining the basic human needs. When the nutritional supply of the body is depleted, for example, the individual is driven to seek and consume food thus restoring a state of equilibrium. Under this assumption, man's behavior is a function of homeostatic balance.

While these three theories help to emphasize the varying positions that have been taken in an attempt to explicate motivation, it is interesting and important to note that they all, to a substantial degree, support a feature of commonality. Each theory, in its own way, describes motivation in terms of a restoration of an "internal balance." Whether this internal balance is of a cognitive, hedonistic, or homeostatic nature is a moot question; the point is that man's behavior can best be described in terms of his efforts to maintain a balance among the overt and covert behaviors of his perceived world.[2] This conception of motivation is vitally important to the person who wishes to be an effective communicator. For herein lies a basic tenet for persuasion, as Gerald R. Miller states: "Since balance is the preferred psychological state, any perception of imbalance will be tension-producing, and the individual will subsequently act—covertly, overtly, or both—in a manner calculated to restore cognitive balance."[3] With this assumption it is logical to propose that the function of a persuasive speech is to (1) present material which will create a state of psychological disequilib-

[1] Edward J. Murray, *Motivation and Emotion* (Englewood Cliffs, New Jersey: Prentice-Hall, Inc., 1964), p. 7.
[2] Gerald R. Miller and Murray A. Hewgill, "Some Recent Research on Fear-Arousing Message Appeals," *Speech Monographs*, XXXIII (November, 1966), 377.
[3] *Ibid.*

rium or imbalance, and then (2) to offer recommendations which, if accepted, will restore cognitive balance. This paradigm of persuasion, however, needs careful analysis. For as we all know, not every persuasive speech which has been successful in creating imbalance has, at the same time, been successful in advocacy. There are disruptive intervening variables.

A first form of interference may arise when the auditors reduce imbalance created by the communication by expressing disbelief, aggressiveness, or lack of trust in the communicator. Through discounting the credibility of the source the auditor may reduce his feelings of anxiety. A second mediating factor which will cause rejection of the communicator's proposal may occur when a listener perceives the communication as unrealistically intense in amount or quality of anxiety-arousing material and simply stops listening. In this case, the person "blocks out" the stimulus and thus avoids the tension-producing state of psychological imbalance. Still another factor may be involved in explaining the failure of a persuasive speech. It may be the case that the members of the audience do not perceive the recommendations advocated by the speaker as being adequate to reduce the anxiety produced by the communicator. Beyond the fact that this form of interference does not relieve the anxiety of the listeners, it may also have the effect of motivating them to "ward off" subsequent exposure to further anxiety-arousing content of a similar nature. As a speaker it is well to be advised that any one or combination of these forms of interference can destroy the effect of your persuasive message. Safeguards must be taken in order to insure success.

Considerable recent research has shown that acceptance of a communication may be induced by the motivational influence of fear-arousing appeals. It is in this area that the combined efforts of researchers in psychology and speech have produced data which are meaningful and useful in describing the success or failure of this type of message appeal.

The pioneering study in the area of fear-arousing appeals was conducted by Irving L. Janis and Seymour Feshbach in 1953 under the auspices of the Yale Communication Research Program. In their study, "Effects of Fear-Arousing Communications," the authors prepared three communications: one incorporating strong fear-arousing material, one moderate fear-arousing material, and one minimal fear-arousing material.[4] The message content, causes of tooth decay and recommendations for better oral hygiene practices, as supported by one of the three levels of fear-arousing material served as the independent variable. Dependent variables were measures of emotional tension, retention of material, attitude toward the communication, conformity to

[4] Irving L. Janis and Seymour Feshbach, "Effects of Fear-Arousing Communications," *The Journal of Abnormal and Social Psychology,* 48 (1953), 78–92.

recommendations, and resistance to counter propaganda. The entire freshman class of a large Connecticut high school served as subjects with the final results based on four equal groups (one group for each of the three experimental speeches and one group as a control group) of fifty students per group.

The major finding was that when the goal of a persuasive communication is to create sustained preferences or attitudes, a relatively low degree of fear arousal will sometimes be optimal. Conversely, a "strong" fear appeal may evoke one of the forms of interference discussed earlier in this article and reduce the effectiveness of the communication. The authors state, "the results definitely contradict the assumption that as the dosage of fear-arousing stimuli in a mass communication is increased the audience will necessarily become more highly motivated to accept the reassuring recommendations contained in the communication . . . for communications of the sort used in the experiment, the optimal dosage appears to be far below the level of the strongest fear appeal that a communicator could use if he chose to do so."[5] This conclusion among others in the study supplied the incentive for additional experimentation.

Before reviewing more recent research which relates specifically to the elements of the communication situation, it is necessary to advance support for an important assumption: the magnitude of imbalance generated depends upon the message variable, in other words, the "stronger" the fear appeal, the "higher" the anxiety. Although this is a seemingly elementary conclusion, the level of an individual's anxiety *is directly proportionate* to the degree of fear-arousing material. Janis and Feshbach found in their experiment that the group who heard the communication with the strong fear appeal felt significantly more worried about the condition of their teeth than did the subjects of the other two groups; the subjects who heard the speech with a moderate level of fear appeal tended to feel more worried than did those subjects who heard the speech with minimal fear-arousing material.[6]

The relationship between fear-arousing material and anxiety is also supported by Berkowitz and Cottingham in, "The Interest Value and Relevance of Fear-Arousing Communications."[7] They found that messages (dealing with the topic of automobile safety belts) with strong fear-arousing material created emotional tensions to a significantly higher degree than did messages with minimal fear-arousing material.

Recalling the tenet of persuasion expressed earlier, one would assume that the "higher" the anxiety, the "greater" the attitude change; however, there appears to be a "tolerance ceiling" beyond which the

[5] *Ibid.*, p. 88.
[6] *Ibid.*, p. 82.
[7] Leonard Berkowitz and Donald R. Cottingham, "The Interest Value and Relevance of Fear-Arousing Communications," *The Journal of Abnormal and Social Psychology*, LX (1960), 37–44.

higher anxiety will no longer motivate the listener in the direction advocated by the communicator. The auditor, once beyond this point, responds with a defensive avoidance reaction negating the effect of the communication. The Janis and Feshbach finding that the moderate and high fear speeches were not as effective as the low fear speech in producing attitude change may be partially explained by the fact that the listeners responded with one of the forms of defensive avoidance. Strong fear appeal, then, will not always be effective in communications in which attitude change is the goal. Other studies which support this view include an unpublished doctoral dissertation by David Haeffner. He noted, after using high- and low-threat versions of a communication on the desirability for the control of nuclear weapons, that the high-fear communication produces greater resistance to attitude change.[8] In another study, by Janis and Terwilliger, the same conclusion was drawn.[9] These investigators attempted to persuade thirty-one adults (ages 18-55) of the danger of developing lung cancer through cigarette smoking with a high- and low-threat communication. They concluded that as a result of psychological resistance, "the strong-threat version tended to be less effective than the mild-threat version."[10] Therefore, the conclusion that a defensive avoidance reaction may develop as a result of high fear-arousing material is supported. However, it is important to understand that data from other investigations indicate that the so-called tolerance point fluctuates within the total speech complex of source, medium, message, and auditors. It may be concluded, then, that effective use of anxiety to motivate subjects toward a desired response depends upon the ability of the communicator to select fear appeals with optimum emotional tension which do not trigger defensive avoidance reactions. A review of specific research findings will demonstrate this point.

THE SOURCE AND FEAR-AROUSING APPEALS

The first element of the communication situation to be considered is the speaker. The question here is: What is the effect of the credibility of the communicator delivering a persuasive speech which contains fear-arousing material? Murray A. Hewgill and Gerald R. Miller investigated this question by employing the following three hypotheses:

1. If a source has high credibility with a listener, appeals that elicit strong fear for persons highly valued by the listener will effect greater attitude change than appeals that elicit mild fear.

[8] David Haeffner, "Some Effects of Guilt-Arousing and Fear-Arousing Persuasive Communications on Opinion Change" (Ph.D. dissertation, University of Rochester, 1956).

[9] Irving L. Janis and Robert F. Terwilliger, "An Experimental Study of Psychological Resistance to Fear-Arousing Communications," *The Journal of Abnormal and Social Psychology*, 65 (1962), 403-410.

[10] *Ibid.*, p. 407.

2. If a source has low credibility with a listener, appeals that elicit mild fear for persons highly valued by the listener will effect greater attitude change than appeals that elicit strong fear.

Taken together, these two hypotheses lead to the prediction that:

3. The level of fear appeal and the credibility of the source will interact.[11]

Although the results of their study failed to support contentions two and three, the first hypothesis was supported. This finding helps to emphasize one condition, namely, a highly credible source, in which strong fear appeal can be used successfully. With regard to the conclusion that high fear appeals can not be used, the authors state:

These findings place clear restrictions on the widely accepted generalization that strong fear messages are relatively ineffective in producing the desired audience effect. It would seem that such a sovereign statement represents an over-simplification of complex psychological processes, and that other variables—here, the credibility of the message source—will affect the recipients' response to the total persuasive situation.[12]

THE MEDIUM AND FEAR-AROUSING APPEALS

Public speakers find it necessary to use a wide range of media. Concern is often expressed about the efficiency of the medium of transmission employed. In this case the question of interest is: Will the medium have an effect on fear-arousing appeals used to support a persuasive communication? Frandsen provides some insight into the above question in his study, "Effects of Threat Appeals and Media of Transmission," reported in the June, 1963, *Speech Monographs.*[13] One of the goals of this author was to determine the difference, if any, between using a taped, a televised, or a live presentation of a communication containing different levels of threat appeals in a study designed to test shift of opinion and immediate information recall. Frandsen reported the following finding: none of the three media produced a significantly greater amount of immediate recall or effected greater shift of opinion than any other. Therefore, there is experimental evidence to support the conclusion that any one of the three above-mentioned forms of transmission may be used without concern for a loss of efficiency or effectiveness in dealing with fear arousal and attitude change.

[11] Murray A. Hewgill and Gerald R. Miller, "Source Credibility and Response to Fear-Arousing Communications," *Speech Monographs,* XXXII (June, 1965), 95–96.

[12] Gerald R. Miller and Murray A. Hewgill, "Reduction of Cognitive Imbalance Following Exposure to Fear-Arousing Communication." Paper presented to the National Convention of the Speech Association of America, Chicago, Illinois, December 28, 1964, pp. 28–29.

[13] Kenneth D. Frandsen, "Effects of Threat Appeals and Media of Transmission," *Speech Monographs,* XXX (June, 1963), 101–104.

THE MESSAGE AND FEAR-AROUSING APPEALS

Topic. In a doctoral dissertation entitled, "An Experimental Study of the Relationship Between Fear Appeal and Topic Importance in Persuasion," Colburn investigated the question: Is the persuasive effect of a speech a function of the relationship between the importance of the topic and extremeness of its supporting material?[14] Nine speeches were composed with each of three levels of fear-arousing material as support for three topics. The topics, which were carefully tested to insure that they did represent various degrees of importance, were cancer, tuberculosis, and tooth decay. The effectiveness of the recommendation that the subjects have an annual health checkup was measured by a multiple-item and a single-statement Likert scale. Based upon a statistical analysis of the evaluations of three hundred and sixty subjects the author concluded: (1) there is a high interaction between the intensity of fear-arousing appeals and speech topic, and (2) as the importance of the topic is increased the level of fear-arousing material may also be increased. Generalized conclusions that high levels of fear-arousing material are ineffective in persuasion are shown once again by the findings of this study to be in error. High level fear-arousing material may be successfully employed in support of highly important propositions.

Information. Whether or not high anxiety would temper or in some way "block" information is an important consideration in analyzing the use of fear-arousing material. Information is a basic element in persuasion and therefore its transmission must not be distorted. DeWolfe and Governale in a combined field-experimental study entitled, "Fear and Attitude Change," have noted the strong relationship between information and attitude change.[15] With forty-five student nurses, just beginning a six-week training program in the tuberculosis ward of Veterans Administration Hospital in Hines, Illinois, as subjects and with a carefully designed pre- and post-training period questionnaire, the experimenters found that subjects fearful of contracting T.B. before beginning the training lessened their anxiety as training progressed. At the end of the six-week period the student nurses were significantly less fearful of contracting T.B. than they were before starting the program. The authors state, "This study, then, evaluated the change of highly personally meaningful attitudes toward the fear-

[14] C. William Colburn, "An Experimental Study of the Relationship Between Fear Appeal and Topic Importance in Persuasion" (Ph.D. dissertation, Indiana University, 1967).

[15] Alan S. DeWolfe and Catherine N. Governale, "Fear and Attitude Change," *The Journal of Abnormal and Social Psychology*, 69 (1964), 119–123.

provoking agents and the stability of the changed attitudes under conditions where the subjects were confronted concurrently with both the threat, fear of contracting tuberculosis, and information about threat-averting actions."[16] This study shows a highly significant lowering of anxiety as the training session progressed and as the student nurses gained more information about tuberculosis and its treatment. In a very similar study, Hicks and Spaner found that student nurses developed a more favorable attitude toward the mentally ill as they progressed through a three-month training session in a Veterans Administration Hospital in Downey, Illinois. The authors concluded, "Favorable attitudes toward the mentally ill developed as a function of intimate exposure to the mental hospital environment."[17]

In another experimental study, Janis and Milholland investigated the immediate verbatim recall of the content of communications with either strong or minimal amounts of fear-arousing material.[18] In their study, using communications with the message content "causes of tooth decay and recommendations concerning oral hygiene practices," Janis and Milholland found no significant difference in the subjects' capability of immediate verbatim recall after listening to the experimental communications. This study confirms the notion that immediate recall of content is not affected by the level of fear appeal.

The studies cited in this section, concerning fear appeal and information as related to attitude change and verbatim recall, indicate that high anxiety does not interfere with the perception and evaluation of information.

Personal or Impersonal Appeals. Fredric A. Powell, School of Public Communication, Boston University, explored the following hypotheses:

1. A greater change in attitude will occur when the anxiety appeal is directed at members of the listener's family than when it is directed at the listener himself.

2. An anxiety appeal threatening the nation will produce a lesser change in attitude than one directed at the listener or his family.

3. A strong anxiety appeal directed at the listener will produce *less* change in attitude than one that is mild.

4. A strong anxiety appeal posing a threat to the listener's family will produce a *greater* change in attitude than will one that is mild.

[16] *Ibid.*, p. 120.
[17] Jack M. Hicks and Fred E. Spaner, "Attitude Change and Mental Hospital Experience," *The Journal of Abnormal and Social Psychology*, 65 (1962), 120.
[18] Irving L. Janis and Harry C. Milholland, "The Influence of Threat Appeals on Selective Learning of the Content of a Persuasive Communication," *Journal of Psychology*, XXXVII (1954), 75–81.

5. A strong anxiety appeal presenting an impersonal threat to the listener will produce a *smaller* change in attitude than one that is mild.[19]

Using as independent variables, (1) high and mild levels of threat and (2) the listener, the family, and the nation as persons or groups endangered, Powell examined the effect on the subjects' attitudes toward a proposed program of community fallout shelters. The principal findings were: one, anxiety appeals will change attitudes significantly only if explicitly directed at the listener or at those with whom he is personally and closely involved and, two, a strong anxiety appeal posing a threat to the listener's family will produce a greater change in attitude than will one that is mild in level of anxiety.[20]

These findings, once again, represent experimental evidence which supports the conclusion that, under certain conditions, a high-anxiety appeal is more effective in producing greater positive attitude change than a mild- or low-anxiety appeal.

THE AUDITORS AND FEAR-AROUSING APPEALS

Goldstein, in "The Relationship Between Coping and Avoiding Behavior and Response to Fear-Arousing Propaganda," published in *The Journal of Abnormal and Social Psychology,* noted:

In their comprehensive study of the effectiveness of fear-arousing propaganda, Janis and Feshbach attempt to explain the failure of the strong fear appeal by recourse to the concept of a "defensive reaction." . . . However, recent research on defense mechanisms suggests that there is no uniform defensive reaction to the heightening of emotional tension. . . . The defensive reaction of subjects seems to reflect a habitual way of dealing with tension-producing material.[21]

Goldstein investigated the proposition that individuals differ in their defensive reactions to fear-arousing propaganda. He hypothesized that acceptance or nonacceptance of the recommendations contained in a propaganda appeal is related to the subject's characteristic reaction to tension-producing stimuli. In order to test this hypothesis, Goldstein divided his test population into two groups by using Mainord's highly emotionally-charged Sentence Completion Test (SCT). Persons who were sensitized to the sexual and aggressive implications of the various

---

[19] Fredric A. Powell, "The Effects of Anxiety-Arousing Messages when Related to Personal, Familiar, and Impersonal Referents," *Speech Monographs,* XXXII (1965), 102.

[20] *Ibid.,* p. 106.

[21] Michael J. Goldstein, "The Relationship Between Coping and Avoiding Behavior and Response to Fear-Arousing Propaganda," *The Journal of Abnormal and Social Psychology,* LIX (1959), 247.

sentence stems and could relate them to their own needs and emotions were identified as "copers"; "avoiders," on the other hand, were those who characteristically failed to recognize the implications of the sentence stems and were unable to perceive the feelings suggested in the stems as being related to themselves. After conducting a carefully controlled experiment, Goldstein concluded that "a strong fear appeal receives greater acceptance among copers than among avoiders, while the minimal fear appeal receives greater acceptance among avoiders than among copers."[22] The obvious importance of the study is that it may be of value to discriminate between different types of defensive reactions and different individual tolerance levels in attempting to predict and explain the eventual acceptance or rejection of a propaganda appeal.

SUMMARY

The complexity of the communication situation is clearly shown by the research which has been conducted in the area of fear-arousing appeals. Conclusions of this research emphasize the importance of high source credibility, of a thoroughly analyzed and carefully prepared message, and of judicious assessment of the auditors. In other words, no aspect of the communication situation, with the exception of the media of transmission, can be discounted in the preparation, delivery, and analysis of a persuasive message.

As a final note, it must be emphasized that the research which has been conducted in the area of fear appeals is of value only as it describes the function of fear-arousing material in relation to the variables of the communication situation. Decisions which lead to the actual use of fear appeals are judgmental questions which must be resolved by the communicator. Understanding the research findings in this area, however, is the basis of reaching sound decisions concerning the selection of fear appeals.

PREDICTIVE GENERALIZATIONS

III-A   Listeners or readers will not comprehend or accept a communication unless they first pay attention to it.

III-A-1   A listener's attention will be seized *momentarily* by such things as the speaker's vocal inflection, volume, movement, gesture or position because, perhaps, elements of novelty in the environment direct listener's attention to events that are potentially dangerous.

III-A-2   A listener's attention will be *sustained,* however, only by information that touches his experiences and interests.

[22] *Ibid.,* p. 252.

III-A-3   Anti-climactic order of information will usually be more effective than climactic in *seizing* the attention of listeners or readers initially uninterested in the subject; where interest in the subject is high, a climactic order of materials may prove more effective in *sustaining* attention.

III-B   Personal characteristics of listeners or readers will determine whether information will be accurately perceived.

III-B-1   Those who regard new information as potentially useful will open themselves to it; those who regard new information as potentially dangerous or threatening will either avoid or distort it.

III-B-2   The interests of listeners or readers will sometimes cause them to distort information either by perceiving greater agreement with the statements of friends or greater disagreement with the statements of enemies than is actually the case.

III-B-3   Listeners or readers who know how their group perceives an object may, if they value membership in the group, tend to see it in the same way.

III-B-4   Aroused emotion may affect listeners' or readers' abilities to perceive, thereby producing the reaction of perceptual defense, that is, resistance to the perception of unpleasant objects.

III-B-5   Those who are alerted to perceive certain objects will perceive them more quickly than those who are not alerted, but will tend to miss other events.

III-B-6   Familiar language or language associated with the values held by listeners will improve the accuracy and speed of perception.

III-B-7   Neutral language, rather than emotionally loaded language, will help forestall distortion of information.

III-B-8   The best insurance against distortion of one's information is the introduction of redundancy, either by verbal restatement or re-exemplification, or by gesture, vocal inflection, or supplementary materials such as photographs, charts, objects or demonstrations.

III-C   Listeners or readers will comprehend a communication when they are familiar with its words and other cues and are able to associate, in some useful way, new ideas with familiar ideas.

III-C-1   The association of new ideas with familiar ideas is dependent on the complementary processes, concept formation and concept attainment. That is, one must be familiar with the categories into which new experiences are to be fitted (or must devise such categories), and must be able to identify the characteristics of a new instance that permit it to be placed in one of the established categories.

III-C-2   Speakers and writers facilitate comprehension by reporting the results of concept formation (indicating the existing categories into which this corner of experience has been divided), and by providing practice in concept attainment (providing experience in fitting new instances into the existing categories).

III-C-3   The sequence in which information is presented does not seem to be important to comprehension as long as discussions of individual categories are kept distinct, that is, as long as "political" advantages of free trade are distinguished from the "economic" and "social" advantages.

III-C-4   Since comprehension, like attention, is a form of motivated behavior, the speaker or writer will improve comprehension insofar as he relates new information to the interests of listeners or readers.

III-C-5   By explicitly stating his conclusions rather than allowing listeners or readers to infer those conclusions, the speaker or writer invariably facilitates comprehension.

III-D   A listener or reader accepts the recommendations of a speaker or writer because he respects the person making the recommendations, because information provided him demonstrates that those recommendations are consistent with other things he believes and does, and/or because acceptance promises to lead to the achievement of one or more of his personal goals.

III-D-1   Listeners will judge a speaker to be competent if they see him as having equal or higher social status than themselves, or if they see him as a member of a group to which they also belong. Clues provided by a man's speech, clothes, reputation and what he says about himself permit these judgments. Other factors are presumably also involved.

III-D-2   Listeners will judge a speaker to be trustworthy if they judge his manner to be sincere and his motives not entirely selfish. Clues provided by a man's voice, appearance, reputation and his fairness in treating opposing advocates and arguments permit these judgments.

III-D-3   Since the effects of the speaker's or writer's prestige in inducing acceptance tend to deteriorate in time, he will gain maximum effect if he secures commitment from listeners shortly after they have heard his communication, or if he reminds listeners of his prestige just before they are called upon to act.

III-D-4   Since listeners and readers may regain cognitive balance by other means than opinion change, speakers or writers may be advised that, the greater the change in opinion they recommend, the more likely listeners will be to discredit them rather than change their opinions, especially when they already have strong opinions on the matter and do not regard the speaker highly. However, when they have the high respect of an audience with relatively weak opinions on the issue, speakers may expect greater changes in opinion the greater the change they recommend.

III-D-5   Because many people hold opinions without having much information, they will tend to seek information that supports such opinions. Speakers or writers seeking action from audiences tacitly disposed to accept their propositions, by providing such information in the form of examples, illustrations, statistical data or authority-based assertion, may so strengthen the belief that it may find expression in consistent action.

III-D-6   Where listeners or readers hold no clearly formulated opinion on an issue, the information presented by a communication may produce acceptance by showing that the new proposition is consistent with other things they believe and do.

III-D-7   Testimony in the form of statistical data may induce acceptance by demonstrating that the new proposition is consistent with accepted ways of knowing.

III-D-8   Testimony in the form of authority-based assertion may induce acceptance by demonstrating that acceptance of the new proposition is consistent with prior evaluation of the advocate and, ultimately, with other propositions already accepted.

III-D-9   Since listeners or readers may accept recommendations advocated in a communication if acceptance promises to lead to attainment of one or more personal goals, speakers and writers who first remind listeners of the worth of the goal, and then indicate that acceptance will lead to attainment of the goal, may induce acceptance.

III-D-10   A corollary is: if listeners or readers fear that non-acceptance will result in the frustration of goal-attainment, they may be induced to accept the speaker's or writer's recommendations.

III-D-11   When fear-arousing appeals are used, speakers and writers will be more likely to gain acceptance of their recommendations if the strength of those appeals is proportionate to the importance of the issue in listeners' minds.

DISCUSSION QUESTIONS

1. Which would you say is the strategy more frequently used to seize attention by magazines distributed chiefly through newsstand sales— exploitation of novelty or appeal to interests?

2. Under what circumstances will repetition of some form of stimulation arrest attention? Will repetition have other effects?

3. Are there certain subjects of communications that may be more likely than others to encourage listeners to distort what is said? Can any principle be derived for classifying subjects that will and will not tend to encourage distortion?

4. Experiments with radar watch-keepers and others performing vigilance tasks have demonstrated that accuracy of perception under such conditions can be improved by "rest" periods. What do you suppose is the function of such "rest" periods? Do you see any application to communication?

5. Can you think of any circumstances in which comprehension of information is not related to concept formation and concept attainment? What other activities may take place?

6. We have declared that sequence of items does not affect listeners' or readers' abilities to comprehend information. If that is so, what value

have such orders as chronology, simple-to-complex, problem-solution, or familiar-to-unfamiliar?

7. Is there any reason to suppose that irony or satire may be dangerous methods of exposition insofar as ease and accuracy of perception and comprehension are concerned?

8. What can possibly be the aim of communications that apparently seek no active response from listeners or readers—many sermons, anniversary addresses and commencement addresses, editorials about Christmas and other "inspirational" pieces? What function, if any, do they perform?

9. Does your experience with information-seeking confirm the notion that opinions are formed prior to the possession of much information?

10. Several studies of the differential effects of arguments supported with good and bad evidence, using such issues as the abolition of capital punishment and the prohibition of religious instruction in public schools, have found that weak evidence, inconsistent evidence, undocumented evidence or no evidence at all produced no more or less opinion change than "good" evidence. How do you explain these results? Do you believe that the *quality* of informational support for opinions is irrelevant?

11. Will some people be more likely to accept communications confirmed by testimony composed of statistical data and others be more likely to accept those confirmed by authority-based assertion? What general hypothesis would you propose for investigation?

12. Recall some recent instance in which you were induced to change an opinion. What part did evidence play in that decision? What part the prestige of the communicator?

13. Someone has declared that people are more inclined to accept the recommendations of an honest man of mean intellect than those of a highly competent man whose trustworthiness is in doubt. How might one confirm that observation?

14. Some of the more obvious efforts at motivating acceptance of communicators' recommendations are to be seen in advertisements for perfumes and other cosmetic products. Where lies the chief weakness of such motivational efforts? Could that weakness be removed?

SECTION IV

Limits of
communication effects

THE LIMITS OF COMMUNICATION EFFECTS

HOWARD H. MARTIN

THE IMAGE of the *Brave New World* cast by Aldous Huxley in 1932 was intended to frighten western readers into resistance against a standardized slavery imposed by a Soviet-style totalitarian elite aided and sustained by the technology of the great capitalist nations, Britain and the United States, "Our Ford." Material affluence would render men docile while medical and psychological technology would enforce their slavery. A College of Emotional Engineering and various Bureaus of Propaganda using techniques of "neo-Pavlovian conditioning" and "hypnopaedia" would standardize feelings and attitudes. The drug, *soma,* freely distributed, would blot out uncomfortable reality. Nothing, Huxley seemed to say, stood in the way of this anti-Utopian future but the temporary imperfection of our understanding of human behavior and our primitive technology for controlling it.

George Orwell's *1984* played variations on the same theme. And Huxley, in the preface to a subsequent edition of *Brave New World,* declared that an efficient technology was all that was required for complete social control. "To bring about that revolution," he said, "we require, among others, the following discoveries and inventions. First, a greatly improved technique of suggestion—through infant conditioning and, later, with the aid of drugs, such as scopolamine. Second, a fully developed science of human differences, enabling government managers to assign any given individual to his or her place in the social and economic hierarchy. (Round pegs in square holes tend to have dangerous thoughts about the social system and to infect others with their discontents.) Third (since reality, however Utopian, is something from which people feel the need of taking pretty frequent holidays), a substitute for alcohol and other narcotics, something at once less harmful and more pleasure-giving than gin or heroin. And fourth, . . . a foolproof system of eugenics, designed to standardize the human product and so to facilitate the task of managers."[1]

Vance Packard's 1957 best-seller, *The Hidden Persuaders,* declared that technology had already placed immensely effective tools in the hands of those seeking to manipulate people—advertisers, public relations counsels, psychotherapists and political campaigners—and that these tools were being used, "often with impressive success, to channel

---

[1] Aldous Huxley, *Brave New World* (New York: Bantam Books, 1958), p. xiii.

our unthinking habits and purchasing decisions, and our thought processes. . . . " The terrible danger, cried Packard, was that "typically, these efforts take place beneath the level of our awareness; so that the appeals which so often move us are, in a sense, 'hidden'." We are already in "the chilling world of George Orwell and his Big Brother," Packard concluded, when "we please them [the manipulators] with our growing docility in responding to their manipulation of symbols that stir us to action."[2] The bulk of his book documented with excited editorial urgency the powerful underhanded techniques currently in use to merchandise political candidates, to mold the minds of workers to fit the needs of business and to sell unwanted products and services to unwitting consumers.

Huxley, Orwell and Packard agreed in their view of men as helplessly exposed pawns of a power elite armed with increasingly powerful tools with which to render communication effects, sooner or later, completely predictable. Once communication could be carried on in an entirely scientific fashion, social control would become a reality, and when that had happened, human intelligence, responsibility and freedom would have been destroyed.

There are those who look on this new era of "social engineering" with anticipation and zest, one of the best known of whom is the Harvard psychologist, B. F. Skinner. In his novel, *Walden Two*, Skinner's protagonist, Frazier, declares that the means of social control are at hand and wait only to be seized by the Planners who will direct the rebuilding of society more to the heart's desire:

No, Mr. Castle, the science is there for the asking. But its techniques and methods are in the wrong hands—they are used for personal aggrandizement in a competitive world or, in the case of the psychologist and educator, for futile corrective purposes. My question is, have you the courage to take up and wield the science of human behavior for the good of mankind?[3]

Although the book is in the tradition of the Utopian novel, the social image and the views of Frazier agree with Skinner's professional statements. He argues consistently that with increasing scientific understanding of human behavior come opportunities for social control that ought to be seized with zest, not rejected in fear or distaste.[4] Such a view, like those of Huxley, Orwell and Packard, seems to stress the efficiency of communicative techniques without considering the defenses people hold against them or the absence, in this society at least, of effective control over the circumstances in which people hear or

[2] Vance Packard, *The Hidden Persuaders* (New York: David McKay Co., 1957).

[3] B. F. Skinner, *Walden Two* (New York: The Macmillan Co., 1948), p. 214.

[4] B. F. Skinner, "Freedom and the Control of Men," *The American Scholar*, 25 (Winter, 1955–56), 47–65.

read messages of these would-be manipulators. There may be reason to worry about the conduct of some persuaders, perhaps even to erect restraints on their activities, but there may also be less reason for panic when we understand that the power of the spoken or written word to re-make society is much more limited than either the frightened student of mass communication or the eager social engineer would have us believe. This chapter and its associated readings develops some of those limitations on communication effects.

PERSONAL DEFENSES

Far from being pawns helplessly exposed to the powerfully efficient tools of communication elites, individuals possess a number of defenses against manipulation efforts. The most obvious of these is the freedom to turn off the radio and put down the newspaper. We simply do not pay attention to most of the messages directed at us. By exercise of choice, we expose ourselves only to those communications we suppose will provide information we need or will shore up the beliefs and attitudes we already possess. Our experiences determine our interests, and our interests dictate what we will attend. We can afford to listen to radio or watch television only so many hours a week; there is evidence that we select the entertainment of those hours. We turn off a tedious or offensive program, and advertisers read their messages while we are in the bathroom. Therefore, the obvious freedom we possess to shut off most messages designed to influence us is probably the severest limitation on the manipulator. Since we have already developed the importance of *selective exposure* on page 63 there is no need to say more here.

A second personal defense is *inattention*. Although listeners may expose themselves, voluntarily or involuntarily, to new information, there is still no guarantee that the information will be received unless closely attended. As the writer of a recent summary of the field of perception declares, "an observer's perception of the field, or of any particular aspect of it, may be more rapid and accurate insofar as his attention is directed towards it."[5] The corrolary is obvious: what one does *not* pay close attention to will *not* be perceived either rapidly or accurately. The repetitious nature of some television and radio commercials is designed to overcome the habitual defense of inattention thrown up by most listeners.

A third defense against communications is the phenomenon of *perceptual sensitivity* and its counterpart, *perceptual defense*. Several laboratory experiments discovered that words flashed upon a screen were more quickly identified by people who prized values to which the

---

[5] M. D. Vernon, *The Psychology of Perception* (Baltimore: Penguin Books, 1962), p. 165.

words related, while words unrelated to such values were either missed or were less quickly identified. For instance, one person with high aesthetic, theoretical and social values had trouble identifying the word "income," and saw it instead successively as "learning," "tomorrow," "learning," "knowledge," "literature," "learning," "loving," and finally, "income," as the exposure time was increased.[6] In other experiments where sexual words were used, some respondents seemed to resist perception of such words while others who seemed *sensitized* to such words perceived them more quickly than neutral words.[7] Such findings suggest that people may be armed with another defense against communications.

Even after one has paid attention to the words of a speaker or writer, he seems to have a fourth defense, *selective remembering and forgetting*. Private experience and considerable experimental evidence has shown that many things we learn are soon forgotten, not simply because of the passage of time, but, we now believe, because other experiences crowd out the original learning. It may seem that forgetting under such conditions is accidental, rather than intentional; but a deliberate effort may be implied by the tendency already discussed to expose ourselves usually to experiences and ideas we expect to be pleasant and reinforcing rather than the reverse. A particularly offensive speech lampooning our favorite candidate may make us eager to get the bad taste out of our mouth by reading about the candidate's warm reception among people we respect. The later information will tend to produce what learning theorists call *retroactive interference* which will push the unpleasant information into the shadow.[8]

Another side of selective remembering is the individual tendency to remember things the way we want to remember them. Such distortion of information is related to the way emotional and motivational factors affect our perception of what we see and hear. If we admire the speaker, we are likely to hear him say things we agree with, even if his views are, in fact, slightly different from ours. If we dislike him or disagree with him, we are likely to understand him as holding a position further away from our own than it actually is. These phenomena have been called *assimilation* and *contrast* effects.[9] The same thing occurs with information accessible in memory; we remember

[6] Leo Postman, Jerome S. Bruner, and Elliot McGinnies, "Personal Values as Selective Factors in Perception," *Journal of Abnormal and Social Psychology*, 43 (April, 1948), 153.

[7] Vernon, *Perception*, p. 216.

[8] Ernest R. Hilgard and Gordon H. Bower, *Theories of Learning*, 3rd edition (New York: Appleton-Century-Crofts, 1966), pp. 498ff.

[9] These "assimilation" and "contrast" effects have been discussed in C. I. Hovland, O. J. Harvey and M. Sherif, "Assimilation and Contrast Effects in Reactions to Communication and Attitude Change," *Journal of Abnormal and Social Psychology*, 55 (September, 1957), 244–252.

it as we wish to remember it, making qualitative modifications in it to make it conform more closely to our needs and interests.

What we hold in memory is closely related to our lasting interests. Frederick Bartlett in the pioneering experimental report on *Remembering* observed that "Very broadly speaking, the matter of recall is mainly a question of interest . . . interests, regarded as a development of individual mental life, may decide what it is that a person remembers."[10] Our interests, needs and habits may act more or less without conscious effort to produce the defense of selective forgetting.

Finally, there does seem to be some consciously willed *repression* of information that threatens to produce anxiety. In much the same way, but not to the same extent as those suffering from mental illness, normal people repress threatening information. The experiences of normal people following free association with an analyst seem to confirm the existence of some *willed* forgetting. This, too, serves as a personal defense against manipulative communications.[11]

Several investigators have asked the question: "Are some people more easily persuaded by communications than others?" or, to put it the other way around, "Are some people more immune to persuasive communications than others?" If those questions can be answered affirmatively then some people possess a fifth *general defense* against communicative manipulation. The studies summarized in the accompanying essay by Carl Hovland and Irving Janis seem to confirm the suspicion that some people are more or less immune to persuasive communications, and that this immunity is related to certain personality traits rather than to the topic of the communication, the identity of the communicator or the setting.

The most decisive personality trait of the generally persuasible person seems to be low self-esteem. If a man is not sure of his position among his associates, feels inadequate to his task or believes that he has not reached the goals he set for himself, he may be more susceptible to influence from others than is the person who feels socially adequate. This relationship was confirmed by the experience of American soldiers in Chinese prisoner of war camps during the Korean War. Edgar Schein reports that "the man who was most vulnerable *ideologically* was he who had never enjoyed any kind of secure or rewarding status position either in his home community or in the Army."[12]

That women seem generally more susceptible to persuasive communications than men is apparently related to the cultural determination of sexual roles, for girls do not differ from boys in general

[10] Frederick C. Bartlett, *Remembering: a Study in Experimental and Social Psychology* (Cambridge: The University Press, 1932, reprinted 1961), p. 256.

[11] Ian M. L. Hunter, *Memory, Facts and Fallacies* (Baltimore: Penguin Books, 1957), pp. 121–122.

[12] Edgar Schein, "The Chinese Indoctrination Program for Prisoners of War," *Psychiatry*, 19 (May, 1956), 167.

persuasibility. As they grow to womanhood, females in our culture are drawn to accept a submissive role, that is, tend to define themselves more in terms of their relations with other people—their husbands and families—than do men, with the result that men are generally more immune to persuasive communications than their wives or mothers, sisters or daughters.[13]

A sixth personal defense against communications aimed at manipulating opinion is one's sense of the *private importance of the belief* or opinion under fire. Milton Rokeach, in the accompanying lecture to a group of advertising men, sees an individual's beliefs as a series of levels, pictured as concentric circles expanding from a center of *primitive beliefs* to a periphery of *inconsequential beliefs*. These inconsequential beliefs, the ones with which advertisers mostly deal, are easiest to change, but beliefs in each inner circle are successively more difficult to change until the innermost primitive beliefs are practically impossible to alter.[14] Rokeach's scheme suggests that personal investment in a particular belief or opinion makes one more resistant to efforts by communicators to change that belief. Moreover, the occasional success of advertisers in altering inconsequential beliefs can hardly be thought dangerous, especially when that success has been haphazard and impermanent.[15] Other writers have defined the private importance of a belief in terms of *ego-involvement* which, on the whole, determines what they call *latitudes of acceptance* and *latitudes of rejection* of a communication. If a listener strongly holds a position which is quite discrepant from that expressed by a communicator, he will classify the communication for rejection and thereby defend himself against it.[16]

Several studies have found that a person who meets arguments that run counter to his position may be forced to defend his view by devising defensive arguments. This act of defending his own belief by

[13] Studies of persuasibility have shown women more persuasible than men only on certain issues such as voting choices. Perhaps men would be found to be more persuasible than women on such matters as child-care and -rearing or home decoration, issues about which men would be less well-informed than women and which they would find less salient. The blurring of the social roles of men and women may be reducing the differences in persuasibility between the sexes.

[14] Milton Rokeach, "Images of the Consumer's Mind on and off Madison Avenue," *Etc: A Review of General Semantics*, 21 (September, 1964), 267–273.

[15] An inconsequential belief in this context would be the conviction that one deodorant will last longer in preventing perspiration odor than another. We do not mean to suggest in this discussion that advertisers do not profoundly affect our attitudes and values by emphasizing the importance of youthfulness, of free sexual expression, of physical beauty, of self-indulgence, among other values. But much of their effect in fixing or altering our values is accidental and cumulative rather than specifically calculated. We have mentioned these effects upon the standardization of American life on page 241.

[16] Carolyn W. Sherif, Muzafer Sherif and Roger E. Nebergall, *Attitude and Attitude Change* (Philadelphia: W. B. Saunders Co., 1965), p. 228.

developing supportive arguments seems to immunize him against sub-sequently encountered stronger counter-arguments. For this reason, ad-vocates who presented their opponents' views as well as their own (rather than only their own position) proved more successful in per-suading their audiences and especially in preventing them from shift-ing when later subjected to the opponents' arguments.[17] Therefore, those who run into views that disagree with their own may find that the exercise of developing argumentative support for their own views, by immunizing them against disagreeable positions, provides an addi-tional defense against later persuasive communications. One would suppose, although there is no evidence on the point, that a Lutheran who had been brought into contact with other doctrinal views during his years in public schools would be more immune to a skeptical col-lege roommate's attacks on his beliefs than another young man who had been isolated from opposing views by his attendance in parochial schools.

That a variety of options, besides changing his opinion, exist for the person exposed to persuasive communications constitutes another personal defense. Several writers have discussed the process of opinion change in terms of what has been called *balance theory*. The notion is this: when a person encounters a piece of information which contra-dicts something else he already knows, he will try to bring these two pieces of information into a consistent relationship with each other. For example, if a liberal spokesman whom you have always respected were publicly to declare his opposition to the extension of social security benefits, two cognitive elements—your prior belief in social security and the admired liberal's opposition to social security—would be inconsistent or out of balance. Leon Festinger has called this situation *cognitive dissonance* and presumed that the discomfort you feel as a result of these inconsistent pieces of information will motivate you to act in order to regain cognitive consistency or balance.[18] One way of regaining balance is to change your opinion to match that of the ad-mired liberal spokesman. But if the original belief was strong or closely tied to other important beliefs, you might regain cognitive balance in several other ways:

1. You might *alter your opinion of the liberal spokesman*: "Maybe he's not as liberal as I thought he was!"
2. You might *refuse to believe the reports* that he opposed the exten-sion of social security benefits.
3. You might *distort the view of the spokesman*: "I see what he means:

---

[17] Hovland, Janis and Kelley summarize several studies in *Communication and Persuasion*, pp. 105–110; see also William J. McGuire, "Persistence of Resistance to Persuasion Induced by Various Types of Belief Defense," *Journal of Abnormal and Social Psychology*, 64 (April, 1962), 241–248.

[18] Festinger, *A Theory of Cognitive Dissonance*, p. 264.

Let's not commit ourselves to the extension of benefits until we can be certain that increased contributions and tax support will meet the expense."

4. You can *rearrange the importance of the conflicting pieces of information*: "Well, maybe he does oppose extending social security benefits, but he is such a staunch supporter of civil rights legislation which is, after all, a more important reflection of the liberal's interest in human values."

The availability of these options other than opinion change represents another personal defense against persuasive communications.

A final limitation upon the effects of the communication is the possibility that the listener will be able to test the claims of the persuader by tentatively taking the recommended action. If the promised rewards are not forthcoming, he can then reject the proposal. Where the commitment is minor—buying a package of soap or a tube of toothpaste—this may provide a defense against persuasion.

ENVIRONMENTAL LIMITATIONS

Beyond these personal defenses against persuasive communications, there are features of the environment in which communication occurs that restrict its effectiveness. Or, to look at the matter from the point of view of the persuader, unless some control can be exercised over the listener's environment, the effect of his communications will be small. For this reason, totalitarian leadership seeking to preserve its popular consensus clamps down on the free distribution of information. Approved ideas saturate radio and television fare, fill newspapers and magazines, appear on wall posters and in the mouths of party members. Contrary ideas are at first suppressed by force and ultimately excluded because no one wants to hear them. By these means, a homogeneity of opinion is preserved more easily than it might be in an environment where variety of public views is the rule. The censorship imposed by a dictator inevitably provokes indignant criticism, and well it might; as listeners, we are obviously interested in protecting ourselves against harmful communicative influence.

But our horror at the idea of censorship hardly alters the fact that communicators seek, insofar as they are able, to control the environment so that their messages are favored and competing messages are minimized. The advertiser who buys up all the commercial spots during the evening of a national election when he knows millions will be watching, seeks to create, for the six or eight hours of that night, a controlled environment in which his messages dominate. Of course, his degree of control is slight indeed, but control is his aim. Parochial schools were founded and are maintained on the principle of environmental control. If children, the reasoning goes, spend most of their time with other members of their religious group under the guidance of men and women who are doctrinally correct, the children will develop a deeper and more enduring attachment to their church than they might if they attended public schools where there is no homogeneity of religious views. Some parents still choose to send their sons and daughters to colleges that have a sectarian religious environment in the hope that the young people may not as easily grow skeptical of their traditional faith as sometimes happens in a large and unreligious university. By excluding contrary ideas, an institution or nation may help maintain certain beliefs, but it may ignore the task of immunizing people against conflicting views, in the manner discussed on page 236, and may, therefore, render the desired beliefs vulnerable to change when contrary ideas are encountered outside of the protective environment. Unless homogeneity of expressed opinion could be perpetually preserved, it might be a mistake to attempt to maintain it only for a short time.

The democratic nation, too, in the interest of its own self-preservation seeks to set some environmental controls. The brashest and severest criticism is sometimes hard to bear, therefore alien and sedition laws or Communist control acts are devised in order to prevent contrary ideas from destroying political consensus. That such legislation may be undesirable and unnecessary need not be argued here; the point to be made is this: many groups who seek to influence the opinions and beliefs of other people realize that the efficacy of their messages may be enhanced by a degree of environmental control.

Two questions may be raised here about the relation of environmental control to the limitations of communication effects. 1) Just how much does a high degree of environmental control increase the effectiveness of messages? 2) Is it possible for communicators to exert much control over the environments in which their messages are broadcast? An answer to the first question is explicit in Edgar Schein's report on the Chinese indoctrination program to which we have referred.

Americans were shocked to learn that U.S. soldiers captured in Korea were actually induced to broadcast Chinese charges that American troops were using germ warfare in Korea. When some of the prisoners returned from POW camps to reveal the intense indoctrination they had endured, the name *brainwashing* seemed an accurate label for the devilish process of *thought control* practiced by the Chinese. Careful study of the returned prisoners' accounts of their experiences and their behavior in camp and back home has made clear that the indoctrination program was neither "new" nor nearly as effective as was first believed. But the experience is instructive, for the Chinese enjoyed almost maximum environmental control, and even under such conditions were able to affect the beliefs and significant behavior of only a handful of men for only a limited time.

The Chinese sought to "gain complete control over those parts of the physical and social environment which sustained attitudes, beliefs, and values," Schein observed, and therefore substituted their own information for prisoners' usual information, manipulated the delivery of mail from home, undermined personal contacts between prisoners by segregation and the cultivation of suspicion and distrust, broke up all established or spontaneous groups that were not of their own creation.[19] They subjected prisoners to long daily lectures, to various propaganda leaflets and films, to testimonials from collaborating prisoners, to group discussions of the ideological themes of lectures, and to lengthy and fatiguing interrogations in which prisoners were encouraged to participate by writing out confessions, by copying Communist doctrine from books, or by writing original defenses of Communist propositions. Prisoners who were willing to assist the Chinese in small or large ways were rewarded with food, cigarettes, undemanding duties and social rank and status.

And what were the results? While most of the men *collaborated* by helping the enemy in some way, few seem to have collaborated "to a sufficient extent to be detrimental to the United Nations cause," and those who did collaborate did not necessarily defect from democratic values or ideology.[20] Even fewer men were *converted* to the Communist cause, as measured by overt behavior, although the measurement of ideological change and its permanence after the men returned to the United States is difficult or impossible. Only 21 men refused repatriation; subsequently, all but 3 returned (as of April 1967) to the United States. Such evidence as this brought Schein to the conclusion that "considering the effort devoted to it, the Chinese program was a failure."[21] Given almost unlimited environmental control, the program was still "a failure"!

There were several reasons for the ineffectiveness of the indoctrination program. One which is suggested in Schein's report is that the Chinese did not exert all the control they might have exerted, or exert it continuously. While the breaking up of formal and spontaneous organizations deprived prisoners of social support, "it was never sufficiently extended to make the prisoners completely dependent on the Chinese."[22] And, the Chinese did not have enough trained indoctrinators who could establish close and personal relationships with individual prisoners. Nor could their captors completely exclude contrary facts from the prisoners' environment; prisoners took the poor conditions in the villages in which they lived as evidence of the failure of Communist promises to their people. Moreover, the Chinese may have made some mistakes in their efforts at control. The segregation of Negro prisoners, which was apparently done to facilitate indoctrina-

[19] *Psychiatry*, Vol. 19, p. 153.
[20] *Ibid.*, p. 169.
[21] *Ibid.*
[22] *Ibid.*, p. 170.

tion in the failures of democratic promises to minority groups, seems to have backfired; most Negroes could see no difference between Chinese and American segregation.

Implicit in the reports of Chinese indoctrination is the fact that even rigid environmental control is insufficient to insure the success of communications. Few men actually changed their minds about democracy or Communism, but went along with the Chinese in order to survive or to gain privileges, or because they thought of themselves as infiltrators, or because they wanted to let their families know they were alive. Those who did convert were often men of low status who thought they had everything to gain and nothing to lose by accepting rewards from their captors. To persuade such men would hardly have required the elaborate environmental controls enforced by the Chinese, for those of low status and low self-esteem are most exposed to the blandishments of a would-be manipulator.

Moreover, converts did not remain pro-Chinese or pro-Communist after they returned home to an environment non-supportive of the beliefs the Chinese had hoped to inculcate.[23] The same sort of reversion to accustomed ways has been observed in hospitalized patients who return to active life after a long confinement. Although they have grown acquiescent and dependent in the hospital, docilely accepting the direction of the professional staff, it is not long after they return to their homes and lives that they resume their former self-sufficiency and pre-hospitalization attitudes and opinions.[24]

We may now take up the second question, Is it possible for communicators to exert much control over the environments in which their messages are broadcast? A partial answer is that, in the Western Democracies at least, no group other than the state has the power to control the environment to an appreciable degree, and the state refuses, as a matter of principle, to use its power to insure homogeneity of political or social belief.

Realizing that a message is more effective where there are none to contradict it, the television advertiser who is introducing a new product saturates peak viewing time with 15-second spot announcements. If he can produce a situation approaching the ideal—the presence of his message to the exclusion of others—he may increase the chance that his message will be heard and comprehended, and may even facilitate its acceptance. The increased density of television spot announcements as the political campaign nears the end suggests that promoters of candidates recognize the importance of a homogeneous environment of expressed opinion. But such control is puny at best. Because society

---

[23] Edgar Schein, *Coercive Persuasion* (New York: W. W. Norton, 1961), p. 189.

[24] See, for example, Rose Laub Coser, "A Home Away from Home," in *Sociological Studies of Health and Sickness*, Dorian Apple, editor (New York: McGraw-Hill Book Co., Inc., 1960), pp. 154–172.

encourages diversity of opinion, it is all but impossible to shut out competing ideas and claims.

It might be argued, however, that television and films do a surprisingly effective job of standardizing the reference groups against which listeners measure their own acts. The style of life exhibited in commercial messages is quite unrelievedly middle-class to upper middle-class in the usual details of furnishings, clothes, household appliances, play and other aspects of living. That much of American life has become standardized across class boundaries suggests that advertisers have been unintentionally effective in picturing for us a homogeneous material environment from which there are almost no dissenters.

Efforts to manipulate behavior by having listeners participate in the communication have often been tried. Groups such as the Daughters of the American Revolution and the Women's Christian Temperance Union have sponsored essay contests for money prizes hoping to encourage large numbers of young people to write arguments supporting the positions of these groups on the premise that they would learn about the group's purposes and begin to commit themselves to them by making public statements. The principle is the same one used by Chinese interrogators. Nor have advertisers ever given up the notion that if people can be enticed to write praise of the product they may also buy it. The person who declares that "I like Swan because . . ." in 25 words or less is making a public declaration of an opinion which he may later feel the need to justify by behaving accordingly. The experiments in *forced compliance* reported by Festinger and others are similar to the plan of the advertiser who offers a reward or chance of reward to the contestant to get him to declare an opinion he may not actually then hold, for experimenters paid their subjects to write arguments in defense of positions with which they were known to disagree.[25]

Rewards are often used by advertisers to get consumers to buy products or services rather than simply express approval of them. Money or the illusion of money reward is the most common: if you buy one product, you get another different product free; if you buy one item at the regular price, you get a second for less; if you buy ten gallons of gasoline at once, you get double-value in savings stamps. Because money rewards of this size are hardly as important to the buyer as were the rewards of status, food, or relieved duties to American prisoners of the Chinese, we are forced to conclude that such opportunities for significant environmental control are meager in this society.

Communicators cannot usually affect the important social props on which most of us lean, cannot break up the groups to which we belong or substitute dependence on the communicator for our dependence on those groups. The only sort of dependence possible is that based on

[25] Festinger, *A Theory of Cognitive Dissonance*, pp. 104–122.

convenience or habit. Because the catalogue is always at one's elbow may make it easier to buy many things from Sears, or to depend, in a way, upon a particular source of information about goods and prices. Some newspapers and magazines develop that kind of dependence. But dependence on the *New York Times*, for example, reflects dependence on a source of information identified as part of an important reference group to which we already belong (independent political liberals), rather than a substituted dependence such as the Chinese provided for confused and suspicious prisoners.

Opportunities for any effective control by communicators over the environment are, in fact, intentionally restricted by acts of the federal and state governments and by the activities of independent professional and consumer groups. Several federal commissions supervise the communicative activities of many business firms. The Federal Trade Commission, acting under the Wheeler-Lea Act of 1938, controls the advertising of foods, drugs, cosmetics and therapeutic devices by means of "cease and desist" orders requiring changes in advertising claims or deceptive practices. Trick photography in television commercials, the use of French names for domestically manufactured perfume, the advertisement of inexpensive products that were not truly for sale have been practices enjoined by the FTC.[26] As a preventative measure, the FTC also publishes guides for advertisers of cigarettes and tires covering such matters as "bait" advertising and deceptive pricing.

The Food and Drug Administration supervises the branding of products offered in interstate commerce in order to prevent manufacturers from offering misleading information about an item, concealing the name and address of the maker, or reducing in size the required descriptions of contents or warnings about excessive or improper use.

The Federal Communications Commission, operating under the Federal Communications Act of 1934, is charged with granting broadcast licenses in accordance with the public interest and necessity. Although few licenses have ever been suspended or revoked for cause, the threat probably has some effect on the programming of broadcasters. The requirement that broadcasters grant equal time to competing political candidates has the effect of frustrating possible efforts of one candidate to shut off the speeches of his opponents by gaining support of network or station owners. In order for the Kennedy-Nixon debates to be held in 1960, Congress had to pass special legislation freeing broadcasters of the requirement to grant equal time to the Prohibition Party candidate or the Farmer-Labor party candidate where they were on the ballot.

The Post Office Department controls use of the mails for fraudulent or obscene purposes. The Securities and Exchange Commission over-

---

[26] I have relied on the summary provided by Edward L. Brink and William T. Kelley, *The Management of Promotion, Consumer Behavior and Demand Stimulation* (Englewood Cliffs, New Jersey: Prentice-Hall, 1963), pp. 335ff.

sees the dissemination of information about securities and has power to punish those who mislead or seek to defraud investors. Moreover, the laws against libel and slander inhibit those speaking against people or institutions by providing legal redress for those charged untruthfully or abusively.

In addition to federal restraints, there are laws in many states prohibiting "bait" advertising, regulating the advertising of liquor, controlling the advertising of physicians, funeral parlors, loan companies and sellers of oleomargarine, and regulating all billboard advertising.

Where state or federal law offers insufficient protection to consumers, private groups of citizens exert restraints on certain communicative activities. Better Business Bureaus, for example, keep watch on misleading advertising and fraudulent business practices. The League of Women Voters seeks to insure that voters have full and accurate information about candidates and issues in local, state and federal elections. And the journals of the American Medical Association and the American Dental Association as well as other publications have adopted standards for advertising that also prevent certain efforts at environmental control by sellers.

Opportunities for communicators to exert control over the environment are, at best, transient and insignificant in this society, and are frequently frustrated by federal and state law or by the concerted action of private groups. Even where the communicator enjoyed considerable control, as the Chinese did in prisoner of war camps in Korea, the effectiveness of communications still proved modest and often impermanent. While these facts need not sap our vigilance, they may allay any sense of panic at the supposed dangers of social control by an unscrupulous elite.

SUMMARY

Once we feared—or hoped—that increased understanding of the strategies of communication would place great power for social control in the hands of an enterprising elite. Now we have come to understand that there are serious limitations on the effects produced by communications. These limitations derive from such *personal defenses* as selective exposure, inattention, perceptual defense, selective remembering and forgetting, general resistance to persuasion, ego-involvement in particular issues, alternative options to opinion change, and reality testing; and derive from *environmental limitations* such as the difficulty, the expense, and the unacceptability of many efforts at environmental control as well as the very modest advantage which even a considerable amount of environmental control confers upon a communication.

GENERAL PERSUASIBILITY

CARL I. HOVLAND AND IRVING L. JANIS

THE QUESTION TO BE ANSWERED IS: To what exent is the trait of persuasibility actually found experimentally and what degree of generality does it exhibit?

CONSISTENCY OF INDIVIDUAL DIFFERENCES

The present series of studies indicates that there is such a factor as general persuasibility, although there are certain limitations to its generality imposed by the experimental procedures employed. There is evidence that persuasibility exists as a "content-free" factor; that is, it exists independently of the subject matter or appeals presented in any particular persuasive communication.

General persuasibility is demonstrated in the studies of Janis and Field. The procedure devised by these experimenters to assess general persuasibility consisted of (1) an Initial Questionnaire measuring opinion on 15 items, (2) a booklet (I) containing five persuasive communications on widely varying topics, each followed by three questions identical with the questions included in the Initial Questionnaire, and (3) another booklet (II) presenting a second series of five persuasive communications on exactly the same topics as the first series but taking diametrically opposite positions. After each communication in Booklet II, the subjects were asked the same opinion questions as in the Initial Questionnaire and Booklet I.

The communications were intentionally varied with respect to type of appeal and arguments. They were all attributed to an identical type of source—reporters writing on "Opinions in the News." The existence of widespread diversity of opinion on the topics was stressed for the subjects, and they were encouraged to express their own views. A general Persuasibility score was assigned to each subject on the basis of his opinion changes in response to both booklets. In order for an opinion change to be counted as such, the subject who had changed his Initial opinion in one direction in response to the communication in

---

Reprinted with permission from Chapter 11 of Irving L. Janis, Carl I. Hovland, et al, *Personality and Persuasibility* (New Haven: Yale University Press, 1959).

Booklet I must change following the Booklet II communication all the way back to his original position or beyond on the provided scale.

The results from this procedure showed consistent individual differences in persuasibility, some subjects shifting first in one and then in the other direction following receipt of the conflicting communications in Booklets I and II. A factor analysis was computed from the intercorrelations between persuasibility subscores on each communication. The results support the hypothesis of a general factor in persuasibility and indicate that the predisposition to change opinions is not wholly specific to the topic or subject matter of the communications.

An investigation of the consistency of individual differences in susceptibility to persuasion by majority opinion was reported by King. His procedure for measuring persuasibility used first a Before questionnaire consisting of 45 opinion items on which subjects checked their scale position from "Agree strongly" to "Disagree strongly." The After questionnaire was identical to the Before questionnaire except that, as a persuasive "communication," each item was checked at a prearranged scale position by the experimenter. The check marks were attributed to one of three sources: a majority of 400 parents of high school students, a majority of 400 high school teachers, and a majority of 400 high school students.

Results from this procedure provide evidence of consistent susceptibility to majority communications over different sources and different content areas. This was demonstrated by the significantly high positive correlation between opinion changes on odd and even items for each subject (split-half reliability score).

A different type of measure of persuasibility was employed by Abelson and Lesser, using first-grade children for subjects. Defining persuasibility as the tendency to seek a state of agreement on matters of opinion, these authors devised three tests of general persuasibility:

1. The Persuasibility Booklet, consisting of pairs of unfamiliar objects, was administered either in group form by the teacher (Teacher Persuasibility measure) or in individual session by the experimenter (Experimenter Persuasibility measure). The communicator showed each pair of pictures to the subjects, first indicating her own preference for one of the objects and then asking the subjects to state their preferences.

2. The Incomplete Stories test was administered individually by the experimenter. Each story described a situation involving a mother (or father) and child, in which the parent figure stated a novel opinion, fact, or bit of advice. The subject was asked to tell what the child in the story would think or do in response.

3. The Recorded Opinions measure, also administered in individual session, was represented as an opinion poll. Unusual opinion questions were posed to the subjects. Before giving their views, the subjects

heard a tape recording on which either two adult voices (one male and one female) or peer voices expressed unanimity of opinion in favor of one choice. Subjects were then asked to state their own preferences.

Two additional measures were obtained, one a Parent Rating of the subjects on persuasibility and the other a Teacher Rating of the same trait.

The results of these procedures yielded statistically significant inter-correlations among the various measures, showing a tendency toward persuasibility, or lack of it, over various topics and in relation to various sources (parents, teachers, experimenters, peers). Significant correlations were obtained for both boys and girls between the Teacher Persuasibility measure and (1) the Teacher Ratings of persuasibility and (2) the Mother Persuasibility measure. The Parent Rating of persuasibility yielded low reliability; nevertheless, there was a significant positive correlation between Parent Ratings and the Teacher Persuasibility measure for the boys in the sample, although not for the girls.

In the Experimenter Persuasibility test subjects were presented with an actual disagreement between their preferences and those of the experimenter and then asked to give their choices again. The results were significantly correlated with the Mother Persuasibility test. The pupils were tested not only immediately but also after a week's delay. At the later session, no effort was made to reinstate the experimenter's preferences or the subject's previous choices; the subject was simply asked to give his present preferences. The correlations between Mother Persuasibility and Experimenter Persuasibility were almost the same for the Immediate and Delayed measures among the boys in the sample, but among the girls there was a significantly higher correlation for the Delayed measure than for the Immediate one.

PERSONALITY CORRELATES OF PERSUASIBILITY

As a further analysis of individual differences in persuasibility, the studies in this volume have attempted to determine what other personality variables are concomitant with high and low responsiveness to verbal communications. Certain variables, such as self-esteem, hostility or aggressiveness, and intelligence, have been investigated by several methods and replicated in more than one study. Other personality correlates are suggested by the evidence from single studies.

Self-Esteem

Janis and Field investigated the hypothesis that high persuasibility is related to low self-esteem. Using a self-rating personality inventory, these authors measured three types of inferiority feelings: feelings of inadequacy, social inhibitions, and test anxiety. Their results showed significant correlations between high persuasibility and the measures of inadequacy feelings and social inhibitions; the correlation between persuasibility and test anxiety was in the expected direction but not significant. These results were obtained from the male subjects in the sample; with the female sample the self-esteem hypothesis was not supported.

The same hypothesis was investigated by Janis and Rife with institutionalized male mental patients, employing the identical personality inventory and persuasibility measure as in the previous study. The correlation between persuasibility and the scores on feelings of inadequacy and guilt proved to be significantly higher than the correlation for the normal sample. This finding, together with the fact that personality scores of the patients showed greater variance than those of the normals, lends some weight to the authors' assumption that the personality predispositions underlying persuasibility in the population at large may be more pronounced in emotionally disturbed persons and therefore more readily observable.

In view of the importance of the self-esteem variable as a concomitant of persuasibility, Cohen performed a study analyzing some of the components of self-esteem as well as its effect on the social influence process. Self-esteem was defined in terms of the value an individual places upon himself, which is assumed to be a function of past success and failure experiences. For experimental purposes, self-esteem was measured by the correspondence or discrepancy between a subject's ideals and his achievement of them, the subjects being sorted into high and low self-esteem groups on this basis.

The effect of level of self-esteem on social influence was measured in a set of interpersonal rather than mass-media persuasion situations. Results showed persons of high self-esteem to be less susceptible to influence from persons of low self-esteem than vice versa and also to be more active in attempting to exert influence. Individuals of high self-esteem were better able in general to protect themselves against unfavorable reactions from their social group and reacted less to any specific group expectations communicated to them.

An investigation of the relation of self-esteem to persuasibility in children made by Lesser and Abelson is reported. In view of their definition of persuasibility as the desire to seek agreement with others they hypothesize that low self-esteem and high persuasibility stem from the same type of previous experience, viz. negatively reinforced instances of disagreement or discrepancy.

In one experiment, three measures of self-esteem were taken, based on sociometric techniques: (1) Each child was asked to name those classmates he regarded as "nicer," "smarter," etc. than he. (2) Each was asked to judge which classmates liked him or would choose to sit next to him. (3) A measure was taken of the direction and extent of discrepancy between the subject's judgment on the second measure and his actual position of popularity in the class.

Correlations between the three measures of self-esteem and the Teacher Persuasibility measure were in the predicted direction. However, only the correlation between the rank-discrepancy self-esteem score (measure 3) and Teacher Persuasibility was statistically significant, and that only for the boys in the sample.

A second experiment related subjects high and low in self-esteem, divided on the basis of measures 1 and 2 above, to an Experimenter Persuasibility measure. The later was based on a test in which the experimenter stated her preferences for certain objects after the subject had stated his. The experimenter contradicted the majority of the choices of some subjects; with others the experimenter agreed. The child was then asked to state his preferences for new objects after hearing the experimenter's preferences. Results from this experiment showed that children below the median in self-esteem were significantly more persuasible than those above the median. A qualifying condition was evident from the interaction effect with the variable of preliminary agreement or disagreement between the subject's choices and those of the experimenter. Low self-esteem children were more persuasible than high self-esteem children when the experimenter had agreed with their choices; under conditions of previous disagreement, however, those low in self-esteem were not significantly more persuasible than the highs. The authors interpret these results in terms of the sensitivity of the low self-esteem child to both approval and rebuff.

Hostility and Aggressiveness

The hypothesis that hostile personalities tend to be relatively less persuasible than nonhostile ones was tested by Janis and Field. Three measures of aggressiveness were taken from the self-rating questionnaire: items relating to hyperaggressiveness, argumentativeness, and suspiciousness. A fourth measure was based on a projective Judgment of Motives test, in which the subject could attribute hostile motives or motives of manipulative intent to persons in ambiguous situations.

Results showed no significant correlations between Persuasibility scores and scores on the four measures of aggressiveness for either male or female subjects. In fact, two correlations, Persuasibility with Hyperaggressiveness and with Argumentativeness, approached significance in the opposite direction for the male subjects. The authors suggest the following interpretation for this finding: Many subjects who rate themselves low on self-esteem may have a general tendency toward self-derogation and therefore also rate themselves high on aggressiveness. There was, in fact, an unexpected significant positive correlation between scores on feelings of inadequacy (low self-esteem) and argumentativeness for both males and females.

Janis and Rife studied the same relationship among male mental patients. Using the identical self-rating questionnaire measures of aggressiveness, no significant correlations with persuasibility were found. The authors suggest, however, that these self-rating items may involve a mixture of opposing personality tendencies, because many of the aggressiveness items refer to strong negative emotions that are likely to be regarded as socially undesirable. An investigation of the relation between strong negative emotions and persuasibility revealed a significant correlation: Persons who more readily admitted having unpleasant emotional reactions, such as episodes of intense anger, irritability, and worry, also proved to be more persuasible. This relationship would obscure the hypothesized negative relation between persuasibility and aggressiveness. The most crucial evidence came from clinical records bearing on the subjects' paranoid symptoms and antisocial aggressive behavior. Large and statistically significant differences were found in the incidence of antisocial behavior among high, medium, and low persuasibility groups: the antisocial patients fell predominantly in the low persuasibility category. Thus the expected inverse relationship with persuasibility emerged when aggressiveness was assessed from observations of overt behavior rather than from self-appraisals.

Further support for the hypothesized relation between aggressiveness and low persuasibility is offered by Linton and Graham. They report that subjects who did not change their views in response to mass-media communications scored significantly higher on a questionnaire scale of self-assertive aggression than subjects who changed their opinions.

In investigating correlates of persuasibility among adolescents, King included a questionnaire item on feelings of rebelliousness which might be relevant to the findings on aggressiveness. King sorted his subjects by both sex and parental domination variables and then made comparisons between the percentages of the low and high rebellion subgroups who showed large Susceptibility scores. He found a significant difference only for boys who perceived a high degree of parental domination; among them, those in the low rebellion category were significantly more susceptible to persuasion than those who were highly rebellious.

Evidence concerning the relationship between aggressiveness and persuasibility in children is given by Lesser and Abelson. These authors advance the theoretical proposition that aggressiveness is related to low persuasibility by virtue of their both stemming from the same antecedent factors: parental rejection and/or low firmness of parental control.

An aggressiveness score and a submissiveness score was assigned to each child on the basis of the number of times he was mentioned by his classmates on a "Guess Who" test. Children were asked to mention those classmates who say "mean things" and act aggressively, both verbally and physically, as well as those who exhibit submissive behavior. The correlation between the Teacher Persuasibility measure and the measure of aggressiveness was significantly negative for the boys in the sample, whereas the correlation between submissiveness and Teacher Persuasibility was significantly positive. Neither correlation was significant for the girls.

Other Personality Correlates

Neurotic defensiveness. The evidence from the Janis and Field study failed to support the hypothesis that neurotic defensiveness is related to low persuasibility. Two earlier studies (Janis, 1954, 1955) had yielded contradictory results with respect to this hypothesis. The present study, attempting a more precise assessment of the neurotic-defensiveness hypothesis, included self-rating measures of (1) obsessive-compulsive symptoms and (2) symptoms of acute neurotic anxiety. These measures showed no relationship to scores on the Persuasibility test.

Perceptual dependence. The relation between persuasibility and perceptual-field dependency was investigated by Linton and Graham. *Field dependency,* as measured by Witkin's tilting-room–tilting-chair test, is defined as the extent to which an individual's perceptions are affected by the surrounding field. These authors found that persuasibility correlated with field dependency. The subjects whose opinions were changed by the communication were more affected by the interfering aspects of the stimulus field than nonchangers.

Authoritarianism. No over-all relationship was found between scores on the Authoritarian Personality questionnaire and persuasibility in the study by Linton and Graham. They found, however, a significant correlation between persuasibility and questionnaire responses on all the subscales the authors of *The Authoritarian Personality* (Adorno et al., 1950) consider as reflecting personality patterns predisposing the individual toward authoritarianism. In contrast, the two subscales that directly reflect social attitudes (Politico-Economic Conservatism and Ethnocentrism) did not correlate with opinion change measures.

Inner- and other-directed attitudes. Persuasibility in relation to inner- or other-directed orientation, in Riesman's terms, was also investigated by Linton and Graham. *Inner-direction* was defined as a value system stressing personal goals and standards as against *other-direction,* which places more emphasis on group conformity and adaptation. The two value orientations were measured in a questionnaire presenting hypothetical dilemmas for which the subject could choose an inner-directed or an other-directed solution. A significant positive correlation was found between degree of other-direction and degree of persuasibility, as measured by the Opinion Change test.

Social isolation. From their work with children, Lesser and Abelson advance the hypothesis that social isolation will correlate positively with persuasibility. They base this expectation on the assumption that social isolation of a child from his peers will accentuate an agreement-seeking process, and hence lead to greater persuasibility. In their research on this problem, they measured social isolation by an extension of the sociometric technique used to assess other personality variables, and they assumed that a child who is mentioned neither favorably nor unfavorably by his classmates is a socially isolated individual. Results indicated a significant positive correlation between the Teacher Persuasibility measure and the measure of social isolation for the boys in the sample. Among the girls, no significant relationship was found.

The results with children differ from the findings with adults, who appear to be relatively less persuasible when socially isolated (cf. Hovland, Janis, and Kelley, 1953, pp. 195–196). Abelson and Lesser suggest that the relationship may vary at different ages. Children ignored by their peers in early grade school may initially place high valuation upon entry into the group, but those who remain isolated may come in time to lower their valuation of all groups, with an attendant change in persuasibility.

Interpersonal attractiveness. Among the boys in their sample, Lesser and Abelson found a tendency for children to select as their friends other children who had similar ratings on the persuasibility dimension. Thus relatively persuasible children preferred other persuasible children, while unpersuasible ones selected friends low on the persuasibility dimension. These results found support both on the Teacher Persuasibility and Peer Persuasibility measures for boys but not for girls.

Richness of fantasy. Janis and Field postulated a relation between richness of fantasy and persuasibility on the theory that a major mediating mechanism in attitude change is the anticipation of rewards and punishments explicitly or implicitly conveyed by the communicator. Individuals with a rich fantasy life would presumably have greater facility than others in imagining these anticipated results. As a measure of richness of fantasy, eleven questionnaire items were devised concerning vividness of daydreams, ease of imagining future events, etc. Results showed a significant positive correlation between the fantasy score and persuasibility for male subjects but not for females.

The same relationship was tested on a male hospital population by Janis and Rife. This study yielded a correlation approaching significance ($p = .07$), thus partially supporting the Janis and Field findings.

Intelligence

None of the studies presented has found a relationship between persuasibility and level of general intelligence either with normal subjects or with mental patients. These negative findings are consistent with the results from earlier studies of the relationship between responsiveness to persuasibility and general intelligence (Murphy, Murphy, and Newcomb, 1937, p. 930; Hovland, Janis, and Kelley, 1953, pp. 181–184). There is some reason to expect, however, that differentiated measures of various types of intellectual ability may yield significant relationships.

Sex Differences

Two of the three studies in this volume which used both male and female subjects found significant differences in general persuasibility related to sex. Janis and Field, working with high school students, found the mean persuasibility of female subjects to be significantly higher (at the .01 level of confidence) than that of male subjects. King, also using high school students, found a greater over-all susceptibility to influence on the part of girls than of boys (difference at the .02 level of confidence).

Abelson and Lesser, on the other hand, with first-grade children as subjects, found no significant differences between boys and girls with respect to general level of persuasibility on any of their persuasibility measures.

The fact that sex differences in degree of persuasibility do not emerge in young children is not necessarily incompatible with the finding that there are clear-cut differences between older males and females. A developmental factor may account for both sets of findings: During early childhood the social norms and verbal training which influence responsiveness to communications may be essentially the same for both sexes; but then, at a later phase of development (perhaps during puberty), there may be powerful social pressures, associated with sex-typing and differentiated sex roles, which could give rise to somewhat different predispositions in young men and women.

The relation of sex to persuasibility is most clearly evidenced in assessing personality correlates of general persuasibility. Here marked differences between male and female subjects appear at all the age levels studied.

Janis and Field report that although there were significant relationships between personality factors and persuasibility for the males in their sample of adolescents, there were no significant relationships for the female subjects. For two personality correlates (fantasy and social inhibitions), the sizable differences between the male and female correlations approached significance. The authors suggest that if these results are supported by future research evidence, it may be necessary to postulate two classes of predispositional variables affecting persuasibility: one based on personality factors and the other on cultural sex-typing influences.

King, in his study of high school adolescents, found that the relationship between parental domination and general persuasibility varied according to the sex of the subject. For boys, scores indicating perception of low or high parental domination were not related to susceptibility. For girls, however, high parental domination scores were associated with a significantly greater degree of susceptibility.

With first-grade children, Abelson and Lesser also found marked differences between boys and girls on their measures of the personality correlates of persuasibility. The correlation between the measure of firmness of parental control and the Experimenter Persuasibility measure, which is important to their developmental theory of persuasibility discussed below, was significant for the boys in their sample but nonexistent for the girls. Similarly, the correlations between the Teacher Persuasibility measure and the personality variables of self-esteem, aggressiveness, social isolation, and friendship orientation were all significant for the boys in the sample but were nonsignificant for the girls. Of ten pairs of independent correlations between persuasibility measures and developmental or personality measures, nine were greater for boys in the expected direction, and for three correlations the differences were statistically significant.

The disparity between male and female subjects in the personality correlates of persuasibility is interpreted by the authors of all three studies (Janis and Field, King, Abelson and Lesser) as indicating the influence of culturally sex-typed roles which outweigh personality differences in relation to persuasibility. It has been suggested that personality differences may serve as indicators of level of persuasibility in boys since the cultural sex role for boys is less definitive in prescribing how to react to persuasive influences. However, the culture seems to demand of girls greater acquiescence in relation to prestigeful sources of information and a pattern of frictionless social relationships, with the result that girls on the whole are more susceptible to influence regardless of their personality traits. Especially under conditions of high parental domination, girls may feel less able to act out their rebellious feelings than boys, a difference which carries over into the communication situation, where rejection of suggestions from high-prestige sources would constitute a form of rebellion.

Developmental Factors

Abelson and Lesser propose a developmental theory of persuasibility in terms of reinforcement and learning principles. Defining persuasibility as the probability of obtaining a response from the subject which will produce agreement between himself and the communicator, these authors point out that such instances of agreement or disagreement may be either positively or negatively reinforcing for the subject. As a primary antecedent to persuasibility, they postulate that positively reinforced instances of agreement or negatively reinforced instances of disagreement will tend to increase general persuasibility, whereas the reverse conditions will tend to decrease it.

In fitting these general propositions into a developmental framework, the authors first examine those parent-child interactions in which opinion agreement is at issue. These fall into two broad categories: control situations and acceptance situations. In control situations the child is required to do something he did not intend to do and, in meeting this requirement, he may either agree with the demand or disagree with it. The following relationships are postulated between degree of parental control and level of persuasibility in the child:

1. Low firmness of parental control (where firm control is defined as the reinstatement of a parental demand once the child has expressed disagreement) tends to decrease persuasibility. Firmness of control, therefore, should correlate positively with persuasibility.

2. The greater the frequency of parental control attempts, the higher the relationship between firmness of control and persuasibility.

These postulated relationships are derived from the negative or positive reinforcement which is assumed to accrue to instances of agreement or disagreement between child and parent.

In acceptance situations, the second broad category of parent-child interaction, the child initiates a request or demand on the parent. For these situations it is postulated that parental acceptance correlates positively with child persuasibility.

Research evidence is presented in support of these propositions. To substantiate the view that persuasibility may profitably be considered as agreement-seeking, Abelson and Lesser found a remarkably high correlation between scores on the Mother Persuasibility measure and scores on an Attribution of Agreement test, in which the subjects were first asked to indicate their own preferences and then to pick the objects they thought the experimenter would prefer. A significant relationship was shown between the subjects' attitude of agreement toward the mother and their assumption of agreement between themselves and the experimenter.

Research evidence also supports the proposition that previously reinforced agreement tends to produce persuasibility. In this procedure a female experimenter varied the extent of her agreement with the subjects' choices, following which the subjects were tested for persuasibility. The difference between the agreement and disagreement conditions in mean persuasibility scores was again highly significant.

Firmness of control proved a difficult variable to measure. Parental responses to questionnaire items were not discriminating, and the authors had recourse to a Firmness of Control test administered to the children. This again made use of incomplete stories, and the subjects were given a choice of parental behavior sequences in situations of conflict between the wishes of parent and child. In these fixed choices the parent either reinstated his demand or let his request drop after disagreement from the child. Partial support for the proposed positive correlation between firmness of parental control and persuasibility was evidenced by the correlation between scores on this test and on the Experimenter Persuasibility measure. The correlation was significantly positive for the boys in the sample but not for the girls.

A test of the relation between parental acceptance and persuasibility was also made. Subjects were given the Teacher Persuasibility and Mother Persuasibility measures and also a Favorable Image of Mother test, which consisted of another set of incomplete stories, this time giving the child an opportunity to attribute either supporting or rejecting responses to the mother figure. The correlations between both persuasibility measures and the Favorable Image of Mother scores were significant for both boys and girls in the sample.

The above findings provide tentative support for the theoretical assumptions put forth by Abelson and Lesser concerning the way in which individual differences in persuasibility arise from parent-child interactions.

REFERENCES

ADORNO, T. W., FRENKEL-BRUNSWICK, ELSE, LEVINSON, D. J., AND SANFORD, R. N., 1950. *The Authoritarian Personality.* New York, Harper.

HOVLAND, C. I., JANIS, I. L., AND KELLEY, H. H., 1953. *Communication and Persuasion.* New Haven, Yale University Press.

JANIS, I. L., 1954. Personality correlates of susceptibility to persuasion. *J. Pers.*, 22, 504–518.

JANIS, I. L., 1955. Anxiety indices related to susceptibility to persuasion. *J. Abnorm. Soc. Psychol.*, 51, 663–667.

MURPHY, G., MURPHY, LOIS B., AND NEWCOMB, T. N., 1937. *Experimental Social Psychology*, rev. ed. New York and London, Harper.

IMAGES OF THE CONSUMER'S MIND
ON AND OFF MADISON AVENUE

Milton Rokeach

THE ADVERTISING MAN is not the only person who seeks to shape and change other people's beliefs, attitudes, and behavior. There are many kinds of people in our society, professional and non-professional, working for pay and for free, who for various combinations of altruistic and selfish reasons are vitally interested in the theory and in the practice of shaping and changing other people's values, beliefs, attitudes, and behavior. Let me point, by way of illustration, to the psychotherapist, to the teacher, the missionary, the politician, and the lobbyist. All these have in common, with the advertising man, the desire to influence and to persuade others to believe and to act in certain ways in which they would not otherwise believe and act.

This does not mean that the advertising man wants to change the same sort of beliefs which, say, the therapist or the politician wants to change. Every human being has many different kinds of beliefs, and every advanced society seems to have encouraged the growth of different kinds of persuaders who specialize in trying to change some kinds of belief and not other kinds.

What, then, are the different kinds of beliefs which all men have and what kinds of beliefs does the advertising man wish most to influence? What are the properties of the different kinds of beliefs, and how easily is one kind changed compared with another kind? And what are the special problems which arise to plague the advertising man because of the fact that he specializes in trying to change certain kinds of beliefs and not other kinds, and what can he do about these problems?

To answer these questions, I would like to tell you about five kinds of beliefs which we have thus far isolated in our work at Michigan State University. This work is part of a larger, on-going program of research extending over the past decade on the nature of man's systems of belief: how such systems of belief are formed, organized, and modified, and how such systems differ from one person to the next.

To begin with, all persons are assumed to have belief systems, and each belief system contains tens of thousands of beliefs. These beliefs can not all be equally important to the person possessing them. It is necessary to assume that beliefs vary along a continuum of importance or centrality. Further, we must assume that the more important a belief the more it will resist change and the more trivial a belief the more easily it can be changed. And, finally, we must assume that the more important a belief which is changed, the more widespread the repercussions in the rest of the person's belief system, because many of the beliefs "hooked up" with it will change too.

THE FIVE KINDS of beliefs which I will describe may be represented by five concentric circles, with the key beliefs at the center, and the more inconsequential beliefs along the outside circle. To help keep track of them let me call the innermost beliefs Type A, which is then followed by Type B, and so on, until we get to Type E along the outside circle.

At the core are Type A beliefs which I call primitive beliefs. These are beliefs we all share with one another about the nature of physical reality, social reality, and the self. For example, *I believe this a table. I believe this is an audience listening to a speech. I believe my name is Milton Rokeach.* These are all supported by one hundred percent social consensus. Type A beliefs are our taken-for-granted axioms which are not subject to controversy because we believe, and we believe everyone else believes. Such primitive beliefs are fundamental and we have evidence which shows that they are more resistant to change than any other type of belief. And we have obtained additional evidence suggesting that we become extremely upset when Type A beliefs are seriously brought into question.

And then there is a second kind of primitive belief—Type B—which is also extremely resistant to change. Such beliefs do not depend on social support or consensus but, instead, arise from deep personal experience. Type B beliefs are incontrovertible and we believe them regardless of whether anyone else believes them. Many of these unshakable beliefs are about ourselves and some of these self-conceptions are positive ones—Type B+—and some are negative ones—Type B—. The positive ones represent beliefs about what we are capable of, and the negative ones represent beliefs about what we are afraid of.

Let me illustrate some Type B+ beliefs which most of us here probably have. Regardless of what others may think of us, we continue to believe ourselves to be intelligent and rational men, able and competent, basically kind and charitable. Type B+ beliefs represent our positive self-images which guide our aspirations and ambitions to become even better, greater, wiser, and nobler than we already are.

But many of us also have Type B— beliefs—negative self-conceptions—which we cling to primitively, regardless of whether others may agree with us. We are often beset by phobias, compulsions, obsessions, neurotic self-doubts and anxieties about self-worth, self-identity and self-competence. These are the kinds of primitive beliefs which we only wish we were rid of, and it is these Type B— beliefs which the specialized psychotherapist is often asked to change. Other specialized persuaders are generally not trained or interested in changing Type B— beliefs, but they may be interested in exploiting them without trying to change them.

A third kind of belief, Type C, we call authority beliefs—beliefs we all have about which authorities to trust and which not to trust. Many facts of physical and social reality have alternative interpretations, are socially controversial, or are not capable of being personally verified or experienced. For these reasons, all men need to identify with authorities who will help them to decide what to believe and what not to believe. Is communism good or bad? Is there a God or isn't there? How do we know the French Revolution actually took place? What about evolution? No man is personally able to ascertain the truth of all such things for himself. So, he believes in this or that authority—parents, teachers, religious leaders, scientists—and he is often willing to take some authority's word for many things. Thus, we all develop beliefs about which authorities are positive and which are negative, differing from one person to the next, and we look to such authorities for information about what is (and is not) true and beautiful, and good for us.

A fourth kind of belief, Type D, we call peripheral beliefs—beliefs which are *derived* from the authorities we identify with. For example, a devout Catholic has certain beliefs about birth control and divorce because he has accepted them from the authority he believes in. I believe Jupiter has twelve moons, not because I have personally seen them, but because I trust certain kinds of authorities who have seen them. I am quite prepared to revise my belief about Jupiter's moons providing the authorities I trust revise their beliefs. Many people adhere to a particular religious or political belief system because they identify with a particular authority. Such peripheral beliefs can be changed, providing the suggestion for change emanates from one's authority, or, providing there is a change in one's authority.

Finally, there is a fifth class of beliefs, Type E, which I call inconsequential beliefs. If they are changed, the total system of beliefs is not altered in any significant way. I believe, for example, that you can get a better shave from one brand of razor blade than another; I believe that a vacation at the beach is more enjoyable than one in the mountains; I believe Sophia Loren is prettier than Elizabeth Taylor. But, if you can persuade me to believe the opposite, the change is inconsequential because the rest of my belief system is not likely to be affected in any important way.

LET ME NOW briefly summarize the five kinds of beliefs: every person's total system of beliefs is composed of beliefs that range in importance from the inconsequential, through the peripheral, to beliefs about authority and, finally, at the core, to primitive beliefs which are extremely resistant to change, either because they do not at all depend on social support or because they enjoy universal social support. All these five kinds of beliefs, considered together are organized into a remarkable piece of architecture which I call the belief system. It has a definable content and a definable structure. And it has a job to do; it serves adaptive functions for the person, in order to maximize his positive self-image and to minimize his negative self-image. Every person has a need to know himself and his world insofar as possible, and a need not to know himself and his world, insofar as necessary. A person's total belief system, with all its five kinds of beliefs, is designed to serve both functions at once.

You might wonder what objective evidence there may be that the five kinds of beliefs I have just described really exist. There is not enough time here to tell you about all our research addressed to this question, but I would like to report that the best evidence we have comes from a study as yet unpublished in which we tried to change the five kinds of beliefs I have described through hypnotic suggestion. This work was done in collaboration with my colleagues Dr. Joseph Reyher and Dr. Richard Wiseman at Michigan State University and the results we obtained are quite clear. Our data show that all five kinds of beliefs change under hypnosis. But as we had expected, the amount of change in belief varies with the centrality of belief: the primitive beliefs, Type A and B, changed the least as a result of hypnotic suggestion. Beliefs about authority, Type C, changed more. Peripheral beliefs, Type D, changed yet more. And inconsequential beliefs, Type E, changed the most.

The results also show that changing one kind of belief leads to changes in the other kinds of beliefs, but changes in Types A and B beliefs exert the greatest consequences on other beliefs. Changes in Type C beliefs exert lesser consequences, changes in Type D beliefs exert yet lesser consequences and, finally, Type E beliefs—inconsequential beliefs, the ones most easy to change—exert the least effect on other beliefs.

Now, given these five kinds of beliefs as a frame of reference, it is possible to obtain a somewhat clearer picture of what society's specialized persuaders are trying to do, and which kinds of beliefs they wish most to act upon, to influence, and to change. As far as I can tell, there are no specialized persuaders whose main business it is to change the first kind of belief I have described—the Type A beliefs which are universally supported by social consensus. But, as already stated, it is the business of the professional psychotherapist to change the second kind of primitive belief. The psychotherapists' job is to help us get rid of our negative self-conceptions—Type B— beliefs—and to strengthen our positive self-conceptions—Type B+ beliefs.

Then, there are other specialized persuaders—the political and religious partisans and ideologists of various persuasion. What sorts of beliefs are they mostly concerned with? I would suggest that their main focus is on the Type C and Type D beliefs—those I have called authority beliefs and peripheral beliefs.

By now, you can perhaps anticipate what I am about to say next about the kinds of beliefs which that specialized persuader—the advertising man—tries to form and to change. Without in any way wishing to deny that the results of advertising may have important economic consequences, it could be stated from a psychological standpoint that the advertising man has concentrated mainly on changing Type E beliefs—inconsequential beliefs—to the extent that his purpose is to meet the competition, and he has concentrated mainly on Type D—peripheral beliefs—to the extent that his purpose is to give information. Furthermore, the more competitive the advertising, the more it addresses itself to changing psychologically inconsequential beliefs about the relative merits of one brand over another. . . . Inconsequential beliefs are generally easier to change than other kinds of beliefs. This does not mean, however, that the consumer will passively yield to others' efforts to change such beliefs. We generally resist changing *all* our beliefs because we gain comfort in clinging to the familiar and because all our beliefs, as I have tried to suggest, serve highly important functions for us.

So the advertising man, while he has a psychological advantage over other persuaders specializing in changing more central beliefs, still has to find economical ways of changing the less consequential beliefs in which he specializes. This he has often tried to do by developing methods for shaking the consumer loose from his belief regarding the inconsequential virtues of a particular brand over a competitor's in order to make him believe instead that the difference does make a difference. He tries to convince the consumer that there are important benefits to be gained by changing brands, that deeper beliefs and needs will be better satisfied. The advertising industry has frequently been successful in achieving this aim and, sometimes, miraculously so.

How? In line with my analysis, I would suggest that the advertiser's goal is achieved by associating the fifth kind of belief, Type E—the inconsequential beliefs—with other kinds of beliefs tapping psychologically more consequential beliefs and wants.

But what are the other kinds of beliefs which are most frequently associated with Type E beliefs? Theoretically, it is possible to associate the inconsequential beliefs with Type D, or C, or B+, or B—, or A beliefs, but the advertising industry does not use all these combinations with equal frequency. The associations which seem to come up most often in competitive advertising are those between Types E and C (the authority beliefs, as in testimonials) and between Types E and B— (as in the old Lifebuoy ads on B.O. or in the more sophisticated Maiden-form Bra ads which exploit primitive fears or primitive self-conceptions concerning insufficient femininity).

Why should these two combinations come up more often than the other possible combinations? I suspect that this is due to the fact that the advertising industry has been heavily influenced by two theories in psychology—behaviorism and psychoanalysis—both having in common an image of man who is fundamentally an irrational creature, helplessly pushed around on the one hand by irrational guilt, anxiety, self-doubt, and other neurotic self-conceptions (B— beliefs) and, on the other hand, helplessly pushed around by external stimuli which, through reward and punishment, he is conditioned to from arbitrary associations. Advertising has borrowed from psychoanalysis its laws of association, and from behaviorism its principles of conditioning. Psychoanalysis tells you what to associate with what, and behaviorism tells you how to stamp it in. I would suggest that it is because the advertising profession has taken over such an irrational image of man from behaviorism and psychoanalysis that the inconsequential beliefs have been so often associated with the authority beliefs (Type C) and with the primitive beliefs (Type B—). In doing so, the advertising industry has come in for a great deal of criticism—to my mind, justified—from various sources for a style of advertising which encourages conformity, which is exploitative, debasing, lacking in taste, and insulting to the dignity of man. . . .

Since the end of World War II, an increasing number of distinguished psychologists have revolted against the image of Irrational Man which behaviorism and classical psychoanalysis have both helped build. Contemporary psychoanalysts talk more about the conflict-free sphere of ego functioning. The Gestalt psychologists have, for a long time, emphasized man's search for meaning, understanding, and organization. Carl Rogers has emphasized the drive for growth and maturity within all individuals. Abraham Maslow has familiarized us with man's drive for self-actualization. Gordon Allport and the existentialists talk about being and becoming. Robert White, Harry F. Harlow, D. E. Berlyne, Leon Festinger, and many others, have pointed to the fact that man has a need to know, to understand and to be competent.

I would say that the major way in which contemporary psychology differs from the psychology of twenty years ago is that Man is now seen to be not only a *rationalizing* creature but also a *rational* creature —curious, exploratory and receptive to new ideas. . . .

But the irrational image of man still predominates in the advertising world. The more inconsequential the benefits of one brand over a competitor's the more desperately the industry has harangued and nagged and, consequently, irritated its mass audience. It's not easy work to convince others that psychologically inconsequential matters are consequential. The fact that the advertising industry attracts such highly talented people, pays them fabulous salaries, and puts them under such terrific pressure—these can all be attributed to the kinds of beliefs it specializes in changing. It is, consequently, no wonder that the advertising profession is reputed to be among the most guilt-ridden, anxiety-ridden, ulcer-ridden, and death-ridden profession in America. I think it significant that four speakers from the academic world were invited to speak to the Eastern Conference of the American Advertising Agencies about the *consumer's* interests, and I think it also significant that on no less than three separate occasions was I reminded in the process of being invited to address this group that the agency leaders who organized this meeting "are in no way seeking a whitewash of the advertising business." These facts would seem to suggest the advertising industry's alarm over its predicament, an eagerness to face up to its social responsibility, a search for conviction, and a courage somewhat in excess of conviction.

In closing, therefore, let me emphasize again—constructively, I hope —that the advertising man's image of the consumer requires revision in order to bring it more in line not only with the broader and newer image of man I have all-too-briefly outlined here but also with the advertising man's image of himself. To the extent that the advertising man can bring himself to do so, he will gain a new respect from the consumer and in the process gain a renewed respect for himself.

LIMITS OF PERSUASION

The hidden persuaders are made of straw

RAYMOND A. BAUER

MAN SEEMS TO LIVE in perpetual hope and horror that infallible means have been developed whereby one man can control another's behavior. As usual, the hope and the horror are opposite sides of the same coin:

On the hopeful side, some selfishly see the possibility of advantage for themselves in gaining control over their fellow men. Others, more idealistically, look to a "science of man" as the basis for establishing a Utopia which will be optimally efficient in the production of both material goods and human happiness.

On the side of horror, some fear that they themselves will be "manipulated" to the advantage of someone else. Others fear the motives for their own relations to their fellow men. The image of a potential Utopia gets turned inside out, and we see that the reverse image is that of *1984*—the totalitarian state of George Orwell's novel—in which the best qualities of man are lost.

Recent developments in the science of psychology, and the publicity given to some of its more sensational applications—such as "subliminal advertising" or "brainwashing"—have strengthened our anxiety. The significance of these developments is of particular concern to businessmen, for they, along with politicians, will be responsible for the use of the new techniques. But there is no reason for panic. Anxiety stems, in part, from ignorance of the causal relations between the "persuaders" and the "persuaded." To show this relationship, and the limitations it imposes on the techniques, we must consider three broad areas of application:

- Propaganda and human relations.
- Appeals to "noneconomic" motives.
- Appeals to "unconscious" motives.

With a better understanding of the functioning of these techniques, we will be in a stronger position to evaluate them realistically.

Reprinted with permission from *Harvard Business Review*, 36 (September-October, 1958), 105–110.

NEW FEAR OR OLD SCARE?

The specter of "manipulation" and "hidden persuasion" has stalked all the lands that man has ever inhabited. The most primitive manifestation of the deep anxiety which we feel on this issue is represented by Nightmare Alice, the witch of Li'l Abner Land. From time to time, Nightmare Alice makes an effigy of one of the "good people" of Dogpatch and places this person under her hidden control. Black magic is found among most nonliterate peoples, and the fear of it persists. In the Middle Ages, people were "possessed by the devil"; in our own colonial times we went back to "witches."

In recent decades, to be sure, we have done away with such superstitions and become more "scientific." Or have we simply dressed up our old fears in modern fashions? Remember how during the 1920's and 1930's we worried about the mysterious powers of the mass media, particularly as manipulated by such practitioners as George Creel and Ivy L. Lee? My point is that although this century has led to tremendous progress in our knowledge of the human mind, our fear that this knowledge will be misused is as old as the history of man.

But what are the facts? Does modern psychology give us the tools to control each other? The full range of considerations is, of course, beyond our purview here. Moreover, any discussion of psychological techniques of persuasion and manipulation must, of course, be done without knowing what new knowledge may be developed. It is my belief, however, that what I have to say must hold in principle for almost any conceivable situation that may develop.

RATIO OF RESISTANCE

Let me begin my positive assertions with what may seem like a paradoxical statement. Without doubt we have, largely on the basis of improved social science knowledge in the fields of psychology, sociology, and anthropology, developed increasingly refined and effective means of persuasion. It does not follow, however, that even in the field of advertising we are able to effect more persuasion. How can this be? Simply because the increased knowledge benefits not only the persuader but also the target of persuasion. As the persuaders become more sophisticated, so do the people to be persuaded.

One way of reading the history of the development of techniques of persuasion is that the persuaders have been in a race to keep abreast of the developing resistance of the people to be persuaded. Thus:

In the decades following World War I, we were very excited about the power of propaganda. We came close to saying that if it were possible to get a story in the newspapers or on the radio, people would automatically believe it and act on it. But what happened? Many people became so suspicious of propaganda that they would scarcely believe the news on the sports page.

As a result, World War II propaganda in the Western countries was markedly different from that of World War I. Propagandists—that is, "persuaders"—were scrupulously careful not to test the credulity of their readers and listeners; they also avoided more blatant emotional appeals.

Why? People had become more sophisticated, and more resistant to "persuasion." Social science research on the effects of communications, by the beginning of World War II, had pretty well destroyed the myth of propaganda's omnipotence.

We see today similar developments in advertising. There is still some advertising that is reminiscent of the old-fashioned pitchman selling snake oil. However, the development of the "soft sell" seems to me a tacit acknowledgment of the developing resistance of the potential consumer.

MANIPULATION MORE DIFFICULT

Within business and industry we have witnessed the evolving concern with human relations and communication. These events also have been viewed with horror as evidence of the growth of manipulation. But the viewers-with-horror naively assume that the knowledge on which this presumed manipulation is based is limited to the manipulators. Without in any way deprecating the desirability of the human relations approach—I not only favor it but even try to practice it—I doubt if it has produced any increase in manipulation.

As a matter of fact, all this new concern must have made the process of interpersonal communications more complicated. It is traditional that, as people become more diplomatic, their communications become more subtle. Perhaps we are all reaching the point of the diplomat who, on being informed of the death of his opposite number, queried: "I wonder what he meant by that." So in the absence of any long-run trend statistics on the number of effective persuasive and manipulative acts in business and industry, I shall remain content with pointing to the obvious mechanisms of resistance to persuasion; noting that manipulation has become more difficult; and suggesting there is no more reason to believe that the actual practice of manipulation has increased than that it has lessened. The data to prove me wrong are unobtainable.

HIDDEN PERSUADERS?

Our main fear, however, is not that we will be taken in by the persuasive logic of a Madison Avenue salesman but that, through appeals to deep, unconscious motives, we can be manipulated without even knowing it.

A book such as Vance Packard's *Hidden Persuaders*[1] generates a

[1] New York, David McKay Company, Inc., 1957.

good deal of soul searching, both among the general public and within professional circles. This book, for the benefit of the fortunate few who are not familiar with it, tells *a* story, though certainly not *the* story, of how psychology has been applied in market research. By determining people's unconscious motives "via the principles of modern dynamic psychology," researchers are able to devise methods whereby mysterious and miraculous marketing results are produced. The consumer is powerless to resist these techniques, and he just buys and buys without knowing why. From this it is, of course, only one step to applying these techniques in politics, and *1984* will arrive at least twenty years ahead of schedule. Packard's picture, needless to say, is a trifle stylized.

Packard wrote his book to warn the public. The net impact of the volume is that there has been a complete revolution in market research in the form of motivation research, the term for the intensive exploration of the psychological factors involved in consumer behavior and product usage. But it is only the *intensity of concern* that is new. So far as I can see, the major practical result has been—as one might expect—an increased and unrealistic demand for motivation research. Packard succeeded in painting the picture of psychological demonology so persuasively that motivation researchers are now concerned with giving their clients a more realistic notion of what they can do.

But Packard also succeeded in creating again the primitive anxiety that we are on the verge of being able to establish complete control over human behavior to the extent that the victims of this control will not have a chance to resist it because they do not realize it is there.

NONECONOMIC MOTIVES

In the first place, people *do* have some chance to resist the motives associated with the new techniques. People buy many things for *noneconomic* reasons, but such motives are not necessarily *unconscious*. It is a serious mistake to equate the two; and the use of the term *irrational* makes the confusion even worse. Once you label noneconomic motives irrational, you imply they are unreasonable, and you are well on the way to assuming they are unconscious.

When I say that people do things for noneconomic reasons (what others might call "irrational"), I am talking about the fact that people may buy a particular automobile because they desire status, the esteem of themselves and others; because they like products which fit their own self-image; or even because a man likes the feeling of potency which comes from driving an overhorsepowered vehicle. But I can see no reason to say a man is more "rational" to want transportation than to want self-respect and the esteem of others—though if it helps you to understand why he is doing what he is doing, you can say he is being less economic.

It is true that most of the motives I have just mentioned are not usually cited in response to the direct question: "Why did you buy that product?" In our culture, the accepted reasons for buying a product bear on its primary economic function: for instance, the cost of transportation provided by the car, the cleaning effectiveness of a soap, and so on. Accordingly, we are not as likely to think of the noneconomic motives as reasons for buying, bearing as they do on the secondary functions (or "added value") of products. Or, if we do, perhaps we feel a little ashamed and so are reticent about them. But in no meaningful sense are these motives unconscious. With a little stimulation almost every one of us recognizes their existence.

PRACTICAL CONSEQUENCES

This is no mere quibble. The fact that people can and do acknowledge the existence of these motives has considerable practical consequence. The use of appeals directed to such motives—as well as the widespread discussion, which we have already witnessed, of the concern given such motives in product design and merchandising—is bringing them into the center of consciousness as buying motives even if they were not there before. Some people will come to accept these as proper buying motives, and will probably learn to shop as astutely for the product that gives them the most prestige as for the product that has the lowest price, best mechanical qualities, and so on. Other people will resist these appeals, not accepting the secondary functions as a legitimate reason for buying.

Appeal to such motives may still serve, as in the past, to win the merchandiser a temporary advantage. However, as such appeals become customary and the public becomes generally aware of them, they will leave the merchandiser just about where he was to start with as far as his "persuasive advantage" is concerned.

Just because marketing and product design are based increasingly on psychologically oriented market research, it does not follow that products will continue to be sold increasingly on the basis of their secondary functions or "added value." At this time merchandisers are becoming more and more alert to the power of the secondary characteristics of products to satisfy consumer wants. As a psychologist I can have no conceivable objection in principle to people's noneconomic wants being satisfied. But we must look seriously at the possibility that this trend may reach the point of saturation.

Even now, the "irrationality"—a word I detest—of the consumer may be grossly overestimated. In few, if any, of the discussions of consumer motivation is there any mention of the growth of such consumer information services as Consumer's Research and Consumer's Union. The notion that people are not concerned with and do not understand the technical aspects of the products they buy may have to be tempered in the future. Today's consumers are almost certainly more interested and better informed on the technical features of products than they have been in the past.

There is something ironical in depicting the housewife shopping in the supermart as being indifferent to economy, being cozened by hidden persuaders into spending 15% more for her market basket than some stringent criterion says is necessary. Remember, the corner grocery store offers the housewife psychological rewards that the supermart does not. Yet in the interests of economy housewives have deserted the corner grocery store for the more impersonal, but more economical, supermart. This very same group of housewives has patronized discount houses, which scarcely give them the same psychological satisfactions as do department and high-class specialty stores.

One of the established arguments for stressing the secondary functions of a product is that all products in a given line are virtually identical with respect to their primary economic function. But suppose all automobiles in a given price range become virtually identical with regard to their symbolic value: this might drive the manufacturers to strive again for differentiation on the basis of the primary function of transportation. This notion is far from facetious. While Chrysler may indeed have gotten into difficulty a few years ago by de-emphasizing styling, today it is the small economical car—American Rambler or a foreign make—that is making inroads into the market, not the cars with "sex appeal."

This is not to brush aside the importance of the motives that the motivation researchers have stressed. I am merely suggesting that we keep our image of the consumer in somewhat clearer perspective. The merchandiser who concentrates too much on the secondary characteristics of products will find himself in as much difficulty as the one who ignores them completely. Motivation research may indeed become indispensable *because* of the very trends in the population I have been describing. The merchandiser will probably need increasingly detailed psychological knowledge of consumers as the years go on, if only to know what difficulties he is up against and how far he must stay away from noneconomic appeals.

UNCONSCIOUS MOTIVES

This is not the whole picture. All that I have said to this point is that many of the motives with which motivation research deals are *not* unconscious *in any meaningful sense;* and that, as these particular motives are appealed to, the consumer recognizes them more explicitly as motives linked to consumer behavior, and develops the capacity for a critical appraisal of appeals to such motives.

But there *are* some truly unconscious motives—that is, motives which the individual would not acknowledge consciously to *himself* even if, or especially if, they are called explicitly to his attention. To illustrate:

One of the most spectacular of the claims for the exploitation of unconscious motives is the development of the hardtop convertible. The hardtop is labeled as a compromise between the male buyer's dual attachment to the stable, reliable wife, symbolized by the sedan, and the flashy, unreliable mistress, symbolized by the convertible.

Certainly, in psychoanalytic thinking, it is accepted that the male child has conflict over thinking of his mother as a sexual object, and develops a split image of women. But I cannot conceivably take a stand on whether or not this is the complete story of the hardtop, or what substantial portion of the story it may comprise. I use it only as an example of appealing to a motive that is meaningfully referred to as unconscious.

There is something very plausible in the notion that if we understand another person's unconscious motivation, then we can appeal to his motives and get him to do something without his knowing why he did it. Certainly, he ought to be powerless to resist. To some extent this is true. But the entire picture is more complicated. Remember that there is a reason for certain motives remaining unconscious; in general, conscious acknowledgment of these motives would produce intolerable anxiety. Hence, appeal to such motives may backfire, and backfire violently. Thus, on an *a priori* basis, combining the "mistress and the wife" in the form of the hardtop convertible *could* have aroused anxiety and caused people to stay away from this model in droves.

My concern is not hypothetical. Research projects give us evidence that this happens, as in the following cases:

One of the most deep-seated motives that is postulated in Freudian psychology is fear of castration. Furthermore, our anxiety over dental work is asserted to be due to a displacement of this castration anxiety. Again, I ask you to take this interpretation on its face value. It is only if you take it seriously that there is any issue at all. Presumably any message directed at relieving this anxiety ought to be met with prompt and vigorous positive response. Thus, instructions on oral hygiene ought to be listened to attentively, remembered, and acted on. However, experiments at Yale show that highly emotional messages on oral hygiene are less effective than detached, less emotional ones in conveying information on proper methods of preserving teeth.[2] Furthermore, the persons who heard the more emotionally charged lectures were *less* resistant to counterpropaganda.

While the psychologists who did this work have been conservative in interpreting these results, in the context of this discussion I am willing to put myself out on a speculative limb. I would argue that this finding sug-

[2] Carl I. Hovland, Irving L. Janis, and Harold H. Kelley, *Communication and Persuasion* (New Haven, Yale University Press, 1953), pp. 56–98.

gests that what I have already indicated may be true, that strong appeals to unconscious motives *may* evoke a great deal of anxiety, with resultant strong resistance to the message directed at the person. Thus, appeal to unconscious motives is a subtle and complex business which may well backfire.

Much has been made of the possibilities of subliminal advertising—the presentation of messages at an intensity low enough so that the individual at whom they are directed is not aware of their presence. Work on subliminal perception is extremely controversial within the profession of psychology, and the particular data on which subliminal advertising was promoted are more questionable than most. However, what is significant is that Professor George Klein of New York University, on whose basic research subliminal advertising was built, reported in the public press that his own experiments gave evidence that some people responded *negatively* to the purportedly unseen stimuli.

There are innumerable difficult technical problems involved in subliminal advertising, and I do not want to pass judgment one way or another on the effectiveness of this phenomenon—although I have some profound doubts. All I want to point out is that to the extent we have firm knowledge in this area, some of that knowledge at least suggests that the individual may resist even "unperceived" messages. My guess would be that extensive use of subliminal advertising—again begging the technical question of what it is and whether it could be pulled off—would increase the strength and pervasiveness of resistance.

POWER TO RESIST

I am not arguing for or against the effectiveness of any of these techniques of persuasion. I have merely indicated that individuals have the capacity to resist even on the unconscious level. I *am* arguing that the individual's resistance to persuasion probably increases in proportion to the efforts made to persuade him against his own perceived interest. We may even go further than that. Our primitive anxiety concerning the possibility of being manipulated leads us to resist persuasion by others, even in some instances where it may be *in our own interest.* Thus we have the automatic response, "Nobody's going to tell me what's good for me."

My guess is that over the years the American people have developed resistance to manipulation at about the same rate that our techniques of persuasion have become more sophisticated and effective. I mean, of course, that *if the audience had remained the same,* our new techniques would be more effective than our old ones. But the audience has not remained the same. The pace of the race has grown swifter, but it is difficult to say who has gained on whom.

Another point to remember is that merchandising is a competitive activity, and any technique of research or persuasion is about equally available to anyone who wants to make use of it. Even the vaunted subliminal advertisements would tend to cancel out each other if all refrigerator manufacturers, for example, were to use them on television.

Competition among persuaders, indeed, is very much like that between the persuader and the object of his persuasion. Adoption of a new technique may well give a momentary competitive advantage, but this advantage lasts only until competitors have also adopted that technique. As long as there is a multiplicity of advertisers, it is difficult to see how the public at large can become the passive puppets of "hidden persuaders."

OMNIPOTENT CONTROL?

But there is still one other dread possibility to dispose of, if we can. Let us consider what might happen if there were *no* competition—if the tools of manipulation were in one group's hands. This would be *1984*, the society in which an elite group will direct the behavior of everyone else, in so subtle a way that no one is aware that it is happening. Perhaps it has already happened? How could we tell when it began?

I would not say for a moment that there are no situations in which one person can exercise absolute control over another. Give one man a gun (known in the vernacular as a "persuader"), and he can do a pretty good job of directing the activities of an unarmed man. True, some people in such a situation have escaped, taken the gun from the man, or got themselves shot. But I would not like to quibble about such a small minority, particularly in view of the fact that the effectiveness of this persuader depends on its presence being known, not hidden.

Accounts of brainwashing and similar phenomena indicate that—with a considerable expenditure of effort, careful control of a man's environment (which includes isolating him and getting him in a state of fatigue), good intuitive psychological insight, and a great deal of patience—it *is* possible to change the beliefs of a large proportion of one's victims. There is even some threat in the offing that the use of drugs and of electrodes implanted in the brain may make such procedures more effective.

Although I have some modicum of competence on such subjects, I frankly do not know exactly how far one can go now or in the immediate future with such procedures of influencing people. But look at how remote this is from the notion of controlling *a large society* via psychological techniques. Not only is it doubtful if strictly psychological practices would effect a considerable amount of brainwashing in the absence of all the other factors of control over the individual's environment, but there is the very practical matter that the amount of time and energy expended on each individual must be at least equal to his own time and energy. In short, the influencing of a single individual in a confined situation and by a large number of people is an entirely different case from that of a small number of people influencing a large number of people on a societal level. The Soviet Union is the closest approximation to this latter circumstance that we have seen, and I can say from my own studies of that society that the persuasion was far from hidden, far from total, and, possibly, far from desirable for the efficient functioning of the society.[3]

To be quite realistic, I do not see how anyone who has observed or operated any large-scale organization can take seriously the notion of complete control of behavior. In particular, social science has taught us at least as much about the *necessity* of permitting initiative—which a *1984* society by definition cannot do—as it has taught us about directing behavior.

CONCLUSION

In sum, I am skeptical about the extreme pictures of "hidden persuasion" that have been drawn for either the present or future of business or politics. This does not mean I am indifferent to the prospects of individual instances of the unscrupulous use of psychological or other social science knowledge. What I have been attacking is the notion of the possibility of omnipotent control over the behavior of large numbers of human beings. That such a notion rears its head repeatedly comes, I believe, from our primitive anxiety over manipulation. This anxiety is caused, on the one hand, by our fear that other people may be doing it to *us,* and therefore that we have lost control over our own destiny. It comes, on the other hand, from the notion that *we* may be doing it to others; and here we have a sense of guilt concerning our own motives and behavior toward those others.

I may be fighting a straw man in the sense that this particular *object* of people's fears is not real. But the *fears* exist; they are real. To date most people have not recognized that the threat of omnipotent control over man's behavior *is* a straw man. It may be that my contribution here is that of pointing out that the "hidden persuaders" in their exaggerated form are, in fact, made of straw.

PREDICTIVE GENERALIZATIONS

IV-A   He who expects to influence people by means of communication, even when he possesses considerable knowledge and skill together with a degree of environmental control, should expect no more than modest results.

IV-B   Listeners or readers possess a number of defenses against persuasive communications, the operation of which severely limits the effecness of those communications.

[3] See, for example, Raymond A. Bauer, "Brainwashing, Psychology or Demonology," *Journal of Social Issues,* Vol. 13, No. 3, 1957, p. 41.

IV-B-1 Unless a listener expects a communication to satisfy his needs or agree with what he already believes, it is likely that he will avoid exposing himself to it either by staying out of earshot, by failing to read the message, or by inattention to it.

IV-B-2 Having exposed himself to a communication that he discovers does not meet his needs or runs counter to his beliefs, a listener or reader may weaken its impact by distorting it in his memory, by crowding it out of his memory with more agreeable information, or by actually repressing it.

IV-B-3 A listener or reader may defend himself against persuasive communications by adopting some alternative to opinion change; he may change his assessment of the speaker, refuse to believe reports that he took a divergent position, distort the view of the speaker, or rearrange the importance of conflicting pieces of information.

IV-B-4 By exposing himself to opposing arguments and being forced to develop arguments supportive of his opinions, a listener or reader may immunize himself against subsequently encountered opposition arguments.

IV-B-5 Some listeners or readers, because of certain personality traits, may be especially resistant to persuasive communications. Those with strong self-esteem may feel less need to follow the recommendations of others; women because of their social role may be more easily persuaded than men.

IV-B-6 The more important a belief is in the listener's or reader's organized system of beliefs, the more difficult it will be to change in response to communications.

IV-B-7 Some beliefs assume special importance because they are held in common with others in a group. Where membership in such a group is important to a listener or reader, group support of his opinions renders them resistant to change.

IV-B-8 The decision of a listener or reader to accept the advice of a communicator may be reversed as soon as experience proves the communication to have been misleading or wrong.

IV-C Control by the communicator of some aspects of the listener's or reader's environment may enhance the effectiveness of communication.

IV-C-1 The exclusion of contradictory information will often increase the effectiveness of the communicator's message.

IV-C-2 The destruction of normal social supports for beliefs may increase the effectiveness of the communicator's message, especially if acceptance of the message promotes a new system of social supports —new friends or a new sense of group membership and solidarity.

IV-C-3 But, since this society offers almost no opportunity for environmental control by a communicator, the effects of communications are greatly curtailed.

IV-C-4 In the United States, the exclusion of contradictory information will be almost impossible for advertisers, political campaigners or any persuader other than the therapist who can institutionalize his patient.

IV-C-5   The destruction of the social supports of beliefs will be practically impossible because of social restraints on such radical manipulative efforts.

IV-C-6   In an environment which the listener feels is forced upon him, the effect of communications may prove to be superficial or temporary; in an environment chosen or approved by the listener or reader, and in which he feels some responsibility for group decision-making, the effect of communications may be more fundamental and lasting.

IV-C-7   A person who is compelled to write or speak ideas contrary to his beliefs may subsequently readjust his beliefs to accommodate the ideas he was compelled or persuaded to express, but the usual impossibility of compulsion and the persuasive inadequacy of most financial rewards for such behavior, as well as the difficulty in predicting success, make these means of achieving effect generally unpromising.

IV-C-8   Because of the alternatives to opinion change that are open to a listener or reader, it is often difficult to know whether specified communications will have predictable effects upon specified audiences.

DISCUSSION QUESTIONS

1. A few years ago a great stir was caused by film and television experiments with "subliminal advertising"—messages or images flashed across the screen so rapidly that they were not noticed but allegedly had the effect of increasing sales of popcorn and soft drinks. You may have to go beyond the materials of this book to discover whether these fears of subliminal manipulation were warranted or not.

2. Is too much effort devoted by advertisers to overcoming inattention with the result that little effort is given to providing reasons for acting? For example, the Volkswagen ads amuse but may not stress advantages in the product or touch strong motives for buying.

3. What do you suppose a study of the relative persuasibility of elementary school children as opposed to college students would reveal? What hypotheses would you offer for testing by such an investigation?

4. It has been proposed that a person without any fixed opinion on a particular proposition will be easier to influence than one who has an opinion already. Does this hypothesis seem true? How might it be tested?

5. How might an individual who expects to be exposed to persuasive communications immunize himself against such efforts? Could you propose a program for soldiers going to Korea in 1950 that might have rendered them more resistant to the persuasive efforts of their Chinese captors?

6. Can you make some judgment about your tolerance for dissonance as compared with that of your friends or parents? How could such a phenomenon be observed?

7. Radio Free Europe which broadcasts news and American propaganda to the Soviet Union and the other eastern European countries aims at breaking the communication monopoly of the Communist governments. How effective, on theoretical grounds, would you expect such an effort to be? Might some other effort be more useful?

8. Can what has been said about the efficacy of environmental control be applied to the public school, the private summer camp, the social fraternity, the college residence hall, the military school, the "senior citizen's" housing settlement, the prison, the hospital or the home?

9. Perhaps we have been too quick to conclude that the dangers of manipulation by an unscrupulous elite are remote if we recall the effectiveness of Senator Joseph McCarthy's efforts to stifle free discussion in the nineteen-fifties and the alleged suppression of dissent from Viet Nam war policies by those associated with the Johnson administration. What do you think?

10. Would a study of the persuasibility of women performed today turn up different results than those reported in the Hovland and Janis essay? Why or why not?

SECTION V

*Assessment of
communication effects*

THE ASSESSMENT OF COMMUNICATION EFFECTS

Howard H. Martin

SINCE MOST WRITING AND SPEAKING aims at having some influence on a reader or listener, it is not surprising to find critical observers preoccupied with *effects*. The speaker naturally wants to know whether he moved his listeners in the way he had hoped to do. Others, who have their own persuasive intentions, look on in order to learn what kinds of communications have what kinds of effects on variously disposed listeners. The discovery of an *effect* means that a causal relationship has been inferred between something a speaker or writer says or does and some subsequent statement or act by a listener. Like all such inferences, the reliability of our declarations about causal relationships will depend on the frequency with which the supposed relationship has been observed and the degree to which we can separate the communication from all other kinds of stimulation that might also have produced the effect. We should admit right away that the complexity of the communicative act makes it extremely difficult for us to be comfortably assured that we have, in certain instances, actually observed an unambiguous causal relationship.

Before considering the ways of assessing communication effects, we ought to consider what constitutes an *effect*. In general, two kinds of changes are looked for as indications that a communication has had an effect: changes in the state of mind or feeling of a reader or listener (cognitive or affective changes), and change in his manifest behavior. For evidence of the first kind of changes we have to depend on the testimony of listeners or readers themselves, the occasional unreliability of which tests the investigator's ingenuity in devising measures that will produce honest responses. We are interested in how much attention a listener paid to a message, how well he comprehended it, and whether or not he accepted it. Some communications may alter a listener's perception of a proposition—allow him to see Medicare as "public medicine," for example, rather than "socialized medicine." Finally, communications produce feelings of pleasure, anxiety, anger or other emotions. Some writers have talked about these changes of mind or feeling as *instrumental effects* which operate to produce ultimate changes in behavior, while some psychologists speak of these effects as *mediating processes* that take place between the initial stimulation of the listener or reader by means of the communication and his behavioral response to it.[1] In both cases, discussions of these cognitive

278

and affective changes become a part of theoretical explanations of what happens when a person, for example, casts a vote against an open housing referendum after having been exposed to several mail appeals from an organization of real estate brokers.

The second kind of change which we take as indication that a communication has had an effect—change in manifest behavior—is subject to observation. Cheers, applause, hissing and disorder during a speech may be good momentary indications of listeners' approval or disapproval of the speaker or his proposition. But, much immediate behavior is ambiguous; a serious and alert look may mean that the listener is paying attention, or it may mean that he would like the speaker to think he is paying attention in order to be free to pursue his own thoughts. How much a listener or reader can remember of a communication, indicated by his ability in an interview or in a paper-and-pencil test to recognize or recall information presented in a communication, may also be an indication of effect. Probably the most dependable indication that a communication has produced an effect is the listener's or reader's having initiated action recommended by the communicator.

The two kinds of changes we have considered may be observed in the reactions to a communication of a single listener. But since speakers and writers are not usually satisfied with having evoked response from a single random listener, we ought to expand our concept of "effect" by making two qualifications. First, it makes a difference who is affected. Many Democratic partisans reacted strongly against Richard Nixon after his famous "Checkers" speech defending himself against charges that he misused campaign funds. But, since Nixon was not really addressing those strong Democratic partisans and had no intention of affecting their votes by his speech, the effects produced on them were irrelevant to Mr. Nixon, and were probably not unanticipated. A more surprising instance was Federal Reserve Board Chairman William McChesney Martin's speech to a Columbia University alumni luncheon in June, 1965, apparently intended by Martin as a warning against excessive speculation, but which frightened many investors with the specter of economic dangers and sent the stock market into a spin that lasted for months.[2] In this case, the supposed effects of Martin's speech, although largely unanticipated and unintended, were quite relevant to the aims he seems to have had.

Second, how many people respond to a communication is relevant to a determination of whether an effect has been produced. One cannot, of course, ignore the speaker's or writer's declared intentions, but

[1] Wallace C. Fotheringham discusses instrumental effects at length in *Perspectives on Persuasion* (Boston: Allyn and Bacon, Inc., 1966), chapter 3.
[2] Some have argued that the stock market spin was not entirely due to Martin's statements; others have seen the speech as chiefly responsible.

need not accept those declarations uncritically. A host of radio evange-
lists may be able to justify the expense of their broadcasts on the
ground that "if one lamb is brought home to the fold" their efforts have
been successful, but a critic may wonder whether one person "saved"
constitutes an effect. Advertisers who purchase expensive television
time adopt other standards of coverage and penetration in deciding
what constitutes an effect.

THEORETICAL PREDICTION

When other information about the responses to a speech or piece of
writing is unavailable, a critic may guess at its probable effects from
what he finds in the text. Since we are not entirely ignorant of what
sorts of language strategies strike certain listeners in certain ways, we
may sometimes infer with fair accuracy the effects of a particular speech
or play, novel or essay. Critics have speculated for years about the reception of Shakespeare's plays by the groundlings. Since we shall
probably never have any more information about the immediate reactions of Globe audiences than we have now, we must be content with
the considered judgments of those who have studied the plays relative
to the general traits of Elizabethans. There is a temptation for a latter-
day reader of Edmund Burke's remarks in Parliament on "Conciliation
with America" to assume, unintentionally, that his own reactions to the
speech mirror the reactions of the original parliamentary audience.
While such an assumption might produce misleading judgments, it
might also produce wise ones if the reader had successfully immersed
himself in the lives of the Georgian M.P.s and the events that affected
their decisions. Still, the imaginative recreation of the event is complicated by the fact that hearers were not all of one mind on Burke's
proposition, and their responses would have to be assessed by the reader's identifying himself first with one group and then with another until
he could arrive at some cumulative response or collection of responses.

Such efforts at projecting the effect of a discourse usually produce
judgments about the speech as a whole rather than the effects of certain strategies within the speech. Perhaps that should satisfy us. But
if we are genuinely interested in discovering more reliable generalizations about what kinds of talk produce certain responses in certain
listeners, we need more specific judgments. Was it his order of attack
that forced some M.P.s to agree with Burke—his closing off of the
alternatives before offering conciliation as the only remaining option?
Many have studied and admired this tactic of Burke, but we really
cannot be sure that it had the effect it may have been intended to have,
or the effect then that it often has upon a modern reader.

Jonathan Edwards' sermon, "Sinners in the Hands of an Angry
God," has been the focus of critical commentary by historians, literary

critics, psychologists and rhetoricians, many of whom have tried to guess at its effects or tie subsequent events to it as a cause. The temptations are apparent. We can see that this sermon is not altogether like others Edwards preached in the early seventeen-thirties, and we know, too, that it was preached during a period of revival in New England, a revival attended by tremendous enthusiasm and remarkable psychological manifestations, many of which Edwards himself has recorded in his *Faithful Narration*. Edwards was invited to Enfield because of his local reputation as a revival preacher; those who invited him expected him to "get results." We put these and other facts together to help us understand the effectiveness of Edwards' sermon. We read it today and guess that his description of the plight of the unredeemed sinner hanging by a thread over the fiery pit must have frightened his congregation, that his personal applications must have riveted their attention, that the building horror and anxiety must have produced some cries and gestures from the people of the church, and that some of them must have been moved to public confession and renewed commitment. These may be awfully good guesses, but there is no way of knowing how good they are. And, such attribution of results does not advance our understanding of what sorts of communication tactics produce what kinds of effects upon what kinds of listeners.

But there are occasions when such theoretical prediction of effects is the only sort of assessment we can make of a communication. The text of John Kennedy's November 22, 1963, speech in Dallas can be judged in terms of its probable effects although it was never delivered. We could decide whether it would have been understood, well-received, likely to have caught national attention, or to have been influential in strengthening support for the president's policies among those who were to have heard the speech. In fact, this seems to be the only method by which we assess the effects of ceremonial speeches at college commencements or on important anniversaries. We know, for example, that the keynote speaker at the Republican nominating convention aims at making delegates feel proud of the party's record and resolute in the coming campaign, so, when no contrary evidence is presented, we readily assume that the man had the effect he intended. If we looked more closely at such events, we might discover that fewer of those kinds of communications succeed than we have supposed.

CONTEMPORANEOUS REPORTS

Where some record has been made of responses shortly after listeners heard a speech, readers read a pamphlet or broadside, or spectators saw a play, it is sometimes possible to reconstruct the effects of a communication. Tom Paine's incendiary pamphlet, *Common Sense*, it has been said, "was to the American Revolution what *Uncle Tom's*

Cabin was to the Civil War."[3] How was such a judgment reached? Morison and Commager summarize the evidence: "The influence of this amazing pamphlet cannot well be exaggerated. Within a few months it had been read by or to almost every American. It rallied the undecided and the wavering, and proved a trumpet call to the radicals."[4] In a more detailed study of Paine's pamphlet, we would be shown the records and estimates of sales of the piece, the attention it received in daily and weekly newspapers, the number of other pamphlets it inspired, and the extent of its distribution as indicated by references to it in the correspondence of Revolutionary leaders. From such evidence we might be able to judge that "it rallied the undecided and the wavering, and proved a trumpet call to the radicals."

The sort of evidence relied on in such an assessment of the relationship between a speech or other communication and subsequent responses made by people privately or in groups is, of course, the same as that sought by the historian seeking to interrelate any collection of events. The more evidence and more direct testimony that people took the speech as a *cause* for their subsequent opinions and actions, the more confident he is in his inference. The fact that patriotic *acts* followed the appearance of the pamphlet strongly suggests that there was an intervening change of heart or strengthening of resolve among colonials; without such corroborative acts, we would be less certain that the publication "rallied the undecided and the wavering." In fact, this example probably should make us cautious about assuming a relationship between a communication and a subsequent act without a close look at the intervening reactions of listeners or readers. In any event as complex as the Revolution there are whole constellations of contributory events, some insignificant, some important, some crucial, and many so woven together or simultaneous that one can only say that this collection of prior events seems to have caused these later acts. But, while we can admit the fact of multiple cause, if we are interested in discovering useful generalizations about the effects of particular kinds of communications on particular audiences, we cannot abandon the search for more precise attribution of causal relationships where evidence exists that might make such inference possible.

Another kind of contemporaneous record of audience response that may assist in more specific attribution of effect is the comment of a reporter on audience reactions during a speech. The reporter of Wendell Phillips' speech on "The Murder of Lovejoy" noted interruptions of applause, laughter and the like. Newspapers reporting Andrew Johnson's appearances in Cleveland and other cities on the "Swing around the Circle" recorded the cheers and taunts that greeted the President, the cries of "Grant!" (the popular general who had left the

[3] Samuel E. Morison and Henry S. Commager, *The Growth of the American Republic* (New York: Oxford University Press, 1942), I, 193.
[4] *Ibid.*, p. 194.

entourage), 'Stop! Go on! No, no, we want nothing to do with traitors! Grant! Grant!" groans and other cries of "Shut up! We don't want to hear from you, Johnson."[5] Electronic recordings of contemporaneous speeches provide us with the same kind of evidence of audience responses during a speech. Where the reporter has been conscientious in indicating not only the kind but the degree of response—"sustained applause," "enthusiastic cheers," "scattered applause," "applause from the Republican side"—such a report may permit some inferences about reactions to particular tactics of the speaker. But often such reports are suspect. Partisan newspapers—and in the nineteenth century, newspapers made no pretenses of objectivity—may have presented their favorite in a good light and his opponent in an unfavorable one. Press reports in Democratic and Republican papers well illustrate the effect of bias on reporting of the Lincoln-Douglas debates. Another difficulty with assessments of the effect of a speech based on such evidence is that immediate responses may or may not be related to subsequent decisions. One could cheer one of Lincoln's deft parries but vote for Douglas; no doubt many did. In spite of these difficulties, such reports of immediate audience reactions constitute another bit of evidence on which may be based inferences about the effects of communications.

PUBLIC OPINION POLLS

Since the Great Depression we have had another kind of evidence available from which to infer communication effects. Several permanent organizations employing statistically validated sampling techniques take the public pulse fairly regularly on matters of public policy and the standing of public leaders. George Gallup's American Institute of Public Opinion, Elmo Roper and Associates, the Louis Harris poll, the Survey Research Center of the University of Michigan, the National Opinion Research Center of the University of Chicago, the California Poll conducted by Mervin D. Field, and a great many other surveys conducted from time to time by newspapers, magazines or other private institutions have supplied a mountain of data from which the cautious observer may draw probable inferences about the effects of certain communications. In every case, such surveys investigate a small sample of the electorate or of the potential consumers, the size and method of selection of which is determined by mathematical considerations of probability. Individual households are interviewed by men and women guided by a previously devised questionnaire. The wel-known surveys which are sometimes reported in local newspapers commonly ask for a "yes," "no," and "don't know" response to ques-

[5] Claude G. Bowers, *The Tragic Era* (Cambridge: The Riverside Press, 1929), pp. 136–137.

tions. Other scientific surveys measure intensity of opinion by asking respondents whether they "strongly agree," "moderately agree," or "slightly agree," "strongly— ," "moderately— ," or "slightly disagree" or are "undecided" about statements such as, "The Republican candidate will be more able than the Democratic candidate to end the Viet Nam fighting." The summation of interview responses is commonly expressed in percentages of the sample agreeing or disagreeing with the statements presented by the interviewer. Polls regarding voter preferences for candidates are expressed in the same way; for example, the 1964 presidential preference polls reported their results in this way:[6]

Nationwide Polls	Johnson	Goldwater	Undecided
Gallup poll	61	32	7
Harris poll	62	33	5
(Actual vote	61.4	38.6)	
Statewide Polls			
California poll	60	34	6
(Actual vote: California	59.8	40.2)	
Oliver Quayle poll	51	36	13
(Actual vote: Indiana	56.1	43.9)	

Where the intention of the research organization is larger than the prediction of election results, the opinions of the people in the sample may be analysed in terms of income groups, age groups, partisan groups, urban or rural groups, sex, racial or ethnic background, newspaper reading or television watching habits, or any number of other factors.

Since most polls do not aim specifically at measurement of the effects of particular speeches or public statements their use requires caution and judgment. But the same demands are made of the interpreter of any of the previously mentioned sources of information. Obviously, survey information may only suggest that a speech or other communication contributed to a later event; no indication of its importance in producing that effect will be possible. Moreover, since poll percentages generalize the responses of a large number of people, some of whom may have been exposed and some not exposed to a particular speech, many inferences about effects will be tentative.

The series of national television debates in the autumn of 1960 be-

---

[6] William C. Selover, "How the Polls Fared," *Christian Science Monitor*, November 14, 1964, quoted by Edward C. Dryer and Walter A. Rosenbaum, *Political Opinion and Electoral Behavior* (Belmont: Wadsworth Publishing Company, Inc., 1966), p. 22.

tween John F. Kennedy and Richard M. Nixon, which was one of the most closely examined speech events of all time, provides us with a nearly ideal picture of what can be done with opinion survey evidence in assessing the effects of communication. Advance notice of the debates allowed survey researchers to plan their investigations to coincide with the debates, thereby raising the probability that subsequent opinions were the result of one or more of the debates. Comparisons of opinions expressed before the debates with those expressed after the first debate and after each of the other three debates allowed inferences about the influence on voters of each man in each debate or in the entire series of four debates. For example, the Gallup Poll assessed opinion early in the 1960 campaign, before the first debate, after the first debate, and after the fourth debate, using a sample that varied between 1,500 and 8,000 people of voting age in order to discover who won. The results of most of the 31 studies that sought to discover the effects of the debates are summarized by Elihu Katz and Jacob J. Feldman in a reading accompanying this section.

LABORATORY EXPERIMENTATION

The historical critic and often the survey researcher want to know why certain events took place, what produced them and what were the causes that operated. They are more interested in understanding the event once it has occurred than in predicting whether a similar result can be expected in subsequent similar circumstances. A laboratory researcher, on the other hand, is less interested in understanding past events than in developing the means by which future events can be predicted. By testing the effects of specific communications in the laboratory he hopes to refine tentative generalizations about the relationship between communications having specified characteristics and the responses of listeners or readers also having specified characteristics.

The hallmarks of laboratory experimentation in communication effects are *system, control,* and *measurement* or *quantification.* Casual observation, it is argued, is undependable because accidental. Not until the researcher has declared what he is looking for, identified the places to look for it, and observed with some care and constancy in order to remove the element of accident, can he be satisfied with his generalizations. Therefore, some system is required; unless the experimental design can pass muster by providing for systematic observation of stated phenomena, whatever results are produced by such experimentation will be suspect.

Control implies both the act of simplifying the communication so that one aspect at a time may be looked at, and the provisions for comparing the behavior of people who have been exposed to the communication with that of those who have not. The first kind of control involves attempts to identify all of the possible aspects of the communication situation that might produce effects and eliminate or neutralize all but those which can be observed conveniently in a single experiment. In order to observe the effect of deductively patterned argument, one would wish to exclude or neutralize such other matters as the prestige of the communicator, the importance of the issue of the argument to the listener or reader, the emotional loading of the language, and all other potentially effective matter or manner. The second kind of control involves the observer's providing himself with the means of comparing later behavior of those exposed to the communication with the behavior of those who did not hear or read it, so that he may be sure that subsequent behavior was attributable to the communication and not to some other factor such as the personality traits of the people used as subjects or the mere passage of time.

The most distinctive characteristic of laboratory experimentation, although opinion surveyors aspire to it as well, is measurement. In some instances, measurement is necessary to verify that a supposed effect did in fact occur. More often the experimenter wants to know *how much* of an effect is produced in listeners or readers by specified aspects of the communication situation. Organization has an effect, but how much of an effect under each of several conditions? Certainly it makes a difference whether the plea is made by the President or the Vice-President, but how much difference and why?

Of the two kinds of effects produced by communications, manifest behavior and changes in one's state of mind, only the last has posed serious problems of measurement. Several procedures have been refined over the past four decades for use by the experimenter seeking to measure the effects of communications. One is the now familiar Likert-type scale which listeners mark after having heard a communication by indicating their current state of mind toward a proposition as "strongly agree," "moderately agree," "undecided," "moderately disagree," or "strongly disagree." By supplying listeners with a number of propositions bearing on the same attitude complex, experimenters expect to derive a fairly dependable measure of the direction and intensity of the listener's attitude. A second variety of attitude measure is the Thurstone scale or the scale of equal-appearing intervals. Here, respondents are asked to identify one of a range of statements as representative of their attitude toward a specified object, the statements having been previously arranged by judges in order between two stated extremes of attitude. A third instrument is the Bogardus social distance scale originally devised to discover the intensity of a person's attitudes toward various racial or national groups. Respondents were asked to indicate which of seven positions they would adopt toward a racial group from "I would accept members of this group to close kinship by marriage," "to my club as personal chums," "to my street as neighbors," "to employment in my occupation," "to citizenship in my country," "as visitors to my country," and "I would exclude from my country."[7] A fourth measuring device is the *semantic differential* developed by Charles Osgood, George Suci and Percy Tannenbaum for the discovery of elements of meaning but which also has proved useful in assessing attitudes. The semantic differential is a list of contradictory adjective pairs—"strong-weak," "wise-foolish," "clear-vague," etc.—arranged so that the respondent may check his position on a seven-point continuum between the two extremes. By having listeners check their positions on a scale composed of three, four or more bi-polar adjectives relevant to the subject under investigation, investigators have found that they can describe the direction and intensity of a listener's attitudes before and after a communication.[8]

With these and other measuring instruments, investigators in the laboratory have generally proceeded in two ways to assess the effects of communications. The most common approach has been to expose selected listeners or readers to some communication created or selected by the experimenter and, by testing attitudes before and after the communication, to infer the effect of the message. Such a method permits the investigator to change elements in the message (order of items, amount of fear-arousing material, difficulty of language), to alter the conditions under which it is heard or read (accidentally overheard, heard in presence of group, heard in a state of personal anxiety), to vary the person or persons said to be responsible for the message (a highly respected source, an unknown source, a disliked source), and to vary other components of the communication event in order to assess the specific effects of specific characteristics. A second approach has been to require those participating in the experiment to do something beyond merely listening to a communication—to copy a passage written by someone else, to write out an argument of their own, to read such an argument aloud to a group of other people. Attitude tests administered before and after the exercise serve as a measure of the effect of the communicative behavior on subjects' attitudes. These tactics have been designed to test the effect of interaction on the attitudes of persons thought of as the objects of communicative manipulation.

A number of examples of laboratory experiments are provided by Carl Hovland in his accompanying essay on the problems of reconciling conflicting results of survey and experimental studies. Hovland sees no necessary incompatibility between the two approaches, and explains the special virtues and limitations of each.

---

[7] William Albig, *Public Opinion* (New York: McGraw-Hill Book Co., 1939), p. 195.
   [8] Charles E. Osgood, George J. Suci and Percy H. Tannenbaum, *The Measurement of Meaning* (Urbana: University of Illinois Press, 1957).

CHANGED BEHAVIOR

The assessment of communication effects either by reference to contemporaneous reports, public opinion surveys or much laboratory experimentation accepts a declaration of the listener's state of mind as evidence of the impact of the speech. The speaker often assumes that a changed state of mind—firmer conviction or the stirrings of contrary ideas—may sooner or later lead to some concrete action in the form of a vote or a purchase. While there is some reason to suppose that beliefs express themselves in action and that the speaker who gains the listener's mental assent is on the way to achieving the behavioral change he seeks, other ideas or events may forestall or prevent the listener from acting in accordance with his changed or changing mind.[9] Actions may argue a prior state of mind consistent with the action, but the presence of the state of mind is no assurance that the action will follow. For example, people who voted for Barry Goldwater in 1964 no doubt believed that he would be better for the country than Lyndon Johnson; but there were probably a number of people who, at one time or other during the campaign, thought well of Goldwater but did not cast their vote for him. Since the relationship between belief and action is not always predictable, taking verbal statements of belief as a measure of effect or as a step toward the desired effect may be undependable. The best evidence of effect is behavior of those addressed consistent with that urged by the speaker—a check for the United Fund, an affirmative vote on the proposed tax millage increase, a dollar on the counter for the recommended book. The next two approaches to the assessment of communication effect look to concrete behavioral change as the measure of success.

Students of political behavior and consumer behavior have displayed a lively interest in the effects of communications. In both politics and marketing, the end product of communication is an overt act —a vote or a purchase. No problem of measurement arises; actions are decisive and can simply be counted. We are not troubled by the complicated relationship between declared state of mind and subsequent behavior for the action represents an understood behavioral commitment to a state of mind. Of course, the two actions are not equally important to most people. A decision to buy a tube of toothpaste does not commit one to very much for very long and, unless the product becomes important for the buyer or he is continually re-persuaded to buy

---

[9] An interesting report on the hiatus between actions and words is Richard LaPierre's account of travelling with a Chinese couple without encountering any discrimination, but having many innkeepers who had served them later say they would not accept orientals. See "Attitudes vs. Actions," *Social Forces*, 13 (1934), 230–237; Leon Festinger makes the same point in "Behavioral Support for Opinion Change," *Public Opinion Quarterly*, 28 (Fall, 1963), 404–417.

it, he may turn around next month and buy another brand. A vote is more important not only because it is a choice one has to live with for several years, but because the beliefs involved in such a decision, as Milton Rokeach pointed out in an earlier essay, are more central to the individual than those touched by most advertisers. We will want to argue in the last pages of this essay that the permanence of a decision (continuing to buy a certain brand of razor blade or sticking to a particular legislative solution) may be an important measure of the effectiveness of the communications that induced it. For the moment, we wish to consider techniques for assessing *immediate* effects of communication represented by voting studies and market research.

The vote in a state or national election reflects the impact of an entire communication campaign spreading over many months and reaching voters via several media. Although the outcome at the polls is the measure of effects that is most important to the candidate, an examination of the vote may not tell him which of his communications were most effective and which were least effective. Therefore candidates and others have used survey interview techniques to supplement the information provided by election data. Since survey techniques have been considered, only the interpretation of election results will be discussed here insofar as they serve to indicate the effect of the candidate's communicative efforts.

One pointed effort to use voting behavior as a measure of speaker effectiveness examined the Illinois congressional vote of 1858 in counties where Lincoln and Douglas debated.[10] Disturbed by the interpretations of the election which presumed that, because Republicans polled more votes than Democrats, Lincoln was the winner of the debates although antiquated apportionment robbed him of the election victory, Forest Whan proposed to compare the vote for Lincoln in the counties where he spoke with the vote in counties where he did not speak. These were the results:

In the Republican counties in which the two men spoke in the north, Douglas gained in 4; Lincoln in 3. In those in which they did not speak, Douglas gained in 1, and Lincoln gained in 7. In the great, doubtful, central section, where the two men spoke, Douglas gained in 18; Lincoln did not gain in a single county. Where they did not speak in this area, Douglas gained in 5, and Lincoln in 4. In the Democratic strongholds of the south, Douglas gained in 2 in which they spoke; Lincoln gained in 2. Where they did not speak, Douglas gained in 2 and Lincoln in 8. For the state as a whole, then, Douglas gained strength of 10 per cent or more [over 1854] in 24 counties in which the two men spoke; Lincoln gained in 5. In counties where they did not speak, Douglas gained in only 8 and Lincoln in 19.[11]

---

[10] Forest L. Whan, "Stephen A. Douglas," in *A History and Criticism of American Public Address*, William N. Brigance, ed. (New York: McGraw-Hill Book Co., 1943), II, 822–824.

[11] *Ibid.*, p. 823.

Although Illinois was moving toward the Republican party, Whan points out, the speaking of Stephen Douglas "was one of the sustaining factors in keeping the Democratic legislature in Illinois in 1858."[12] Recognizing the difficulty of attributing the outcome entirely to the speaking of either man, he argues that the debates were an important, perhaps decisive, factor: "to assume otherwise is to place an unusual reliance on coincidence or to argue that neither man had the ability to determine in which counties speaking would influence the election."[13]

In a sense, all elections are partly a measure of the effectiveness of communications, for the political campaign is simply a large and coordinated effort at communicating to the voter that the candidate is an able and responsible man whose views on current problems and capacity to deal with them are deserving of the voter's approval. Where certain communications within a campaign can be shown to be crucial, election results may reflect in part the impact of such events. An example might be Franklin Roosevelt's speech to the Teamsters' convention in Chicago in 1944 where, in a single speech, he exploded the Republican-sponsored notion that he was an aging and tired man unable to sustain the burdens of the Presidency. Not only did this single speech in which he ridiculed the rumors that his dog, Fala, had been flown home from Alaska by a special air force mission reassert Roosevelt's vigor and keenness, but it so provoked candidate Dewey that the Republican lost his composure in a subsequent speech in Oklahoma City, thereby injuring his standing with some voters. Another instance was Richard Nixon's famous televised address in response to newspaper charges that he made dishonest use of a secret fund provided him by wealthy California businessmen who hoped to gain political favors. In part, the election results indicated Nixon's success in reassuring voters that the Republican ticket had the moral vigor to clean up alleged corruption discovered in the Democratic administration. Of course, in the case of this speech, there were other more immediate measures of effect in the numbers of telegrams, telephone messages and letters that reached the Republican National Committee and Republican campaign headquarters within two or three days of the telecast, and in the public responses of Republican committeemen, congressmen and the party's candidate, General Eisenhower.

The importance of the television debates between Richard Nixon and John Kennedy in 1960 on the election outcome was stressed by Theodore H. White. Although, as we have seen, there were other measures of the impact of the debates, the voting results exhibited the "personal victory" of Kennedy who "ran ahead of his party or even with his party in the states of his most important victories."[14] Such a

[12] *Ibid.*, p. 824.
[13] *Ibid.*
[14] Theodore H. White, *The Making of the President 1960* (New York: Atheneum Publishers, 1961), p. 364.

result is a direct indication of the effectiveness of his personal campaign and of all the communicative efforts of which it was composed.

Most of the voting studies of national elections have set out to discover reasons for the result rather than the effects of communicative efforts which constituted the campaign.[15] But many of these studies by political scientists have evidence to offer about the effects of particular speeches, of a series of television or radio spot announcements, of newspaper advertisements or other dominant or distinctive communicative efforts. Because the vote represents an important overt behavior that is related in some way to the communications of the candidate, critics will continue to measure the effectiveness of communication by means of voting behavior.

Advertising agencies or their employers also seek to measure the effect of communications by means of the behavior of consumers—purchase of the product or, at least, an obvious display of interest in it. Although advertising agencies and market research organizations make use of survey procedures just as do students of political behavior, many companies and agencies are skeptical of such measures of communication effectiveness. The interview technique is used, for example, by Daniel Starch whose organization sends out a staff of researchers with a recent issue of a national magazine to ring doorbells until the surveyor finds someone who says he read the magazine. The interviewer leafs through the magazine asking the housewife which of the ads she can remember having seen. The assumption is that if people *recognize* the ads, they must have paid some attention to them when they read the magazine. Another organization, Gallup and Robinson, has its interviewers probe for what and how much their respondents can *recall* about specified advertisements on the assumption, as before, that the *penetration* of an advertisement can be assessed by the amount of information people can remember about it.[16] The skeptics argue that recognition and recall of information in their advertisements is not the effect they are after; they expect advertising to produce sales. Is there a predictable relationship, they want to know, between *learning* what the ad says and forming a favorable opinion of the product and actually buying it? A review of 28 advertising and non-advertising studies bearing on this question found only two exhibiting a positive relationship between knowledge changes and attitude or behavior changes,

---

[15] Representative voting studies are: Edmund A. Moore, *A Catholic Runs for President* (New York: The Ronald Press, 1956), on the 1928 campaign; Lazarsfeld, Berelson and Gaudet, *The People's Choice*, discussed in Section II, on the campaign of 1940; Angus Campbell, Gerald Gurin and Warren E. Miller, *The Voter Decides* (Evanston: Row, Peterson and Co., 1954), on the campaign of 1952; and the two studies by Theodore White of the campaigns and elections of 1960 and 1964, *The Making of the President* (New York: Atheneum Publishers, 1961 and 1965).

[16] Martin Mayer, *Madison Avenue, U.S.A.* (New York: Harper and Brothers, 1958), pp. 257–268.

while two actually exhibited a negative relationship and the remainder left the relationship ambiguous. The writer was forced to conclude that, "Learning and recall of factual information from mass communications does occur. However, recall and retention measures seem, at best, irrelevant to the ultimate effects desired."[17] In other words, ads that are remembered do not necessarily sell products.

Many advertisers would rather measure the effect of their communications by the number of inquiries received in response to specific advertisements or by the number of sales that can be related to specific advertisements or campaigns. Various ways of promoting inquiries have been used including return coupons for gifts or discounted premiums, offers of catalogues either free or for a price, and of additional information about the product. Requests for more information about the product are the surest and perhaps the only genuine indication of communication effectiveness by the inquiry measure; other replies may be unrelated to subsequent purchase of the product as Lucas and Britt point out in an accompanying reading. Pitney-Bowes company, manufacturer of postage meters, for example, used the numbers of inquiries for information as a measure of the effectiveness of alternative advertisements appearing in several publications. Coded return addresses permitted the company to identify the ad and publication which drew each inquiry.[18]

The acid test of advertising effectiveness is sales. Although no foolproof means has yet been devised for relating advertising efforts to subsequent sales, there are a number of techniques in use that offer some help in measuring advertising effectiveness. The best of these approaches seems to be the market area test. The Johnson wax company introduced its new air freshener, "Glade," in its northeast marketing area, New England and northern New York, with newspaper advertisements and television commercials inserted in its two programs, "Robert Montgomery Presents" and "The Red Skelton Show." The Benton and Bowles organization research staff conducted store audits in Syracuse, Springfield, Binghampton and Boston recording monthly shelf and storeroom inventories, receipts, and returns for all brands of air fresheners in order to determine unit sales and distribution figures. Presumably, the advertising effort was instrumental in producing the computed sales.[19] If the Johnson company had at the same time introduced the product in another area using different advertising material and media, the differences in sales would have provided some indication of the relative effectiveness of the two communication campaigns.

[17] Jack A. Hawkins, "Factual Recall as a Measure of Advertising Effectiveness," *Journal of Advertising Research*, 4 (March, 1964), 7.

[18] Neil H. Borden and Martin V. Marshall, *Advertising Management, Text and Cases*, rev. ed. (Homewood, Illinois: R. D. Irwin, 1959), pp. 944–946.

[19] *Ibid.*, p. 541.

Sales figures, which most merchandisers are certain bear some relationship to advertising efforts, may not tell the seller what he wants to know. He may conclude from sales figures that "we must be doing something right" (or wrong) without having any idea what. For example, the Dow Chemical Company, after having marketed Saran Wrap for nearly two years, was dissatisfied with sales growth and sought further information from three sources. One was the Nielsen Drug-Food Index data on inventories of various food wraps in food markets; the other two were consulting organizations, Ernest Dichter's Institute of Motivational Research and Nowland and Company. The report from the Dichter organization revealed that advertising claims of reuse had backfired because people had trouble reusing the product although they felt they ought to, and that word of mouth advertising seemed most effective which suggested that future advertisements should duplicate that situation by showing one woman telling another about the virtues of Saran Wrap. The Nowland and Company investigations of sales identified "light" and "heavy" users. Heavy users, for example, were fond of cooking and kitchen work while the light users were not. The report suggested that women be given reasons for using Saran Wrap, declaring that the "Housewife cannot be expected to perceive the relationship between the abstract ability to cling, and the fact that wrapping silver in Saran Wrap will keep the silver from tarnishing."[20] The advertiser was urged to show appropriate uses for the product; believability of commercials was not the problem but "relevancy to consumer interests and uses."[21] Such additional information about the effective and ineffective aspects of advertising communications for Saran Wrap allowed Dow to redirect its efforts, using sales to assess the influence of specific changes in its advertising program.

A number of techniques have been devised for pretesting the effect of particular advertisements. Two representative approaches will illustrate. The Schwerin Corporation hit upon a simulated sales situation as a means of testing the effectiveness of television commercials. People invited to a theater were asked to select gifts (a six months' supply of razor blades or $25.00 worth of baking powder) from an assortment of brands. After they had made their selection, they were shown a commercial for one brand. The numbers who, in a subsequent selection, picked the brand advocated in the commercial were taken as a measure of the effectiveness of the commercial message.[22] Another technique for measuring the effectiveness of television and radio commercials and print advertising is that used by the Ward J. Jensen organization. Shoppers on their way to a supermarket are interviewed

[20] *Ibid.*, p. 578.
[21] *Ibid.*, p. 582.
[22] Mayer, *Madison Avenue, U.S.A.*, pp. 270–271.

and supplied with a packet of discount coupons for a variety of products. Some of the shoppers are invited to view brief commercial films in a trailer-theater in the shopping center parking lot before they enter the store. A comparison of the coupons redeemed by shoppers who see the advertising films with those redeemed by shoppers who do not see the films provides a measure of the effectiveness of the advertisements.[23]

Measures of effect in terms of changed behavior seem a surer index that the communication has succeeded than measures of attitude change or of ability to recall information, in spite of the obvious difficulty of discovering what aspect of the communication situation produced the effect. Perhaps, as more efficient detection tools are devised, we may be able to put our finger on the differential effects of characteristics of the message, traits of the speaker, personality differences of readers or listeners, and the settings in which communication occurs. As we have seen, the combination of observed behavior *and* inquiry into the listener's state of mind or feeling seems to provide the clearest interpretation of communication effects.

PERSISTENCE OF BEHAVIOR

Many communications advocate that listeners or readers make a choice and act on it. Once the choice has been made, the fact that it proves satisfying for some time may argue the effectiveness of the original communications. If, on the hand, the choice is found to be unsatisfactory and is rescinded almost as soon as it is made, the communicator can hardly consider his efforts successful. Of course, the lasting satisfaction of the choice cannot depend entirely on the communications that induced it; the world may change and present new alternatives that were not at hand when the choice was made. We cannot blame the insurance broker for the fact that his clients turned from his recommended health insurance policy to Medicare when the federally sponsored plan became law. But we can raise some questions about the effect of the salesman's communication when most of those who were pressed to purchase a bargain on a trial basis returned it for refund almost immediately. From one point of view, we could say that the listener found out that the product did not live up to its billing; relative to the communication, we can say that it did not have the intended effect. Many buyers were led to expect qualities which, when they could inspect the merchandise, they found it did not possess. Had they been led to expect only what was forthcoming, fewer would have returned the goods. In any event, since the advertiser wished to dispose of his merchandise, the communication he employed to accom-

[23] Ward J. Jensen, "Sales Effects of TV, Radio and Print Advertising," *Journal of Advertising Research*, 6 (June, 1966), 2–7.

plish that aim was apparently ineffective if he did not, in fact, dispose of the goods. The same test could be applied to some social changes precipitated by written or spoken communications or communication campaigns. While we may wish to examine the initial causal inference, the permanence of pure food and drug legislation that followed publication of Upton Sinclair's book, *The Jungle,* which described unsanitary conditions in the Chicago meat-packing district, seems to indicate the effectiveness of Sinclair's effort. Recently, a similar effect has been attributed to Rachel Carson's *The Silent Spring,* a book that warned of the dangers to plant and animal life of chemical fertilizers and insecticides, the publication of which was followed by federal and state regulatory legislation still in force. Detroit auto makers have blamed Ralph Nader's book, *Unsafe at Any Speed,* which dramatized injurious and dangerous design features of automobiles, for the list of federal safety regulations affecting cars manufactured after January 1, 1968. If such standards are maintained and refined over the years ahead, that fact will argue the effectiveness of Nader's efforts to alert Americans to a potential hazard.

Similarly, those legislative changes which do not endure may cause us to question the effectiveness of the original persuasive efforts that brought them about. Detroit's experience with referendum ballots on the issue of fluoridation of the city's water supply suggests that neither the advocates nor the opponents of fluoridation have been dramatically successful in satisfying voters that fluoridation is either good or bad. That a 1966 vote favoring fluoridation was almost immediately questioned in the courts and plans laid for another referendum on the same question indicates that communications favoring the proposal did not build a strong enough consensus to discourage the unconvinced opponents. Permanence of public policy demands consensus; when such consensus is created by a communication campaign, it will be judged successful. Where the change advocated is achieved, but consensus is too weak to discourage immediate attack, the communication effort is likely to be judged ineffective. Advocates of the prohibition of alcoholic beverages who pushed through the eighteenth amendment to the Constitution during World War I failed to gain a preponderance of support as the history of the nineteen-twenties and the repeal of Prohibition in 1933 testify. Perhaps a similar test could be applied to the Missouri compromisers of 1820, although the world changed much between 1820 and 1854 when "popular sovereignty" brought the old agreements about slavery's territorial limits into question once again.

Assessing communication effects by considering the persistence of those effects joins ethical and pragmatic tests of effect. The fraudulent advertiser who carelessly or cynically misleads potential buyers may discover that he has not achieved his object. The opponent of fluoridation who frightens voters with spurious tales of poisoning and subversion may shortly discover that such tactics are ultimately ineffective; reality may intrude where there is no way for the communicator to hide it from his listeners.

SUMMARY

Two kinds of changes in listeners or readers are considered to be "effects" of communications, changes in the state of mind or feeling (cognitive or affective changes), and changes in directly observable behavior. These two kinds of effects have been assessed in several ways: by theoretical predictions based on inspection of the speech or document, by reliance on contemporary reports of audience responses to a discourse, by opinion polls and other survey interview data, by controlled experiments in laboratory situations, by field observations of changed behavior, especially in voting or buying advertised products, and by observations of the persistence of changed behavior over months and years.

WHO WON THE KENNEDY-NIXON TELEVISION DEBATES?

ELIHU KATZ AND JACOB J. FELDMAN

IN CONTRAST to the paucity of specific questions concerning the format of the debates, it is surely revealing that so many of the studies asked, unabashedly, "Who won?"—or words to that effect.

Again, the studies are very consistent concerning the results (see Table 3). The first debate was clearly won by Kennedy. That is, a plurality of respondents in every one of the thirteen applicable studies reported this result. The second debate was very close. The third debate was won by Nixon. And the final debate, again, was very close.

TABLE 11—3. WHO WON?

(per cent of all viewers[a])

STUDY		QUESTION	FIRST DEBATE		SECOND DEBATE		THIRD DEBATE	
			RMN	JFK	RMN	JFK	RMN	JFK
3	California Poll	"Made better impression"	24	35				
5	Carter	"Who benefited"						
7	Deutschmann	"Won votes"	7	26				
9	Gallup Poll	"Better job"	23	43				
11	Iowa Poll	"Gained most"	23[b]	35[b]				
14	Kraft		31	40	42	41	39	34
18	Minnesota Poll	"Gained the most"						
21	Opinion Research Corp.	"Best job stating his case"	25	39	31	36	46	28
22	Roper	"Best job"						
23	Schwerin	"Outscored"	23	39	28	44	42	39
25	Sindlinger	"Who won"	24	26	31	28	40	23
29	Texas Poll	"Best job"	26[b]	46[b]				
31	Wallace	"Better impression"						

[a] The difference between sum of totals and 100 represents "no choice."

[b] Question was asked following second debate and referred to first two debates.

Reprinted with permission from Elihu Katz and Jacob J. Feldman, "The Debates in the Light of Research: A Survey of Surveys," in Sidney Kraus, editor, *The Great Debates* (Bloomington: Indiana University Press, 1962).

TABLE 11—3 *cont.*

STUDY	QUESTION	FOURTH DEBATE		ALL DEBATES	
		RMN	JFK	RMN	JFK
3 California Poll	"Made better impression"				
5 Carter	"Who benefited"			11	49
7 Deutschmann	"Won votes"				
9 Gallup Poll	"Better job"			30	42
11 Iowa Poll	"Gained most"			21	32
14 Kraft				30	42
18 Minnesota Poll	"Gained the most"			17	51
21 Opinion Research Corp.	"Best job stating his case"	39	35		
22 Roper	"Best job"	31	36	21	37
23 Schwerin	"Outscored"	27	52		
25 Sindlinger	"Who won"	35	36		
29 Texas Poll	"Best job"				
31 Wallace	"Better impression"			23	54

(Only the Schwerin study disagrees that the second and fourth debates were inconclusive. In both cases, the New Yorkers in the Schwerin laboratories declare Kennedy the winner by large margins.) Over-all, when the question was asked about the debates as a whole Kennedy was far ahead.

Table 4 provides some insight into the major basis upon which people decide who won. Examining results for the first debate only, several things are evident from the table: (a) With the exception of two local studies, individuals with a party affiliation or with a specific voting intention declare their own candidate the winner more often than they choose the opposition candidate. (b) More Republicans and Nixon supporters choose Kennedy as the winner than Democrats and Kennedy supporters choose Nixon; this is true of every one of the studies. (c) More of the former than the latter insist that they cannot decide who won. In other words, there is a marked tendency to choose one's own candidate as the winner, though among the relatively small number who concede to the opposition (5 to 10 per cent in the state and national polls), there is a greater proportion of Republicans and Nixon supporters. Republicans, too, are more likely than Democrats and Kennedy supporters to say that they have no choices. (d) Finally, note that the Undecided—those who had not yet made up their minds between the candidates—choose Kennedy more often than Nixon, though most of them report no choice.

TABLE 11—4. "WHO WON" FIRST DEBATE: PERCENTAGE DISTRIBUTION OF CHOICE OF WINNER ACCORDING TO VOTING INTENTION OR PARTY AFFILIATION [a]

(each row equals 100%)

			WINNER		
STUDY	QUESTION	INTENTION OR AFFILIATION	Nixon	Kennedy	No Choice[b]
3	California Poll	"Made better impression"	Republican	39	17	44
			Democratic	11	51	38
7	Deutschmann	"Won votes"	Republican	10	27	63
			Democratic	4	30	66
			Independent	4	19	67
9A	Gallup	"Better job"	Pro-Nixon	45	17	38
			Pro-Kennedy	3	71	26
			Undecided	12	26	62
11	Iowa Poll[c]	"Gained most"	Pro-Nixon	39	16	45
			Pro-Kennedy	3	62	35
			Undecided	8	30	62
14	Kraft[c]		Pro-Nixon	59	17	24
			Pro-Kennedy	7	65	28
			Undecided	25	31	44
21	Opinion Research Corp.	"Best job stating his case"	Pro-Nixon	52	8	40
			Pro-Kennedy	2	73	25
			Undecided	4	22	74
23	Schwerin	"Outscored"	Pro-Nixon	47	6	47
			Pro-Kennedy	4	79	17
			Undecided	7	39	54
31	Wallace	"Better Impression"	Republican	28	46	26
			Democratic	2	87	11
			Independent	26	48	26

[a] Information on voting intention and party affiliation was obtained during the same interview as evaluation of the debates. It is conceivable, therefore, that some people aligned their party affiliation or voting intention according to their evaluation of who won the debate. Although several studies have pre-debate information available, only the Kraft study actually employs voting intentions obtained in an earlier interview.

[b] No Choice and/or Don't Know.

[c] Question was asked following second debate and referred to first two debates.

Most of the other factors which differentiate between those who thought that Kennedy won and those who thought that Nixon won (education, occupation, age, religion, etc.) are confounded with voting intention and, therefore, we shall not report them. Only sex (happily) tends to be relatively free of statistical contamination. As it turns out, Nixon's debate performance seems to have impressed proportionately more women than men.

Roper asked those who named one or the other candidate as having won the final debate, "In what ways would you say that (Kennedy, Nixon) was better?" and the answers were cross-tabulated by voting intention. Three categories of reasons characterize the loyal partisans as compared with those who conceded defeat: they said that the winner was better, first of all, because they *agreed with his views;* secondly, because he was *better informed;* and, finally, because he was more *sincere,* honest, truthful, etc. Those who decided for Kennedy were much more likely than those who decided for Nixon to emphasize that their choice was *specific,* gave facts, answered questions directly rather than evasively. Comparing only the two (very small) groups of conceders, it appears that Nixon supporters who conceded that Kennedy had won did so primarily on personality grounds: they liked his personality, they said. And they concurred in his partisans' admiration for his specificity.[1] Kennedy supporters who conceded that Nixon had won the debate were unique in attributing the victory to his having kept his opponent on the defensive, and they were much more likely than Nixon's own partisans to feel that he had displayed greater confidence in presenting his position.

Although there are various ways in which the many categories of response classified by Roper might be combined and recombined, it seems that a candidate's general informedness and his style of presentation of facts and arguments were more important criteria for judgment than either what he said or his personality as a whole. In other words, if these attributes are separable at all, the Roper data seem to argue that style of presentation was more important than either the content of the presentation (issues) or the personality of the debater (image).[2] This is in contrast to those who have speculated that the audience was interested only in the personalities of the candidates.

[One of the studies] feels that *both* personality and style of presentation were important frames of reference and agrees that the subject matter of the debate—the issues—was rarely mentioned as a factor which "counted in favor of" or "counted against" each candidate. Thus, "the questions we asked here were carefully worded so as to allow

[1] Still, pro-Kennedy people and those who leaned toward Nixon (but not those "for" or "strongly for" Nixon) apparently would have liked Kennedy to be even more specific. Asked by Market Psychology, Inc. to complete the sentence, "I would like Kennedy a little more if he would only . . . ," large proportions of these groups (in New Brunswick, N. J.) said, "If he would only be more specific," especially about details of his foreign policy. Sizable proportions of the same groups said he should be "less rash, less double-talking, more mature, time his phrases, speak more slowly and more clearly, speak right to us, not end so abruptly, show the sense of the Presidency as an awful trust rather than merely a political goal, etc."

[2] The Kraus-Smith paper finds the "images" attributed to each candidate closer to the "images" of some issues than of others, e.g., it is suggested that the "profile" of the Democratic image of Kennedy matches the "profile" of Catholicism, federal aid to education, and the U.N.

respondents to talk either about what the candidates said or about the two men themselves and how they performed. . . . The fact that so little comment was directed at the subject matter of the debate or at any of the arguments involved, and so much more at the candidates themselves and the general quality of their respective performances as debaters, would seem to confirm what some commentators have already suggested. This is that a television debate of this kind, which focuses attention so sharply on the contestants themselves, leaves a mass audience with (as we have seen) some very distinct impressions of the capabilities of the two men as debaters and as persons, but (as our results suggest) with very little idea of what the debate was all about."

LEARNING FROM THE DEBATES: THE ISSUES

That does not mean that people learned nothing from the debates about the issues. Indeed, Carter gave a 16-item information test to his respondents based on statements made by the candidates in the first debate and found not only that at least some of what was said was remembered but, even more, that there was no evidence that a process of "selective recall" was operating. That is to say, Democratic viewers were no more likely to recognize statements made by Kennedy than statements made by Nixon and the same thing holds true for Republican viewers. This is an extraordinary finding, suggesting that the debates not only overcame the well-established tendency toward selective exposure (which insulates one from opposition arguments) but also— at least as far as information is concerned—the tendency to perceive and recall selectively.

A related study by Sebald also finds respondents—sociology students at Ohio State, in this case—equally able to identify correctly statements made by either candidate (regardless of their own preferences). Sebald's concern, however, was rather different from Carter's. Respondents were presented with a set of statements made by the two candidates and were asked, first, to agree or disagree with each statement and, second, to name its author. While the over-all attribution of statements to the two candidates was equally correct, statements with which a respondent disagreed were most often attributed to the opposition candidate—even when actually made by the respondent's own candidate—while statements with which the respondent agreed were much more accurately attributed to the candidate who made them. This implies that it may be more painful to disagree with one's own candidate than to agree with some statement of the opposition. In still another aspect of the same study, respondents were asked to recall spontaneously statements made by the candidates. Here, the students tended to recall those of their own candidate's statements with which they personally agreed and statements of the opposition candidate with which they disagreed.[3] It is not clear, however, whether the students' opinions on the issues preceded or followed exposure to the candidates.

Of course, there is plenty of other evidence to illustrate the workings of selective perception in audience reaction to the debates. The distribution of votes on "who won" according to voting intention or political affiliation (Table 4) provides an obvious example; and there are many others. An especially pertinent example is reported by Kraft, who finds that those who say that the most important thing discussed in the (second) debate was foreign policy were much more likely to be pro-Nixon than pro-Kennedy, whereas those who say that some domestic matter was the most important topic discussed tended to be for Kennedy.

The evidence suggests that foreign affairs was the paramount issue during the entire campaign and, according to Sindlinger, it increased in importance following the second, third, and fourth debates. Since Nixon was generally conceded to be the more expert and experienced in foreign affairs—he was far ahead of Kennedy in perceived ability at "handling the Russians" and "keeping the peace"—the focus on foreign affairs was clearly to Nixon's advantage. In the debates themselves, the Quemoy-Matsu issue seemed to work for Nixon. Roper asked specifically, "How do you feel about this—that Nixon scored against Kennedy in these discussions about the offshore islands of Quemoy and Matsu . . . or that Kennedy scored against Nixon or that neither one of them handled this issue well?" While partisans said that their own candidate had outscored the other, the Nixon supporters were surer of this than were the Kennedy supporters. Similarly, in Carter's study, California Republicans were much surer than Democrats that their man got "the best of the argument" over issues such as "peace," "Cuba," "U-2 flights," and "disarmament."[4] Public perception of Kennedy's ability in foreign affairs did increase as a result of the debates but, even so, Nixon might well have won, if perceived ability at handling foreign affairs had influenced more votes.

There seems to be little doubt that the debates made some issues more salient, as all campaigns do. Quemoy and Matsu (from which Nixon profited), U.S. prestige (which benefited Kennedy), and domestic issues such as unemployment, old-age medical insurance, aid to education, and farm policy (all of which benefited Kennedy) were the major ones. But the Kraus-Smith study, which investigated the extent of actual changes in opinion on the issues as a result of the debates, found no change at all, while the Carter study found high proportions insisting, on most issues, that neither candidate had gotten "the best of the argument."

[3] This line of analysis is developed in Berelson, Lazarsfeld, and McPhee, *Voting*, chapter 10.

[4] Citations to Carter in this and the following paragraph are based on material omitted from Carter's chapter in this book.

Still, it is worth bearing in mind that people seemed to remember some of the content of the debates. Moreover, when asked, 27 per cent of the respondents in one study assert that the debates helped them learn something about the issues, and this is not far from the percentage that say they learned something about the candidates (35 per cent) or that the debates generally increased the level of their information and interest in the campaign (17 per cent).

As far as issues are concerned, then, the debates seem to have (a) made some issues salient rather than others (the issues made salient, of course, may or may not have been the most "important" ones); (b) caused some people to learn where the candidates stand (including the stand of the opposition candidate); (c) effected very few changes of opinion on the issues; and (d) focused more on presentation and personality than on issues.

LEARNING FROM THE DEBATES: THE CANDIDATES

Sixty-one per cent of the Kennedy voters said they learned "a great deal . . . about the candidates and what they stand for" from the TV debates. Only about half as many said they learned "a great deal" from other TV appearances of the candidates, from news in the newspapers, from columnists or editorials. The Nixon voters are more grudging about the debates—since their outcome is so clearly associated with the victorious Kennedy. Still, 35 per cent of the Nixon voters say they learned a "great deal"—as large a percentage as for any other source of information.

We have already seen that viewers learned something about the issues, though perhaps not very much. But there is considerably more reason to believe that they learned something about the candidates themselves. They discovered how well each candidate could perform in a debate and they formed images of each candidate's character and abilities.

Many will argue that this is unfortunate learning in the sense that whether a candidate is perceived as sincere, or tough, or quick on his feet is, first of all, probably not an important qualification for the office of president and, secondly, probably misperceived anyway. (Some would say similar things about the issues as they were presented in the debates.) But is it altogether unfortunate? Is it irrational to assume that the observation of two men interacting (albeit with many restrictions) under extreme pressure may be somewhat diagnostic of performance in a high-pressure job? Is the candidates' manner of handling rhetoric or statistics really so remote from the American voter's task of evaluating the qualifications of the man, as much as of the party, for the presidency? It is certainly much more rational than judging an automobile by its body or a book by its cover, but—as some sympathetic soul has pointed out—even these actions may not be as demented as they seem. People are not so foolish as to equate an automobile with the design of its body but, when mechanical sophistication is lacking, they use the body, and whatever other clues are available to them, as indices of the quality of the car.

Whatever the case, there is evidence from several studies that Kennedy fared far better than Nixon as far as positive images are concerned. Of course, Kennedy had the "advantage" of being all but unknown. Nixon had to maintain his image; Kennedy had to attain his—and the latter (or so it seems after the event) is the easier thing to do.

The most elaborate of the several image studies is that of Tannenbaum, in which respondents are asked to choose the attributes of their Ideal President in terms of a set of scales such as weak-strong, agitated-calm, old-young, and the like, and then—before and after the first debate and, once more, following the last debate—they were asked to rate the two candidates in terms of the same scales. The first debate moved the ratings of Kennedy, on all twelve scales, in the direction of the Ideal President, the most important shift being on "experienced-inexperienced." Changes in the before and after ratings of Nixon seemed random and inconsistent by comparison. Both men moved away from Ideal by the end of the debates but Nixon moved away more decisively than did Kennedy. Tannenbaum concludes that "Kennedy did not necessarily win the debates, but Nixon lost them. . . ."

Both Tannenbaum and Carter find that Kennedy's performance in the first debate impressed Democrats and Republicans alike as far as positive images are concerned. Over the entire period of the debates, the Carter findings indicate that the Democrats boosted Kennedy higher and higher while the Republicans' appreciation of Kennedy increased almost as much. Nixon barely maintained his original position. Two studies of university students identified a decline in the favorability of the Nixon image among pro-Kennedy people as the major change and one of the studies found a corresponding improvement in the image of Kennedy among pro-Nixonites.

Not so in Chicago, however. Creative Research Associates found that Nixon's image improved even more than Kennedy's in the second, third, and fourth debates and that Nixon lost ground not so much in the debates but outside them ("between" them).

But this is the only exception and, in any case, CRA does not discuss the first debate, which apparently, made most of the difference. The first debate seems to have served, primarily, to rally the doubting Democrats. A respondent in the Langs' study is quoted as saying that, as a result of the first debate, he "switched from being an anti-Nixon Democrat to a pro-Kennedy Democrat." According to the Langs, many Democrats expected Kennedy to do less well and, in anticipation, were prepared to discount the connection between performance in the debates and qualification for the role of president. Kennedy's victory

TABLE 11—5. IMPACT OF DEBATES ON FAVORABILITY TOWARD CANDIDATES
ACCORDING TO POLITICAL PREDISPOSITIONS (VIEWERS ONLY)

Note: Read this table as follows: Considering the California Poll, for example,
33% of Republican viewers became more favorable to Nixon, 8% less favorable,
and (not shown in the table) 59% remained unchanged. Among Democratic
viewers, 15% became more favorable toward Nixon, 33% less favorable, and (not
shown in the table) 52% remained unchanged.

STUDY	QUESTION		% more favorable		
			Rep	Dem	Ind.
3 California Poll (first debate)	"Did seeing the debate make you more favorable or less favorable toward Nixon? Toward Kennedy?"	Toward Nixon	33	15	
		Toward Kennedy	25	54	
5 Carter (after four debates)	"Did your feelings about either candidate change in any way as a result of the television debates? In what way?"	Toward Nixon	25	14	
		Toward Kennedy	19	39	
18 Minnesota Poll (after three debates)	"Has your opinion of Kennedy (Nixon) changed in any way as a result of the debates? In what way?"	Toward Nixon	29	13	20
		Toward Kennedy	6	23	19
23 Schwerin[a] (first debate)	"Having seen this debate, what is your attitude toward Vice-President Nixon? Toward Senator Kennedy?"	Toward Nixon	57	13	16
		Toward Kennedy	25	72	36
27 Survey Research Center[b] (after four debates)	"Was your feeling about (Kennedy) (Nixon) any different after you watched those programs?"	Toward Nixon (against Kennedy)	40	11	17
		Toward Kennedy (against Nixon)	19	56	40
		Neither	41	33	43

[a] In the Schwerin study, political predisposition was indexed by preference for
candidates rather than for party.
[b] Whereas the other studies percentaged changes in favorability separately for
each candidate, the SRC study combined pro-Kennedy and anti-Nixon changes
and pro-Nixon and anti-Kennedy changes and percentaged these over the total
viewers of each party.

TABLE 11—5 cont.

STUDY	QUESTION		% less favorable		
			Rep	Dem	Ind.
3 California Poll (first debate)	"Did seeing the debate make you more favorable or less favorable toward Nixon? Toward Kennedy?"	Toward Nixon Toward Kennedy	8 19	33 4	
5 Carter· (after four debates)	"Did your feelings about either candidate change in any way as a result of the television debates? In what way?"	Toward Nixon Toward Kennedy	17 32	29 16	
18 Minnesota Poll (after three debates)	"Has your opinion of Kennedy (Nixon) changed in any way as a result of the debates? In what way?"	Toward Nixon Toward Kennedy	2 17	12 2	8 11
23 Schwerin[a] (first debate)	"Having seen this debate, what is your attitude toward Vice-President Nixon? Toward Senator Kennedy?"	Toward Nixon Toward Kennedy	2 14	31 6	11 2
27 Survey Research Center[b] (after four debates)	"Was your feeling about (Kennedy) (Nixon) any different after you watched those programs?"	Toward Nixon (against Kennedy) Toward Kennedy (against Nixon) Neither			

not only strengthened confidence in him among partisans and potential partisans but, by making the performance criterion universally legitimate, made the institution of the debates more important than they otherwise might have been and the defeat of Nixon all the more serious.[5]

These changes in the image of Kennedy surely account for the increase in the over-all favorability toward Kennedy over the period of

[5] An analysis of the Tannenbaum data subsequent to the one reported in the present volume tends to confirm the notion that the first debate was especially influential for Democrats and Independents. Of particular interest here is the marked improvement in the eyes of Democrats and Independents in Kennedy's position relative to Nixon's with respect to such traits as "experience" and "strength." While Kennedy's image as a "TV performer" showed particular improvement with respect to these traits, there was also improvement in the corresponding components of his "presidential" image. The results are reported in Bradley S. Greenberg, "The Political Candidate Versus the Television Performer," a paper read at the annual meeting of the Pacific Chapter, American Association for Public Opinion Research, Los Angeles, January, 1962.

the debates. Five studies inquire specifically into the generalized attitudes of voters toward the two candidates, and the results are summarized in Table 5. Just as in the evaluation of "who won," it is evident from the table that (a) the Democrats reported that their opinion of Kennedy had improved more often than Republicans reported an improvement in their general opinion of Nixon; (b) Republicans became more favorable to Kennedy than Democrats to Nixon; (c) indeed, two of the studies suggest that the Democrats became much more unfavorable to Nixon following the first debate than the Republicans did to Kennedy; (d) Independents moved more toward Kennedy than Nixon. Important as these figures are, however, it is no less important to note that close to half of the respondents in each of these studies reported no change at all.

IMPACT OF THE DEBATES ON VOTING DECISIONS

But did this affect any votes? That is a hard question to answer.

Ideally, to test for the impact of a given debate on voting intentions it would be necessary (a) to have before and after measures of the voting intentions of the same group of respondents; (b) to compare viewers and non-viewers. And, in order to assess the impact on actual voting, it would be necessary (c) to establish that a change in voting intention resulting from exposure to the debate had persisted until Election Day.

But this is very elusive information. Most studies are not based on panels of the same respondents (trend studies, of course, reveal only changes in the total distributions and conceal internal changes). Furthermore, even a panel study cannot focus so narrowly on the debates as to be sure that it was a debate rather than some other campaign event which best explains changes in voting intention. Then, too, it is almost impossible to compare viewers and non-viewers since these were somewhat different kinds of people to begin with and, what's more, non-viewers got the word so quickly. For example, Deutschmann finds a certain amount of change presumably as a result of the first debate but no difference between viewers and non-viewers.

Bearing all these limitations in mind, let us look at the evidence.

First of all, it seems safe to say that the debates—especially the first one—resulted primarily in a strengthening of commitment to one's own party and candidate. This was much more the case for Democrats than Republicans but the former had much greater room for improvement. Thus, according to ORC, the 63 per cent of Republicans who were "strongly committed" to Nixon in August dropped upon re-interview following the first debate to 59 per cent, whereas the percentage of Democrats "strongly committed" to Kennedy increased from 39 to 46. Similarly, the Langs found that most of the changes following the first debate were those of undecided Democratic party sympathizers whose votes had "crystallized" as a result of the debates.

TABLE 11—6. CHANGE IN COMMITMENT FROM DEBATE TO DEBATE[a]

DEBATE	WINNER	% CHANGE IN "STRONG COMMITMENT" TO OWN PARTY'S CANDIDATE	
		Republicans	Democrats
First	Kennedy	−4	+7
Second	Tie	+9	+8
Third	Nixon	+7	−1
Fourth	Tie	−4	+2
	Net Change	+8	+16

[a] Adapted from ORC study. Note that successive interviews are with different sub-samples of original August sample of respondents, nationwide, and thus the changes reported are essentially "trend" data rather than "panel" data.

Secondly, trend data on changes in strength of commitment from debate to debate follow the pattern of evaluation of "who won." Consider Table 6, based, again, on the ORC study. In the two debates with a clear-cut winner (first and third) there is an increase in strength of commitment to the winner and a decrease in commitment to the loser. Between the first and second debates (the second being a tie) both candidates gained strength equally. The fourth debate (also a tie) fits the pattern somewhat less well, though the net gain for Kennedy results from Nixon's loss of Republican strength-of-commitment rather than an increase in commitment among Democrats.

Finally, still drawing on the same study, Table 7 compares the pre- and post-debate positions (on a nine-point scale) of viewers and non-viewers.[6] The first thing to note in the table is that viewers of the debates, if anything, changed *less* than non-viewers. This is not as surprising as it sounds considering the fact that the non-viewers were far less interested in the election and far less committed to a candidate than the viewers. Previous election studies have shown that these are the people who are most open to influence, who are least likely to vote, and whose responses, in any case, are of dubious reliability. The second important point to note in the table is that among those who did change their voting intentions, by and large, neither candidate gained; this is true for both viewers and non-viewers of the final three debates. *Only in the first debate* is there evidence that viewing made a difference for one of the candidates. The net gain for Kennedy among viewers of the first debate is 8 per cent, compared with the usual negligible difference (2 per cent) among the non-viewers.[7]

[6] These data are based on before-and-after comparisons of the *same* respondents. There are four sets of comparisons, one for each debate. Any movement on the scale (e.g., from "leaners" toward Kennedy to "strongly committed" to Kennedy) is classified as a change—in this case, of course, a pro-Kennedy change.

[7] The absence of a clear-cut net gain for Nixon among viewers of the third

TABLE 11—7. CHANGES IN COMMITMENT OF VIEWERS AND NON-VIEWERS[a]

	FIRST DEBATE		SECOND DEBATE		THIRD DEBATE		FOURTH DEBATE	
	Viewers	Non-Viewers	Viewers	Non-Viewers	Viewers	Non-Viewers	Viewers	Non-Viewers
	%	%	%	%	%	%	%	%
Unchanged	58	52	65	66	73	69	70	67
Change to Kennedy	25	25	17	17	14	15	16	16
Change to Nixon	17	23	18	17	13	16	14	17
Net gain for Kennedy	+8	+2	−1	0	+1	−1	+2	−1

[a] Based on special tabulations by ORC of before-and-after interviews with the *same* individuals. Before and after the first debate, for example, 58% of the viewers indicated precisely the same commitment (on a 9-point scale), while 25% made a change in Kennedy's favor (e.g., from "leaning" to "strongly committed") and 17% changed in favor of Nixon.

As previously noted, Deutschmann's report is rather similar. He found no difference in the extent of change among viewers and non-viewers of the first debate. He also found that 25 per cent of his panel made a change (on a seven-point scale) before and after the first debate, of whom 11 per cent crossed over from one candidate to the other. Kennedy profited slightly more than Nixon from the net result of these moves. Again, the Creative Research study found that non-viewers changed at least as much as viewers of the second, third, and fourth debates. There is a whisper of a suggestion that there was more movement from undecided to a specific voting intention among the viewers than among the non-viewers.[8]

From these studies it appears a reasonable inference that the debates did have some effect or, more exactly, that at least the first debate accelerated Democratic support for Kennedy among viewers.

To put these findings in a somewhat different perspective, however, it is instructive to consider the long-term trend within which the above-mentioned changes were going on. Consider Table 8, in which the trend results of the Gallup Poll are reported for the entire campaign. The results reported on September 25 were obtained immediately before the first debate and the interviewing for the report of October 12

debate conflicts with Table 6. It is difficult to reconcile these two sets of data.

[8] The ORC and Deutschmann data just presented were analyzed as "panel" data, comparing the response each individual gave before the debate with his post-debate response. Creative Research Associates also interviewed the same respondents before and after each debate but presented only the over-all marginal distributions at each point in time and therefore could measure only the "net change."

was conducted immediately after the first debate, during the period September 27–October 4. Here, too, it appears that Kennedy scored a net gain in the debates, advancing three percentage points while Nixon lost one. But consider the long-term trend, which suggests that Kennedy was gradually advancing anyway!

TABLE 11—8.   THE GALLUP POLL[a]

(*each row equals 100%*)

Release date	Kennedy Johnson	Nixon Lodge	Undecided
August 17	44	50	6
August 31	47	47	6
September 14	48	47	5
September 25[b]	46	47	7
October 12[c]	49	46	5
October 26	48	48	4
November 4 (adjusted for probable voters)	51	45	4
November 7	49	48	3
Actual vote	50.1	49.9	

[a] "If the election were held today, which ticket would you vote for—Nixon and Lodge or Kennedy and Johnson?" Results reported above include those registered and intending to vote who were more or less certain of their choice. Note further adjustment of November 4.

[b] Before first debate.

[c] After first debate.

Did the debates really affect the final outcome? Apart from strengthening Democratic convictions about their candidate, it is very difficult to say conclusively.

But if you *ask* people whether the debates influenced their voting decision, they say yes. As Table 9 reveals, a sizable proportion of the voting population feels that the debates helped them decide. This is more true for Democrats than for Republicans, as has already been pointed out.[9] But consider the 6 per cent in the national Roper study who say that the debates "made them decide" or the 39 per cent in the Bruskin study who mention the debates in answer to a very different question concerning "the one most important thing" that led to Kennedy's victory.[10] Even these people, almost certainly, were reinforced

[9] A study of University of Washington students by Edelstein finds 5 to 6 per cent who consider the debates the "most important" factor in their decisions and some 35 per cent who feel that the debates were at least "fairly important." There is little, if any, support here, however, for the finding of other studies that the debates were considered more important by Democrats than by Republicans.

[10] ORC asked a question only slightly different from Bruskin's but with very different results. To the question, "What do you think were the most important issues or factors in deciding who won the election?" only 8 per cent mentioned the debates, while 18 per cent mentioned religion, 12 per cent mentioned labor vote, 10 per cent mentioned personality, and, in addition, a large number of specific

by the debates in their prior inclinations rather than converted. On the other hand, who is to say that the doubts and reservations which existed among Democrats regarding Kennedy might not have been dispelled at all if it had not been for the debates?

TABLE 11—9. PERCEIVED ROLE OF DEBATES IN DECISION-MAKING PROCESS ACCORDING TO VOTING INTENTION [a]

	Study	Question
11	Iowa Poll[b] (after two debates)	"Do you feel that these television debates between Nixon and Kennedy have helped YOU DECIDE which candidate you will vote for or haven't the debates made any difference?"
22	Roper (after four debates	"Different people have said the debates did different things for them. Some say the debates made them *decide* who they'll vote for; some say they made them *more sure* their choice was right; some say they left them *less sure*, and others say the debates had practically no effect on them one way or the other. Which is *most* true for you?"

[a] Per cent of pro-Nixon, Pro-Kennedy, Undecided, and all respondents.

[b] The Iowa Poll also reports on results of a similar question asked after all four debates were over: helped, 29%; no difference, 63%; don't know, 8%. No breakdown is given according to voting intention. Note the decline in the proportion claiming that they were helped in their decisions.

TABLE 11—9 *cont.*

Answer	Pro-Nixon %	Pro-Kennedy %	Unde-cided %	Total %
Yes, helped decide	28	42	34	34
No, no difference	70	57	64	64
Don't know	2	1	2	2
	100	100	100	100
Made them decide	3	9	1	6
Made them more sure	39	49	4	41
Made them less sure	5	3	24	5
No effect	49	35	52	43
Don't know	4	4	19	5
	100	100	100	100

issues were named. A phenomenon similar to the difference between the Roper and Bruskin results noted in the text has been often observed in survey research. In studies of medical care, for instance, very few people ever attribute their *own* failure to have an illness attended by a physician to a fear of the diagnosis, while a large proportion of the same people ascribe this motive to "most people."

RECONCILING CONFLICTING RESULTS DERIVED FROM EXPERIMENTAL AND SURVEY STUDIES OF ATTITUDE CHANGE

CARL I. HOVLAND

Two QUITE DIFFERENT types of research design are characteristically used to study the modification of attitudes through communication. In the first type, the *experiment*, individuals are given a controlled exposure to a communication and the effects evaluated in terms of the amount of change in attitude or opinion produced. A base line is provided by means of a control group not exposed to the communication. The study of Gosnell (1927) on the influence of leaflets designed to get voters to the polls is a classic example of the controlled experiment.

In the alternative research design, the *sample survey*, information is secured through interviews or questionnaires both concerning the respondent's exposure to various communications and his attitudes and opinions on various issues. Generalizations are then derived from the correlations obtained between reports of exposure and measurements of attitude. In a variant of this method, measurements of attitude and of exposure to communication are obtained during repeated interviews with the same individual over a period of weeks or months. This is the "panel method" extensively utilized in studying the impact of various mass media on political attitudes and on voting behavior (cf., e.g., Kendall & Lazarsfeld, 1950).

Generalizations derived from experimental and from correlational studies of communication effects are usually both reported in chapters on the effects of mass media and in other summaries of research on attitude, typically without much stress on the type of study from which the conclusion was derived. Close scrutiny of the results obtained from the two methods, however, suggests a marked difference in the picture of communication effects obtained from each. The object of my paper is to consider the conclusions derived from these two types of design, to suggest some of the factors responsible for the frequent divergence in results, and then to formulate principles aimed at reconciling some of the apparent conflicts.

Reprinted with permission from *The American Psychologist*, 14 (1959), 8–17, published by the American Psychological Association, Inc.

DIVERGENCE

The picture of mass communication effects which emerges from correlational studies is one in which few individuals are seen as being affected by communications. One of the most thorough correlational studies of the effects of mass media on attitudes is that of Lazarsfeld, Berelson, and Gaudet published in *The People's Choice* (1944). In this report there is an extensive chapter devoted to the effects of various media, particularly radio, newspapers, and magazines. The authors conclude that few changes in attitudes were produced. They estimate that the political positions of only about 5% of their respondents were changed by the election campaign, and they are inclined to attribute even this small amount of change more to personal influence than to the mass media. A similar evaluation of mass media is made in the recent chapter in the *Handbook of Social Psychology* by Lipset and his collaborators (1954).

Research using experimental procedures, on the other hand, indicates the possibility of considerable modifiability of attitudes through exposure to communication. In both Klapper's survey (1949) and in my chapter in the *Handbook of Social Psychology* (Hovland, 1954) a number of experimental studies are discussed in which the opinions of a third to a half or more of the audience are changed.

The discrepancy between the results derived from these two methodologies raises some fascinating problems for analysis. This divergence in outcome appears to me to be largely attributable to two kinds of factors: one, the difference in research design itself; and, two, the historical and traditional differences in general approach to evaluation characteristic of researchers using the experimental as contrasted with the correlational or survey method. I would like to discuss, first, the influence these factors have on the estimation of overall effects of communications and, then, turn to other divergences in outcome characteristically found by the use of the experimental and survey methodology.

Undoubtedly the most critical and interesting variation in the research *design* involved in the two procedures is that resulting from differences in definition of exposure. In an experiment the audience on whom the effects are being evaluated is one which is fully exposed to the communication. On the other hand, in naturalistic situations with which surveys are typically concerned, the outstanding phenomenon is the limitation of the audience to those who *expose themselves* to the communication. Some of the individuals in a captive audience experiment would, of course, expose themselves in the course of natural events to a communication of the type studied; but many others would not. The group which does expose itself is usually a highly biased one, since most individuals "expose themselves most of the time to the kind of material with which they agree to begin with" (Lipset et al., 1954, p. 1158). Thus one reason for the difference in results between experiments and correlational studies is that experiments describe the effects of exposure on the whole range of individuals studied, some of whom are initially in favor of the position being advocated and some who are opposed, whereas surveys primarily describe the effects produced on those already in favor of the point of view advocated in the communication. The amount of change is thus, of course, much smaller in surveys. Lipset and his collaborators make this same evaluation, stating that:

As long as we test a program in the laboratory we always find that it has great effect on the attitudes and interests of the experimental subjects. But when we put the program on as a regular broadcast, we then note that the people who are most influenced in the laboratory tests are those who, in a realistic situation, do not listen to the program. The controlled experiment always greatly overrates effects, as compared with those that really occur, because of the self-selection of audiences (Lipset et al., 1954, p. 1158).

Differences in the second category are not inherent in the design of the two alternatives, but are characteristic of the way researchers using the two methods typically proceed.

The first difference within this class is in the size of the communication unit typically studied. In the majority of survey studies the unit evaluated is an entire program of communication. For example, in studies of political behavior an attempt is made to assess the effects of all newspaper reading and television viewing on attitudes toward the major parties. In the typical experiment, on the other hand, the interest is usually in some particular variation in the content of the communications, and experimental evaluations much more frequently involve single communications. On this point results are thus not directly comparable.

Another characteristic difference between the two methods is in the time interval used in evaluation. In the typical experiment the time at which the effect is observed is usually rather soon after exposure to the communication. In the survey study, on the other hand, the time perspective is such that much more remote effects are usually evaluated. When effects decline with the passage of time, the net outcome will, of course, be that of accentuating the effect obtained in experimental studies as compared with those obtained in survey researches. Again it must be stressed that the difference is not inherent in the designs as such. Several experiments, including our own on the effects of motion pictures (Hovland, Lumsdaine, & Sheffield, 1949) and later studies on the "sleeper effect" (Hovland & Weiss, 1951; Kelman & Hovland, 1953), have studied retention over considerable periods of time.

Some of the difference in outcome may be attributable to the types of communicators characteristically used and to the motive-incentive conditions operative in the two situations. In experimental studies communications are frequently presented in a classroom situation. This may involve quite different types of factors from those operative in the more naturalistic communication situation with which the survey researchers are concerned. In the classroom there may be some implicit sponsorship of the communication by the teacher and the school administration. In the survey studies the communicators may often be remote individuals either unfamiliar to the recipients, or outgroupers clearly known to espouse a point of view opposed to that held by many members of the audience. Thus there may be real differences in communicator credibility in laboratory and survey researches. The net effect of the differences will typically be in the direction of increasing the likelihood of change in the experimental as compared with the survey study.

There is sometimes an additional situational difference. Communications of the type studied by survey researchers usualy involve reaching the individual in his natural habitat, with consequent supplementary effects produced by discussion with friends and family. In the laboratory studies a classroom situation with low postcommunication interaction is more typically involved. Several studies, including one by Harold Kelley reported in our volume on *Communication and Persuasion* (Hovland, Janis & Kelley, 1953), indicate that, when a communication is presented in a situation which makes group membership salient, the individual is typically more resistant to counternorm influence than when the communication is presented under conditions of low salience of group membership (cf. also, Katz & Lazarsfeld, 1955, pp. 48–133).

A difference which is almost wholly adventitious is in the types of populations utilized. In the survey design there is, typically, considerable emphasis on a random sample of the entire population. In the typical experiment, on the other hand, there is a consistent over-representation of high school students and college sophomores, primarily on the basis of their greater accessibility. But as Tolman has said: "college sophomores may not be people." Whether differences in the type of audience studied contribute to the differences in effect obtained with the two methods is not known.

Finally, there is an extremely important difference in the studies of the experimental and correlational variety with respect to the type of issue discussed in the communications. In the typical experiment we are interested in studying a set of factors or conditions which are expected on the basis of theory to influence the extent of effect of the communication. We usually deliberately try to find types of issues involving attitudes which are susceptible to modification through communication. Otherwise, we run the risk of no measurable effects, particularly with small-scale experiments. In the survey procedures, on the other hand, socially significant attitudes which are deeply rooted in prior experience and involve much personal commitment are typically involved. This is especially true in voting studies which have provided us with so many of our present results on social influence. I shall have considerably more to say about this problem a little later.

The differences so far discussed have primarily concerned the extent of overall effectiveness indicated by the two methods: why survey results typically show little modification of attitudes by communication while experiments indicate marked changes. Let me now turn to some of the other differences in generalizations derived from the two alternative designs. Let me take as the second main area of disparate results the research on the effect of varying distances between the position taken by the communicator and that held by the recipient of the communication. Here it is a matter of comparing changes for persons who at the outset closely agree with the communicator with those for others who are mildly or strongly in disagreement with him. In the naturalistic situation studied in surveys the typical procedure is to determine changes in opinion following reported exposure to communication for individuals differing from the communicator by varying amounts. This gives rise to two possible artifacts. When the communication is at one end of a continuum, there is little room for improvement for those who differ from the communication by small amounts, but a great deal of room for movement among those with large discrepancies. This gives rise to a spurious degree of positive relationship between the degree of discrepancy and the amount of change. Regression effects will also operate in the direction of increasing the correlation. What is needed is a situation in which the distance factor can be manipulated independently of the subject's initial position. An attempt to set up these conditions experimentally was made in a study by Pritzker and the writer (1957). The method involved preparing individual communications presented in booklet form so that the position of the communicator could be set at any desired distance from the subject's initial position. Communicators highly acceptable to the subjects were used. A number of different topics were employed, including the likelihood of a cure for cancer within five years, the desirability of compulsory voting, and the adequacy of five hours of sleep per night.

The amount of change for each degree of advocated change is shown in Fig. 1. It will be seen that there is a fairly clear progression, such that the greater the amount of change advocated the greater the average amount of opinion change produced. Similar results have been reported by Goldberg (1954) and by French (1956).

But these results are not in line with our hunches as to what would happen in a naturalistic situation with important social issues. We felt that here other types of response than change in attitude would occur. So Muzafer Sherif, O. J. Harvey, and the writer (1957) set up a situation to simulate as closely as possible the conditions typically involved

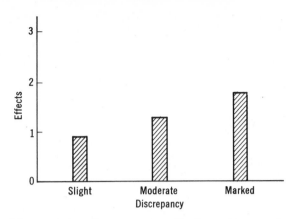

Figure 1. Mean opinion change score with three degrees of discrepancy (deviation between subject's position and position advocated in communication). [From Hovland & Pritzker, 1957.]

when individuals are exposed to major social issue communications at differing distances from their own position. The issue used was the desirability of prohibition. The study was done in two states (Oklahoma and Texas) where there is prohibition or local option, so that the wet-dry issue is hotly debated. We concentrated on three aspects of the problem: How favorably will the communicator be received when his position is at varying distances from that of the recipient? How will what the communicator says be perceived and interpreted by individuals at varying distances from his position? What will be the amount of opinion change produced when small and large deviations in position of communication and recipient are involved?

Three communications, one strongly wet, one strongly dry, and one moderately wet, were employed. The results bearing on the first problem, of *reception*, are presented in Fig. 2 [p. 318]. The positions of the subjects are indicated on the abscissa in letters from A (extremely dry) to H (strongly wet). The positions of the communication are also indicated in the same letters, B indicating a strongly dry communication, H a strongly wet, and F a moderately wet. Along the ordinate there is plotted the percentage of subjects with each position on the issue who described the communication as "fair" and "unbiased." It will be seen that the degree of distance between the recipient and the communicator greatly influences the evaluation of the fairness of the communication. When a communication is directed at the pro-dry position, nearly all of the dry subjects consider it fair and impartial, but only a few per cent of the wet subjects consider the identical communication fair. The reverse is true at the other end of the scale. When an intermediate position is adopted, the percentages fall off sharply on each side. Thus under the present conditions with a relatively ambiguous

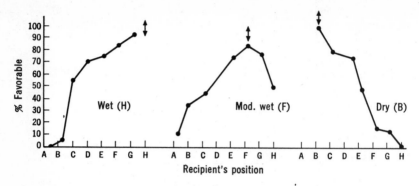

Figure 2. Percentage of favorable evaluations ("fair," "unbiased," etc.) of wet (*H*), moderately wet (*F*), and dry (*B*) communications for subjects holding various positions on prohibition. Recipient's position range from *A* (very dry) to *H* (very wet). Position of communications indicated by arrow. [From Hovland, Harvey, & Sherif, 1957.]

communicator one of the ways of dealing with strongly discrepant positions is to *discredit* the communicator, considering him unfair and biased.

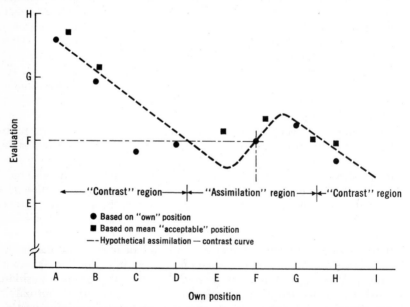

Figure 3. Average placement of position of moderately wet communication (*F*) by subjects holding various positions on the issue, plotted against hypothetical assimilation-contrast curve. [From Hovland, Harvey, & Sherif, 1957.]

A second way in which an individual can deal with discrepancy is by distortion of what is said by the communicator. This is a phenomenon extensively studied by Cooper and Jahoda (1947). In the present study, subjects were asked to state what position they thought was taken by the communicator on the prohibition question. Their evaluation of his position could then be analyzed in relation to their own position. These results are shown in Fig. 3 for the moderately wet communication. It will be observed that there is a tendency for individuals whose position is close to that of the communicator to report on the communicator's position quite accurately, for individuals a little bit removed to report his position to be substantially more like their own (which we call an "assimilation effect"), and for those with more discrepant positions to report the communicator's position as more extreme than it really was. This we refer to as a "contrast effect."

Now to our primary results on opinion change. It was found that individuals whose position was only slightly discrepant from the communicator's were influenced to a greater extent than those whose positions deviated to a larger extent. When a wet position was espoused, 28% of the middle-of-the-road subjects were changed in the direction of the communicator, as compared with only 4% of the drys. With the dry communication 14% of the middle-of-the-roaders were changed, while only 4% of the wets were changed. Thus, more of the subjects with small discrepancies were changed than were those with large discrepancies.

These results appear to indicate that, under conditions when there is some ambiguity about the credibility of the communicator and when the subject is deeply involved with the issue, the greater the attempt at change the higher the resistance. On the other hand, with highly respected communicators, as in the previous study with Pritzker using issues of lower involvement, the greater the discrepancy the greater the effect. A study related to ours has just been completed by Zimbardo (1959) which indicates that, when an influence attempt is made by a strongly positive communicator (i.e., a close personal friend), the greater the discrepancy the greater the opinion change, even when the experimenter made a point of stressing the great importance of the subject's opinion.

The implication of these results for our primary problem of conflicting results is clear. The types of issues with which most experiments deal are relatively uninvolving and are often of the variety where expert opinion is highly relevant, as for example, on topics of health, science, and the like. Here we should expect that opinion would be considerably affected by communications and furthermore that advocacy of positions quite discrepant from the individual's own position would have a marked effect. On the other hand, the types of issues most often utilized in survey studies are ones which are very basic and involve deep commitment. As a consequence small changes in opinion due to communication would be expected. Here communication may have little effect on those who disagree at the outset and function merely to strengthen the position already held, in line with survey findings.

A third area of research in which somewhat discrepant results are obtained by the experimental and survey methods is in the role of order of presentation. From naturalistic studies the generalization has been widely adopted that primacy is an extremely important factor in persuasion. Numerous writers have reported that what we experience first has a critical role in what we believe. This is particularly stressed in studies of propaganda effects in various countries when the nation getting across its message first is alleged to have a great advantage and in commercial advertising where "getting a beat on the field" is stressed. The importance of primacy in political propaganda is indicated in the following quotation from Doob:

> The propagandist scores an initial advantage whenever his propaganda reaches people before that of his rivals. Readers or listeners are then biased to comprehend, forever after, the event as it has been initially portrayed to them. If they are told in a headline or a flash that the battle has been won, the criminal has been caught, or the bill is certain to pass the legislature, they will usually expect subsequent information to substantiate this first impression. When later facts prove otherwise, they may be loath to abandon what they believe to be true until perhaps the evidence becomes overwhelming (Doob, 1948, pp. 421–422).

A recent study by Katz and Lazarsfeld (1955) utilizing the survey method compares the extent to which respondents attribute major impact on their decisions about fashions and movie attendance to the presentations to which they were first exposed. Strong primacy effects are shown in their analyses of the data.

We have ourselves recently completed a series of experiments oriented toward this problem. These are reported in our new monograph on *Order of Presentation in Persuasion* (Hovland, Mandell, Campbell, Brock, Luchins, Cohen, McGuire, Janis, Feierabend, & Anderson, 1957). We find that primacy is often *not* a very significant factor when the relative effectiveness of the first side of an issue is compared experimentally with that of the second. The research suggests that differences in design may account for much of the discrepancy. A key variable is whether there is exposure to both sides or whether only one side is actually received. In naturalistic studies the advantage of the first side is often not only that it is first but that it is often then the only side of the issue to which the individual is exposed. Having once been influenced, many individuals make up their mind and are no longer interested in other communications on the issue. In most experiments on order of presentation, on the other hand, the audience is systematically exposed to both sides. Thus under survey conditions, self-exposure tends to increase the impact of primacy.

Two other factors to which I have already alluded appear significant in determining the amount of primacy effect. One is the nature of
the communicator, the other the setting in which the communication is
received. In our volume Luchins presents results indicating that, when
the same communicator presents contradictory material, the point of
view read first has more influence. On the other hand, Mandell and I
show that, when two different communicators present opposing views
successively, little primacy effect is obtained. The communications setting factor operates similarly. When the issue and the conditions of
presentation make clear that the points of view are controversial, little
primacy is obtained.

Thus in many of the situations with which there had been great
concern as to undesirable effects of primacy, such as in legal trials,
election campaigns, and political debate, the role of primacy appears to
have been exaggerated, since the conditions there are those least con-
ducive to primacy effects: the issue is clearly defined as controversial,
the partisanship of the communicator is usually established, and different communicators present the opposing sides.

Time does not permit me to discuss other divergences in results
obtained in survey and experimental studies, such as those concerned
with the effects of repetition of presentation, the relationship between
level of intelligence and susceptibility to attitude change, or the relative impact of mass media and personal influence. Again, however, I
am sure that detailed analysis will reveal differential factors at work
which can account for the apparent disparity in the generalizations
derived.

INTEGRATION

On the basis of the foregoing survey of results I reach the conclusion that no contradiction has been established between the data provided by experimental and correlational studies. Instead it appears
that the seeming divergence can be satisfactorily accounted for on the
basis of a different definition of the communication situation (including
the phenomenon of self-selection) and differences in the type of communicator, audience, and kind of issue utilized.

But there remains the task of better integrating the findings associated with the two methodologies. This is a problem closely akin to
that considered by the members of the recent Social Science Research
Council summer seminar on *Narrowing the Gap Between Field Studies
and Laboratory Studies in Social Psychology* (Riecken, 1954). Many
of their recommendations are pertinent to our present problem.

What seems to me quite apparent is that a genuine understanding
of the effects of communications on attitudes requires both the survey
and the experimental methodologies. At the same time there appear to
be certain inherent limitations of each method which must be under-

stood by the researcher if he is not to be blinded by his preoccupation with one or the other type of design. Integration of the two methodologies will require on the part of the experimentalist an awareness of the narrowness of the laboratory in interpreting the larger and more comprehensive effects of communication. It will require on the part of the survey researcher a greater awareness of the limitations of the correlational method as a basis for establishing causal relationships.

The framework within which survey research operates is most adequately and explicitly dealt with by Berelson, Lazarsfeld, and McPhee in their book on *Voting* (1954). The model which they use, taken over by them from the economist Tinbergen, is reproduced in the top half of Fig. 4. For comparison, the model used by experimentalists is presented in the lower half of the figure. It will be seen that the model used by the survey researcher, particularly when he employs the "panel" method, stresses the large number of simultaneous and interacting influences affecting attitudes and opinions. Even more significant is its provision for a variety of "feedback" phenomena in which consequences wrought by previous influences affect processes normally considered as occurring earlier in the sequence. The various types of interaction are indicated by the placement of arrows showing direction of effect. In contrast the experimentalist frequently tends to view the

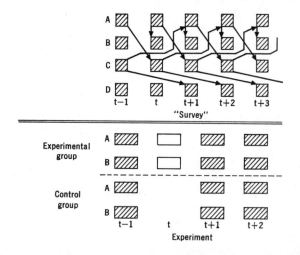

Figure 4. TOP HALF: "Process analysis" schema used in panel research. (Successive time intervals are indicated along abscissa. Letters indicate the variables under observation. Arrows represent relations between the variables.) [From Berelson, Lazarsfeld, & McPhee, 1954.]

BOTTOM HALF: Design of experimental research. (Letters on vertical axis again indicate variables being measured. Unshaded box indicates experimentally manipulated treatment and blank absence of such treatment. Time periods indicated as in top half of chart.)

communication process as one in which some single manipulative variable is the primary determinant of the subsequent attitude change. He is, of course, aware in a general way of the importance of context, and he frequently studies interaction effects as well as main effects; but he still is less attentive than he might be to the complexity of the influence situation and the numerous possibilities for feedback loops. Undoubtedly the real life communication situation is better described in terms of the survey type of model. We are all familiar, for example, with the interactions in which attitudes predispose one to acquire certain types of information, that this often leads to changes in attitude which may result in further acquisition of knowledge, which in turn produces more attitude change, and so on. Certainly the narrow question sometimes posed by experiments as to the effect of knowledge on attitudes greatly underestimates these interactive effects.

But while the conceptualization of the survey researcher is often very valuable, his correlational research design leaves much to be desired. Advocates of correlational analysis often cite the example of a science built on observation exclusively without experiment: astronomy. But here a very limited number of space-time concepts are involved and the number of competing theoretical formulations is relatively small so that it is possible to limit alternative theories rather drastically through correlational evidence. But in the area of communication effects and social psychology generally the variables are so numerous and so intertwined that the correlational methodology is primarily useful to suggest hypotheses and not to establish casual relationships (Hovland et al., 1949, pp. 329–340; Maccoby, 1956). Even with the much simpler relationships involved in biological systems there are grave difficulties of which we are all aware these days when we realize how difficult it is to establish through correlation whether eating of fats is or is not a cause of heart disease or whether or not smoking is a cause of lung cancer. In communications research the complexity of the problem makes it inherently difficult to derive causal relationships from correlational analysis where experimental control of exposure is not possible. And I do not agree with my friends the Lazarsfelds (Kendall & Lazarsfeld, 1950) concerning the effectiveness of the panel method in circumventing this problem since parallel difficulties are raised when the relationships occur over a time span.

These difficulties constitute a challenge to the experimentalist in this area of research [not only] to utilize the broad framework for studying communication effects suggested by the survey researcher, but to employ well controlled experimental design to work on those aspects of the field which are amenable to experimental manipulation and control. It is, of course, apparent that there are important communication problems which cannot be attacked directly by experimental methods. It is not, for example, feasible to modify voting behavior by manipulation of the issues discussed by the opposed parties during a particular campaign. It is not feasible to assess the effects of communications over a very long span of time. For example, one cannot visualize experimental procedures for answering the question of what has been the impact of the reading of *Das Kapital* or *Uncle Tom's Cabin*. These are questions which can be illuminated by historical and sociological study but cannot be evaluated in any rigorous experimental fashion.

But the scope of problems which do lend themselves to experimental attack is very broad. Even complex interactions can be fruitfully attacked by experiment. The possibilities are clearly shown in studies like that of Sherif and Sherif (1953) on factors influencing cooperative and competitive behavior in a camp for adolescent boys. They were able to bring under manipulative control many of the types of interpersonal relationships ordinarily considered impossible to modify experimentally, and to develop motivations of an intensity characteristic of real-life situations. It should be possible to do similar studies in the communication area with a number of the variables heretofore only investigated in uncontrolled naturalistic settings by survey procedures.

In any case it appears eminently practical to minimize many of the differences which were discussed above as being not inherent in design but more or less adventitiously linked with one or the other method. Thus there is no reason why more complex and deeply-involving social issues cannot be employed in experiments rather than the more superficial ones more commonly used. The resistance to change of socially important issues may be a handicap in studying certain types af attitude change; but, on the other hand, it is important to understand the lack of modifiability of opinion with highly-involving issues. Greater representation of the diverse types of communicators found in naturalistic situations can also be achieved. In addition, it should be possible to do experiments with a wider range of populations to reduce the possibility that many of our present generalizations from experiments are unduly affected by their heavy weighting of college student characteristics, including high literacy, alertness, and rationality.

A more difficult task is that of experimentally evaluating communications under conditions of self-selection of exposure. But this is not at all impossible in theory. It should be possible to assess what demographic and personality factors predispose one to expose oneself to particular communications and then to utilize experimental and control groups having these characteristics. Under some circumstances the evaluation could be made on only those who select themselves, with both experimental and control groups coming from the self-selected audience.

Undoubtedly many of the types of experiments which could be set up involving or simulating naturalistic conditions will be too ambitious and costly to be feasible even if possible in principle. This suggests the continued use of small-scale experiments which seek to isolate some of the key variables operative in complex situations. From synthesis of component factors, prediction of complex outcomes may be practicable. It is to this analytic procedure for narrowing the gap between laboratory and field research that we have devoted major attention in our research program. I will merely indicate briefly here some of the ties between our past work and the present problem.

We have attempted to assess the influence of the communicator by varying his expertness and attractiveness, as in the studies by Kelman, Weiss, and the writer (Hovland & Weiss, 1951; Kelman & Hovland, 1953). Further data on this topic were presented earlier in this paper.

We have also been concerned with evaluating social interaction effects. Some of the experiments on group affiliation as a factor affecting resistance to counternorm communication and the role of salience of group membership by Hal Kelley and others are reported in *Communication and Persuasion* (Hovland et al., 1953).

Starting with the studies carried out during the war on orientation films by Art Lumsdaine, Fred Sheffield, and the writer (1949), we have had a strong interest in the duration of communication effects. Investigation of effects at various time intervals has helped to bridge the gap between assessment of immediate changes with those of longer duration like those involved in survey studies. More recent extensions of this work have indicated the close relationship between the credibility of the communicator and the extent of postcommunication increments, or "sleeper effects" (Hovland & Weiss, 1951; Kelman & Hovland, 1953).

The nature of individual differences in susceptibility to persuasion via communication has been the subject of a number of our recent studies. The generality of persuasibility has been investigated by Janis and collaborators and the development of persuasibility in children has been studied by Abelson and Lesser. A volume concerned with these audience factors to which Janis, Abelson, Lesser, Field, Rife, King, Cohen, Linton, Graham, and the writer have contributed will appear under the title *Personality and Persuasibility* (1959).

Lastly, there remains the question on how the nature of the issues used in the communication affects the extent of change in attitude. We have only made a small beginning on these problems. In the research reported in *Experiments on Mass Communication*, we showed that the magnitude of effects was directly related to the type of attitude involved: film communications had a significant effect on opinions related to straightforward interpretations of policies and events, but had little or no effect on more deeply intrenched attitudes and motivations. Further work on the nature of issues is represented in the study by Sherif, Harvey, and the writer (1957) which was discussed above. There we found a marked contrast between susceptibility to influence and the amount of ego-involvement in the issue. But the whole concept of ego-involvement is a fuzzy one, and here is an excellent area for further work seeking to determine the theoretical factors involved in different types of issues.

With this brief survey of possible ways to bridge the gap between experiment and survey I must close. I should like to stress in summary the mutual importance of the two approaches to the problem of communication effectiveness. Neither is a royal road to wisdom, but each represents an important emphasis. The challenge of future work is one of fruitfully combining their virtues so that we may develop a social psychology of communication with the conceptual breadth provided by correlational study of process and with the rigorous but more delimited methodology of the experiment.

REFERENCES

BERELSON, B. R., LAZARSFELD, P. F., & McPHEE, W. N. *Voting: A study of opinion formation in a presidential campaign.* Chicago: Univer. Chicago Press, 1954.

COOPER, EUNICE, & JAHODA, MARIE. The evasion of propaganda: How prejudiced people respond to anti-prejudice propaganda. *J. Psychol.*, 1947, *23,* 15–25.

DOOB, L. W. *Public opinion and propaganda.* New York: Holt, 1948.

FRENCH, J. R. P., JR. A formal theory of social power. *Psychol. Rev.*, 1956, *63,* 181–194.

GOLDBERG, S. C. Three situational determinants of conformity to social norms. *J. abnorm. soc. Psychol.*, 1954, *49,* 325–329.

GOSNELL, H. F. *Getting out the vote: An experiment in the stimulation of voting.* Chicago: Univer. Chicago Press, 1927.

HOVLAND, C. I. Effects of the mass media of communication. In G. Lindzey (Ed.), *Handbook of social psychology.* Vol. II. *Special fields and applications.* Cambridge, Mass.: Addison-Wesley, 1954. Pp. 1062–1103.

HOVLAND, C. I., HARVEY, O. J., & SHERIF, M. Assimilation and contrast effects in reactions to communication and attitude change. *J. abnorm. soc. Psychol.*, 1957, *55,* 244–252.

HOVLAND, C. I., JANIS, I. L., & KELLEY, H. H. *Communication and persuasion.* New Haven: Yale Univer. Press, 1953.

HOVLAND, C. I., LUMSDAINE, A. A., & SHEFFIELD, F. D. *Experiments on mass communication.* Princeton: Princeton Univer. Press, 1949.

HOVLAND, C. I., MANDELL, W., CAMPBELL, ENID H., BROCK, T., LUCHINS, A. S., COHEN, A. R., McGUIRE, W. J., JANIS, I. L., FEIERABEND, ROSALIND L., & ANDERSON, N. H. *The order of presentation in persuasion.* New Haven: Yale Univer. Press, 1957.

HOVLAND, C. I., & PRITZKER, H. A. Extent of opinion change as a function of amount of change advocated. *J. abnorm. soc. Psychol.*, 1957, *54,* 257–261.

HOVLAND, C. I., & WEISS, W. The influence of source credibility on communication effectiveness. *Publ. opin. Quart.*, 1951, *15,* 635–650.

JANIS, I. L., HOVLAND, C. I., FIELD, P. B., LINTON, HARRIETT, GRAHAM, ELAINE, COHEN, A. R., RIFE, D., ABELSON, R. P., LESSER, G. S., & KING, B. T. *Personality and persuasibility.* New Haven: Yale Univer. Press, 1959.

KATZ, E., & LAZARSFELD, P. F. *Personal influence.* Glencoe, Ill.: Free Press, 1955.

KELMAN, H. C., & HOVLAND, C. I. "Reinstatement" of the communicator in delayed measurement of opinion change. *J. abnorm. soc. Psychol.,* 1953, 48, 327–335.

KENDALL, PATRICIA L., & LAZARSFELD, P. F. Problems of survey analysis. In R. K. Merton & P. F. Lazarsfeld (Eds.), *Continuities in social research: Studies in the scope and method of "The American Soldier."* Glencoe, Ill.: Free Press, 1950. Pp. 133–196.

KLAPPER, J. T. *The effects of mass media.* New York: Columbia Univer. Bureau of Applied Social Research, 1949. (Mimeo.)

LAZARSFELD, P. F., BERELSON, B., & GAUDET, HAZEL, *The people's choice,* New York: Duell, Sloan, & Pearce, 1944.

LIPSET, S. M., LAZARSFELD, P. F., BARTON, A. H., & LINZ, J. The psychology of voting: An analysis of political behavior. In G. Lindzey (Ed.), *Handbook of social psychology.* Vol. II. *Special fields and applications.* Cambridge, Mass.: Addison-Wesley, 1954. Pp. 1124–1175.

MACCOBY, ELEANOR E. Pitfalls in the analysis of panel data: A research note on some technical aspects of voting. *Amer. J. Sociol.,* 1956, 59, 359–362.

RIECKEN, H. W. (Chairman) Narrowing the gap between field studies and laboratory experiments in social psychology: A statement by the summer seminar. *Items Soc. Sci. Res. Council,* 1954, 8, 37–42.

SHERIF, M., & SHERIF, CAROLYN W. *Groups in harmony and tension: An integration of studies on intergroup relations.* New York: Harper, 1953.

ZIMBARDO, P. G. Involvement and communication discrepancy as determinants of opinion change. Unpublished doctoral dissertation, Yale University, 1959.

MEASURING ADVERTISING EFFECTIVENESS:
INQUIRIES AND SALES MEASURES

Darrell B. Lucas and Steuart H. Britt

Many advertisements aim at ultimate response in the form of buying behavior or some intermediate step, such as making an inquiry. Advertisements that explicitly request such overt responses are relatively easy to evaluate, assuming that the solicited response is immediate and is the only major objective.

The evaluation is further facilitated if the advertisement contains an order form or coupon or if the responses are in any way keyed to specific advertisements. Most order forms and coupons bear some identification of the specific advertisement and medium.

INQUIRIES

The reasons for soliciting inquiries vary. Usually the inquiry is intended to aid the selling process directly, but sometimes inquiries are solicited primarily to test the effectiveness of the advertising message. Sales may be aided by using inquiries as leads for salesmen, or by following up directly with literature and samples designed to convert inquiries into sales.

If, on the other hand, inquiries are sought primarily for the purpose of testing copy, the strategy is quite different. The number of inquiries is often a very small fraction of the total number of people the advertiser expects to stimulate. A few thousand inquiries may become the basis for estimating advertising impact upon millions of prospective buyers. This discussion is chiefly concerned with soliciting inquiries for the purpose of testing copy.

How Inquiries Relate to Advertising Effect

When a national advertiser invites inquiries primarily to test copy, it is assumed that he does not expect to make a profit solely from sales to respondents. Instead, the overt actions of those who respond are taken as evidence that some useful impressions were made on a much larger audience.

If the responses appear to reflect genuine interest in the product, the advertiser probably assumes that a great many more people were at least partially interested, but not enough to make an inquiry. If returns from two or more advertisements are compared under similar circumstances, the advertiser may assume that the advertisement producing more inquiries has also done a better job with the whole audience, but this is not necessarily true.

One of the determining factors in any response is the attractiveness of the offer. If the offer is too good, people will tell others about it. This may lead to requests from people who had no contact with the advertisement at all. When this happens, it gives little evidence of the merit of the advertising message under test.

At the opposite extreme is the offer which is so unattractive that practically no one responds. When response is too low, the advertiser finds himself without adequate data to make a decision. If inquiries are to be meaningful at all, it is first necessary to design an offer which is relevant and which is neither too attractive nor too unattractive.

Logical offers include small product samples, additional product information, and gifts. Novelty gifts should be used only when their intrinsic value is small and when it can reasonably be assumed that the respondent made thorough examination of the advertisement. Only inquiries requesting additional product information are likely to ensure that the response is motivated by genuine interest aroused by the advertising message. It is quite difficult to obtain a substantial number of bona fide inquiries for additional information on most products, although a return coupon is usually helpful.

The Return Coupon

Mail order advertisements or those seeking immediate sales leads make regular use of boxed-in return coupon forms in order to make responses easier and more numerous. Advertisers interested in testing broader copy appeals may also use return coupons, but this may give too much emphasis to the offer. The number of replies is likely to be more than doubled, but the evidence of impact of the copy is less clear. There are several reasons why return coupons increase responses to an offer, even though the copy may not be basically designed for direct action.

The psychological advantages of a coupon form begin with the fact that the coupon draws attention to the offer. It is not even necessary for the reader to go through copy details in order to discover the coupon. Many coupon-carrying advertisements include captions and visual devices directing the reader to the offer. The normal attention-getting power of the coupon, coupled with extra emphasis in the copy, helps to explain the great increase in inquiries to offers accompanied by coupons.

The coupon not only draws attention to an advertising offer, but also suggests that the reader take action. To a degree, a reader must psychologically reject the offer in order to pass by the coupon provided for his response. Frequently the advertiser compounds his suggestion by means of captions and copy, urging the reader to mail the coupon. In this way, the inherent suggestive influence of the coupon is heightened by the suggestions made in the surrounding copy.

Another psychological factor favoring response to a coupon form is present when the respondent is relieved of further obligation. When an advertiser invites an inquiry, he assumes any related obligation. Very often, the advertiser explicitly relieves the respondent of obligation, using such words as, "Without obligation, please send me . . ." The word "free" may also be featured in the headline, in the copy text, and in the coupon itself. The relief from obligation, inherent in a coupon response, is fortified by these explicit assurances given by the advertiser.

The most obvious psychological advantage of the return coupon is its convenience for making the proper request. It provides both the physical form and the exact verbal instructions for obtaining the thing offered to the reader. The advertiser may further simplify the response by suggesting that it be pinned to the reader's letterhead or pasted on a postcard. Some publications make it possible simply to tear off a franked self-addressed coupon after inserting the reader's address and to drop it in the mailbox. Another possibility is to invite readers to telephone or telegraph collect.

The theory of measurement through coupon returns may be stated quite simply. If two advertisements for the same product are identical except for a headline or lead element designed to attract attention and to "get people into the ad," then the number of returns of the coupons from one advertisement as compared with the returns from the other advertisement provides useful information. In fact, this is quite a sensible method of determining the relative value of a headline (or lead illustration) as compared with a different headline (or lead illustration).

On the other hand, the use of coupons for measurement would be undesirable in many, if not most, advertisements; they would get in the way of the basic advertisement itself. It would be out of place to add a coupon to the usual advertisement for cigarettes, automobiles, and most other commodities.

Inspection of coupon returns on consumer magazine advertisements will quickly reveal the techniques used to draw attention to the offer, to urge the response, to relieve the respondent of obligation, and to make the response as easy as possible. . . .

MEASURES RELATED TO SALES

Since nearly all advertisements are intended to facilitate sales, it is clear that any direct measurement of selling influence is of interest in copy research. If the national advertiser had a practical procedure for measurement of the sales influence of individual advertisements, he could quickly achieve mastery over his advertising techniques heretofore enjoyed only by retailers and mail-order advertisers.

Basically, there are three approaches to sales evaluation of specific advertisements and of entire advertising campaigns. Although no one of the three methods has proved to be a complete evaluator of the sales influence of general national advertisements, all three can contribute helpful evidence.

The *first* method is a direct questioning approach, in which customers are asked to report the influence of advertisements on their purchases. A *second* approach attempts to relate product purchases or ownership to advertising exposure or expenditure, and this includes the application of mathematical analysis and the technique of correlation. A *third* method is the application of controlled experiments to limited markets or areas as a means of estimating later sales impact on the total market, and sales area tests will be discussed in the latter group.

Each of these methods will be discussed in the following three sections.

INTERVIEWING CUSTOMERS

There are many reasons why it is difficult to get comprehensive information from customers which will reveal the influence of specific advertisements on their purchases.

One obstacle which we immediately encounter is that most people believe they generate their own decisions and will actually deny the influence of advertisements. Social barriers to the admission of certain influences have arisen, and it has become popular to disavow the acceptance of advertising. Since the accumulated advertising contribution to any single purchase may go back over a period of years, it is understandable why direct probes of the consumer's motivation have tended to be so fruitless.

Much advertising expenditure is assumed to help hold loyal customers, but the effects are more dynamic when people are induced to try new products or brands. Consumer-purchase panels, wherein families report a continuous record of purchases, provide information on changes of brands. If an investigator is quick to follow up brand changes with an interview, there is an increased likelihood of learning the underlying causes of change. Even under these favorable conditions, direct questions about the influence of advertising on the purchase of small items have revealed little to justify advertising costs.

George Gallup . . . has reported success with a different approach for obtaining testimony from new buyers of brands and products.[1] Women in a probability sample of households were asked in detail about circumstances surrounding recent product brands purchased for the first time. They were asked to try to recall where they got the idea leading to the new purchase. Questioning goes *from* the purchase *to* the advertising, instead of the more traditional method which tries to go from the advertising to the purchase. Advertising is treated as a cause for action, and hence the name *Activation* research, as used by George Gallup.

Much of the Gallup & Robinson activation interview is devoted to documentation of the initial testimony as to advertising effect. Respondents are required to recall what the advertising looked like and said and where it appeared. If television was the medium, people are probed for program name, date, content, and other means of verification. Physical proof of the possession of products is also requested. If a product is missing from the shelf because it has already been consumed, the housewife is asked to give a detailed account to support that fact. Elaborate inventories, especially of pantry and bathroom articles, are sought in order to ensure maximum coverage of possible purchases of all related products.

Activation surveys lead to the development of an index number for each reported product brand; and the relationship between index numbers and sales is studied. There has been notable success in tracing brand switches and new product introductions, especially where heavy television advertising has been used. Results for magazines and other national media are also reported.

According to George H. Gallup, more recent activation explorations have aimed at measurement of advertising influence on three major categories of customer. Not only is the new brand buyer studied but also the repeat buyers and those who fluctuate in their choices of brands. Mathematical analysis is applied to the survey data in order to establish the weights of these three categories in evaluating the total advertising effort.

While Gallup & Robinson have reported a considerably higher level of advertising effect by these methods than have other investigators, people in the advertising industry have been somewhat cautious in their acceptance of the method and the findings. It is difficult to assess the promise and the value of consumer testimony on the sales influence of advertising. One basic objection is that the method seems to measure change in buying, but if a woman has been buying Kellogg's Corn Flakes (for example) for her family for a good many years, she is not nearly so likely to answer that she was influenced by the advertisement to buy this product as would another woman who is buying the product for the first time.

Most research investigators in this area of buying behavior have given up before finding sufficient evidence to justify more than a small part of advertising costs. Others have obtained such a disproportionate advantage of broadcasting over other media as to suspect their own findings.

Certainly television is a dramatic medium; and when a commercial message is closely associated with a program, it is relatively easy to recall and identify it in an interview. High television scores may reflect poor interviewing technique, but may also simply reflect the strength of the broadcasting medium.

Paul F. Lazarsfeld of Columbia University has expressed a strong belief that interviews made with customers can identify those who bought a product brand as a result of advertising or of advertising in a specific medium.[2] It would first be necessary through a process of detailed questioning to bring out references to advertising influence and then to trace and confirm each influence. This means that the respondent would have to be capable of recalling advertising impressions. Lazarsfeld has recommended a procedure for gathering actual sales data or experimenting. His plan calls for comparison between people exposed and not exposed to advertising, for application through comparative evidence obtained by treating major sales territories differently, and for mathematical analysis of the data. All these factors will be brought into the discussion in the next section.

CORRELATION OF ADVERTISING AND SALES

While most national advertisers find it extremely difficult to measure the sales impact of specific advertisements, it is comparatively easy to obtain evidence of the exposure or penetration of their advertising messages. It is also possible to find out what brands of products people have in their homes. These types of evidence and the manufacturer's own knowledge of advertising expenditures and product sales may be studied to see whether there are logical relationships between advertising efforts and sales responses.

National advertising typically operates over extended periods and in combination with many other types of promotional activity. The simple

---

[2] Paul F. Lazarsfeld, "Evaluating the Effectiveness of Advertising by Direct Interviews," in Paul F. Lazarsfeld and Morris Rosenberg (editors), *The Language of Social Research* (Glencoe, Ill.: Free Press, 1959), pp. 411–419.

relationships between advertising cost or opportunity and accomplished sales can seldom be taken as proof that specific advertising caused the observed sales. Nevertheless, the correlation between advertising exposure and product possession is a useful type of evidence, when interpreted with caution. In this context, correlation refers to relationships, varying from those which can be directly observed in the data to those requiring complex mathematical analyses of many variables. Precautions need to be stressed as much as procedures.

Since media are responsible for providing advertising with opportunities for exposure of ideas for prospective buyers, media have a considerable incentive to provide evidence of sales effects. One of the earliest correlation studies was made—although not published—by a major magazine. Readers and nonreaders were compared on possession of products advertised in the publication. More importantly, people claiming to have seen from one to five advertisements in a campaign series were compared with issue readers who claimed to have seen none of the advertisements. In almost every instance, those reading the issues and those seeing one, two, or more of the advertisements showed progressively more product possession than nonreaders of the issues. The gains were extremely favorable in relation to advertising costs.

When it comes to assessing increases in product ownership as direct effects of seeing or reading printed advertisements, one basic question has to be settled. As compared with the extent that people buy products because they have read advertisements, to what extent do they read advertisements because they have already purchased the product? It is a common experience, especially after having made an important brand choice, to feel a heightened interest in advertisements of that brand.

Actually, a high correlation between product purchase and advertising readership may result from either of two kinds of cause-effect relationships—readership may help to lead to purchase, or purchase may help to give rise to readership.

High correlation coefficients may also result from a third kind of causation—probably the most important of the three possibilities. If a person is interested in and "sold on" a given product (or service) for whatever reason or reasons, he is inclined both to look for the product (or service) and for advertisements about it simply because he is interested in the possibility of purchasing it. Thus, there would be a high correlation between the eventual purchase of a product and readership of the advertising, since both kinds of behavior are concomitants of being interested in and sold on the product. In other words, both purchase and readership may be the results—without either being the cause—of some of these high correlations.

There is far less likelihood that new purchasers of particular brands will give attention to product-sponsored broadcast programs than that they will read printed advertisements because of recent product purchases. This may explain the long procession of correlation studies in the field of radio and then television, with their implied measurement of advertising effects. Broadcast media have sometimes claimed direct sales evaluation and have, on other occasions, made more modest claims of attitudes built up through communication of advertised ideas. Two decades of such correlation surveys have met with skepticism and often rejection on the part of technically trained research people.

An example of a simple division of viewers and nonviewers of sponsored broadcasts, where product possession is also known, as presented in Table 3.

TABLE 3. PER CENT OF VIEWERS OF SPONSOR'S PROGRAM POSSESSING BRAND

BRAND AND PRODUCT	FREQUENT VIEWERS	OCCASIONAL VIEWERS	NONVIEWERS
R brand of razor blades	11	8	7
M brand of mouth wash	13	11	8
T brand of toilet soap	27	22	19
C brand of cake mix	21	18	16
B brand of breakfast cereal	9	7	4

These typical margins of difference in product ownership at first appear to be exclusive outcomes of advertising on particular programs, but internal analysis of the survey data may reveal that brand ownership is only one of the differences between viewers and nonviewers of a sponsored program. The nonviewers may have less money or less need and may be further from store outlets. Many other factors may contribute to the situation.

Anyone who believes in the power of advertising usually assumes that some sales advantages reported in correlation studies are genuine advertising effects. The great problem is that of controlling the influence of variables, many of which are probably not even known. Investigators have tried to match samples on many characteristics, including exposure to all major media. The advent of television, with stations opening up one market at a time, permitted additional controls based on observations before and after stations were built. This provided more of an experimental design, disturbed chiefly by the fact that television stations came first to the most promising markets. Following are a few of the recognized factors which should be considered when interpreting correlations of television advertising penetration or product possession among exposed and unexposed population groups:

The broadcast signal may be better for homes in areas where the product is also most accessible.

Viewing a program usually involves staying at home, and this same tendency may favor product use.

Size of family is one factor related to both program viewing and usage of many products.

Viewers, as individuals, may normally be faster or slower consumers of the advertised product.

Advertisers usually try to advertise their products by using media which are most likely to reach people who are most likely to buy the products. A correlation of advertising exposure and product use may simply reflect a degree of success in selecting media on this basis.

Nonviewers include many types of nonprospects, such as those too poor for the sponsored products.

The early owners of television sets or color sets are venturesome or prosperous people who may be more responsive to advertising of all kinds.

The ownership of a product brand should make it easier to remember both the brand and the program which it sponsors.

People who are inclined to make excessive claims of product possession may also tend to overclaim familiarity with programs and with advertising messages.

Despite the competition of various media for audience time, the viewers of a particular program may be "consumers" of more other media than are nonviewers.

When manufacturers increase their media expenditures to buy television in selected markets, they may step up the whole program of sales promotion at the same time.

When comparisons are made before and after television stations or programs enter a new market, there are opportunities for independent changes in the responsiveness of the market during the measuring interval.

While many of the above variables can be controlled by matching survey samples, this process often destroys the projectability of the results to a whole population.

The problem of matching samples and establishing a defensible basis of comparisons between exposed and unexposed populations has been dramatically attacked by Irwin M. Towers, Leo A. Goodman, and Hans Zeisel in a proposal to measure the effects of *nonexposure*.[3] They would simply draw two parallel random samples of the population. Each sample would include the normal percentage of viewers of a

[3] "Nonexposure: What It Can Tell the TV Advertiser," *Printers' Ink*, Vol. 278 (March 30, 1962), pp. 64–66.

particular program. One sample would continue without change, while the second sample would be *denied exposure* to the program and its commercials. Just how to control this nonexposure is, of course, a problem; but the two samples would then be comparable except that one would no longer be exposed to the particular advertising messages. The influence of nonexposure could thus be measured under scientifically comparable conditions. No other published proposal has heretofore provided for truly comparable test groups, but it should also be said that the proposed study is theoretical at this time and has not been carried out.

Media have not been alone in the attempt to establish meaningful correlations between specific advertising efforts and sales or possession of products. Independent research operators have worked out ingenious systems of sales measurement, even for single insertions of an advertising campaign. Daniel Starch, in particular, set up elaborate controls in an attempt to sift out exclusively advertising influence on sales.[4] Purchases of products by magazine readers—both before and after issuance—divided according to claims of reading or nonreading of brand advertisements were offered as evidence of sales effects. This approach logically represented an advance in control of related variables, but slow acceptance by the advertising industry may have been caused by the problem of obtaining accurate field data on advertisement reading and on dates of product purchases. Certainly the method has not been generally accepted as a sales evaluator of national advertisements in magazines.

Daniel Starch has presented additional evidence that readership of advertising is closely related to the attracting of prospective buyers.[5] He discusses the assertion that high-readership ads tend to attract nonprospects for the products and services advertised. This is not so, he says, and he presents a good deal of evidence indicating that the more readers an advertisement has, the more the actual number of prospects. (Also, the more prospects, the greater likelihood there is of more readers.) "The data clearly show that as advertising (either for your own brand or for competition) is stepped up, reduced, or stopped, there are marked effects on the number of buyers and current users."[6] There is the likelihood, of course, that advertising appropriations often are either increased or decreased largely in anticipation of what sales trends are expected to be.

In 1961 Starch added to his analyses on the correlation method of

[4] Daniel Starch, "Advertising's Sales Power Can Be Measured," *Advertising and Selling*, Vol. 41 (February, 1948), pp. 33–68.

[5] Daniel Starch, "Ad Readership Scores Can Be Equated with Attracting Prospective Buyers, Starch Asserts," *Advertising Age*, Vol. 31 (October 31, 1960), pp. 77–78.

[6] Daniel Starch, "Do Ad Readers Buy the Product?" *Harvard Business Review*, Vol. 36 (May–June, 1958), pp. 49–58, at p. 58.

estimating the sales influence of advertising.[7] By comparing the findings of several of his approaches to this type of analysis, he was able to demonstrate a degree of consistency which he felt confirmed the relatively simple "Netapps" (NET Ad Produced PurchaseS) method. This requires magazine issue readers or television program viewers merely to report on whether the advertisements were seen and whether the product had been purchased within one week after noting.

If 15 per cent of 30 ad-noters bought the product, this would account for 4.5 purchases. If 10 per cent of 70 non-ad-noters bought the product, this would account for 7 purchases. The total number of reported purchases is known to be 4.5 + 7.0, or 11.5.

However, if the 30 ad-noters had not seen the ad, and if 10 per cent would have bought as did the non-ad-noters, this would account for 3 of the 4.5 purchases they did make. Thus, only 1.5 purchases seem direct outcomes of ad-noting or reading, which would be 1.5 out of a total of 11.5, or 13.04 per cent. In this case, the advertising would be credited with 13.04 per cent of the reported purchases within the week after publishing or broadcasting the advertisement.

The present authors find insufficient consideration given by Starch to certain factors which he treats too lightly or not at all. There is the possibility that noters of specific advertisements are generally better ad-noters and buyers of advertised products. In fact, the Advertising Research Foundation has demonstrated that prospective buyers were 50 per cent better noters of advertisements in *Life* magazine than the nonprospects were.[8]

It is also possible that noting of advertisements makes it easier to remember and report products purchased or that purchase of a product makes it easier to remember noting the advertisement. Perhaps more important is the fact that Starch Readership Service data are not sufficiently accurate to justify such precise analysis. As with other correlation studies, there is always the possibility that other factors which are not isolated or identified may vitiate the entire approach.

The work of Harry Deane Wolfe of the University of Wisconsin in isolating the influence of advertising also deserves comment.[9] Wolfe discusses his explorations with this precautionary statement:

It is doubtful that complete advertising measurement is likely to be attained. There are too many variables, complicating factors, and uncontrollable influences acting on the mind of the consumer. But an "all or nothing" complex in research seems childish; a combination of 50% fact and 50% hunch seems a far better basis for decision than is 100% hunch.[10]

---

[7] Daniel Starch, *Measuring Product Sales Made by Advertising* (Mamaroneck, N.Y.: Daniel Starch & Staff, 1961).

[8] Darrell B. Lucas, "The ABCs of ARF's PARM," *Journal of Marketing*, Vol. 25 (July, 1960), pp. 9–20, at p. 14.

[9] Harry Deane Wolfe, "A New Way to Measure Advertising Effectiveness," *Tide*, Vol. 32 (February 14, 1958), pp. 51–57.

[10] Page 52 of citation in footnote 9.

His final estimate of how much of sales ads "produce" depends upon a comparison of latest brand usage among those who could recall that brand's advertising messages and those who could not. His correlation analysis indicated that slightly over 25 per cent of $15 million in sales bore a relationship to knowledge of present advertising. One of Wolfe's most interesting contributions is the summary of other factors which contributed to the total sales of $15 million:

1. Consumers like the product.
2. Consumers know it is a nationally advertised product.
3. Consumers know the brand name.
4. Consumers *once* knew the advertising.
5. Consumers can find the product in their favorite store.
6. Consumers took advantage of a special promotion such as mailed coupons, in-box coupons, off-price sales in store.
7. Consumers were influenced by store advertising and store display.
8. Consumers bought it on impulse.
9. Consumers bought it because of *communal influence* (or word of mouth, if you will) exerted by parents, relatives, friends, dealers, professional people (doctors, dentists), and others.[11]

The correlation approach, with respect to these and other factors, may result in the assertion: "But all of these factors were the same for both the exposed and unexposed groups." And the response is: "If there are all of these and possibly more factors influencing the sale, then how can correlation evidence be more than a crude estimate of advertising's effect?" Wolfe has met this rebuttal by his statement that 50 per cent fact is better than no facts at all.

However, it needs to be pointed out that if people abandon judgment which is 55 per cent right in favor of leaning on research which is 50 per cent right (and this often does happen at one accuracy level or another), there has been a loss in decision-making efficiency. Moreover, this is usually done with an overt acknowledgment of the research inaccuracies. The poor research is often set forth as being "at least as right as it is wrong." But the real difficulty is to try to balance the likely accuracy of the research with the likely validity of judgments made *without* the research.

In any case, it is more conservative to evaluate whole campaigns than to rate each advertising insertion. Sales trends over a period of months or years may show a parallel with advertising expenditures or readership ratings.[12] When magazine readers are separated into those noting and those not noting particular brand advertisements, the differential may show a convincing pattern.

11 Page 57 of citation in footnote 9.
12 Page 58 of citation in footnote 7.

But there remain possible influences other than advertising. People who do not see the magazine advertisement of a particular brand, for example, must obviously include those who noted few advertisements of any kind. The people who read few advertisements may act quite differently as consumers in comparison with people inclined to read a great many advertisements. This does not deny the importance of the evidence, but raises a serious question about crediting *all* sales advantages to advertising alone. . . .

PRETESTING IN SELECTED SALES AREAS

The possibility of testing out advertisements in limited markets was suggested in the previous discussion.

This method of *sales-area testing* has long been a part of advertising research. Groups of cities or markets are selected, using some cities as controls without advertising changes. The sales pattern for the product is checked through store inventories for several weeks before the test. Then new advertisements are introduced, each variation being tried in several cities and checked for sales results in many stores. Inventories of stock are kept during the test period and may be extended some weeks thereafter to study the normal sales pattern. If certain advertisements are followed by sales increases well above the normal fluctuations in the same markets, they have an increased prospect of proving effective in later national coverage.

No two cities or markets are actually identical, and the selection of test cities is extremely important for sales-area tests. Cities should be comparable in such population characteristics as economic levels, occupational distribution, national origins, and permanence of residence. Types of industry and everything related to the purchase pattern for the product should be matched. Naturally, the selection of cities should be aimed at matching the characteristics of the total market in which the product is sold.

Dealers play a crucial role in the test, particularly if they keep the stock inventories necessary for measuring sales. Since all competing products should be checked, it is possible to keep the dealers from knowing the identity of the brand under test. Otherwise, they may be *too cooperative* and "push" the product.

Even if the investigator keeps track of inventory, which is the wiser procedure, he must keep account of all stock coming to the shelves from elsewhere within the stores, from warehouses, wholesalers, drop shippers, wagon distributors, the manufacturer, and even through loan from other sources.

Ready availability of stock at all times is also highly important. Two or more inventories before the test period, frequent inventories during the test, and two or more inventories following the test are recommended. The final inventories, especially in control cities, can help to ensure that the effects of the test advertisements are not confused with normal sales variations.

The timing of a sales-area test, the selection of media, the schedule of insertions, and the advertising plan must all be well coordinated. The test should be scheduled at such a time that the results will be most significant for the particular time at which the advertising is to be released generally. Buying trends for the product and its competition, as well as general business trends, should be considered. The local media being used should relate as closely as possible to the national media for later use. The rate of insertions should not be speeded up to a point which might distort the relative normal performances of different test advertisements. Even more important, the test copy should not be designed exclusively for immediate sales unless this is the strategy intended for the national campaign, and this last point clearly limits the kinds of advertising for which sales-area tests are adapted.

Sales-area tests always produce differences. The problem, then, is to *evaluate the differences* and to estimate the sales effectiveness of each advertising design.

Early applications of this method led to unsupported conclusions, because normal sales variations by store and by community were not examined. There was little internal analysis of the data. After "winning" advertisements were selected and extended to national markets, there was often reason to believe that results were poor. Reexamination of the sales-area test data, in the majority of such cases, showed that the differences obtained under test were smaller than the usual sales fluctuations in the same markets!

Sales-area tests should be used mostly for new products which are frequently purchased. If the product is purchased after long intervals or if the purchase pattern tends to be erratic, it is not practical to measure the effects of ordinary changes in advertising. Since sales-area tests necessarily cover brief periods, the results cannot be helpful in evaluating the campaign buildup and cumulative effect typically sought through national advertising.

An interesting idea was used by a manufacturer who was willing to be patient in getting the results of some advertising tests. He had developed a new drug product never before advertised, and he faced real competition in breaking into already saturated markets. Instead of just allocating X dollars for an overall campaign, he began to experiment with different types of advertising in different test markets. Local newspapers in the test cities carried different advertisements for the product—and *the product was not displayed in stores, so that the only way consumers could know about the product was through advertising* (and, of course, word of mouth). This sort of testing and retesting resulted in the collection of considerable amounts of sales data as to the pulling power of the advertising dollars spent in different ways.

There has been a growing effort on the part of users of sales-area tests to extend their test areas to major regional markets and to seek fuller control of all promotional efforts in assigned regions. George H. Brown of the Ford Motor Company has given a broad description of such efforts in the evaluating of advertising copy and media.[13] Such efforts are still in their infancy, but if prominent advertisers are willing to permit experimental control of all advertising in large, naturally isolated markets which are capable of separate coverage by all types of media, there are heightened possibilities of actual sales evaluation of advertisements and campaigns. It would seem that the possibilities of payoff are high enough to merit such a policy for many companies. . . .

IMPLICATIONS

The preceding treatment of direct measurement of the sales influence of advertising and indirect sales evaluation through inquiry response may seem to have overstressed the limitations and the fallacies. This has been done deliberately—despite the fact that any direct evidence based on overt response is extremely valuable to advertisers insofar as it is a valid indicator of sales influence. It is all the more important to examine the logic of all such approaches, to look for the pitfalls which abound in this area, to label the limitations restricting each method, and to note the specific products and advertising situations to which each sales evaluator may safely apply. All of this is clearly in accord with the current state of research practice and with current business judgment.

There are some national advertising situations to which coupon returns or other inquiry responses are a reasonably sure sales guide. There are other circumstances, campaign strategies, and product categories which seem to call for serious consideration of a properly executed sales test in comparable areas or markets. New convenience products, designed for frequent repeat purchase in a mass national market, are likely to fit into such a program. Many other products which are already widely advertised through national media seem almost incapable of adaptation to sales-area tests in single city markets that cannot be separately covered by most national media.

It is to be observed, of course, that successful application of a valid sales measurement of most national advertisements would obviate the need for the many test methods discussed previously. Even though readership ratings, attitude research, and the many specialized ap-

---

[13] George H. Brown, *Measuring the Sales Effectiveness of Alternative Media,* paper presented to the Seventh Annual Conference of the Advertising Research Foundation, Inc., New York City, October 3, 1961.

proaches might give a more direct gauge of success in attaining some of the intermediate goals of advertising, the ultimate objective is usually related to the sales process. As is the case with much retail advertising, a true sales measure would provide most of the required basis for intelligent planning and selection of advertising materials.

The fact is that little has yet been learned about the actual measurement of the sales influence of most national advertisements. This is especially true in trying to predict future buying behavior.

Much advertising works so slowly and shares with so many other sales influences that the national advertiser is unlikely to succeed in isolating the effects of each individual unit. Only a scientifically conceived program of genuine advertising experiment, supported by favorable policies over long periods, seems likely to contribute materially toward the solution of the problem of sales evaluation.

Meanwhile, many useful approaches are available for probing specific areas of advertising effects, for establishing the degree of success in attaining certain intermediate objectives, and for reinforcing the process of decision making at almost every stage. Preceding chapters have dealt with the most prominent and most promising of these techniques. The more direct attack through inquiry testing and actual sales evaluation has met with greater obstacles, but none of the evidence needs to be wholly rejected. Rather, every method included in this chapter can be used to throw light on the sales productivity of advertising, providing it has the benefit of the best available procedures combined with intelligent interpretation of the meaning of the results.

PREDICTIVE GENERALIZATIONS

V-A   The assessment of effects of a communication, because of the complexity of the environment in which it takes place and of the act itself, may often be difficult.

V-A-1   Where the effect is presumed to be an altered state of mind or feeling in the listener or reader—attention, comprehension, acceptance, altered perception, anxiety or some other emotional state —testimony of the listener or reader will provide evidence of effect.

V-A-2   Where the effect is changed behavior in the form of immediate response (laughter, jeers, etc.), the ability to recall information presented in the communication, or initiation of action consistent with the recommendations of the communicator, direct observation will provide evidence of effect.

V-B   Theoretical predictions of effects may sometimes be reliable where past experience permits generalization and the communicative event is relatively uncomplicated.

V-C   Listeners' or readers' recollections of the impact of a communication, if substantial and in agreement, may indicate the effect of a communication.

V-D   Reports of audience responses during a speech, even if accurate, may not be an indication of subsequent action, although they may be a good indication of immediate reactions to a speaker's strategies.

V-E   The results of opinion polls and other survey research interviews may be helpful indexes of the effect of a communication, if interviews took place shortly after the communication and exposure to the communication of those interviewed can be established.

V-F   Laboratory experimentation provides a better means of assessing the effect of specified characteristics of a communication than the effects of the speech or essay as a whole or of planned sequences of communications.

V-G   Since there is no dependable relationship between cognitive or affective changes and subsequent behavior, it cannot be assumed that a listener's favorable response in a paper-and-pencil test of his attitude toward the speaker's proposition will predict action consistent with that attitude.

V-H   Voting behavior and consumer behavior studies are often a significant measure of the effect of a communication in terms of the communicator's ultimate objectives.

V-I   The effect of a communication may also be indicated by the permanence of the change in observed behavior of people exposed to the communication.

DISCUSSION QUESTIONS

1. Communications, it is presumed, may alter one's perception of some object and thereby affect subsequent views of the same object. Does your experience confirm this expectation?

2. How might one go about discovering whether there is ever a significant relationship between a listener's immediate responses to a communication and his later behavior consistent with the recommendations of the speaker?

3. After having looked at Jonathan Edwards' account of the reactions of his parishioners to revival preaching, can you say whether all or most of the effects he noticed could be attributed to the communications addressed to them?

4. What do you think of the effort made by one writer to define *persuasion* not as a process but as an effect? The definition was: "Persuasion is conceived as that body of effects in receivers, relevant and instrumental to source-desired goals, brought about by a process in which messages have been a major determinant of those effects."—Wallace C. Fotheringham, *Perspectives on Persuasion* (Boston: Allyn and Bacon, Inc., 1966), p. 7.

5. A cynic might observe that ceremonial speakers protect themselves against "failure" by not declaring specific communication objectives. Would it be possible to gather information about the intentions and effects of such communications?

6. Can anything useful be learned from audience noises one hears in a tape recording of a speech at a public meeting?

7. Discover some information campaign or major political speech of the past few years on the effects of which public opinion poll data might cast some light.

8. Consumer behavior and voting behavior are unlike not only in the degree of importance of the decisions involved. What other differences would affect communicative attempts to influence these kinds of behavior?

9. Can some means be devised for measuring the effectiveness of a classroom speech in terms of the subsequent behavior of listeners?

10. What do you make of the fact that television and radio listeners form strong opinions about certain commercial messages, either of irritation or strong dislike? Will such reactions prevent messages from having an effect?

FOR FURTHER EXPLORATION

Writings about communication and its effects are so abundant that a casual reader may be overwhelmed. In this volume, we have tried to represent the various groups interested in the subject, their approaches and general findings. A reader who wishes to forage on his own might begin by looking at general summaries of research such as Arthur R. Cohen, *Attitude Change and Social Influence* (New York: Basic Books, Inc., 1964), Joseph T. Klapper, *The Effects of Mass Communication* (Glencoe, Illinois: The Free Press, 1960), Carl I. Hovland, Irving L. Janis and Harold H. Kelley, *Communication and Persuasion* (New Haven: Yale University Press, 1953), or the survey by Wayne N. Thompson, *Quantitative Research in Public Address and Communication* (New York: Random House, 1967). Claude E. Shannon and Warren Weaver, *The Mathematical Theory of Communication* (Urbana: University of Illinois Press, 1949) develops the information theory approach to communication. An ambitious inventory of scientific findings on certain facets of communication is Bernard Berelson and Gary A. Steiner, *Human Behavior* (New York: Harcourt, Brace and World, Inc., 1964). The approaches of several disciplines to the study of communication are suggested in a dozen original essays in Frank E. X. Dance (ed.), *Human Communication Theory* (New York: Holt, Rinehart and Winston, Inc., 1967).

Discussion of the settings for communication is not to be found in one place. Jerome D. Frank, *Persuasion and Healing* (Baltimore: Johns Hopkins Press, 1961) exposes the dimensions of private face-to-face communication in psychotherapy. Elihu Katz and Paul F. Lazarsfeld compare the relative importance to opinion formation of several settings in *Personal Influence* (Glencoe, Illinois: The Free Press, 1955). Edward C. Banfield illuminates the nature of several communication settings by means of case studies of Chicago city government in *Political Influence* (Glencoe, Illinois: The Free Press, 1961). Wilbur Schramm's collection, *The Process and Effects of Mass Communication* (Urbana: University of Illinois Press, 1948) is an early but still useful volume. Studies of wartime morale-building efforts are reported in Carl I. Hovland, Arthur A. Lumsdaine and Fred D. Sheffield, *Experiments on Mass Communication* (Princeton: Princeton University Press, 1949). V. O. Key, Jr., *Public Opinion and American Democracy* (New York: Alfred A. Knopf, 1963) provides a behavioral political scientist's view of opinion formation, persistence and change.

Although the studies of Hovland, Janis and Kelley, of Klapper, of Cohen and others already mentioned consider communication strategies, detailed attention is given to special topics in other places. Attention and perception are discussed in M. D. Vernon, *The Psychology of Perception* (Baltimore: Penguin Books, 1962), William N. Dember, *The Psychology of Perception* (New York: Holt, Rinehart and Winston, Inc., 1960), and Donald Broadbent, *Perception and Communication* (Oxford: Pergamon Press, 1958). We have relied in our discussion of comprehension on Jerome S. Bruner, Jacqueline J. Goodnow and George A. Austin, *A Study of Thinking* (New York: John Wiley and Sons, Inc., 1956). Many studies of the process of persuasion have stressed means of gaining acceptance. Thomas S. Scheidel, *Persuasive Speaking* (Glenview, Illinois: Scott, Foresman and Co., 1967) is a useful brief account founded on a behavioral view of social judgment. Wallace C. Fotheringham provides a provocative discussion of message effects and persuasive campaigns in *Perspectives on Persuasion* (Boston: Allyn and Bacon, Inc., 1966). Gerald R. Miller and Thomas R. Nilsen (eds.), *Perspectives on Argumentation* (Chicago: Scott, Foresman and Company, 1966) takes a modern look at the place of evidence and reasoning in opinion formation and change. Theodore M. Newcomb, Ralph H. Turner and Philip E. Converse, *Social Psychology* (New York: Holt, Rinehart and Winston, Inc., 1965) emphasizes communicative interaction as the foundation of interpersonal and group psychology. The most influential statement of the balance theory of attitude change is Leon Festinger, *A Theory of Cognitive Dissonance* (Stanford: Stanford University Press, 1962). The effects of personality differences on receptivity of information and persuasive communications are discussed in Milton Rokeach, *The Open and Closed Mind* (New York: Basic Books, Inc., 1960) and in Irving L. Janis and Carl I. Hovland (eds.), *Personality and Persuasibility* (New Haven: Yale University Press, 1959).

Many of the studies already mentioned discuss the effects of communications and limitations upon those effects. A reader might be especially interested in the voting studies mentioned in Section V, as well as some of the cases of advertising efforts cited in Neil H. Borden and Martin V. Marshall, *Advertising Management: Text and Cases* (Homewood, Illinois: R. D. Irwin, 1959). A readable account of advertising techniques is Martin Mayer, *Madison Avenue, U.S.A.* (New York: Harper and Brothers, 1958). A number of the volumes suggested here are available in paperback editions.

Index

Index

Index of Names